Structure and Meaning in English

Structure and Meaning in English: A Guide for Teachers

Graeme Kennedy

PEARSON
Longman

Harlow, England • London • New York • Boston • San Francisco • Toronto • Sydney • Singapore • Hong Kong
Tokyo • Seoul • Taipei • New Delhi • Cape Town • Madrid • Mexico City • Amsterdam • Munich • Paris • Milan

PEARSON EDUCATION LIMITED

Edinburgh Gate
Harlow CM20 2JE
Tel: +44 (0)1279 623623
Fax: +44 (0)1279 431059
Website: www.pearsoned.co.uk

First edition published in Great Britain in 2003

ISBN 0 582 50632 8

British Library Cataloguing in Publication Data
A CIP catalogue record for this book can be obtained from the British Library

Library of Congress Cataloging in Publication Data
A CIP catalog record for this book can be obtained from the Library of Congress

10 9 8 7 6 5 4 3 2 1

Set in 9/12pt Stone serif by Graphicraft Limited, Hong Kong
Printed in Malaysia

The Publishers' policy is to use paper manufactured from sustainable forests.

Contents

Acknowledgements

We are grateful to the following for permission to reproduce copyright material:

Table 1.4 from The Frequency of Occurrence of Speech Sounds in Southern English in *Archives Néerlandaises de Phonetique Experimentale*, XX, published and reprinted by permission of Royal Holland Society of Sciences and Humanities (Fry, D. B. 1947); Table 3.1 adapted from *Investigating Linguistic Acceptability*, published and reprinted by permission of Mouton De Gruyter, a division of Walter de Gruyter GmbH & Co. KG Publishers (Quirk, R. and Svartvik, J. 1966); Table 3.2 adapted from Recurrent verb complement constructions in the London-Lund Corpus in *English Language Corpora: Design, Analysis and Exploration. Papers from the Thirteenth International Conference on English Language Research on Computerized Corpora, Nijmegen 1992* edited by J. Aarts, P. de Haan and N. Oostdijk, published and reprinted by permission of Rodopi BV (Altenberg, B. 1993); Chapter 5, p. 180; list adapted from *Longman Grammar of Spoken and Written English*, published and reprinted by permission of Pearson Education Ltd (Biber, D. et al. 1999).

In some instances we have been unable to trace the owners of copyright material, and we would appreciate any information that would enable us to do so.

Preface

This book has been written to help teachers develop an understanding of those aspects of English that are especially relevant when teaching learners who speak other languages. It provides an overview of the forms, structures and functions that frequently occur in English and need to be known by learners. The word 'grammar' is used here to describe not only how words and sentences fit together, but also how English is structured at other levels of the language, including sounds, vocabulary and texts.

Standard reference grammars of English contain rich descriptions of the language. This book complements these descriptions by drawing attention to those items and processes which research has shown are often hard for learners, or which occur frequently enough to justify learning. Where appropriate, corpus-based research is used to identify the frequently occurring items or processes. In general, the terminology and descriptive frameworks of modern, comprehensive descriptions of English are used here, including the grammars of Quirk et al. (1985), Greenbaum (1996) and Biber et al. (1999).

The material in the book is designed to form the basis of about 50 hours of class instruction. Specific learning objectives are listed at the beginning of each chapter. The book can also be used for self study, with the notes, tasks and discussion topics being worked through without formal classes. The chapters are best studied in the order presented here, but chapters 1, 2 and 8 can be studied before or after chapters 3–7. The tasks are intended to help you check your understanding of particular aspects of the grammar. Answers or possible solutions for many of the tasks are given at the end of the book.

While recognising that it should be an advantage to know as much as possible about the structure and use of English, teachers often differ a great deal in the amount of explicit knowledge they already have about the language they teach. By working through this book you should acquire pedagogically relevant knowledge about English grammar, how it is used, and the nature of learners' errors or problems.

I am grateful to those colleagues and students who, over many years, have given me ideas on pedagogical grammar. It is not possible to trace the source of all the comments or suggestions that have improved the material that appears here. Special thanks are due, however, to John McCaffery for permission to use the sample of children's speech in Text 8.1, to Janet Holmes and Bernadette Vine for permission to use material from the *Wellington Corpus of Spoken New Zealand English*, to Ave Coxhead for permission to reproduce her Academic Word List on pages 104–106, and to Adam Gadsby for arranging for the use of analyses and texts from the *Longman Corpus of Spoken and Written English* and the *British National Corpus*. Paul Nation, Anna Adams, Sara Cotterall, Alastair Ker, Alan Kirkness, Johanne McComish, Caroline McGhie, Jonathan Newton, John Read, Paul Warren and Jane Dudley are also among those who have contributed in various ways and at various times, but who, of course, bear no responsibility for the outcome.

Introduction

What is grammar?

People sometimes say that they don't know any grammar. But, if we did not know the grammar of our language, we would not be able to understand or speak or read or write. This knowledge of grammar is not necessarily explicit, but it underlies our use of language. The grammar of a language is a set of cognitive rules or principles for combining words (and parts of words) to express certain notions or ideas. For example, we combine words to explain where things are, what happened to them, who did what to whom; when, where, why, or how something happened. In this sense, grammar is a system that enables us to get meaning out of sound. *The man bit the dog* does not mean the same as *The dog bit the man*, even though the sounds and words are similar.

The grammatical systems underlying all languages can be thought of as being related or fundamentally similar. This is sometimes called 'universal grammar': that is, all languages have ways of expressing when events occurred and where they happened; ways of comparing things; ways of asking questions; ways of expressing causation; and so on.

When children begin to acquire language and can only speak short sequences of words, they express particular, possibly universal, relationships between these words. Brown (1973) showed that certain relationships are expressed by children very early in their grammatical development regardless of which language they are learning, and even when their word sequences contain as few as two words. Here are some grammatical relationships which children typically express quite early in their language development.

Grammatical relationship	Example
1 Agent and action	Sara break
2 Action and receiver of the action	break cup
3 Agent and receiver of the action	Sara cup
4 Action and place	drink table
5 Thing or person and place	cup floor
6 Possessor and possession	Sara cup
7 Thing or person and some characteristic	dirty floor
8 Action and instrument	sweep broom

Children later begin to add particular ways of being more specific because sentences of only two or three words can be highly ambiguous. Consider, for example, how many meanings the sequence *drink table* can have. Articles, prepositions, tenses and other items can make the meaning of such an utterance much clearer, e.g. *I had a drink from the cup on the table* or *I want to drink at the table* or *I spilt my drink on the table*. By about 12 years of age, native speakers of a language have typically learned the grammar of that language. Usually, however, they cannot explain what they know, nor do they need to be able to explain what they know in order to be able to be fluent users of their language. Some users may wrongly assume that just because they have not studied grammar, or cannot explain how the language works, they do not know any grammar.

What is 'bad grammar'?

The word 'grammar' is also used by some people to refer to linguistic etiquette. For example, some users of English who say *I'm not* dislike the fact that some other people say *I aren't* or *I ain't* and condemn this as 'bad grammar'. From a descriptive point of view, *I'm not, I aren't* and *I ain't* are all used by groups of speakers, consistently and systematically, and both are well formed (or 'grammatical') in different varieties of English. Their use is a phenomenon associated with particular social, occupational or regional varieties of English, and is not a matter of correctness or a moral issue. Languages change over time, and particular words and structures become associated with particular groups of language users and uses, including levels of formality. English is not a single, monolithic system. Whereas incomplete sentences and contractions are normal characteristics of spoken English, for example, they are much less acceptable in written English. From a linguistic perspective, systematic grammatical differences between varieties of a language are not 'bad grammar'. The notion of 'bad grammar' typically reflects prejudiced preconceptions and attitudes about the linguistic behaviour of other groups of people.

Learners of English, whether as young first language learners, or as learners of English as a second or foreign language, often produce utterances that are 'ungrammatical'. It is quite natural for language learners to make errors as part of the learning process, as they try things out, make false generalisations, or draw incorrect conclusions about how the language works. The material in this book is designed to help teachers understand the kinds of problems that learners face in coming to terms with the grammar of English.

What is a grammar?

A grammar is a linguist's description of a language, usually expressed in terms of 'rules'. Grammars are written by linguists for various purposes. Most grammars are descriptions of linguistic structure and use – how words are put together in a particular language to make phrases and sentences. Grammars can be narrowly defined as dealing with word forms ('morphology') and word order or sentence structure ('syntax'). In this book, grammar is defined more widely to also include description of English sounds, vocabulary, text types and text structures, as part of a 'description of English'.

Grammars attempt to describe what every native speaker of that language already knows unconsciously. All grammars of English are incomplete because we do not yet have comprehensive and accurate descriptions of the vast number of rules that even six-year-olds have acquired. Since the 1970s many language teachers and their students have not been expected to study these grammatical rules. This is partly because it has been recognised that teaching grammar in this sense of 'teaching about the structure of a language' is rarely the most effective way of developing communicative competence in a language. However, many language teachers are also aware that one part of being a professional includes having as rich a knowledge as possible of the structure and use of the language they teach as a foundation for teaching practice.

What is a pedagogical grammar?

A pedagogical grammar of English is a particular kind of descriptive grammar which draws attention to those parts of English that are important for second or foreign language learners of English because they are especially hard to learn or because they occur frequently. A pedagogical grammar for teachers concentrates on those aspects of grammar that are sources of comprehension or produce difficulty for learners. Analyses of errors made by learners of English have helped identify the items that learners find difficult. For example, Close (1962), a celebrated teacher of English to speakers of other languages, listed the following as particularly difficult aspects of grammar for learners of English:

- when to use or omit *the* or *a*
- whether to say *I write* or *I am writing, have written* or *wrote, wrote* or *had written*
- how to use *have been writing* and *had been writing*
- how to use *could, would, should, might, must*
- whether to use the infinitive or the form of the verb ending in *-ing*
- which preposition to use after a verb or before a noun
- whether to use *some* or *any, each* or *every*
- where to put adverbs in a sentence
- whether to use *say* or *tell, do* or *make*.

Of course, learners typically make errors or have learning difficulties that are characteristic of their particular language background. However, experienced teachers of English have found that students from many different language backgrounds also tend to have certain problems in common when they learn English. The following aspects of English grammar seem to be among the most difficult to learn how to use:

- articles and other determiners
- prepositions
- verb use (including tenses, modal verbs, participles, infinitives, phrasal verbs)
- subordinate clauses and verb complements
- ellipsis.

Common areas of difficulty such as these tend to cause particular problems for learners regardless of their language background, and therefore it is these problem areas that receive particular focus in this book.

As well as showing what word forms or sequences of words are possible, pedagogical grammars also try to give information on probabilities of occurrence – what users of the language are most likely to say or write. Statistical information on how often items are used by speakers of English is included in a pedagogical grammar to help teachers reach decisions about whether particular items are worth teaching. Nowadays, analysis by computer of large collections of texts known as 'corpora' helps identify the most frequently used words and structures of English. In this book, the following corpora have been used as sources of texts for illustrating points of grammar, and for distributional information on items: the 40-million-word *Longman Corpus of Spoken and Written English (LCSWE)* (which contains texts from spoken and written sources in American and British English), the 100-million-word *British National Corpus (BNC)*, the *Brown Corpus* of written American English, the *Lancaster–Oslo–Bergen Corpus (LOB)* of written British English, and the *Wellington Corpora of Spoken and*

Written English. Exercises in the book are, where appropriate, based on such texts, and can be easily supplemented by the choice of other texts from appropriate genres.

However, as experienced teachers know, while frequency of use, as revealed by the analysis of corpora, is one indication of usefulness, it should not be the only basis on which language teaching is planned and organised. For this reason, the book is corpus-informed rather than corpus-based. It takes account of information on the distribution and frequency of linguistic items and processes that corpus-based research has made available, but it also takes account of learning difficulty and learning goals. Further, in order to focus as clearly as possible on particular points of grammar or use, 'made-up' examples, rather than 'authentic' examples from corpora, are frequently used throughout the book.

Studying grammar

The incredible complexity of the grammar of English (or any language) is only partly understood by linguists, so you should not be surprised if there are no simple or straightforward answers to some of your questions about English. There are sometimes different ways of describing or analysing a point, and grammarians sometimes cannot adequately account for particular phenomena.

Although studying grammar can be difficult, teachers may find it useful to keep certain questions in mind when attempting to improve their own understanding of how particular grammatical items of English work. In the examples that follow, and throughout the book, an asterisk denotes an ungrammatical construction.

1 Form

- What forms can the item have? (e.g. *go–went, cannot–can't*)
- What other items can have similar forms? (e.g. *leave–leaves–left–leaf; ring–rang; bring–brought*)

2 Position

- What positions can the item occur in? (e.g. *two old cats; *old two cats*)
- What items can come before or after it? (e.g. *I was writing a letter; *I was write a letter*)
- Where does it come in the sentence? (e.g. *I saw him; He saw me*)
- What other items could be substituted for it? (e.g. *She had dinner at 5pm; She had dinner when she got home*)

3 Function

- What is the item used for? (e.g. *I **went** to see my aunt*)
- What does its use or absence tell us? (e.g. *I'd like a coffee; I like coffee*)

4 Meaning

- Is there another grammatical way of expressing this meaning?
  (e.g. *The kiwi is a bird. Kiwis are birds. A kiwi is a bird.*)
- When can you use different forms to express the same meaning?
  Is there a different function when different forms are used? (e.g.
  compare *Open the door please. Would you mind opening the door?*)

5 Frequency

- How likely are learners or users of English to need to understand or
  produce the item or items?

Teaching grammar to learners of English

The material in this book is designed for teachers – for consciousness-
raising about how English is structured and used. It is not intended that
this material should be taught to learners in this way. However, when you
do teach grammar to your learners, here are some general points:

- Focus first on items that are important in conveying meaning.
  Don't concentrate on trivial grammatical points. Make sure that
  your learners know the frequent items first.
- Focus on your learners' needs. What are these?
  - productive (speaking and writing) or receptive (listening and
    reading)?
  - accuracy or fluency?
  - many structures or fewer structures?
  - simple structures or complex structures?
  - structures with a wide range of uses, or ones with a narrower range?
- Focus on grammatical items that are appropriate to learners' needs in
  the following ways. Where it is possible, teach items in the context
  of use with both brief 'made-up' illustrative examples and more
  complex 'authentic' texts.

  a Show the learners the **form** of the item you wish to teach.

  b Direct your learners' attention to the item in known contexts
    (e.g. text, video, picture) and establish the **meaning** of the item.

c Organise the item in teaching materials so that grammatical patterns become obvious and the **forms** are seen in **position**.

d Help learners to focus on target structures; for instance, it is often useful to mark a text through bold typing or italics.

e Give the learners opportunities to discover a target rule in contexts.

f Give the learners opportunities to judge whether examples are well formed (grammatical). Where necessary, get the learners to change or correct ungrammatical examples.

g Provide opportunities for the learners to practise using an item in simple, formal structured exercises and known contexts. Start with recognition and comprehension exercises and move to production tasks, first 'controlled' and then 'free'.

h Provide opportunities for the learners to practise use of the item with focused exercises in new contexts.

i Keep checking that learners understand.

j Avoid confusing your learners. If you teach at the same time items that are semantically related (e.g. two tenses), you may cause your learners to learn both incorrectly.

k Help learners to make good use of their knowledge of the new grammatical item in their production and comprehension by providing repeated opportunities to use the item in new contexts, with increasingly free production spaced out over a period of time.

It is not always clear whether it is better to treat a learner's particular difficulties as having a grammatical or a lexical (vocabulary) basis. Spoken English and written English are used in ways in which the context, words and grammatical structures interrelate. For example, in response to the question *Where is Sue?* two appropriate answers would be:

1 *She's away from her class.*
2 *She's absent from her class.*

Although Sentences 1 and 2 might seem to have identical structures, they are in fact different. *Away* is an adverb, while *absent* is an adjective. We can say, *Sue is an absent student*, but for the learner who says **Sue is an away student*, we may need to decide whether to say that *away* is not appropriate before a noun, or whether to recommend that the learner omits *a student* and says *Sue is away*. There is often more than one sensible way of helping learners overcome a particular problem.

CHAPTER 1

The sounds of English

This chapter gives an overview of the sounds of English and how they are made. The notes and exercises are to help you understand how the sound system works, rather than focusing on pronunciation problems.

Objectives

When you have finished this chapter you should:

1 Know what **sounds** there are in English.

2 Be able to use **phonemic transcription** to show that you know how many sounds there are in particular words, and what those sounds are.

3 Be able to show you understand the relationship between **letters** and **sounds**.

4 Know which are the most frequent sounds and combinations of sounds in English.

5 Be able to describe the main processes used in making **speech sounds**.

6 Know the main differences between **consonants** and **vowels**.

7 Be able to describe how each of the English consonants and vowels is made.

8 Know the difference between **phonemes** and **allophones**.

9 Know how to read the pronunciation information in a dictionary in order to be able to give advice to learners on how particular words are pronounced.

10 Be able to show how sounds change in the environment of other sounds.

11 Know what the main **word stress** and **sentence stress** patterns are in English.

12 Know which words receive **strong stress** in English and which words do not.

13 Know what the main **intonation patterns** of English are and some of the important meanings they can signal.

14 Be able to describe some of the important differences between the sounds in different **varieties of English** (e.g. UK, US, Australian, NZ), which result in different **accents**.

15 Know some of the main difficulties that learners of English from different language backgrounds have with English pronunciation.

1.1 Speech sounds

1.1.1 Sounds and symbols

Phonetics is the study of speech sounds. We can focus on how the sounds are made (articulatory phonetics), the physics of speech sounds (acoustic phonetics), or how sounds are perceived by the ear and brain (auditory phonetics). For teachers of English, articulatory phonetics is by far the most important branch of phonetics.

The human vocal apparatus is capable of making a huge number of different sounds. Each language makes use of its own small number of sounds known as **phonemes** which mark differences in the meaning of words in that language. The English words *tin*, *din* and *some* each consist of three phonemes. The words *be*, *bee* and *pea* each have two phonemes. Depending on how detailed the analysis is and the dialect being described, English has about 44 phonemes – 24 consonants and 20 vowels and diphthongs. Some varieties of English acquire more status than others. Such is the case with British 'Received Pronunciation' (RP). Although it is spoken by perhaps less than 5 per cent of the population of Britain, RP is often used as a pronunciation model in dictionaries and teaching, or as a point of reference for describing varieties of English. In this chapter, the examples used assume an RP-like pronunciation. In Section 1.7 we will consider ways in which other regional varieties of English differ from RP, and thus characterise different English 'accents'.

The 44 phonemes of British RP are shown in Table 1.1. Each sound is represented by a special symbol. The symbols are based on those used by the International Phonetics Association notation system.

Special symbols are needed because there are more sounds in English than the 26 letters of the written alphabet. Teachers and learners of English need to be careful not to confuse sounds and letters. Letters are part of the writing system (or orthography). Phonemes are about spoken language. There is not a one-to-one relation between phonemes and the letters of the alphabet.

Table 1.1 English phonemes

Vowels and diphthongs

1	iː	as in	*see*	/siː/		11	ɜː	as in	*her*	/hɜː/
2	ɪ	as in	*sit*	/sɪt/		12	ə	as in	*about*	/əbaʊt/
3	e	as in	*ten*	/ten/		13	eɪ	as in	*face*	/feɪs/
4	æ	as in	*sat*	/sæt/		14	əʊ	as in	*home*	/həʊm/
5	ɑː	as in	*arm*	/ɑːm/		15	aɪ	as in	*alive*	/əlaɪv/
6	ɒ	as in	*got*	/gɒt/		16	aʊ	as in	*now*	/naʊ/
7	ɔː	as in	*saw*	/sɔː/		17	ɔɪ	as in	*coin*	/kɔɪn/
8	ʊ	as in	*foot*	/fʊt/		18	ɪə	as in	*near*	/nɪə(r)/
9	uː	as in	*too*	/tuː/		19	eə	as in	*hair*	/heə(r)/
10	ʌ	as in	*but*	/bʌt/		20	ʊə	as in	*fewer*	/fjʊə/

Consonants

21	p	as in	*pot*	/pɒt/		33	s	as in	*same*	/seɪm/
22	b	as in	*bad*	/bæd/		34	z	as in	*zoo*	/zuː/
23	t	as in	*tin*	/tɪn/		35	ʃ	as in	*she*	/ʃiː/
24	d	as in	*dog*	/dɒg/		36	ʒ	as in	*measure*	/meʒə/
25	k	as in	*cat*	/kæt/		37	m	as in	*more*	/mɔː/
26	g	as in	*got*	/gɒt/		38	n	as in	*no*	/nəʊ/
27	tʃ	as in	*chin*	/tʃɪn/		39	ŋ	as in	*bring*	/brɪŋ/
28	dʒ	as in	*jump*	/dʒʌmp/		40	l	as in	*last*	/lɑːst/
29	f	as in	*fall*	/fɔːl/		41	r	as in	*right*	/raɪt/
30	v	as in	*vote*	/vəʊt/		42	w	as in	*waste*	/weɪst/
31	θ	as in	*think*	/θɪŋk/		43	j	as in	*yes*	/jes/
32	ð	as in	*that*	/ðæt/		44	h	as in	*house*	/haʊs/

1 Sometimes several different letters or letter combinations can represent one sound. For example, the sound /ʃ/ is represented in at least 12 different spellings in English – <u>sh</u>oe, o<u>c</u>ean, <u>s</u>ugar, i<u>ss</u>ue, con<u>sc</u>ious, man<u>s</u>ion, fu<u>chs</u>ia, <u>ch</u>aperone, mi<u>ss</u>ion, na<u>ti</u>on, <u>sch</u>ist, suspi<u>ci</u>on. Other examples include:

- /f/   f, ph, gh   (<u>f</u>ish, <u>ph</u>ilosophy, enou<u>gh</u>)
- /e/   a, e, i, o, u   (vill<u>a</u>ge, pr<u>e</u>tty, f<u>i</u>t, w<u>o</u>men, b<u>u</u>sy)
- /z/   s, z   (ro<u>s</u>e, fro<u>z</u>e)

2 Sometimes a letter can represent several different sounds, e.g.

M<u>a</u>ry's f<u>a</u>ther w<u>a</u>nts to m<u>a</u>ke it illeg<u>a</u>l to keep c<u>a</u>ts. /eə, ɑː, ɒ, eɪ, ə, æ/

ki<u>ss</u>, ro<u>s</u>e, A<u>s</u>ia /s, z, ʒ/

3 Some letters do not represent any sound in words as they are currently spoken, e.g.

lim<u>b</u>, com<u>e</u>, <u>k</u>nee, <u>g</u>nat, <u>w</u>hole, par<u>l</u>iament

4 One letter can sometimes represent two sounds (e.g. *six* /sɪks/), and two letters can represent one sound (e.g. sick /sɪk/).

The use of a special system of **phonemic symbols** to represent the 44 sounds of English makes it possible to show the pronunciation of words. It can be very useful for teachers and learners to be able to read the pronunciation information in dictionaries to check how words are pronounced by native speakers of English. It is, of course, worth remembering that writing and even phonemic transcription are normally only poor reflections of speech, being unable to reflect many of the subtle nuances of meaning that are expressed through stress, pitch, volume and speed of delivery.

It is important to note that, although the set of symbols used in this book for the 44 phonemes of English is very widely used, some dictionaries use different symbols to indicate pronunciation. For example, books published in the United States sometimes use /č/ instead of /tʃ/, /š/ instead of /ʃ/, /ž/ instead of /ʤ/ and /y/ instead of /j/.

Task 1.1

Using the list of phonemic symbols in Table 1.1 as a checklist, count the number of sounds in each of the following words when read in a careful 'citation' reading style.

of	off	government	luck
few	ship	sea	write
sheep	mother	thumb	arrow
boy	test	yard	answer
phone	days	saw	banana
rough	thought	then	speed
black	roll	house	church
light	serious	be	bee
some	multiplication	magnificently	although

Task 1.2

Write these words in their ordinary written (orthographic) form.

pɪt	rɪp	ʃɪp	vɪzɪt	gɑːdn
lɪd	wiːt	bɪn	fɪl	liːv
siːk	ʃiːp	θɪk	θɪn	feðə
bet	biːt	bɪt	biːn	fɪʃɪŋ
wɒz	lʌvə	dʒɔː	juː	pɑːk
briːð	lɜːn	bɪgə	wʊl	θɪŋ
sɒŋ	niːd	jɑːd	ðen	diːl
meʒə	mɒθ	tʃɪn	ʃʊgə	nɜːs
mʌðə	vjuː	ɑːm	pɜːs	wɔːkt

11

Task 1.3

Write down the phonemic symbols for the first sound in each of the following words.

1 think	6 ship	11 yacht
2 shame	7 those	12 thought
3 yesterday	8 sugar	13 throat
4 joke	9 that	14 shine
5 cheap	10 yolk	15 the

Write down the phonemic symbols for the last sound in each of the following words.

16 song	20 wash	24 bath
17 beige	21 breathe	25 wrong
18 length	22 splash	26 wish
19 both	23 please	27 lathe

Task 1.4

This exercise gives practice in transcribing all the English consonant phonemes. Using the symbols in Table 1.1, write down the phonemic symbols for the first and the last sounds of each word.

main	file	with	sink
pen	refuse (v.)	said	breath
hot	glove	buses	shame
picks	thief	loose	listens
verbs	short	five	marble
crush	catch	those	judge
breathing	sent	banging	shed
lose	think	could	rouge
long	tongue	sense	bought
breathe	cease	leaf	phase
stomach	straight	rough	ways
young	world	width	dropped

Task 1.5

Write the words below in phonemic transcription. Try to ignore the written form of the word and concentrate on listening to yourself saying the word. If you cannot remember the phonemic symbol for a particular sound, check with the list of symbols in Table 1.1 for a word with the same sound in it.

most	join	national	usually
face	fight	messenger	cricket
main	hear	rather	action
air	mine	business	bitter
almost	noise	brown	fence
cow	own	fire	hurt
fly	idea	bite	ball
fail	frighten	fur	catch
spices	grounded	noises	Christmas
rung	wishes	owner	ugly
better	wrong	fears	impossible
fumes	meditate	gave	rather
splits	used	bridges	flew
sailor	agree	sink	mow
know	pleasant	concentrate	now
no	flow	flower	birth
how	sew	flourish	bury
length	flour	floor	temperature
fill	laugh	liquid	race

When you have finished, check your answers in a current learners' dictionary. If you think you need more practice, you can transcribe any English word and check your transcriptions in the dictionary. The *Longman Dictionary of Contemporary English* and the *Oxford Advanced Learner's Dictionary* both use the same system as Table 1.1.

1.1.2 Practice in reading a phonemic transcription

Note: Word and sentence stress is not marked on these texts. Fast speech can result in sounds being dropped or merged with adjacent sounds.

A /ə njuːz rəpɔːt/
/ə mæn stəʊl mɔː ðən tuː hʌndrəd dɒləz wɜːθ əv əlektrɪkl əkwɪpməntə bɪld ə bɜːglər əlɑːm fə hɪz kɑː az hiː dɪdnt wɒnt enɪθɪŋ stəʊln frəmɪt ðə kɔːt wəz təʊld/

B /ðə lɪtl gɜːl ənd ðə wʊlf baɪ dʒeɪmz θɜːbə/
/wʌn ɑːftənuːn ə bɪg wʊlf weɪtɪd ɪn ðə dɑːk fɒrəst fər ə lɪtl gɜːl tə kʌm əlɒŋ kærɪjɪŋ ə bɑːskət əv fuːd tə hə grænmʌðə faɪnəlɪ ðə lɪtl gɜːl dɪd kʌm əlɒŋ ən ʃiː wəz kærɪjɪŋ ðə bɑːskət əv fuːd ə juː kærɪjɪŋ ðæt bɑːskət tə jɔː grænmʌðə ɑːskt ðə wʊlf ðə lɪtl gɜl sed ʃiː wɒz səʊ ðə wʊlf ɑːskt hə weə hə grænmʌðə lɪvd ən ðə lɪtl gɜːl təʊld hɪm ənd hiː dɪsəpɪəd ɪntə ðə wʊd wen ðə lɪtl gɜːl əʊpənd ðə dɔː əv hə grænmʌðəz haʊs ʃiː sɔː ðət ðeə wəz sʌmbədɪ ɪn ðə bed wɪð ə naɪt kæp ən naɪt gaʊn ɒn ʃiː həd əprəʊtʃt nəʊ nɪərə ðən twentɪfaɪv fiːt frəm ðə bed/

wən ʃiː sɔː ðət ɪt wəz nɒt hə græenmʌðə bət ðə wʊlf fɔːr iːvən ɪn ə
naɪt kæp ə wʊlf dʌz nɒt lʊk enɪ mɔː laɪk jəgræenmʌðə ðən ðə
metrəʊgəʊldwən laɪən lʊks laɪk kælvən kuːlɪdʒ səʊ ðə lɪtl gɜːl tʊk ən
ɔːtəmætɪk aʊt əv hə bɑːskət ənd ʃɒt ðə wʊlf ded mɒrəl ɪt ɪz nɒt əz
iːzɪtə fuːl lɪtl gɜːlz nɑʊədeɪz əz ɪt juːst tə biː/

It has been estimated that about 80 per cent of English words have
a regular relationship between sound and spelling. Nevertheless, some
learners of English may still think that English spelling is a rather chaotic
way of representing the sounds, and various writers have poked fun at the
system and pointed out some possible consequences of spelling reform, as
the examples in 1.1.3 show.

1.1.3 Food for thought on English spelling

1

Dearest creature in creation,
Studying English pronunciation,
I will teach you in my verse
Sounds like corpse, corps, horse and
worse.
I will keep you, Susy, busy,
Make your head with heat grow dizzy;
Tear in eye, your dress you'll tear,
So shall I! Oh, hear my prayer!
Pray, console your loving poet,
Make my coat look new, dear, sew it.
Just compare heart, beard and heard,
Dies and diet, lord and word,
Sword and sward, retain and Britain.
Mind the latter, how it's written!
Mark the difference moreover
Between mover, plover, Dover;
Leeches, breeches; wise, precise;
Chalice, but police and lice;
Camel, constable, unstable;
Principle, disciple, label;
Petal, penal and canal;
Wait, surmise, plait, promise; pal.
Suit, suite; ruin, circuit, conduit
Rhyme with 'shirk it' and 'beyond it'.
But is it not hard to tell
Why it's pall, mall, but Pall Mall.
Muscle, muscular; goal, iron;
Timber, climber; bullion, lion.
Made has not the sound of bade,
Say-said, pay-paid, laid but plaid!
Now I surely will not plague you

With such words as vague and ague.
But be careful how you speak,
Say break, steak, but bleak and streak;
Previous, precious; fuchsia, via;
Pipe, snipe; recipe and choir;
Cloven, oven; how and low;
Script, receipt; shoe, poem, toe.
Hear me say, devoid of trickery,
Daughter, laughter and Terpsichore.
Typhoid, measles, topsails, aisles;
Exiles, similes, reviles;
Wholly, holly; signal, signing;
Thames, examining, combining;
Scholar, vicar and cigar;
Solar, mica, war and far.
From 'desire', desirable – admirable
from 'admire';
Lumber, plumber; bier but brier;
Chatham, brougham, renown but
known,
Knowledge; done, but gone and tone;
One, anemone; Balmoral;
Kitchen, lichen, laundry, laurel;
Gertrude, German; wind and mind;
Scene, Melpomene, mankind;
Tortoise, turquoise, chamois-leather;
Reading, Reading, heathen, heather.
This phonetic labyrinth
Gives moss, gross, brook, brooch,
ninth, plinth;
Billet does not end like ballet;
Bouquet, wallet, mallet, chalet;

Blood and flood are not like food,
Nor is mould like should and would.
Banquet is not nearly parquet
Which is said to rhyme with 'sparky'.
Viscous, viscount; load and broad;
Toward, to forward, to reward;
And your pronunciation is O.K.
When you say correctly croquet;
Rounded, wounded; grieve and sieve;
Friend and fiend; alive and live;
Liberty, library; heave and heaven;
Rachel, ache, moustache, eleven.
We say hallowed, but allowed;
People, leopard; towed but vowed.
Worm and storm, chaise, chaos,
    chair;
Senator, spectator, mayor.
Ivy, privy; famous, clamour
And enamour rhyme with 'hammer'.
Pussy, hussy and possess,
Desert but dessert, address.
Gold, wolf; countenance; lieutenants,
Hoist, in lieu of flags, left pennants.
River, rival; tomb, bomb, comb,
Doll and roll and some and home.
Stranger does not rhyme with anger,
Neither does devour with clangour.
Soul, but foul, and gaunt, but aunt.
Font, front, won't; want, grand
    and grant.
And then singer, ginger, linger.
Real, zeal; mauve, gauze and gauge;
Marriage, foliage, mirage, age.
Query does not rhyme with very,
Nor does fury sound like bury.
Does, lost, post and doth, cloth, loth;
Job, job, blossom, bosom, oath.
Though the difference seems little,
We say actual, but victual.
Seat, sweat; chaste, caste; Leigh,
    eight, height;
Put, nut; granite but unite.
Reefer does not rhyme with 'deafer';
Feoffer does, and zephyr, heifer.
Dull, bull; Geoffrey, George; age, late;
Hint, pint; senate but sedate;
Scenic, Arabic, pacific;
Science, conscience, scientific;
Tour but our, and succour, four;

Gas, alas and Arkansas.
Sea, idea, guinea, area;
Psalm, Maria but malaria;
Youth, south, southern; cleanse
    and clean;
Doctrine, turpentine, marine;
Compare alien with Italian,
Dandelion with battalion,
Rally with ally; yea, ye,
Eye, age, whey, key, quay.
Say aver, but ever, fever,
Neither, leisure, skein, receiver.
Never guess, it is not safe;
We say calves, valves, half but Ralph.
Starry, granary, canary,
Crevice, but device and eyrie;
Face, but preface and grimace,
Phlegm, phlegmatic; ass, glass, bass;
Bass, large, target, gin, give, verging,
Ought, oust, joust, and scour but
    scourging.
Ear, but earn; and ere and wear
Do not rhyme with here, but heir.
Pudding, puddle, putting. Putting?
Yes, at golf it rhymes with shutting.
Respite, spite, consent, resent,
Liable, but Parliament.
Seven is right, but so is even,
Hyphen, roughen, nephew, Stephen,
Monkey, donkey, clerk and jerk,
Asp, grasp, wasp, cork and work
Differ, like diverse and divers,
Rivers, strivers, shivers, fivers.
Once, but nonce, toll, doll, but roll,
Polish, polish, Poll and poll.
Have you ever endeavoured
To pronounce revered and severed?
Demon, lemon, ghoul, foul, soul,
Peter, petrol and patrol.
Hugh but hug, and hood but hoot,
Buoyant, minute (noun), but minute
    (adjective).
Cornice, nice, valise, revise,
Rabies but lullabies.
Gooseberry, goose, and close
    (adjective) but close (verb);
Paradise, rise, rose and dose.
Bonafide, alibi,
Gyrate, dowry and awry.

Pronunciation – think of Psyche! –
Is a piling, stout and pikey;
It's a dark abyss or tunnel
Strewn with stones like rowlock,
    gunwale,
Islington and Isle of Wight,
Housewife, verdict and indict.

Don't you think so, reader, rather
Saying lather, bather, father?
Finally, which rhymes with enough –
Though, through, tough, trough,
    plough, cough or hough?
Hiccough has the sound of 'cup' –
My advice is – give it up!

> Attributed to a Dutch speaker, G. N. Trenite, who wrote under the
> pseudonym 'Charivarius' in *Moderna Språk* (1927)

2

Advocates of spelling reform have sometimes suggested that just a small number of changes be made each year, thus giving people time to absorb the changes. Possible consequences of spelling reform were presented in a letter written to newspapers by M. J. Shields:

> For example, in Year 1, that useless letter 'c' would be dropped to be replased by either 'k' or 's', and likewise 'x' would no longer be part of the alphabet. The only kase in which 'c' would be retained would be in the 'ch' formation, which will be dealt with later. Year 2 might well reform 'w' spelling, so that 'which' and 'one' would take the same konsonant, wile Year 3 might well abolish 'y', replasing it with 'i', and Iear 4 might fiks the 'g–j' anomali wonse and for all.
>
> Jeneralli, then, the improvement would kontinue iear bai iear, with Iear 5 doing awai with useless double konsonants, and Iears 6–12 or so modifaiing the vowlz and the rimeining voist and unvoist konsonants. Bai Ier 15 or sou, it wud fainali bi posibl tu meik ius ov thi ridandant letez 'c', 'y' and 'x' – bai now jast a memori in the maindz ov ould doderez – to riplais 'ch', 'sh' and 'th' rispektivli.
>
> Fainali, xen, aafte sam 20 iers ov orxogrefkl riform, wi wud hev a lojikl, kohirnt speling in ius xrewawt xe Ingliy-spiking werld. Haweve, sins xe Wely, xe Airiy, and xe Skots du not spik Ingliy, xei wud hev to hev a speling siutd tu xer oun lengwij. Xei kud, haweve, orlweiz lern Ingliy az a sekond lengwij et skuul! Iorz feixfuli, M. J. Yilz.

1.1.4 Phonemes and allophones

Every language has its own set of **phonemes**. Phonemes are abstract units which are the names of families of sounds. That is, several different sounds (or 'phones') can be manifestations or variants of one phoneme. These variant forms are called **allophones**. For example, compare how the phoneme /t/ is manifested in *tea*, *too*. Lip rounding (in anticipation of /u/) for the /t/ in *too* makes it different from the /t/ in *tea*, which has more spread lips. These different 't' sounds are allophones of the English phoneme /t/. **Phonetic** symbols are used for showing more precisely the pronunciation of allophonic variants. Whereas phonemes are transcribed within slanting lines / /, allophones are transcribed within square brackets [ ]. The 'broader' phonemic symbols are normally used for English language teaching purposes. It is important for language teachers to be aware that when we speak we speak phones not phonemes. For example, if we say aloud the words *he, her, hot, hand, hardly,* we should be able to notice allophonic differences in the way the phoneme /h/ is made, in lip rounding and the extent to which the tongue is raised towards the roof of the mouth. When we compare the allophones of the phoneme /p/ in *pin, spin, stop, lamp, stopped,* we notice differences in the way the /p/ is made, including aspiration (release of air) and the shape of the mouth.

In each case, the allophones of a phoneme are different from each other, but because the meaning of words is never dependent on this difference, the allophones are classed together as being members of the same phoneme. Allophonic variation is often a reflection of the influence of neighbouring sounds in the phonetic environment, or of age, gender, dialect or individual differences. We often group different entities together in other aspects of our lives. For example, we may group *Sue* and her brothers *Max, Fred* and *John* as *Smiths* (even though they are all different from each other). Similarly, in the written alphabet we have no problem classifying as 'the same' different manifestations of the 'same' letter, e.g. *a, a, A, A*. On the other hand, although the letters *u* and *v* are similar, we do not consider them to be 'the same'.

It is important for language teachers to realise that sometimes phones which in one language are allophones of a single phoneme may belong to separate phonemes in another language. For example, in English, whether or not we release a puff of air (marked ʰ) to 'aspirate' the sound at the beginning of the word *pin* does not change the meaning. That is, whether we say [pɪn] or [pʰɪn] does not change the meaning. The difference between [p] and [pʰ] is allophonic. In Thai, however, /p/ and /pʰ/ are two separate phonemes and, thus, whether or not there is aspiration can change meaning.

paa = forest

pʰaa = to split

In Japanese, [r] and [l] are allophones of a single phoneme. In English, /r/ and /l/ are separate phonemes (cf. /ræp/ and /læp/ or /kərekt/ and /kəlekt/).

In Arabic, [p] and [b] are allophonic variants, as are [v] and [f]. In English, however, these four sounds are separate phonemes. Arabic learners of English may thus tend to say /beɪd/ for *paid*, or /feriː/ for *very*.

In Bahasa Indonesia, [f] and [p] are allophones of the same phoneme, and learners of English may therefore say /pɪʃ/ for *fish*.

In Spanish, there is a phoneme /d/ with two allophones:

[d] at the beginning of words (e.g. *dos* = two)

[ð] between vowels (e.g. *nada* = nothing)

Some Spanish learners of English may confuse the pronunciation of the words *breathing* and *breeding*, pronouncing both as /briːðɪŋ/. On the other hand, English-speaking learners of Spanish are sometimes misled by the spelling of a word such as *nada*, pronouncing it [naːdə] instead of [naːðə].

Task 1.6

Look at the position of the different [k] sounds in the words below. [kʰ] is aspirated, which means that it is pronounced with a small puff of air after it. [k°] is unreleased, which means that the closure in the mouth is not opened before the next sound. Are [kʰ, k, k°] allophones of one phoneme or do they represent different phonemes?

copy	[kʰɒpɪ]	book	[bʊk]	cat	[kʰæt]
take care	[teɪk° kʰeə]	black cat	[blæk° kʰæt]	skill	[skɪl]
duck	[dʌk]	take	[teɪk]	school	[skuːl]
keep	[kʰiːp]	make coffee	[meɪk° kʰɒfɪ]		

Task 1.7

Check the transcriptions of these words. Circle the errors and write the correct transcriptions.

1 clutch   /klʌtʃ/
2 jealous   /jeləs/
3 things   /θɪŋz/
4 incorrect   /nkərekt/
5 leaves   /liːvs/
6 fuse   /fuːz/
7 square   /skweə/
8 these   /ðiːs/
9 sugar   /shʊgə/
10 believes   /bəliːvz/
11 singer   /sɪŋgə/
12 axes   /æksəz/

1.2 The speech process and the organs of speech

Speaking is a very complex neuromuscular activity. If we speak at a moderate rate we produce about 150 words per minute. This is about 2.5 words per second or about 14 phonemes per second. About 100 muscles in our trunk, throat and head are used when we speak. Potentially, therefore, there could be about 1,400 muscular movements per second (or 84,000 per minute) if every muscle is 'charged' for every phoneme. No wonder talking can make us tired! Figure 1.1 shows the parts of the head and neck that are used when we speak.

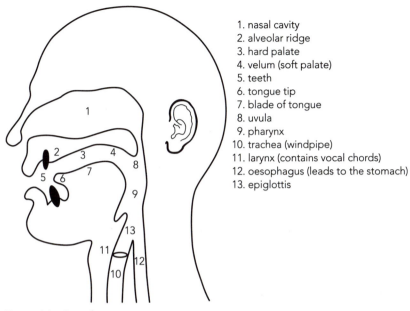

1. nasal cavity
2. alveolar ridge
3. hard palate
4. velum (soft palate)
5. teeth
6. tongue tip
7. blade of tongue
8. uvula
9. pharynx
10. trachea (windpipe)
11. larynx (contains vocal chords)
12. oesophagus (leads to the stomach)
13. epiglottis

Figure 1.1 Speech organs

There are no organs specifically for speaking:

The **lungs** are for oxygenating the blood.

The **trachea** (windpipe) takes air to the lungs.

The **tongue** is used for chewing and swallowing.

The **nose** is used for smelling (and breathing).

The **larynx** is used for strengthening the trunk and arms when we 'hold our breath'.

However, all of these (and other) parts of the body are also used for making speech sounds. Five main mechanisms are involved:

1 the airstream from the lungs

2 voicing (are the vocal chords vibrating?)

3 the oral–nasal process (is the air going out through the nose or mouth?)

4 the place of articulation (where are the tongue, lips, etc.?)

5 the manner of articulation (what is done to the airstream?)

1.2.1 The airstream

Our lungs can contain about 3.5 litres of air. When we breathe normally we expel and take in about half a litre of air every five seconds. For speech, we mainly make use of outgoing lung air (the egressive pulmonary airstream). Some languages also make some sounds using air movement within the mouth (velaric airstream) to make 'clicks'. Lung air travels up the wind-pipe (trachea), through the larynx and out through the mouth or nose.

1.2.2 Voicing

The **larynx** is situated near the top of the windpipe at the 'Adam's apple'. The larynx is made of muscle and cartilage and contains two bands of stretchy tissue (the 'vocal chords') which can close off or restrict the free flow of air to and from the lungs. Figure 1.2 shows the larynx from above:

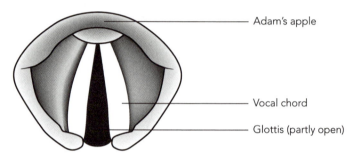

Figure 1.2 **The larynx** (at rest from above)

When the larynx is open at the glottis (the opening between the vocal chords), air can flow in and out relatively unimpeded. When the glottis is narrowed and the vocal chords stretched, the passing airflow causes the chords to vibrate, thus causing 'voicing'. Some sounds are 'voiced' and some are 'voiceless'. We can feel the effect of voicing by putting our fingers in our ears (or by putting a finger on the throat) and making the following pairs of sounds.

/s/	/z/	e.g. *loose, lose*
/f/	/v/	e.g. *feel, veal*
/θ/	/ð/	e.g. *thigh, thy*
/t/	/d/	e.g. *tin, din*

The speed of vibration determines the pitch of our voice. In adult male voices the average pitch is about 120 Hz (120 vibrations per second). In women's voices the average pitch is about 220 Hz, and in children about 260 Hz.

1.2.3 The oral–nasal process

The back of the roof of the mouth is called the **velum** or **soft palate**. Unlike the front of the roof of the mouth (the **hard palate**), the velum is soft, spongy and flexible. When the velum is raised it directs air out through the mouth and prevents air from the lungs going out through the nose, thus resulting in 'oral' sounds. When the velum is lowered, then air can pass through the nose, resulting in 'nasal' sounds. Compare the following pairs of words and note the effect of the nasal sound.

bad   mad

baby   maybe

pig   ping

Behind the top front teeth there is a bony ridge called the **alveolar ridge** which is a very important point of contact for the tongue in many English consonant sounds. The tongue itself is a ball-shaped muscle with a protruding 'tip' and 'blade'. The tongue (and lips) are extremely mobile and can take up many positions to change the size and shape of the mouth, thus affecting sounds.

The place and manner of articulation will be considered in Section 1.3 when we survey English consonants.

1.2.4 Advising learners

To help learners make sounds which do not exist in their own first language, teachers need to understand the speech process and be able to show students how and where individual sounds are made. Some advice can be useful; other advice can be distinctly unhelpful. The following are some examples of **unhelpful** advice to learners of English which have been collected from exams and practicums.

/ɪ/ is like the sound you make when someone punches you in the stomach.

/ð/: to make this sound, put your tongue between your teeth and bite hard.

/ŋ/ is a sound made in the back of the head. Hold on to the sound, think of your nose and say *sing*.

Teachers need to be able to do better than this. For example,

/θ/: to make this sound, put the tip of the tongue between the teeth and breathe out through the mouth without voicing. Watch me do it and listen to the sound.

1.3 English consonants

Consonant sounds have different characteristics from vowel sounds and are described in different ways. Consonants obstruct the flow of air from the lungs, vowels do not. To describe consonants and how to make them, we describe where the tongue or lips move to, what this does to the airflow, and whether there is vibration of the vocal chords (voicing).

The place of articulation and manner of articulation of the English consonant sounds is summarised in Table 1.2. Each of the 24 consonants can

Table 1.2 English consonant phonemes

Manner of articulation	Place of articulation							
	Bilabial	Labio-dental	Dental	Alveolar	Post-alveolar	Palatal	Velar	Glottal
stops	p　b			t　d			k　g	
fricatives		f　v	θ　ð	s　z	ʃ　ʒ			h
affricates					ʧ　ʤ			
nasals	m			n			ŋ	
approximants	w			r		j		
lateral approximant				l				

be described in terms of three parameters – place of articulation, manner of articulation, and voicing. Voiceless consonants are in bold in Table 1.2.

1.3.1 Place of articulation

If the **lips** are involved in articulation, the sound is **labial**; if the **teeth** are involved, the sound is **dental**. Involvement of the tooth ridge produces **alveolar** sounds; the hard palate is associated with **palatal** sounds; the **velum** (soft palate) is associated with **velar** sounds; constriction of the glottis is associated with **glottal** sounds.

1.3.2 Manner of articulation

The flow of air from the lungs can be affected by the lips, tongue, teeth and shape of the mouth.

1 The airflow can be interrupted temporarily to produce **stops** (sometimes called **plosives**). There are six English stops – /p, b, t, d, k, g/. Other English consonants are **continuants**.

2 The airflow can be made turbulent because of narrowing or obstruction in the mouth or throat resulting in friction, thus producing **fricative** consonants. There are nine English fricatives – /f, v, θ, ð, s, z, ʃ, ʒ, h/.

3 The airflow can be stopped temporarily and then released with friction, to produce **affricates**. There are two English affricates – /ʧ, ʤ/. The first consonant in *choose* is an affricate – /ʧ/. Compare this with *shoes* which begins with a fricative /ʃ/.

4 The airflow can be sent out through the nose as a result of a lowering of the velum. This produces **nasal** sounds. For other English consonants the velum is raised so that the breath cannot go out through the nose. There are three English nasal consonants – /m, n, ŋ/, although other sounds can be partly 'nasalised' with the velum partially lowered.

5 **Approximants** include the **lateral** /l/, in which the airstream is blocked in the centre of the mouth, but with air continuing to escape around the sides of the tongue. The **semi-vowels** /w, j/ are continuants and are made like vowels with little or no obstruction of the airflow, but they glide rapidly to the following vowel. They are like consonants in that they require the form *a* not *an* of the indefinite article (*a wish* not **an wish*). /w/ is labio-velar with lips rounded and the tongue raised at the velum. /r/ is also a gliding consonant, but it does not have vowel characteristics as /w/ and /j/ do.

1.3.3 Voicing

Fifteen English consonants (and all vowels) are **voiced**. Table 1.2 shows that eight pairs of consonants have voicing as the only factor that distinguishes them. In fact, however, voiceless sounds are stronger (and louder) than their voiced counterparts, especially in initial positions in words, where there is usually extra air released. It is interesting to note the effect of 'devoicing' all sounds when we whisper words or sentences. There is surprisingly little effect on intelligibility.

Task 1.8

Give the phonemic symbol for the following descriptions.

1 A voiced bilabial stop	/	/
2 A voiced post-alveolar fricative	/	/
3 A voiced velar nasal	/	/
4 A voiced palatal approximant	/	/
5 A voiceless alveolar fricative	/	/

Task 1.9

A description of the articulation of English consonants mentions three features – voicing, place and manner of articulation, e.g. /m/ is a voiced bilabial nasal. Describe the following phonemes.

1 /k/	2 /v/	3 /j/	4 /ʧ/	5 /ð/
6 /p/	7 /ʒ/	8 /ŋ/	9 /s/	10 /θ/
11 /h/	12 /w/	13 /g/		

Task 1.10

Identify each phoneme.

1 The lips are together, the velum is lowered, the sound is voiced and the air passes out through the nose. This sound is / /.

2 The tip of the tongue is placed on the alveolar ridge. The sides of the tongue are against the sides of the hard palate. The soft palate is raised. The pressure of air builds up and, when the tongue tip is lowered suddenly from the alveolar ridge, the air rushes out. The sound is voiceless. The sound is / /.

3 This pair of sounds is made with the tongue tip near the back of the alveolar ridge, higher than for /s, z/. The soft palate is raised so that the air goes out through the mouth. They are continuants. They are / / and / /.

4 This sound is made with the back of the tongue against the soft palate. The soft palate is lowered, with the air escaping through the nose. The sound is voiced. The sound is / /.

5 This is a voiced sound. It is made with the tongue tip between the teeth. It is a continuant, and the soft palate is raised, allowing all the air to come out of the mouth. This sound is / /.

1.4 English vowels

A **syllable** is a unit associated with a pulse of air from the chest. The word *repeat* has two syllables, /rə piːt/. **Vowels** are sounds which 'carry' this pulse of air, and can be described as the 'nucleus' of a syllable. (It should be noted that the 'syllabic consonants' [l] and [n], which can be variants of the /l/ and /n/ phonemes, can also be the core of a syllable as in /teɪbl/ and /kɔːʃn/ rather than /teɪbəl/ or /kɔːʃən/.)

Syllables can have different combinations of consonants and vowels:

closed syllables	CVC	*rip*
	VC	*us*
open syllables	CV	*to*
	V	*a*

Consonants rarely occur alone, but the exclamation /ʃ/ meaning 'be quiet' is one exception.

In the stream of speech, the environment in which the sounds occur can change the syllabic structure of words, e.g.

/rɪp-ɪt-ʌp/ ⇒ /re-pe-tʌp/   (rip it up)

/raɪp-æpl/ ⇒ /raɪ-pæpl/   (ripe apple)

Because the tongue does not touch a specific point in the mouth to make a vowel, we do not describe vowels in terms of a 'place of articulation'. Rather, the tongue helps shape the vocal tract but does not obstruct the mouth when 'voiced' air is released. We describe vowels in terms of the position of the tongue in shaping the vocal tract, the amount of 'rounding' of the lips and the 'length' of the vowel. Whether the vowel is made as an individual sound or forms a **diphthong** is also relevant. Vowels can be made on their own and can be made short or long. They can have variations in pitch and loudness, and can be sung. In contrast, try the impossible task of singing the consonant /s/. Vowel sounds come from resonance (amplification) within the vocal tract of the sound source (which is set up by voicing). The resonance occurs in frequency groups (or **formants**) with frequencies ranging from about 300 to 4,500 cycles per second.

The tongue position for vowels is usually described in terms of the position of the highest point of the tongue. It can be 'high' ('close') or 'low' ('open'), and nearer the 'front' or 'back' of the mouth. Try saying /iː/, /ɑː/ and /uː/. In RP-like pronunciation, you should find that your tongue positions are approximately like those shown in Figure 1.3. With /iː/, the front of the tongue is high and close to the palate. For /ɑː/ the tongue is low at the back. For /uː/ the tongue is high at the back.

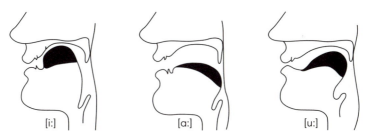

Figure 1.3   Tongue position for three vowels

Early in the twentieth century, the famous British phonetician Daniel Jones suggested that the vowels of any language could be described in terms of eight reference points on a schematised diagram of the mouth which shows the high–low/front–back dimensions. Jones called these positions the **cardinal vowels** to serve as reference points in describing the vowels of particular languages. The cardinal vowels are shown in Figure 1.4.

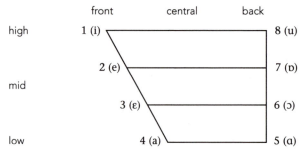

Figure 1.4 The cardinal vowels

The vowels in different varieties of English can be described with reference to these 'cardinal' points. For example, the 12 monophthongal vowels of 'received pronunciation' of British English are approximately as shown in Figure 1.5.

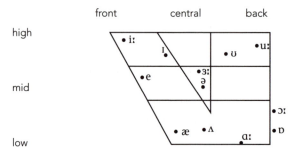

Diphthongs are: /ɪə/ beer; /eɪ/ make; /əʊ/ know; /aɪ/ buy; /aʊ/ cow; /ʊə/ poor; /ɔɪ/ boy; /eə/ hair.

Figure 1.5 The vowel phonemes of British English (RP)

The vowels of General North American English are approximately as shown in Figure 1.6. There is some regional variation on these vowels in different parts of the US and Canada.

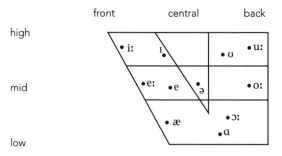

Diphthongs are: /aʊ/ now; /aɪ/ buy; /ɔɪ/ boy; /eɪ/ paint; /əʊ/ home.

Figure 1.6 The vowel phonemes of General North American English

The vowel phonemes of New Zealand English are approximately as shown in Figure 1.7.

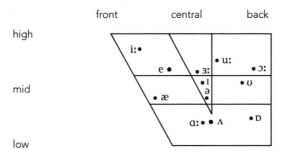

Diphthongs are: /eə/ or /iə/ hear, hair; /eɪ/ make; /əʊ/ know; /aɪ/ buy; /aʊ/ cow; /ɔɪ/ boy.

Figure 1.7 The vowel phonemes of New Zealand English

The description of vowels in this section of the book is a very 'broad' one. There are consistent differences among individual speakers and different sociolinguistic groups. For example, by comparing Figures 1.5 and 1.7, it can be seen that in New Zealand English /ɪ/ tends to be made nearer to /ə/ than in British RP.

Four features are normally mentioned when describing vowels. They are:

1 The length of the vowel

2 The height of the tongue

3 The part of the tongue which is highest

4 The shape of the lips.

For British Received Pronunciation, it can be seen in Table 1.3 that /iː/ is classified as a long high front vowel. It has spread lips. /ɔː/ is classified as

Table 1.3 Classification of the vowels in British Received Pronunciation

		Part of the tongue that is highest		
		Front	Centre	Back
Height of tongue	High	iː ɪ		uː ʊ
	Mid	e	ə ɜː	ɔː
	Low	æ	ʌ	ɒ ɑː

Short vowels are /ɪ, e, æ, ə, ʊ, ʌ, ɒ/.
Long vowels are /iː, ɜː, uː, ɔː, ɑː/.
Vowels and diphthongs with lip rounding are /ɔː, ʊ, uː, ɒ, əʊ, ɔɪ, uə/.
Vowels with spread lips are /iː, ɪ, e/.

a long mid-back vowel. It has rounded lips. /ɪ/ is classified as a short, high to mid, front to central vowel.

The most frequent English vowel is /ə/. It usually replaces other vowels in unstressed syllables (see Section 1.5). For language learners, it has often been pointed out that vowels may best be learned by listening and imitation rather than theory. Some vowels are easy to learn because they occur in many languages, e.g. /iː, uː, ɑː/. Some vowels are easily confused and hard to learn, e.g. /ɜː, ɪə, eə/ (cf. *her, hear, hair*); /e, æ/ (cf. *fellow, fallow*).

Task 1.11

Vowel phonemes
In this exercise there is a test word on the left in phonemic transcription. There are four columns of words on the right. Decide which of these words (there may be more than one) contain the same vowel sound as the test word.

	Test word	1	2	3	4	Answers
1	/sed/	reed	weather	head	lie	
2	/hɪl/	pail	sit	peat	tide	
3	/ɔɪl/	boy	gale	hate	or	
4	/stiːp/	heap	tip	cream	ceiling	
5	/sʊt/	pull	pool	foot	put	
6	/ʃaʊt/	ago	cut	out	taught	
7	/mɑːkt/	park	father	alarm	cat	
8	/hɪə/	here	hear	appear	sincere	
9	/hɜːt/	cup	furniture	sport	her	
10	/sprɔːld/	all	more	hot	claw	
11	/blɒt/	wash	hotel	up	drop	
12	/feə/	ear	air	there	here	
13	/həʊm/	numb	fault	hope	row	
14	/saɪd/	said	beside	eye	tied	

Task 1.12

The neutral or unstressed vowel sound schwa (/ə/)
Each of the following words includes the unstressed vowel sound /ə/. Underline the part(s) of each word containing /ə/.

about	finger	custom	dangerous	absent
island	consider	disappear	husband	other
correct	elephant	policeman	worker	neighbour
banana	quarter	yesterday	allowed	forgive
open				

Task 1.13

Transcribe the following words containing diphthongs.

about	myself	ago	though
endure	fight	fail	hair
how	fatal	mare	enjoy
cried	fear	tour	growl
comb	ache	hope	bough

Task 1.14

Diphthongs

In each row in this task **one** word does not have a diphthong. Underline the word without a diphthong.

1	die	development	describe	divide
2	doubt	down	drive	duty
3	effort	ear	employer	enjoy
4	expensive	explain	explanation	face
5	fail	fact	unfair	famous
6	fierce	family	fight	found
7	fire	floated	finished	flour
8	follow	flower	fly	flew
9	foreign	frighten	game	go
10	gold	great	friend	ground
11	grow	hair	hate	group
12	imagine	idea	inside	iron
13	island	immediately	increase	join
14	joke	journey	kind	knife
15	know	lake	lazy	language

Task 1.15

1 Give the phonemic symbol for the following vowel descriptions. (Do not take account of lip rounding.)

a A long high back vowel   d A long mid central vowel

b A short high to mid back vowel   e A long low back vowel

c A long mid back vowel   f A short low front vowel

2 Describe the features of the following vowel phonemes.

a /iː/   b /ɒ/   c /ə/   d /æ/

1.5 The distribution of English sounds

The items and processes of a language are not all used with equal frequency. Some English sounds are used more than others, and they occur in different positions in words and in combination with other sounds.

1.5.1 Frequency of English phonemes

The frequency of the 44 sounds of English calculated by Fry and cited by Gimson (1980: 149, 217) is shown in Table 1.4.

Higgins has published on the Internet (www.marlodge.supanet.com/wordlist/phonfreq.html) an analysis of the distribution of English phonemes as they occur in the *Oxford Advanced Learner's Dictionary*. The frequencies refer to the headword entries in the dictionary, not to actual use in the language. Higgins's analysis shows that in the 70,646 dictionary entries, the average word length is 6.98 phonemes. There is an average of 2.55 vowel phonemes per word and 4.43 consonant phonemes per word.

Table 1.4   Frequency of British English (RP) phonemes

Vowels	%	Consonants	%
ə	10.74	n	7.58
ɪ	8.33	t	6.42
e	2.97	d	5.14
aɪ	1.83	s	4.81
ʌ	1.75	l	3.66
eɪ	1.71	ð	3.56
iː	1.65	r	3.51
əʊ	1.51	m	3.22
æ	1.45	k	3.09
ɒ	1.37	w	2.81
ɔː	1.24	z	2.46
uː	1.13	v	2.00
ʊ	0.86	b	1.97
ɑː	0.79	f	1.79
aʊ	0.61	p	1.78
ɜː	0.52	h	1.46
eə	0.34	ŋ	1.15
ɪə	0.21	g	1.05
ɔɪ	0.14	ʃ	0.96
ʊə	0.06	j	0.88
	39.21	ʤ	0.60
		ʧ	0.41
		θ	0.37
		ʒ	0.10
			60.78

Source: Fry, D. B. (1947) 'The Frequency of Occurrence of Speech Sounds in Southern English' in *Archives Néerlandaises de Phonetique Experimentale*, XX, pp. 103–6. Reprinted by permission of Royal Holland Society of Sciences and Humanities.

On the basis of their importance for distinguishing the greatest number of English word pairs, data collected by Denes (1963) suggests that certain distinctions between phonemes might be particularly important in affecting intelligibility. These include:

Vowels: /e æ/, /æ ʌ /, /æ ɒ /, /ʌ ɒ/, /ɔː əʊ/, /e ɪ/, /e eɪ/, /ɑː aɪ/, /ɜː əʊ/

Consonants: /p b/, /p f/, /m n/, /n l/, /l r/, /f h/, /t d/, /k g/

Analysis of Table 1.4 shows that the front and central vowels /ɪ/ and /ə/ are especially frequent, and alveolar and bilabial consonants tend to be more frequent than other consonants. About 80 per cent of English sounds are voiced. Among all the consonants, 20 per cent are nasals, 33 per cent are stops and about 46 per cent are fricatives.

1.5.2 Redundancy

While it is obviously desirable for learners of English to be able to produce all the phonemes, it is not absolutely essential because of **redundancy** or predictability in human languages. As we have seen, letters are not the same as sounds, but we can illustrate the effect of redundancy in general by deleting letters from the following written sentences.

1 D_ __u _e_l_y m__n _ha_.

2 D__snt sh_ l_k_ _c_cr__m.

3 _ou__ _ou _a_e _o_e _o_e _o_ __e o__e__.[1]

In 1, half of the letters (a mixture of vowels and consonants) are missing. In 2, all the vowels have been deleted but it is not too hard to work out what the words are. In 3, all the consonants have been deleted and it is much harder to work out what the words might be. Consonants are less predictable and, as O'Connor (1980: 24) has noted, therefore contribute more to making English understood than vowels do. He points out that if we could omit vowel sounds our speech would still be interpretable (although vowels actually contain certain information that helps identify consonants), but if we could omit the consonants speech would be unintelligible. Vowels, on the other hand, are the main basis of distinctive individual voice quality and accent (although consonant pronunciations can also reveal aspects of dialect).

Redundancy in languages helps protect messages by providing extra 'signal' to overcome lapses in the listener's attention, or masking 'noise' from other sources. Redundancy in English sounds enables some native speakers or second language learners to use fewer than 44 phonemes. For example, some speakers use two phonemes (/f/ and /v/) for /f, v, θ, ð/ and say *fings* for *things*, *vese* for *these*. Some speakers use /t/ and /d/ for /t, d, θ, ð/ and say *deze books* or *He knows many tings*.

[1] 1. Do you really mean that? 2. Doesn't she like ice cream? 3. Would you take some more for the others?

1.5.3 The positions that phonemes can occur in

Phonemes can potentially occur at the beginning, in the middle or at the end of a word. Most English sounds occur in all three positions; some occur in only one or two of the positions. For language learners, it is often the case that although a sound in English is similar to a sound in their first language, the sounds cannot occur in the same environment in the two languages. Table 1.5 gives examples of the occurrence of English phonemes (including diphthongs) in initial, medial and final positions. It can be seen that /h/, /w/, /j/ and most vowels do not occur at the end of isolated English words although they can occur as linking sounds; /ŋ/ does not occur at the beginning of English words.

1.5.4 English consonant clusters

In Section 1.4, four main syllable structures were listed: CVC, VC, CV, V. In fact, consonants frequently occur in clusters. English has about 20 syllable types if we include these consonant clusters. Many languages have only CV. The syllable structures of English include:

CV	no	CCVCCC	stands
CCV	fly	CCVCCCC	twelfths
CCCV	straw	CCCVCC	straps
CVC	sit	CCCVCCC	sprinkle
CCVC	bread	CCCVCCCC	sprinkles
CCCVC	scream	V	a
CVCC	hand	VC	on
CVCCC	tests	VCC	apt
CVCCCC	samples	VCCC	ants
CCVCC	grand		

Consonant clusters occur before vowels (**initial clusters**) or after vowels (**final clusters**). Initial clusters are less frequent and not longer than three consonants. There are about 50 initial consonant clusters and about 350 final clusters in English. Examples are shown in Table 1.6. There are some differences between major varieties of English. These include:

	UK	USA
new	/njuː/	/nuː/
student	/stjuːdnt/	/stuːdnt/
lure	/ljʊb/	/lʊə/
farm	/faːm/	/faːrm/

Table 1.5 The distribution of English RP phonemes

Phonemes		Phonemes		Phonemes	
b	bed habit rob	h	him behind	eə	air fairly pair
p	poor happy crop	tʃ	cheese butcher each	æ	apple glad ....
d	deep body wood	ʤ	jazz pages ridge	ɒ	off lot ....
t	ten letter great	m	mouse coming some	ʌ	ugly but ....
g	girl August flag	n	not any sun	ə	allow understand other
k	cat speaking ache	ŋ	.... singer wrong	ʊ	.... book ....
v	voice never give	l	list sailor wall	iː	easy keep fee
f	five office knife	r	rain very	ɑː	artist lather bra
ð	that mother breathe	w	water lower	ɔː	all ball saw
θ	thank nothing bath	j	young beyond	ɜː	early heard her
z	zinc houses choose	ɪ	it shin (happy)	uː	ooze spoon flew
s	sing lesson face	e	every hen	aɪ	idle five sky
ʒ	genre pleasure massage	ɪə	ear fearing beer	aʊ	out house now
ʃ	sugar nation English	eɪ	April break say	ɔɪ	oil boil toy
		əʊ	over stove ago	ʊə	.... pure

Some common words have complex consonant clusters, e.g. *changed* /tʃeɪndʒd/.

Learning how to produce clusters without inserting vowels between consonants is often difficult for language learners. Some learners (including infant native speakers) might say /gəriːn/ for *green*, /səkʊl/ for *school*, /fɪləm/ for *film*, /pəliːz/ for *please* and so on.

For some clusters containing an initial continuant, teachers can help learners make the cluster by getting them to make the second consonant first, then a lengthened preceding one, gradually reducing the length; then the cluster, e.g.

for   *spin*: pin, s.........., s....., s..., spin

1.5.5 Vowel sequences

Vowels can also occur in 'clusters'. When /ə/ follows a diphthong, the resulting sequence is sometimes called a triphthong.

aɪə	fire
aʊə	flower
eɪə	player
ɔɪə	employer
əʊə	follower

Table 1.6 English consonant clusters

Initial clusters

bj	beautiful	fl	flesh	sw	swim
dj	duty	gl	glad	tw	twig
fj	few	kl	class	θw	thwart
hj	humour	pl	plate	sf	sphere
kj	cube	sl	slang	sk	school
kl	clean	br	bread	sm	small
kr	cream	dr	drink	sn	snow
kw	quick	fr	fresh	sp	sport
lj	lure (UK)	gr	grass	st	stone
mj	music	kr	cry	skj	skew
nj	new (UK)	pr	price	skr	scream
pj	pupil	tr	train	skw	square
sj	suit (UK)	ʃr	shrink	spj	spume
tj	Tuesday	θr	three	spl	split
vj	view	dw	dwell	spr	spring
θj	Thucydides (UK)	gw	Gwen	stj	student (UK)
bl	blood	hw	when	str	stream

Table 1.6 (cont'd)

Final clusters (continued over the page)

bd	robbed	kts	subjects	mpt	jumped
bl	trouble	lb	bulb	mst	glimpsed
bld	troubled	lbz	bulbs	mt	tempt
blz	troubles	ld	hold	mts	tempts
bz	clubs	ldz	holds	mz	rooms
dl	middle	ldʒ	bulge	mθ	warmth
dld	muddled	ldʒd	bulged	nd	hand
dlz	muddles	lf	wolf	ndl	bundle
dn	pardon	lfs	gulfs	ndld	bundled
dnd	pardoned	lft	engulfed	ndlz	bundles
dnt	hadn't	lfθ	twelfth	ndz	hands
dnz	gardens	lfθs	twelfths	ndʒ	change
dz	roads	lk	milk	ndʒd	changed
ʒd	raged	lks	milks	nl	tunnel
dθ	width	lkt	milked	nld	tunnelled
dθs	widths	lm	film	nlz	tunnels
fl	ruffle	lmd	filmed	ns	dance
fld	ruffled	lmz	films	nst	danced
flz	ruffles	ln	kiln	nt	tent
fn	often	lnz	kilns	ntl	mantle
fnd	stiffened	lp	help	ntld	mantled
fnz	stiffens	lps	helps	ntlz	mantles
fs	roofs	lpt	helped	nts	tents
ft	lift	ls	false	ntʃ	lunch
ftn	often (UK)	lst	repulsed	ntʃt	lunched
fts	lifts	lt	result	nz	runs
fθ	fifth	lts	results	nθ	month
fθs	fifths	ltʃ	filch	nθs	months
gd	begged	ltʃt	filched	ŋd	wronged
gl	giggle	lv	solve	ŋgl	single
gld	giggled	lvz	wolves	ŋgld	singled
glz	giggles	lz	falls	ŋglz	singles
gnl	signal	lθ	health	ŋk	drink
gnld	signalled	lθs	healths	ŋkl	uncle
gnlz	signals	mbl	rumble	ŋkld	wrinkled
gz	legs	mbld	rumbled	ŋklz	uncles
kl	bicycle	mblz	rumbles	ŋks	drinks
kld	cycled	md	hummed	ŋkt	instinct
klz	bicycles	mf	triumph	ŋz	sings
kn	reckon	mfs	triumphs	ŋθ	length
knd	reckoned	mft	triumphed	ŋθs	lengths
knz	reckons	ml	normal	pl	apple
ks	parks	mld	trammelled	pld	toppled
ksl	axle	mlz	trammels	plz	apples
kslz	axles	mp	lamp	pn	open
kst	text	mpl	simple	pnd	opened
ksts	texts	mpld	sampled	pnz	opens
ksθs	sixths	mplz	samples	ps	hopes
kt	subject	mps	lamps	pst	collapsed

Table 1.6 (cont'd)

pt	accept	tn	frighten	znd	reasoned
pts	accepts	tnd	frightened	znz	reasons
sk	ask	tnz	frightens	znt	isn't
sks	asks	ts	cats	ʃl	official
skt	asked	tʃt	touched	ʃld	marshalled
sl	whistle	tθ	eighth	ʃlz	officials
sld	whistled	tθs	eighths	ʃn	station
slz	whistles	vd	lived	ʃnd	stationed
sn	listen	vl	shovel	ʃnz	stations
snd	listened	vld	shovelled	ʃt	pushed
snz	listens	vlz	shovels	3d	rouged
sp	grasp	vn	heaven	3n	television
sps	grasps	vnd	leavened	3nz	visions
spt	grasped	vnt	haven't	θs	heaths
st	nest	vnz	heavens	θt	unearthed
stl	pistol	vz	lives	ðd	breathed
stlz	pistols	zd	excused	ðl	betrothal
stn	piston	zl	proposal	ðm	rhythm
stnz	pistons	zld	chiselled	ðmz	rhythms
sts	nests	zlz	proposals	ðn	heathen
tl	title	zm	enthusiasm	ðnz	heathens
tld	entitled	zmz	chasms	ðz	clothes
tlz	titles	zn	reason		

1.5.6 The effect of the environment in which sounds occur

1.5.6.1 Linking

When one word ends in a vowel and the next word begins with a vowel, **linking** often occurs. One of /j, w, r/ may be pronounced between the two vowels, e.g. *may I* /meɪjaɪ/, *how about* /haʊwəbaʊt/, *saw enough* /sɔːrənʌf/. A rule to follow is that if the first word of a pair ends in one of /iː, ɪ, eɪ, aɪ, ɔɪ/, add /j/; if the first word of a pair ends in one of /uː, əʊ, aʊ/, add /w/; if there is a letter *r* at the end of the first word or the sound /ɔː/, then /r/ is sounded between the words. These rules can be flexible (and dialect specific). For example, some North Americans, Australians and New Zealanders may pronounce *This film is now out on video* as /naʊraʊt/ rather than /naʊwaʊt/.

1.5.6.2 Rhoticity

Some dialects of English (e.g. Scots English or General North American English) are **rhotic**. That is, they always pronounce /r/ when it occurs before a consonant (e.g. *hard*) or at the ends of words (e.g. *far*). Other varieties (e.g. British RP) are **non-rhotic** and pronounce /r/ only when it is followed by a vowel sound. Rhoticity can have an effect on the preceding vowel.

		Non-rhotic	Rhotic
[iə]	hear	[hiə]	[hiːr]
[eə]	hair	[heə]	[heɪr]
[uə]	tour	[tuə]	[tuːr]
[ɔː]	pour	[pɔː]	[pəʊr]
[ɜː]	turn	[tɜːn]	[tʌrn]

1.5.6.3 Elision

In the company of particular sounds or words, and sometimes simply through language change, some sounds can disappear. This is called **elision**. For example, the word *library* is often pronounced as /laɪbriː/, not /laɪbrəriː/.

Task 1.16

Transcribe these words as they might be pronounced in normal fluent speech.

1 family
2 history
3 properly
4 deliberate (adj.)
5 postman
6 temporary
7 government
8 parliament
9 secretary
10 company
11 temporarily
12 deteriorating
13 grandmother
14 asked
15 separate (adj.)
16 interest

1.5.6.4 Assimilation

When two or more words are produced in sequence, a sound or sounds in the preceding word can change in anticipation of the place of articulation, voicing, lip position or nasalisation of the second. For example,

of /əv/ becomes [əf] before a voiceless consonant [əfkɔːs]

good /gʊd/ becomes [gʊb] before a bilabial nasal [gʊbmɔːnɪŋ]

has /hæz/ becomes [hæs] before a voiceless sound [hæstəduːɪt]

The following list shows changes that frequently occur: /t, d, n, s, z/ often change so that they are made in the **same place** as the following consonant. But they do not change their voicing.

1 /t/ becomes /p/ before /p, b, m/   e.g. *what money* [wɒpmʌniː]
2 /t/ becomes /k/ before /k, g/   e.g. *bright girl* [braɪkgɜːl]
3 /d/ becomes /b/ before /p, b, m/   e.g. *red pen* [rebpen]
4 /d/ becomes /g/ before /k, g/   e.g. *red car* [regkɑː]

5 /n/ becomes /m/ before /p, b, m/ e.g. *green peas* [griːmpiːz]
6 /n/ becomes /ŋ/ before /k, g/   e.g. *when can she go* [weŋkənʃiːgəʊ]
7 /s/ becomes /ʃ/ before /ʃ, j/   e.g. *what's your name* [wɒtʃjɔːneim]
8 /z/ becomes /ʒ/ before /ʃ, j/   e.g. *where's she now* [weəʒʃiːnaʊ]
9 /t + j/ becomes /tʃ/   e.g. *met you* [metʃuː]
10 /d + j/ becomes /dʒ/   e.g. *fed you* [fedʒuː]

Task 1.17

Transcribe the following phrases to show the effect of elision and assimilation when you say them rapidly.

1 one month
2 next week
3 she's waiting at the <u>main gate</u>
4 we sold <u>ten cups</u> of coffee
5 <u>stand back</u> please

6 <u>ten pencils</u>
7 he's <u>gone back</u> home
8 those are <u>nice shoes</u>
9 he's got a <u>bad cold</u>

Task 1.18

Transcribe these phrases as they would sound when the words are run together.

Phrase	Separate words	Words run together
1 hard problems	/hɑːd prɒblɪmz/	
2 good meal	/gʊd miːl/	
3 good concert	/gʊd kɒnsət/	
4 when pouring milk	/wen pɔːrɪŋ mɪlk/	
5 in cupboards	/ɪn kʌbədz/	
6 this year	/ðɪs jɪə/	
7 nice shape	/naɪs ʃeɪp/	
8 his yacht	/hɪz jɒt/	

Task 1.19

Transcribe these phrases and show the syllables as they might be produced in normal fluent speech, e.g. *a cup of tea* [ə kə pəf tiː].

1 what is it
2 your own house
3 where are you going
4 or any evidence
5 just a minute

6 don't touch it
7 the first floor
8 not at all
9 halfway across
10 my mother ate all of them

1.5.6.5 Vowel length

A distinction is sometimes made by phoneticians between **strong** and **weak** consonants. Strong consonants include /p, t, k, f, θ, s, ʃ, ʧ/. Weak consonants include /b, d, g, v, ð, z, ʒ, ʤ/. Strong and weak consonants have different effects on the vowels that come before them. A vowel sound before a strong consonant is shorter than the same vowel sound before a weak consonant. The /iː/ sound in /biːt/ is thus not the same as the /iː/ sound in /biːd/.

Here are some examples.

Short vowel before a strong consonant	Long vowel before a weak consonant
[æt]	[æːd]
[rəʊp]	[rəʊːb]
[haɪt]	[haɪːd]
[tənaɪt]	[dənaɪːd]
[ədvaɪs]	[ədvaɪːz]
[sæk]	[sæːg]
[mɒp]	[mɒːb]
[wɒnt]	[wɒːnd]
[went]	[weːnd]
[raɪf]	[deraɪːv]
[əʊk]	[vəʊːg]
[hɒp]	[hɒːb]
[pʌlp]	[bʌːlb]

1.6 Prosodic features

Syllables and words can be produced with variations in a number of dimensions, including duration ('length'), frequency ('pitch'), intensity ('loudness') and pausing. Such changes are called prosodic features (or suprasegmental features) of the sound system of a language. Together, prosodic features are perceived as giving **stress** to words and **intonation** to sentences. Prosodic features help express the speaker's emotional state or attitudes, give grammatical information such as distinguishing between statements and questions, and highlight the relative importance of words or parts of a sentence. We will consider stress and intonation in turn. It should be noted that stress and intonation together produce considerable difficulties for many learners of English and frequently have a greater effect on the intelligibility of learners' English than does the pronunciation of individual sounds.

1.6.1 Stress

Word and sentence stress is very important in English. Consider the many ways you can say the following sentences to express different nuances of meaning.

He doesn't like yoghurt.

I'll be the judge of that.

We don't live in Chicago because of the weather.

(What's on TV tonight?) I thought we were going out.

(What are we doing tonight?) I thought we were going out.

Putting stress on particular parts of sentences can be used to show where new or important information is in a sentence. As we will see, there are some general rules for assigning stress, but for learners of English it is a good policy to learn appropriate stress when individual words are learned.

Word stress can be discussed separately for function words, which are usually **not** stressed, and content words, which usually have stress, especially if there is more than one syllable.

1.6.1.1 Function word stress

Most function words such as articles, modal verbs, pronouns and prepositions have only one syllable (e.g. *the, can, do, my, him, on, as*). These function words are very frequent (constituting about half of the words we produce), but they are not stressed. When these function words are produced in sentences their vowel is normally pronounced as /ə/. A number of these unstressed English function words have more than one pronunciation. These are sometimes called 'strong' and 'weak' (or 'reduced') forms. When the words stand on their own they have strong forms but when they are placed with other words in sentences or phrases they have weak forms, e.g.

Word	Strong form	Weak form	Example
as	æz	əz	əzgʊdəzðɪs
but	bʌt	bət	bətðætsnɒtɔːl
and	ænd	ən	juːənmiː
of	ɒv	əv	ðəbestəvɔːl
than	ðæn	ðən	betəðəntɒmz
you	juː	jə	djənəʊ
does	dʌz	dəz	wɒdəzʃiwɒnt
from	frɒm	frəm	ɪtsfrəmsuː
at	æt	ət	lʊkətmiː
his	hɪz	əz	hiːzɒnəzəʊn

Other function words which have unstressed weak forms include: *he, her, him, do, did, some, for, them, am, are, is, was, has, had, have, can, shall, will, would, must, an, the, to, what.* Some function words have more than one weak form, e.g. *him* /ɪm, əm/.

The following high frequency verb + *to* combinations also have strong and weak pronunciations:

	Strong form	Weak form
going to	gəʊɪŋ tuː	gənə
got to	gɒt tuː	gətə, gədə
has to	hæz tuː	hæstə
have to	hæv tuː	əftə
ought to	ɔːt tuː	ɔːtə
used to	juːst tuː	juːstə
want to	wɒnt tuː	wɒnə

There is sometimes an important difference in meaning between strong and weak forms, e.g.

I'm going to be sick.	/aɪmgʌnəbiːsɪk/	(prediction)
I'm going to school.	/aɪmgəʊɪŋtəskʊl/	(destination)
What have we got to take?	/wɒtəvwiːgɒtəteɪk/	(necessity)
What have we got to drink?	/wɒtəvwiːgɒttuːdrɪŋk/	(availability)

1.6.1.2 Content word stress

In English, one or more syllables in a content word are normally stressed. If there is more than one stressed syllable, one gets stronger stress than the other(s). This is called **primary stress** (marked ˈ). Other stressed syllables in a word may then get **secondary stress** (marked ˌ), while remaining syllables are 'unstressed'. For example:

ˈant

ˈinsect

reˈmove

ˈenergy

ˌransporˈtation

ˌmagˈnificently

In this book, the stress mark is placed **before** the stressed syllable. In some dictionaries, the mark is placed **above** the stressed syllable. In others, it is placed **after** the stressed syllable.

For learners of English, the major difficulty with stress in content words with more than one syllable is selecting which syllable or syllables to stress. In French, the last syllable in each word is usually stressed. In Czech, the first syllable of a word is usually stressed. English word stress is much more complex.

A number of general points can be listed to show something of the complexity that learners are faced with but, although factors such as the following influence stress assignment, few can be described as hard and fast 'rules'. By learning correct stress for individual words, learners may be best expected to inductively and unconsciously work out the 'rules' for themselves.

Stress assignment can be influenced by:

1 Whether or not the word has derivational affixes. Compare, for example:

    'politics   po'litical   ,poli'tician

2 The word class of the word. Compare these nouns, adjectives and verbs:

    'con,duct (noun)   con'duct (verb)

    'object (noun)   ob'ject (verb)

    'record (noun)   re'cord (verb)

    'estimate (noun)   'esti,mate (verb)

    'separate (adjective)   'sepa,rate (verb)

    'insult (noun)   in'sult (verb)

Typically the noun (or adjective) has stress on the first syllable, and the verb has stress on the last syllable.

3 Whether the word is of Germanic origin or is from Latin or Greek. Germanic words tend to have primary stress on the first syllable of the root, and this is not affected by affixation, e.g.

    'holy   'big

    'holiness   'bigger

    un'holy   'biggest

Words of Latin or Greek origin do not necessarily have the primary stress on the first syllable. Polysyllabic words tend to have their primary stress on the antepenultimate syllable or, less often, on the penultimate syllable, e.g.

    'origin   o'riginate   origi'nality

    'standard   'standardise   standardis'ation

4 The number of syllables in the word. With two-syllable verbs, adjectives and adverbs, if the second syllable contains a long vowel or diphthong, or if it ends with a consonant cluster, then the stress is typically on the second syllable, e.g. re'ply, a'ttract, be'lieve, a'live.

If there is a short vowel in the final syllable, or the word ends with a vowel or a single consonant, then the first syllable typically has primary stress, e.g. 'open, 'level, 'lovely.

With two-syllable nouns, stress usually falls on the second syllable unless the second syllable contains a short vowel, e.g.

de'sign   'father

i'dea   'dollar

ba'lloon   'table

With content words of more than two syllables, the rules are more complex. If a verb ends with a short vowel or a single consonant, then that syllable is unstressed, and the primary stress falls on the preceding syllable (the penultimate syllable). Otherwise, the stress falls on the final syllable, e.g. de'termine, rede'sign.

With nouns, if the last syllable contains a short vowel it is unstressed. If the second to last syllable (the penultimate syllable) contains a long vowel or diphthong or a consonant cluster, then the primary stress falls on that penultimate syllable, but if it also contains a short vowel then the preceding syllable receives primary stress, e.g. 'intellect, ,quantifi'cation, 'customary.

There is thus a tendency for stress in polysyllabic words to fall on syllables containing a long vowel, or diphthong. Some words have two potential locations for primary stress, e.g. 'contra'diction, e'xamin'ation, 'four'teen, but these are not necessarily exactly equal. Some words have different stress in different regional varieties, e.g. compare the pronunciation of *laboratory, inquiry* and *primarily* in British and US English.

UK	US
la'boratory	'laboratory
in'quiry	'inquiry
'primarily	pri'marily

Much more complicated rules, expressed in terms of the 'quality' of the vowels (tense or lax) and the types of suffix, have been proposed in current phonological theory. From the language teacher's viewpoint, however, most learners will learn stress for individual words by imitation, not theory. Some rough rules which may help learners are:

1 In about 80 per cent of words with more than one syllable, it is the first syllable that receives the primary stress, e.g. 'father, 'any, 'gathering, 'excellently, 'water, 'woman, 'table, 'apple. This applies especially to high frequency nouns and adjectives.

2 In words with a prefix, there is a strong tendency for the second (or third) syllable to receive primary stress, e.g. de'vise, re'new, un'do, under'stand, in'vite, con'clude.

3 Suffixes are rarely stressed, e.g. 'kind<u>ness</u>, 'bak<u>er</u>, ob'sess<u>ive</u>, a'tom<u>ic</u>, pro'pens<u>ity</u>, 'pacif<u>y</u>.

4 English compounds typically have stress on the first word, e.g. 'lawn-mower, a'larm clock, 'grandmother, 'newspaper, 'window cleaner, 'washing machine, 'coffee mug, 'baking powder. But note exceptions such as: electric 'blanket, and 'apple cake and apple 'pie.

1.6.1.3 Sentence stress and rhythm

As we have seen, when content words are spoken on their own, they usually have one syllable with primary stress, and sometimes in longer words there are also other syllables with secondary stress. In connected discourse, a fairly regular 'beat' or **rhythm** occurs in sentences.

1 'Fred will 'paint these 'houses.

2 'Fred can 'fix most me'chanical e'quipment.

In Sentences 1 and 2, syllables with stress are followed by syllables without strong stress. In Sentence 1, each syllable with stress alternates with one without. In Sentence 2 there are one, two or three unstressed syllables between stressed syllables.

English is sometimes described as a **stress-timed** language in which there is approximately the same time interval between stressed syllables. If there are several unstressed syllables in sequence, they have to be spoken more rapidly to 'fit' into the rhythmic time interval.

Stress timing is not a rigid process and research has shown that time intervals between stressed syllables are not as regular as theory suggests. Some words are stressed for emphasis (such as to deny something, e.g. *I told him this wasn't mine*). At times, hesitations or choice of particular words affect any 'regular' rhythm. For language learners whose first language is **not** stress timed, learning English sentence rhythm can be quite a problem, however. In **syllable-timed** (or '**mora-timed**') languages such as French, Japanese, or Mandarin Chinese, all unstressed syllables occur at fairly regular time intervals so that the time between syllables which might be regarded as stressed varies according to how many syllables there are. Learners of English who are unfamiliar with stress timing may seem to give each English syllable equal emphasis, and therefore seem to speak jerkily. Such stress patterns are nevertheless common in some varieties of English, e.g. Singapore English.

One important point about English sentence stress is that, although each individual content word in a sentence may have one syllable with primary stress when we pronounce the word on its own, when we pronounce the sentence as a whole, one content word tends to get a fuller stress than the others and all the other stressed syllables are reduced, and some 'stressed' syllables are not in fact stressed. The strongest stress (or **nuclear** stress) is normally near the end of the sentence, e.g.

3 I 'never be'lieve what I 'read in 'news,papers.

4 I ,never be,lieve what I ,read in 'newspapers.

In Sentence 3, the primary and secondary stress have been marked for each word individually. In Sentence 4, the primary sentence stress is marked as occurring on 'news, and all other stress has thus been reduced (from primary to secondary or from secondary to unstressed).

It is not uncommon for sentences to have more than one nuclear stress, especially when they consist of more than one clause, e.g.

When I get 'home, I'll have a 'shower.

In English, the nuclear stress typically comes near the end of a sentence. The reason for this may be because new (unpredictable) information often comes at the end of a sentence. Extra stress for new information helps protect this information from being masked by irrelevant environmental 'noise'. In Sentence 4 above, it could be argued that *newspapers* is not entirely predictable. It could be replaced by *books*, *magazines*, etc., and it is appropriate that it gets the strongest sentence stress to help ensure that the intended word is heard by listeners.

Task 1.20

A Mark the primary stress on each of the following words. The second member of each pair is related in meaning to the first, and consists of the first word + suffix.

B List the suffixes that alter the stress pattern and those that do not alter the stress.

1 accept, acceptance	16 apply, application
2 amuse, amusement	17 atmosphere, atmospheric
3 convenient, conveniently	18 effort, effortless
4 social, socialist	19 entertain, entertaining
5 cultivate, cultivation	20 ceremony, ceremonial
6 economy, economic	21 familiar, familiarity
7 mathematics, mathematician	22 history, historical
8 profit, profitable	23 incident, incidental
9 sympathy, sympathetic	24 character, characteristic
10 accurate, accurately	25 perfect, perfection
11 active, activity	26 continent, continental
12 alter, alteration	27 industry, industrial
13 approximate, approximately	28 theory, theoretical
14 attract, attraction	29 politics, political
15 aware, awareness	30 responsible, responsibility

Task 1.21

Mark sentence stress in the following sentences. Several answers are possible, depending on the intended meaning.

1 The weather has been absolutely terrible.
2 He was very lucky not to have been hurt.
3 Shall we go to a movie after we get home from work?
4 No-one seemed to know where we could get help.
5 The result of the election was quite unexpected.

Task 1.22

Transcribe the first six lines of the verse in 1.1.3, showing the phonemes and the main word stress.

1.6.2 Intonation

As we saw in Section 1.6.1, variations in stress, pausing and pitch are part of the prosodic aspects of English. The use of rising or falling levels of pitch (known as tone) is very important for expressing meaning. Consider how many ways we can say the following words or phrases. Work with a fluent speaker of English if necessary to see how many different ways you can say them. What does each way mean? Work out a context in which they might be used with close friends, new acquaintances, or people who don't know each other.

Yes.

No.

Hello.

Hurry up.

Where do you think you're going?

Sam doesn't like beer.

I like Mexican food and beer.

Most languages are pronounced with changes of tone that can change the meaning of utterances. Many languages (e.g. Zulu, Yoruba, Thai, Mandarin Chinese) associate tone with individual words. In English, however, tone is usually associated with **groups** of words called **tone units**, which speakers consider are units of information. The syllable with the strongest stress in a tone unit often contains important information, such as the answer elicited by a question, e.g.

> *Where are you going?*
> *Back to 'Fred's house.*

In English, the most important changes of pitch are those that are associated with a stressed syllable (the **nuclear** syllable) and continue over a subsequent group of words, if there are any, in the same tone unit. This produces a kind of tone called an **intonation pattern.**

Brazil (1997) described intonation in terms of three major processes.

1 **Prominence**: We highlight a particular syllable of a tone unit by such processes as lengthening a vowel or changing volume in order to focus on the words that carry the most information. Compare these two exchanges:

> *Will you be 'home this evening?*   *'Only after eight p.m.*
> *Shall I ring you this 'evening?*   *Try me after 'seven p.m.*

2 **Key**: We can adjust the level of pitch of tone units to change meaning, as, for example, to express contradiction:

> *↑You were there. No I ↑wasn't.*

3 **Tone**: We can focus on a prominent syllable through a rapid raising or lowering of pitch. The most frequently used intonation patterns are falling, rising, and falling-rising.

1.6.2.1 Intonation patterns

The falling intonation pattern

The following words, phrases or sentences are typically pronounced with a falling away of the pitch after the main stressed syllable. It has sometimes been suggested that the falling intonation pattern gives an impression of completeness or definiteness, and is used by speakers who think they are presenting new information, e.g.

> *'Good.*
> *See you 'later.*
> *'Thank you.*
> *I ,think they're both 'sick.*
> *They ,don't know what they're going to 'do.*
> *I don't know how we can ,possibly pay all these 'bills.*

The rising intonation pattern

The rising pattern is often used for asking questions which have a yes/no/ don't know answer, and are sometimes said to convey incompleteness or indefiniteness. Rising intonation can also be used to convey politeness or tentativeness, e.g.

Are you 'ready?

Have you 'told her about it?

They're here al'ready?

Can you ring me when you get 'home?

In some varieties of English (including the English spoken in NE England, Wales, Australia and New Zealand) a rising intonation pattern is often used at the end of statements instead of the more usual falling tone, e.g.

I ˌthink it could 'rain.

ˌTV reception is ˌpoor in our part of 'town.

The falling-rising intonation pattern

This is sometimes described as being used by speakers who think they are presenting information which is already known by their listeners, e.g.

'Why?

'That wasn't very ˌnice!

The ˌweather wasn't like this 'last Christmas.

Less frequently used patterns include:

The rising–falling intonation pattern

e.g. *The film was just 'excellent.*

The level intonation pattern

e.g. *'okay*

1.6.2.2 Functions of intonation patterns

Intonation is used for many semantic purposes, including expressing degrees of certainty, as well as 'attitudes' of the speaker. There are, of course, many 'attitudes' that speakers can express, including surprise, shock, impatience, tentativeness, delight, hostility. There is thus potentially a huge number of meanings of intonation patterns. Here are a few examples.

Making statements

- Definiteness: *I need another one.* (falling)
- Reassurance: *I'll be careful.* (rising)
- Correction: *(He's over 60.) No, he's only 58.* (falling–rising)
- Warning: *You'll get wet.* (falling–rising)

Asking wh-questions

- Showing interest: *When's your mother arriving?* (rising)
- Assertive: *Why did you do that?* (falling)

Asking yes–no questions

- Short answers: *She won't be there. – Really.* (falling) (*Really* could also be pronounced with a rising intonation to show surprise.)
- All other yes–no questions (rising)

Directives

- Strong: *Don't interrupt us.* (falling)
- Pleading: *Do have another cup.* (falling-rising)

Exclamations

- Strong response: *Rubbish!* (falling)

Greetings and farewells

- *Hullo.*
- *Goodbye.* (both rising)

As noted earlier, intonation and stress can have a very important effect on intelligibility. It should be made clear to learners, however, that learning to use English intonation is not simply a case of applying 'rules'. The many subtle meanings expressed through the use of stress and intonation result in native speakers' 'tones of voice' which are best learned through participating in discourse with native speakers or carefully observing such discourse.

1.7 Accents

In many parts of the world, speakers of English as a first language use about 44 phonemes, but these speakers do not all sound the same. Even within a single country, there can be many different varieties of English. In the UK, speakers of English from Glasgow, Essex and Liverpool have different **accents**. In the USA, speakers from Texas, New York and Boston typically do not sound the same. Teachers of English are sometimes required to teach particular accents of English or to explain how their own accent differs from other major varieties. There are particular 'prestige varieties'. General American English (GAE), a term used for varieties of US English, especially as spoken in the Mid-West, has by far the largest number of speakers of any variety of English. British Received Pronunciation, although spoken by a very small proportion of British residents, has prestige in many parts of the world. New Zealand English has fewer speakers than almost any other native variety of English, and is often perceived as the same as Australian English by non-native speakers, even though New Zealanders and Australians can discern many differences. Similarly, Canadian English is often perceived by speakers of English from elsewhere as very similar to General American English, although Canadian speakers of English will discern important differences. The various North American varieties are sometimes known as General North American English.

The accent of non-native speakers of English is influenced by many things, including their first language, their age, their attitudes to English and speakers of English, and the amount of exposure they have had to particular varieties of English.

Among native speakers of English, differences between accents can be based on several factors, including the fact that language changes. The main sources of accent characteristics are based on allophonic differences, but the number of phonemes in particular varieties of English, and stress and intonation, also affect accent. Here are some examples of differences between varieties of English which contribute to English accents.

1 General American English varieties often do not make a distinction between /ɑː/ and /ɒ/, with the result that *guard* and *god* sound similar when spoken by speakers of GAE.

2 'r'-dropping: Rhotic accents are those where *r* is pronounced in all environments. Most GAE speakers have rhotic accents. In southern England, Australia and most parts of New Zealand, non-rhotic accents are normal. Speakers drop the /r/ before a consonant or in syllable-final positions. Try pronouncing the following examples with and without rhotic accent.

   car, cart, sister, beard, car engine

3 Speakers of GAE and Scottish English are sometimes described as having an additional voiceless consonant phoneme /hw/ as distinct from the voiced /w/, cf. *witch* and *which*, *watt* and *what*.

4 In GAE but not in British RP, medial /t/ is often pronounced as a voiced flap, e.g.

   butter   /bʌtə/ ⇒ /bʌdər/

5 For many speakers of General American or Australian English, the sound which speakers of British RP or New Zealand English pronounce /ɑː/ in words such as *answer* is pronounced further forward as /æ/, e.g. *answer, chance, ask, can't, dance*. Note, however, that British and New Zealand English speakers pronounce *romance* as /rəʊmæns/ not /rəʊmɑːns/. In the north of England, *pass* is pronounced /pæs/ but *father* is pronounced /fɑːðə/.

6 In GAE there is normally no glide (/j/) between an initial alveolar stop or nasal consonant and /uː/, whereas in British, Canadian, Australian and New Zealand English there is a glide in words such as *tune, new, dune*. In British RP there is also a glide after initial /s/.

7 Sometimes particular words have a distinctive pronunciation in different varieties of English, but there is not necessarily a general rule applying to apparently similar words, e.g.

	General American English	British RP
been	/bɪn/	/biːn/
figure	/fɪg(j)ər/	/fɪgə/
herb	/ɝb/	/hɜːb/
issue	/ɪʃuː/	/ˈɪsjuː/
leisure	/ˈliːʒər/	/ˈleʒə/
process	/ˈprɑses/	/ˈprəʊses/
schedule	/ˈskedʒəl/	/ˈʃedjuːl/
tomato	/təˈmeɪtəʊ/	/təˈmɑːtəʊ/
vase	/veɪs/	/vɑːz/

8 Differences in word stress between General American and British varieties include words such as the following: *research, garage, frontier, ballet, primarily, voluntarily, laboratory, advertisement, Caribbean, necessarily, momentarily*. Celce-Murcia et al. (1996) give further examples of phonological differences between British and American varieties of English.

9 Scottish English speakers have an additional voiceless velar fricative /x/, as in *loch*, which is not in most other varieties of English.

10 Where British RP has two phonemes /ʊ/ and /uː/, some Scottish speakers of English have one phoneme /uː/, with the consequence that *look* and *Luke* sound the same.

11 The velar nasal /ŋ/ in final position in some varieties of English tends to be replaced by an alveolar nasal /n/, e.g. *singing* ⇒ singin. This tends to be a sociolinguistic phenomenon influenced by educational levels.

12 In some varieties of English, /θ/ is pronounced as /f/ or /t/, and /ð/ is pronounced /v/ or /d/, e.g.

three	/θriː/	⇒ /friː/ or /triː/
mother	/mʌðə/	⇒ /mʌvə/ or /mʌdə/

13 Some African varieties of English have merged the high front vowels /iː/ and /ɪ/ and therefore *ship* and *sheep* or *live* and *leave* are pronounced similarly.

14 In parts of Australia, /ɪ/ is pronounced closer to /iː/, in words such as *nil*, *Sydney* or *fish*.

15 In New Zealand English, /ɪ/ tends to be pronounced more like /ə/ or /ʌ/, e.g. *fish, pin, six, fridge*. While many Australians pronounce *Sydney* as /siːdniː/, many New Zealanders pronounce it as /sʌdniː/ or /sədniː/.

16 Caribbean and New Zealand varieties tend to merge the two diphthongs /eə/ and /ɪə/ into one. Many speakers pronounce the words in the following pairs in the same way.

    hair   hear   *bare   beer*   *rarely   really*

17 In New Zealand English, /iː/ tends to be used in final positions where British English uses /ɪ/, e.g. *city, pity*.

18 In New Zealand English, /ɔː/ tends to be used where British English uses /ʊə/, e.g. *poor*.

19 In New Zealand English, /e/ tends to be pronounced closer to /ɪ/, e.g.

    egg may sound like /ɪg/

    century may sound like /sɪntʃəriː/

20 Some speakers of New Zealand English do not make a distinction between /æ/ and /e/, especially before /l/, e.g.

    salary   celery   *accept   except*   *better   batter*

1.8 Learners' difficulties with English sounds

In Section 1.7 we noted some of the ways in which systematic variation in the way sounds are made can lead to different English accents. Learners of English as a second or foreign language can also produce English sounds in different ways, often as a result of the influence of their first language.

1.8.1 Common problems

Certain kinds of pronunciation problems tend to occur fairly generally, regardless of the language background of learners of English. These problems include:

● Individual phoneme substitutions

/θ/	replaced with	/f/ or /t/ or /s/	(e.g. *thing* ⇒ *sing*)
/ð/	replaced with	/v/ or /d/ or /z/	(e.g. *the book* ⇒ *de book*)
/ʊə/	replaced with	/ɔː/	(e.g. *pure* ⇒ *paw*)
/ɪ/	replaced with	/iː/	(e.g. *ship* ⇒ *sheep*)
/ɒ/	replaced with	/ʌ/	(e.g. *operate* ⇒ *upper rate*)
/ʌ/	replaced with	/ɒ/	(e.g. *under* ⇒ *on de*)

● Failure to use schwa /ə/ in unstressed syllables
● Influence of spelling, e.g.

busy /bɪziː/ ⇒ /bɪsiː/

● Primary stress on wrong syllable, e.g. ˈ*situation*
● Too many stressed syllables, e.g. ˈ*suitabili*ˈ*ty*
● Consonant clusters broken up, e.g.

spoon ⇒ /səpuːn/
film ⇒ /fɪlɪm/

● Long vowels not long enough, e.g.

/ɑːftə/ ⇒ /ʌftə/

● Devoicing of voiced consonant, e.g.

/hæv/ ⇒ /hæf/

In certain contexts, devoicing is also widespread among native speakers of English.

1.8.2 Predicting pronunciation difficulties for learners of English

In the 1950s and 1960s it was assumed by many researchers and language teachers that transfer from the first language was the main source of errors and problems in pronunciation and grammar for learners of a second language. It was believed that a **contrastive analysis** of the two languages would enable teachers to predict and explain learners' problems. Since the 1970s the contrastive analysis hypothesis has been supported much less enthusiastically in applied linguistics for many reasons, not least because it could not account for many learners' problems, or the problems could be accounted for in other ways, including for example as evidence of interlanguage learning strategies.

Although contrastive analysis does not work well for predicting all language learning difficulties, Stockwell et al. (1965) formulated a **'hierarchy of difficulty' hypothesis** which can help reveal why certain sounds are easy or hard for learners of particular language backgrounds. That is, it can help explain problems that occur. Stockwell et al. suggested that there were up to eight possible levels in their hierarchy of difficulty when comparing the phonology of two languages. Table 1.7 is a six-level summary of the hierarchy of difficulty hypothesis in ascending order of difficulty, with Level 5 the most difficult (Brown, 1987).

Table 1.7   Hierarchy of difficulty

Level 0	Transfer
Level 1	Coalescence
Level 2	Underdifferentiation
Level 3	Reinterpretation
Level 4	Overdifferentiation
Level 5	Split

Level 0 presents no difficulty because it involves using an item from the first language (L_1) in the second language (L_2). This could be a sound, a word or a grammatical structure.

Level 1 involves two items in the L_1 becoming one item in the L_2. For a speaker of English, with singular and plural forms for nouns (e.g. *car*, *cars*), these two forms coalesce into one form in languages such as Indonesian or Maori which do not mark differences between singular and plural on nouns. An English-speaking person who has the two phonemes /r/ and /l/ will ignore this distinction if learning Japanese, where there is an /r/ phoneme but no /l/ phoneme.

Level 2 involves items of the L_1 which are absent in the L_2, e.g. English learners of Spanish must avoid using /z/ when speaking Spanish because /z/ does not exist in that language.

Level 3: An item in the L_1 is used differently in the L_2, e.g. both English and Maori have a velar nasal sound /ŋ/. In English this sound is not used in initial position at the beginning of a word, whereas in Maori it can occur in initial position. English speakers learning Maori will tend to say /naɪəʊ/ instead of /ŋaɪɔː/ for *ngaio* (a species of tree).

Level 4: New items which do not occur in the L_1 may be required in the L_2. For example, a Japanese learner of English must learn /ð/, a sound that is not used in Japanese, when learning to say /mʌðə/.

Level 5: Sometimes a single item in the L_1 becomes two or more items in the L_2, e.g. an /r/ sound in Japanese becomes two sounds /r/ and /l/ in English, so some Japanese learners of English may not make a distinction between, for example, *correct it* and *collect it*. Indonesian does not have /f/. It is often replaced by /p/ by Indonesian learners of English. That is, a single sound /p/ in Indonesian serves for two sounds in English, /p/ and /f/, resulting in /pɪləm/ *film*, /teləpəʊn/ *telephone*.

Task 1.23

In dictionaries or other sources, get hold of phoneme inventories for one or more languages and compare them with English phonemes. Can you find examples of differences which could illustrate the six levels in the hierarchy of difficulty and which might predict difficulties for learners of English? For a description of the main pronunciation problems of learners of English from over 20 different, widely spoken language backgrounds, Swan & Smith (2001) is an excellent source.

From teachers' and learners' points of view, many accent differences and interlanguage errors made by learners do not greatly affect intelligibility. Whether a speaker pronounces the definite article *the* as /ðə/, /də/ or /zə/ does not necessarily matter at all. Because English is an international language, at a time of great movement of peoples around the world many varieties will inevitably be 'standard', and classes often include learners from several different language backgrounds. Teachers will usually be expected to use their own accent as a teaching model, while at the same time knowing what characterises other varieties of English, and to concentrate on those aspects of learners' pronunciation that seriously affect intelligibility. Stress and intonation will usually be strong candidates for teachers' attention.

CHAPTER 2

Words and their meanings

This chapter describes what is involved in learning a word, and what kinds of explicit and implicit knowledge learners of English acquire when they learn vocabulary. The chapter lists the most frequently used English words, including those words used especially for academic and professional purposes.

Objectives

When you have finished this chapter you should:

1 Understand the difference between **concepts** and **words**.

2 Understand the distinction between **function words** and **content words**.

3 Be able to identify the main **word classes** and their distribution in English.

4 Understand the terms **lemma, word family, word type, word token**.

5 Know the difference between **denotative** and **connotative** word meaning.

6 Know the difference between **sense** and **reference**.

7 Know the difference between **word features** and **prototypes**.

8 Be able to recognise **metaphorical** uses of words.

9 Understand the meaning of **polysemy, homonymy, synonymy, antonymy, hyponymy**.

10 Know the difference between **propositional meaning** and **illocutionary meaning**.

11 Know the difference between **inflectional** and **derivational affixes** on words.

12 Understand basic **word formation processes** in English.

13 Be able to recognise **word compounds**.

14 Understand the notion of **collocation**.

15 Have an overview of the most frequently used words in spoken and written English.

16 Know approximately what proportion of the total number of word tokens in a text are represented by the most frequent 10 words, 100 words, 1,000 words, 3,000 words.

17 Understand the terms **high frequency words, academic words, technical words, low frequency words**.

2.1 Categories of words

2.1.1 What is a word?

Words are sometimes thought of as basic building blocks of a language – the items with a space between them when we write, or the items which get to be listed in a dictionary. When we speak there is, of course, not necessarily a clear, discernible pause between words, and in fact the biggest 'gaps' may come between syllables in the middle of a word.

Most words are labels for cognitive entities called **concepts**. The relationship between concepts and words is complex, but can be characterised as follows. As individuals we receive sensory information from our personal environment (e.g. the trees around us). Each one of us forms our own concept of 'treeness' on the basis of the trees we have seen, heard, smelled or touched – trees grow in the ground, they have trunks, branches, leaves, and so on. The collective concepts of all the individuals in a society become socially standardised – they are said to have 'meaning'. In this case this socially standardised 'meaning' is labelled with a word or words: *tree, arbre, rākau, Baum*, etc. Although a cabbage plant has some of the defining characteristics of a tree (it has roots, it grows upwards, it has leaves, etc.), it is not socially defined as a tree. This process can work in reverse when we learn a language. We can start with a word, and associate the word form with a meaning which has its own individual traits or characteristics as part of our concept of 'tree' in our cognitive structure.

When we discuss words, it is important to be clear about whether we are talking about the word **form** or the **meanings**. Consider whether the following four pairs of items each make up one or two words:

1 *book*   *books*

2 *book*   *booked*

3 *right* (opposite of *left*)   *right* (*correct*)

4 *enough*   *sufficient*

Many people agree that 1 and 2 each consist of a single word, whereas 3 and 4 each consist of two words. In the case of *enough* and *sufficient*, the two words might be said to have one meaning. In Example 1, the *-s* suffix on *book* has meaning as a marker of plural number on a noun. In Example 2, the *-ed* suffix on *book* marks the form as the past tense or past participle of a verb. However, in 1, the *-s* suffix could also be an ending on a verb (e.g. *Ann always books her airline tickets through the Internet*).

Sometimes two or more words together label a single concept, e.g.

Fred Smith

the chief negotiator

ice cream

New word forms are constantly being added to English, and 'old' words often change their meanings over time and gain new uses in new contexts. For example, *program, awesome* and *legless* have all taken on new meanings since the 1990s. Lexicographers attempt to record the new word forms and new meanings that become established in the language.

As we will see, the way we define what a word is has importance for language teaching because it affects how we count words and therefore how we answer questions such as 'How many words do you need to read a newspaper?' Similarly, just as it is not a simple matter to define what a word is, so it is the case that we can classify words in a number of different ways relevant for language teaching.

2.1.2 Function words and content words

In English, there is a fundamental distinction between **function** words (sometimes called 'grammatical words' or 'structural words') and **content** words (sometimes called 'lexical words'). There are about 250 **function words** in English (e.g. *the, and, of, a, in, to, it, is, was, that* – these ten words alone make up over 20 per cent of all the words we ever use). Function words are not only very frequent, they also have an important role in linking content words together and expressing grammatical meanings. Function words are said to belong to 'closed classes', which do not accept new words. Function words typically have many meanings, e.g. the *Oxford English Dictionary* gives over eight meanings of *when*, 40 meanings of *in* and over 60 meanings of *of*. A few function words such as *whence* and *whilst* are not frequent. Some word forms can be used as both function words and content words, e.g.

| *have* | I have read *Hamlet*. (*have* is a function word) |
| | I have three brothers. (*have* is a content word) |

There are hundreds of thousands of **content words** in English. Content words belong to open classes (nouns, verbs, adjectives, adverbs) to which hundreds or even thousands of new members, especially nouns and verbs, are added each year.

2.1.3 Word classes

Word class is a term that is commonly used nowadays by linguists to refer to what used to be called 'parts of speech'. There are eight main word classes, and most teachers will be familiar with them.

nouns	e.g. *chair, book, Fred, idea, frustration, right*
verbs	e.g. *operate, remove, play, should, be*
determiners	e.g. *the, this, any, all, several*
prepositions	e.g. *of, in, on, at, between, by*
adjectives	e.g. *terrible, blue, smooth, outstanding*
pronouns	e.g. *it, they, you, us, which, who*
conjunctions	e.g. *and, but, when, because, or*
adverbs	e.g. *only, then, slowly, eventually*

Many words can belong to more than one word class. We have already seen in 2.1.1, for example, that *book* can be a noun or a verb.

Task 2.1

In a dictionary, look up the word classes that each of the following can belong to:

like, change, rail, opening, when, right

The frequencies of the main word classes in two large 1 million-word computer corpora of written English are given in Table 2.1. It is worth noting that just over a quarter of the words in each corpus are nouns and that there is a higher proportion of nouns in informative prose than in imaginative prose. Consequently there is also a higher proportion of determiners, prepositions and adjectives in informative prose because these word classes are particularly associated with nouns. Only about 5 per cent of the words in each corpus are adverbs. The analyses are from the *Brown Corpus of Written American English* (Francis & Kučera, 1982: 547) and the *Lancaster–Oslo–Bergen (LOB) Corpus of Written British English* (Johansson & Hofland 1989: 15). More detailed analyses of word class distributions are available in Leech et al. (2001), including distributions in spoken British English. Chapters 4–7 below describe the use of each of these word classes and outline particular teaching and learning problems associated with them.

Table 2.1 Frequencies of word classes in written American and British English

	%		%		%	
	Total (1,000,000 words in each corpus)		Informative prose sections		Imaginative prose (fiction) sections	
	US	UK	US	UK	US	UK
Nouns	26.80	25.2	28.50	26.9	21.77	20.0
Verbs	18.20	17.8	17.02	16.4	21.69	21.9
Determiners	14.16	14.2	14.84	15.2	12.11	11.4
Prepositions	12.04	12.2	12.77	13.1	9.87	9.6
Adjectives	7.07	7.3	7.65	7.8	5.35	5.7
Pronouns	6.56	7.1	4.75	5.0	11.94	13.1
Conjunctions	5.92	5.5	5.94	5.5	5.86	5.4
Adverbs	5.23	5.5	4.73	5.0	6.72	7.2
Others*	4.02	5.2	3.80	5.2	8.49	5.8
	100.00	100.00	100.00	100.00	100.00	100.00

* Note: Includes wh- words, not, there, foreign words and interjections. Numerals are included as determiners.

Analysis of the much larger *Longman Corpus of Spoken and Written English* supports the information in Table 2.1 and throws further light on the relative distribution of word classes. The predominance of nouns is especially striking in English newspapers and academic writing and other registers associated with high density of information, and is least common in conversation. Verbs and adverbs, on the other hand, are more frequent in conversation and in fiction (which, although written, often reports conversational interactions between characters). Pronouns are also much more frequent in spoken English and in fiction than in informative writing.

In spoken English but not in informational writing, a special group of words known as discourse items or 'inserts' (Biber et al., 1999: 93) are very frequent. Greetings (*hi, hello*), hesitation markers (*um, er*), initiators (*right, well, yeah*), fillers (*you know, and so on, sort of*) are all characteristic of unscripted, informal conversation, which is of course the dominant context in which language is used.

Task 2.2

Make sure you can identify the word class of each word in Text 2.1. If necessary, check your answers in a modern dictionary for learners of English. Underline the function words and work out approximately what proportion of all the words in the text they make up.

Text 2.1

When I was at school our class spent an interesting afternoon visiting a sanctuary for birds. We walked for about an hour along a narrow track until we reached a large, flat, stony area at the top of steep cliffs. There we found thousands of gulls and other seabirds on nests or in the air. Some headed out to sea to look for food, and others returned to feed young birds. The noise that the birds made was incredible, especially while we were moving towards the sanctuary and the birds seemed uncertain about our intentions. After we had stopped and sat down to watch, the noise subsided considerably and the birds ignored us. Each bird or pair of birds got upset only if another bird came too close. Otherwise the whole colony seemed to function like a well-ordered community.

2.1.4 Word lemmas

It is usual to consider one form of a word as a **headword**. Nouns, verbs and adjectives typically also have inflected forms which can change the meaning of the headword. For example, many nouns have plural and possessive forms, e.g. *owner, owners, owner's, owners'*. Many verbs can be inflected for third person singular present tense, past tense, *-ed* participle, *-ing* participle, e.g. *sing, sings, sang, sung, singing*. Many adjectives have comparative and superlative forms, e.g. *big, bigger, biggest*.

When we count the different words in a text or when we try to estimate the number of words a person knows, it is usual to group together into a **lemma** the inflected forms which belong to the same word class. Thus *sing, sings, sang, sung, singing* could be said to be variants of the same word or **lemma**. A lemmatised word list incorporates all the variants under a single headword. Sometimes, variant spellings (*criticise, criticize*) and negative forms (*could, couldn't*) are included as part of the same lemma. Each word type in the lemma can, of course, be counted separately if desired.

When we lemmatise the words in a word list, it greatly reduces the number of separate word forms or **word types**. The lemma *go*, for example, represents several word types (e.g. *go, Go, goes, went, gone, going, goin', gonna*, etc.). Bauer & Nation (1993) have estimated that the 45,957 different word types in the 1-million-word *Brown Corpus of Written American English* belong to 37,617 lemmas, a reduction of about 20 per cent. Each occurrence of a type is called a **token**. In the 100-million-word *British National Corpus* there are 6,187,276 tokens of the type *the*. That is, the word *the* occurs 6,187,276 times.

2.1.5 Word families

Lemmas typically associate word forms which belong to the same word class. From a language learning point of view, we may wish to classify

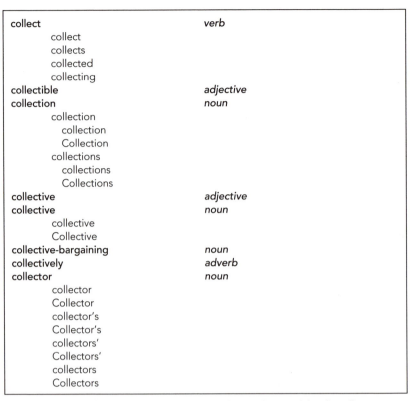

Figure 2.1 Lemmas and word types which make up the word family *collect*

words into bigger units than lemmas. If we consider the lemmatised list in Figure 2.1 we can see that the lemmas *collect, collectible, collection, collective, collective-bargaining, collectively, collector* form a semantically linked **word family**.

Suffixes such as *-able, -er, -ly, -ness, -ation, -ful, -ism, -ist, -ise, -ment* are examples of **derivational affixes** which can change a word stem or headword into a different word class, thus linking words that belong to the same word family. For example, the following words (and the words that are included as part of each lemma) may be considered to be part of a single word family: *criminal, incriminate, decriminalisation, criminally*.

When we 'count' words we can do it in different ways for different purposes. If we are interested in such questions as 'How many words do I need to know to read a newspaper?' then we count **types** – but types conceal different words or senses of words which have the same form, e.g. river *bank* and *bank* for your money are the same type, as are *run* a race and *run* a business. If, on the other hand, we are interested in measuring how many words we can read in an hour, or how fast we can type or how many words are on a typical page, then we count **tokens**.

In teaching English, we thus use the notion of 'word' in different ways, according to whether, for example, we refer to a person's 'vocabulary size' (word families), 'reading speed' (tokens) or 'sight vocabulary' (lemmas).

Task 2.3

Using a dictionary if necessary, compile a list of words which make up the word families for *automatic, person, register, region.*

2.2 Word meanings and functions

In addition to having grammatical functions such as noun or verb, words are associated with many types of meaning in relation to other words and to the world that exists outside of language. **Semantics** is the study of meaning relationships and is a huge field of study in its own right. Many kinds of meanings and meaning relationships have to be acquired for each word we learn. The development of language proficiency includes the piecing together of these levels and layers of meaning associated with word forms. Some of the semantic relationships of particular importance for language learning are outlined in the following sections.

2.2.1 Sense

A word's **sense** is that aspect of its meaning which relates to a particular concept or concepts. Roughly speaking, it is the dictionary definition. Thus, the various senses of the word *change* can include 'making or becoming different', 'coins of low value', 'take off one's clothes and put on different clothes', and so on. We sometimes describe a word's sense as its **denotation**, and the semantic relationship as **denotative meaning**. If we agree that the denotation of *fish* is 'a cold-blooded animal which lives in water', we may nevertheless sometimes find it difficult to decide the limits or boundaries of its denotation, for example whether a lobster, a whitebait or an eel is a 'fish'.

2.2.2 Reference

In particular contexts, words are sometimes described as having **reference**. That is, they refer to particular things. For example, the word *president* refers to different people in different contexts. Similarly, the phrase *my house* has different reference depending on who says it. In the following sentence, the words *Jupiter*, *this planet* and *it* all have the same reference, even though three different words or phrases are involved.

Jupiter is very large but because this planet is so far away it doesn't look to be bigger than the other members of our solar system.

2.2.3 Connotation

The connotative meaning of a word is the personal associations it has for particular users. Connotative meanings vary from person to person, but sometimes they can be common or generalised. For example, *cobra* has the sense of 'variety of snake'. It often also has associated connotative meanings of *dangerous, poisonous, fear*, etc. *Piano* may have a connotative meaning of 'pleasure', 'entertainment' for many people, but 'boredom', 'difficult' for children who are encouraged to practise the instrument against their will. Words can have different connotations in different speech communities, e.g. black cats may be considered 'lucky' in some English-speaking communities but 'sinister' in others.

2.2.4 Word associations

Related to both denotative and connotative meaning is the phenomenon of **association**. For many decades, psychologists and psycholinguists have studied how people and groups of people respond to words as stimuli. When asked to say or write the first word that comes to mind when they are shown a particular word, speakers of English tend to give similar responses. Table 2.2 shows the ten most common responses given to each of the words *butterfly, hungry, salt* in an experiment conducted by Jenkins (1970).

Table 2.2 Common word associations

butterfly	hungry	salt
moth	food	pepper
insect	eat	sugar
wing(s)	thirsty	water
bird	full	taste
fly	starved	sea
yellow	stomach	bitter
net	tired	shaker
pretty	dog	food
flower(s)	pain	ocean
bug	man	lake

These association responses reveal different kinds of relationships. They include:

- **paradigmatic relationships**, in which the response is from the same word class – and might 'replace' the stimulus, e.g. *hungry–starved, butterfly–moth, salt–sugar*. Some of these paradigmatic responses are semantically related through apparent synonymy (e.g. *hungry–starved, butterfly–moth*), while others are linked through less direct relationships (e.g. *salt–sugar, salt–ocean*).

- **syntagmatic relationships**, in which the response is from a potentially adjacent word in a phrase, e.g. *butterfly–pretty, hungry–dog, salt–shaker*. Syntagmatic relationships are discussed further in Section 2.5.

- **hierarchical relationships**, in which the response is a word that includes the stimulus word or is included by the stimulus word, e.g. *butterfly–insect, sugar–food*.

2.2.5 Semantic components of words

Linguists have, at various times, explored the characteristics of some words that appear to be made up of semantic **features** (or 'components' of meaning), which reflect the possible co-occurrence of words in sentences. Thus, the word *girl* may be considered to include features of meaning such as +young, +human, +female, etc., whereas *woman* may include the features ±young, +mature, +human, +female, etc. *Cow*, on the other hand, may be considered to include the features ±young, –human, +bovine, +female, etc.

The verb *criticise* may have features which include that the subject should be +human. Thus, while *The farmer criticised his cows* may be acceptable, *The cows criticised the farmer* is clearly distinctly odd. Whether this is because we know *cow* is not a possible subject for *criticise*, or whether our knowledge of the world includes the fact that cows do not speak, let alone criticise farmers, is a moot point. However, some words can nevertheless be characterised as having semantic features, e.g.

Semantic features	English word
being alive	*alive*
being not alive	*dead*
become not alive	*die*
cause to become not alive	*kill*
cause a human to be not alive	*murder, kill*
cause an important person to be not alive	*assassinate*
cause a possibly disreputable person to be not alive	*rub out/silence*, etc.

Language learners normally find it necessary to fine-tune their use of words to ensure that the scope of a word is comparable to that of other users of the language, and thus to avoid saying or writing *The intruders assassinated the cat*.

Task 2.4

Suggest possible semantic features associated with your concept of each of the following: *car*, *suffer*, *wine*.

2.2.6 Prototypes

Another way of approaching the semantic nature of words is to consider whether they have core or basic meanings. What is it that makes a bird a bird? We might consider such things as feathers, two legs, wings, flight, eyes on the side of the head, a beak, etc. However, kiwis and emus have feathers but cannot fly; owls do not have eyes at the side of the head; bats can fly and yet are not birds; a one-legged parrot is still undoubtedly a bird. Rosch (1975) conducted an experiment in which students were asked to rate items as good (or poor) examples of certain categories such as furniture, birds or tools. *Chair*, for example, was rated as the best example to represent furniture. *Robin* was the prototypical bird, and *hammer* was considered a better example of a tool than *crowbar*. For other varieties of English, or for learners from different first language backgrounds, other items of furniture, birds or tools will prove to be prototypical. Aitchison (1987: 51–62) discusses the significance of prototypes as part of our knowledge of words.

2.2.7 Extended meaning

Word meanings can also be considered from the point of view of their literal use or their extended or metaphorical meanings. Compare these two sentences.

1 *I saw a tiger in a TV programme about India.*

2 *Sue is a tiger for punishment.*

In Sentence 2 Sue is being likened to a tiger. She is not literally a tiger. Here are some further examples of the metaphorical use of words, e.g.

3 *He's head of the company.*

4 *They had to head off the opposition.*

5 *They shot down my argument.*

6 *She flew into a rage.*

7 *In the heat of the debate he abandoned ship and joined the opposition.*

8 *My mind is in top gear.*

There are different kinds of extension of literal word meanings, each overlapping and with many degrees of figurativeness. These include **simile** (where one entity is compared with another, e.g. *He's like a cracked record*), **idiom** (e.g. *This crime is just the tip of the iceberg*), **metaphor** (where a word with literal meaning takes on uses with less literal meaning, e.g. *head of a department, computer mouse, arm of a crane, grasp an idea, prices are haemorrhaging, a menu-driven computer program, between you and me*), **metonymy** (where an attribute of something is used to represent the original thing, e.g. *the crown, new blood, the White House, No. 10*). Examination of texts shows that fluent language use involves a great deal of metaphorical meaning, and learning how to use such extended meaning is a huge part of the language learner's task.

Task 2.5

From a newspaper, magazine or novel, make a list of 20 examples of extended meaning in the use of words or phrases.

2.2.8 Polysemy

Most words have more than one (or even **many**) meanings. This is especially the case with high frequency words. If we compare the following uses of *go* and *by*, we can see that, although each may have certain things in common, there are significant differences in the senses of each.

Go 1 *The covered bridge goes between the two buildings.*

2 *Fred goes between his home and the office every day.*

3 *The river goes from the mountains to the sea.*

4 *I always go by air if I can.*

5 *Your car engine goes well.*

6 *My stereo goes well.*

7 *She goes mad if you mention it.*

8 *It all goes to show that you never can tell.*

9 *This type of yoghurt often goes bad.*

By 1 *The conference was boycotted by the two minor parties.*

2 *This painting is by Picasso.*

3 *I saw him by the river.*

4 *Four by five is twenty.*

5 *What is meant by 'in time'?*

6 *I knew by the look on her face.*

7 *I like travelling by rail.*

8 *By beating England, France won the championship.*

Task 2.6

Look in a learner's dictionary to see how many meanings are listed for each of the following: *on, hard, of.*

2.2.9 Homonymy

While **polysemy** refers to the multiple meanings of words, homonymy refers to cases where words with the same form are not related. Thus, the word form *seal* is listed with up to 25 meanings in some dictionaries. Some of these meanings are related (e.g. *to seal an envelope; to seal off a building*) and are examples of polysemy. However, other uses are not obviously related and represent separate words which just happen to have the same form (e.g. *to seal an envelope; a seal swimming in the sea*). Other homonyms include, for example, *bank* (of a river, a place for money), *bear* (animal, carry), *fine* (weather, a monetary penalty).

Two or more word forms which are pronounced the same but which have different spellings are called **homophones** (e.g. *sea, see; tea, tee; write, right, Wright; peace, piece; bear, bare; ate, eight; or, oar; their, there; red, read; one, won*). **Homographs** are pairs of words which have the same written form but different pronunciations (e.g. *read* – /red/, /riːd/; *row* – /rəʊ/, /raʊ/). Words that can have different grammatical functions are sometimes known as **homomorphs**, e.g.:

run can be a verb or a noun

change can be a verb or a noun

before can be a conjunction or a preposition

2.2.10 Synonymy

Words that have similar meanings are known as **synonyms**. It has been said that there can never be synonyms, because words never have exactly the same context of use, differing for example in levels of formality. For general language teaching purposes, however, it is often convenient to recognise approximate similarity of meaning, and to accept, for example, that *enough, sufficient* and *adequate* mean roughly the same, as do *say again* and *repeat*, or *pull towards* and *drag*. Translation between languages assumes that loose synonymy between word forms is possible.

The use of synonyms is important for avoiding repetition, and thus contributes to cohesion in texts, e.g.

*We rang for a **taxi** at 9 p.m. but the **cab** didn't come till after 10.*

2.2.11 Antonymy

Semantic relationships can also exist between pairs of words which have opposite meanings. These are called **antonyms**, e.g.

wet	*dry*
late	*on time*
same	*different*
more	*less*
kind	*unkind*
direct	*indirect*

Antonyms that are generated by prefixes such as *un-*, *in-*, *im-*, *il-*, *ir-* are a rich source of vocabulary in English.

2.2.12 Hyponymy

Many words can be described as being semantically subordinate or superordinate to other words. Thus, *dog* is subordinate to *mammal*, which in turn is subordinate to *animal*, which in turn is subordinate to *creature*. A word that is subordinate to another in this way is called a **hyponym**. On the other hand, *dog* is also superordinate to words such as *terrier* or *spaniel*, etc. *Apple* is a hyponym of *fruit* which in turn is a hyponym of *food*, and so on. Language learners can get good value from learning superordinate words. The words *thing* and *stuff*, for example, are extremely useful because most common nouns are hyponyms of them.

2.3 Categories of meaning

The many kinds of semantic relationships associated with individual words mentioned briefly in 2.2.1 to 2.2.12 are part of even wider networks of meaning. Linguists sometimes distinguish between the **propositional meaning** (or 'sense') of whole utterances and their **illocutionary meaning** (or 'force'). When someone says *It's been a hot day* a listener might respond by saying *Would you like a beer?* Literally interpreted, the utterance *It's been a hot day* has the 'sense' of being about the weather. The response *Would you like a beer?* suggests that the listener interprets the original statement as having the illocutionary force of being a request. On the other hand, *It's been a hot day* might have a completely different semantic function, as 'small talk' perhaps to open or keep open channels of communication – this is its **phatic function**. Such 'small talk', including comments on the weather, families, food, recreation, greetings and so on, enables us to make contact with the people we meet and opens up the discourse for further communication. Illocutionary meaning and other functions of speech are discussed in more detail in Chapter 8.

2.3.1 Propositional meaning

Propositional meaning is expressed through a number of important semantic categories, especially in terms of metaphors of space, time or quantity. Consider, for example, the description of an earthquake in Text 2.2.

Text 2.2

Almost every year at least one large earthquake occurs without warning on or near a major earthquake fault line, and causes catastrophic damage and human suffering. The most recent earthquake struck just after 10 p.m. Immediately, the whole district was plunged into darkness and many houses collapsed. The noise of falling buildings masked the cries of some of the people trapped and injured in the ruins. Thick clouds of dust rose into a moonlit sky. When rescuers eventually reached the scene some two hours later, it became clear that most buildings within a radius of 60 kilometres from the capital had been damaged or destroyed, and several thousand people had lost their lives.

Task 2.7

Annotate Text 2.2 to show the occurrence of the semantic categories of space, time and quantity. Use single underlining to indicate words and phrases about spatial position, double underlining to indicate words and phrases about time, and parentheses to indic- ate words and phrases about quantity. There is no one 'correct' answer because the boundaries between categories overlap or are not always clear, and some of the uses are metaphorical. However, you should find that you have annotated a substantial part of the text.

Some of the major categories of propositional meaning, expressed through words and grammatical structures, are shown in Table 2.3.

Some academic or professional subjects make especially heavy use of particular categories of propositional meaning. For example, economics, business and journalistic reporting of economic matters frequently use metaphors based on spatial location and motion. In Text 2.3, which illus- trates this tendency, words and phrases expressing spatial position and motion are underlined.

Table 2.3 Some important categories of propositional meaning

Entities	e.g. things, substances, persons, creatures
Classes of entities	e.g. species, groups
States	e.g. existence, presence or absence
Attributes	e.g. shape, dimensions, value, correctness, taste, smell, colour, quality, desirability, usefulness, importance
Quantity	e.g. numerals, totality, absence of quantity, size, approximation, degree, proportion, specific and non-specific quantity, more, equivalence, less, measurement, calculation, parts of a whole, adequacy
Spatial position	e.g. location, motion, direction, separation, exclusion, replacement, distance
Time and temporal relations	e.g. sequence, simultaneity, duration, frequency, points in time, change, development, clock time, subjective time, lateness
Events	e.g. occurrence, schedules
Other relations	e.g. causation, conjunction, hypothesis, condition, comparison (similarity and difference), reason, purpose

Text 2.3

Recovery from the recession in North America is expected to get under way in the middle of next year. Output in Japan was raised considerably in the June quarter but the upswing paused later in the year. Prices of agricultural products entering international trade rose only moderately. In several countries in Europe industrial expansion was brought to a standstill. In parts of Asia the pace of advance also slowed temporarily in the first half of the year, but then export volumes recovered their momentum.

Task 2.8

In a newspaper, find an article about economic matters. Underline or highlight the words and phrases which you think are literal or metaphorical uses of spatial position or motion. There will not be one 'correct' answer because your response will be partly subjective.

It is not possible here to illustrate all major categories of propositional meaning. However, the major semantic categories in Table 2.3 include many of the things we talk or write about when we use language. Language learners need to learn that something caused something to happen, or that two or more things are of different sizes, or belong to different classes or categories. Learners need to be able to express when events occurred, in what order, and how often; who did what to whom, where, and when.

2.3.2 Modal meaning

In addition to using language to express propositional and illocutionary meaning, we can express **modal meaning** through the use of modal verbs and other devices:

● To show how certain we are of the truth of what we say, e.g.

It's likely to rain soon; It could rain soon; It must rain soon.

● To express notions such as obligation, prohibition, permission, e.g.

We have to be home by 10 p.m. You are not allowed to do that. You can take as many lemons as you want.

Modal meaning is discussed in more detail in Chapter 5.

2.3.3 Social meaning

Different settings or contexts and the words we use in them can contribute to degrees of formality, politeness or intimacy and can help establish or mark social distance or solidarity. It can matter a lot whether we say to friends or strangers

Thank you very much	or *Cheers.*
Good morning	or *Hi.*
I've mislaid your keys	or *I've lost your keys.*
Could I have a little sugar?	or *Where's the sugar?*
Would you please hold this rope?	or *Can you hold this rope for a second?*

Whether we sound polite or rude can depend on choosing the appropriate way of speaking to particular people. It normally takes us many years to become really proficient in using language in a socially appropriate way, and some native speakers and second language learners take much longer than others to develop such proficiency.

2.4 Word structure and word formation

Study of the internal structure of words and the processes by which new words are formed is part of **morphology**. A few words in English have only one form and cannot be divided up into parts, e.g.

the   of   so   only

2.4.1 Roots and affixes

Most words, however, can consist of a **root** with one or more **affixes** at the beginning (**prefix**) or end (**suffix**), e.g.

> The word *unify* was borrowed in the sixteenth century from Latin (*unus* = one, + *facere* = make). In English, *unify* is a **root**.
>
> *Unification* consists of the root *unify* + the noun-making suffix *(c)ation*.
>
> *Reunification* consists of the **base** (or stem) *unification* (which contains the root *unify*) with the prefix *re-* which means 'again'.

Huge numbers of English words are composed of roots or base forms and affixes in this way. It is very efficient for language learners to know the meanings of the most frequent affixes. It is important to remember, however, that because of the long history of borrowing and adjustments of spelling and pronunciation it is not always easy to work out what the root of a word is. For example, the word *production* was borrowed from Latin *prōdūcere* (to bring forth) in the fifteenth century. *Dūcere* (to lead) was in turn the base for *prōdūcere*. By the time the word was borrowed into English as 'produce' it was treated as if it was an English root, which in turn, by means of affixes, led to *production, productivity, product, producer, productibility*, etc.

2.4.2 Types of affixes

There are two main types of affixing processes, **inflection** and **derivation**.

2.4.2.1 Inflectional affixes

Inflectional affixes are endings which add extra information to the root but preserve the word class. In English the most frequent inflections are the following suffixes, with the first four being especially frequent and a major source of error among learners. These learning difficulties are discussed in Chapters 4–6.

plural *-s*	(book – book**s**)
past tense *-ed*	(open – open**ed**)
3rd person singular *-s*	(I like it – she like**s** it)
-ed participle	(The letter had been open**ed** by someone else)
-ing participle	(I was eat**ing** my lunch when the phone rang)
possessive *-s*	(My car**'s** value)
comparative *-er*	(a straight**er** line)
superlative *-est*	(the short**est** distance)

Noun and verb inflections with *-s* or *-ed* endings have systematic differences in how they are pronounced, depending on the nature of the sounds that precede them. Consider these endings: in Group 1 the *-s* endings of the verbs or nouns are pronounced /s/; in Group 2 the *-s* endings are pronounced /z/; in Group 3 the pronunciation is /ɪz/.

1	2	3
helps	*cabs*	*boxes*
wants	*dogs*	*kisses*
laughs	*waves*	*bruises*
puffs	*plays*	*causes*
wrecks	*wins*	*faces*
moths	*eyes*	*houses*

The pronunciation rules for *-s* endings are:

1 When the final sound in the stem of the noun is voiceless, the *-s* ending is pronounced /s/.

2 When the final sound in the stem of the noun is voiced, the *-s* ending is pronounced /z/.

3 When the final sound in the stem of the noun is a sibilant sound, the *-s* ending is pronounced /ɪz/ and the word is spelled with an *-es* ending.

The pronunciation of *-ed* endings is also rule-governed. In Group 4 the *-ed* endings are pronounced /t/, in Group 5 the pronunciation is /d/, and in Group 6 the pronunciation is /ɪd/.

4	5	6
laughed	*grinned*	*shouted*
jumped	*applied*	*decided*
locked	*described*	*waited*
missed	*caused*	*graded*
hoped	*carried*	*excited*
passed	*seemed*	*created*

The pronunciation rules for *-ed* endings are:

1 When the final sound in the verb stem is voiceless, the *-ed* ending is pronounced /t/.

2 When the final sound in the verb stem is voiced, the *-ed* ending is pronounced /d/.

3 When the final sound in the verb stem is /t/ or /d/, the *-ed* ending is pronounced /ɪd/.

Table 2.4 Rank order distribution of inflectional suffixes in the *LOB Corpus*

Inflectional suffix	% of words in the *LOB corpus*
plural	5.1
past tense	4.6
-ed participle	3.1
3rd person singular	2.3
-ing participle	1.4
possessive (no pronouns)	0.5
comparative	0.1
superlative	0.1
Total	17.2

In a study of the distribution of affixes, Bauer & Nation (1993) found that 169,265 (about 17 per cent) of the approximately 1 million word tokens in the *LOB Corpus* of written British English have an inflectional suffix, as shown in Table 2.4.

2.4.2.2 Derivational affixes

Derivational affixes typically change the word class of the root or base, e.g.

I asked Fred to itemise his belongings.

(*Item* is a noun. When *-ise* is added it becomes a verb.)

Note that derivational suffixes come before any inflectional suffixes, e.g.

Fred itemised his belongings.

not   **Fred itemedise his belongings.*

Bauer & Nation (1993) found that the *LOB Corpus* contains a total of 59,136 words (about 6 per cent) with derivational affixes, the most frequent being shown in Table 2.5. There are a small number of less frequent derivational affixes not listed in Table 2.5 (e.g. *-atory, -ese, -hood, -ite, neo-, mis-, semi-, sub-*).

If we add the inflectional and derivational affixes together, we might conclude that about 23 per cent of the word tokens in the *LOB Corpus* (which was intended to be a representative sample of written British English) contain an affix. In fact the proportion is somewhat less than this because some words contain more than one affix (e.g. *undoubtedly*). However, we can be confident that about one word in every five in English (20 per cent) has an inflectional or derivational affix, that about 5 per cent of the words we use have a plural suffix, about 5 per cent have a past tense suffix, and about 1 per cent have an *-ly* suffix. Learners of English should become familiar with the use of affixes to help develop their vocabulary.

Table 2.5   Rank order distribution of derivational affixes in the *LOB Corpus*

Derivational affix	% of words in the *LOB Corpus*	Derivational affix	% of words in the *LOB Corpus*
-ly	1.3	-ition	0.05
-ion	0.7	-ward	0.04
-ation	0.4	-less	0.04
-er	0.4	-th	0.04
-al	0.3	-al	0.03
-ment	0.3	-dom	0.03
un-	0.2	-age	0.03
-ity	0.2	-ism	0.03
-ive	0.2	-ship	0.03
-ic	0.1	-ian	0.03
-ness	0.1	-ary	0.02
-y	0.1	-ess	0.02
-ful	0.1	inter-	0.02
-ous	0.1	non-	0.02
re-	0.1	-ise	0.02
-ance	0.1	-ally	0.02
-ence	0.1	-ant	0.01
-ist	0.1	-ee	0.01
-able	0.1	pre-	0.01
-ent	0.1	-ify	0.01
en-	0.1	-ish	0.01
in-	0.1	-an	0.01
		Total	5.8

Note: The negative prefixes *il-, im-, in-, ir-* are very frequent and are often hard for some learners to pick up in spoken English. That is, in context they may hear *illegal* or *irrelevant* as *legal* or *relevant*. There is also potential for confusing *im-* in words such as *impersonal* (a negative prefix) with *im-* in words such as *import* where it is part of the base word borrowed into English.

2.4.3 Greek and Latin affixes

Huge numbers of English words contain Latin and Greek affixes which entered English as part of word borrowings from these classical languages. These affixes include: *a-, ab-, ad-, com-, de-, dis-, ex-, re-, sub-, bi-, non-*. Because of the frequency of Greek and Latin affixes, it is worth focusing on their use, especially with mature or advanced learners.

Task 2.9

In Text 2.4 underline the inflectional affixes and put the derivational affixes in parentheses.

Text 2.4

In the last 30 years of the twentieth century there was unsustainable pressure on the natural environment in most parts of the world. A number of environmental reports all pointed in the same direction. Carbon dioxide emissions doubled and greatly exceeded the ability of the environment to absorb them. Fish consumption also doubled and most fish species are now in decline. Freshwater resources have been more and more exploited, and there is much waste especially in irrigation schemes. The greater consumption of wood for paper, packaging, fuel and timber has resulted in the destruction of rainforests and the life they sustain. Regrettably, governments and citizens have not yet done enough to reverse this assault on the natural world on which all life depends.

2.4.4 Word formation

Some words have been in the English language for a very long time (e.g. *sun*, *they*, *cow*). Sometimes even very old words are given new meanings (e.g. *a fair cow* meaning 'a pity', 'a nuisance' or 'an unpleasant situation'). In addition to the development of new senses and the formation of new words through affixation, as described in 2.4.1, words can have a number of other different origins.

2.4.4.1 Borrowing

Some words have been borrowed virtually unaltered from other languages. The *Oxford English Dictionary* records tens of thousands of such loan words, some of which were 'borrowed' permanently into English centuries ago (e.g. *pork*, *table*). More recent borrowings into English include *pyjamas*, *tortilla*, *karaoke*, *fatwa*, *fettucini*, *merlot*, *mana*, *haka*. Some words which were borrowed earlier with one meaning are later given another. *Menu* was borrowed from French in the nineteenth century to refer to a list of dishes in a restaurant. It is now also used for a list of options on a computer screen. Although it is not a recent borrowing, the word *mouse*, which was used a thousand years ago in Old English (and even earlier in several other European languages) to refer to a rodent, has more recently had a new lease of life in computing.

2.4.4.2 Word combinations

Some words which describe a single concept are constructed from a combination of two or more other words, e.g.

a *fire engine, fire escape, post office, railway station, ice cream*

b *well-meaning, cold-shoulder, dirt-cheap*

c *toothbrush, rainforest, raincoat, seasick*

Words which are borrowed to or from English or which are similar in form in English and a learner's first language may not necessarily have the same meaning. 'False friends' like *sensible* or *sympathetic* in French and English are such examples. Even within English, words can be used with different meanings in different regional varieties, e.g. *thong* can be an item of underwear in some varieties, or an item of footwear elsewhere.

Note that the examples in a, b and c above include some where the two words making up the compound are separated, others where they are hyphenated, and others where there is no space between the words. There is not a lot of consistency in how compounds are written. Many pairs of words, on the other hand (e.g. *falling prices*, *sinking ship*), which go together comfortably, do not label single new concepts and therefore do not have grounds for being considered as new words. The many types of combining (or compounding) processes are discussed in Bauer (1983) and Greenbaum (1996) and also in Section 2.5 of this chapter.

2.4.4.3 Blends

Some words are derived from blending two or more words into one, e.g. *smoke* + *fog*: *smog*; *breakfast* + *lunch*: *brunch*; *information* + *commercial*: *infomercial*.

2.4.4.4 Conversion

New words can also be created by changing a word class without derivational affixes. Thus, the noun *email* (electronic mail) can be used as a verb, e.g. *I'll email her*. There are many thousands of examples of words which began their life as nouns and came to be used as verbs (e.g. *comb, hammer, mother, microwave, ship, cash*). This process is called **conversion**. Other examples of conversion are when verbs come to be used as nouns (e.g. *laugh, run, drink*), or when adjectives come to be used as verbs (e.g. *clean, clear*).

2.4.4.5 Abbreviations

The shortening of words or phrases by means of truncations, abbreviations and acronyms is also quite a common way of forming new words, e.g. *fab, ad, decaf, photo, Euro, scuba*.

2.4.4.6 Acronyms

Acronyms are words formed from the first letters of a string of words, e.g. *CD, AIDS, PC, DVD, ANZAC*.

2.5 Word compounds and collocations

2.5.1 Compounds

As we saw in 2.4.4.2, words for two or more individual concepts can sometimes be put together to form a new single concept. Thus, a new compound 'word' from the original two or more words is formed. Compound nouns are especially frequent in modern English, e.g.

> *tooth pick*
>
> *baked beans*
>
> *ball point pen*
>
> *dust jacket*
>
> *light bulb*
>
> *refrigerator level adjustment screw*
>
> *image display format compatibility*

There are a number of ways of classifying compounds. Bauer (1983) points out that the normal way is according to the function that the compound plays in the sentence as noun, verb, adjective, etc. Other ways of classifying them include according to the word classes that make up the compound (e.g. noun + noun, noun + verb, etc.), or the syntactic relationship between the elements (compare *a washing machine* (a machine for washing clothes) and *a waiting game* (**not** 'a game for waiting')). It is not always clear what word class the elements in a compound belong to. For example, in *birth control, control* can be viewed as a noun or a verb – the *control* (noun) of *births*, or X *controls* (verb) *births*.

Compounds nevertheless have their own internal grammatical relationship between the words. Bauer (1983: 202) describes the main word class relationships in English compounds, with noun + noun being the category with by far the most members. Some categories are rare and have not been included here.

Functioning as nouns:

1 noun + noun (e.g. *light bulb, car cover, credibility gap, television aerial*)

2 verb + noun (e.g. *pickpocket, leapfrog, cut-throat*)

3 noun + verb (e.g. *nose bleed, tooth-pick, sunshine, handshake*)

4 verb + verb (very rare) (e.g. *make-believe*)

5 adjective + noun (e.g. *fast-food, open country, baked beans, busybody*)

6 particle + noun (e.g. *in-joke, off-cut, intake, output*)

7 verb + particle (e.g. *fall-out, drop-out, sit-in*)

8 particle + verb (e.g. *outbreak, downcast, downpour*)

9 verb + -ing + noun (e.g. *washing machine, freezing point, spending money*)

10 noun + verb + -er (e.g. *landowner, hairdresser*)

Functioning as verbs:

1 noun + verb (e.g. *colour-code, typeset, babysit*)
2 adjective + verb (e.g. *fine-tune, double book*)
3 adjective + noun (e.g. *bad-mouth, blacklist*)
4 particle + verb (e.g. *underrate, outdo, overcook*)

Functioning as adjectives:

1 noun + adjective (e.g. *sugarfree, waterproof, duty free*)
2 adjective + adjective (e.g. *deaf-mute, red hot, bittersweet*)
3 adjective + noun (e.g. *blue-collar, high-octane*)
4 particle + noun (e.g. *in-depth, on-site*)
5 adjective + verb (e.g. *quick-change*)
6 verb + particle (e.g. *made-up, put-upon, see-through*)
7 noun + noun (e.g. *seaside, coffee-table*)
8 noun + verb + -ing (e.g. *man-eating, earth-shattering, heart-breaking*)
9 adjective + verb + -ing (e.g. *easy-going, good-looking*)
10 adjective + noun + -ed (e.g. *cold-blooded, thick-skinned*)

2.5.2 Collocations

In addition to compounds which normally label a single concept, there is a tendency for words to keep company with other words. There are a number of terms used to describe this habitual co-occurrence of words, including **set phrases, fixed phrases, routines, lexicalised sentence stems, formulaic expressions, prefabricated patterns, idioms, lexical bundles, collocations.**

For our purposes we will treat these terms as having similar meaning, and use the word 'collocation' to refer to them all. There seem to be millions of collocations in English, and it is not hard to make long lists of possible candidates, e.g.

I don't know	*have a look at*
as far as possible	*How was your day?*
hopeful sign	*Can I get you a drink?*
terribly sorry	*I can't believe it.*
pretty straightforward	*I've got so much to do.*
under these circumstances	*as soon as I get time*
in exceptional circumstances	*for hundreds of years*
at the same time	*the rest of the*

Some of these can be slightly modified (e.g. *as soon as I get a chance/ opportunity*), others are fixed, formulaic and unchangeable (e.g. *it's as easy as falling off a log, I'm at the end of my tether, What's the time?*). Palmer (1938) and Pawley & Syder (1983) are among those who have argued that learning collocations is an enormously important part of the language learner's task.

Biber et al. (1999: 988–1036) provide an important corpus-based account of the extent to which words collocate. For example, their analysis shows that three-word 'bundles' of words occur about 80,000 times per million words in conversation (about ten times more frequently than four-word sequences). About 45 per cent of the words in conversation occur as part of recurrent lexical word sequences, and in academic prose about 21 per cent of the words occur in such recurrent sequences.

Both content words and function words often occur as part of collocations. For example, in the 100-million-word *British National Corpus* (*BNC*) (see 2.6.2), the function word *at* occurs 47,520 times in the 10 million words of spoken text, and 490,473 times in the 90 million words of written text. Table 2.6 lists the 25 most frequent collocations of *at* in the spoken and written texts of the *BNC*. It is worth noting that, in this huge corpus of British English, about a quarter of the 537,993 occurrences of *at* occur only in the collocations listed in Table 2.6.

Collocations are rarely able to be seen as 'logical'. Learners of English simply have to learn them as fixed or semi-fixed phrases. For example, we say:

at least	not	**on least*
tell me the answer	not	**say me the answer*
say what you mean	not	**tell what you mean*

Analysis of large collections of spoken or written English in corpora has shown the extent to which knowing collocations in English is part of the language learning task. Altenberg (1991) showed that about 70 per cent of the words in the half-million-word *London–Lund Corpus* of spoken British English are part of recurrent word combinations of up to five words in length, e.g.

very much	*dead against*
so many	*completely different*
quite clear	*deeply divided*
perfectly willing	*incredibly young*

Collocations can be formed to the left or right of a 'keyword'. Analysis of the *BNC*, for example, shows that the most frequent collocations

Table 2.6 The 25 most frequent right collocates of *at* in the spoken and written texts of the *BNC* arranged in order of frequency

	Spoken English (10 million words)			Written English (90 million words)		
Rank	Collocation	Tokens	%	Collocation	Tokens	%
1	at all	2,812	5.92	at least	23,995	4.89
2	at least	1,693	3.56	at all	12,408	2.53
3	at the moment (of)	1,037	2.18	at the end (of the)	9,129	1.86
4	at home	862	1.81	at the time	7,474	1.52
5	at the end (of the)	811	1.71	at home	6,545	1.33
6	at night	561	1.18	at the same time	6,476	1.32
7	at school	513	1.08	at first	4,605	0.94
8	at that time	487	1.02	at last	4,273	0.87
9	at work	469	0.99	at once	3,912	0.78
10	at the time	416	0.88	at the moment (of)	2,986	0.61
11	at the back (of)	245	0.52	at a time (when)	2,968	0.61
12	at the same time	241	0.51	at present	2,825	0.56
13	at this stage	241	0.51	at work	2,620	0.53
14	at a time (when)	223	0.47	at night	2,551	0.52
15	at the bottom (of)	200	0.42	at the top	2,544	0.52
16	at the beginning (of)	190	0.40	at the beginning (of)	2,448	0.50
17	at one time	174	0.37	at that time	2,066	0.42
18	at the top	170	0.36	at school	2,020	0.41
19	at first	157	0.33	at times	1,998	0.41
20	at Christmas	132	0.28	at the back (of)	1,795	0.37
21	at times	129	0.27	at this time	1,772	0.36
22	at this time	126	0.27	at about	1,704	0.35
23	at about	125	0.26	at this stage	1,629	0.33
24	at this point	113	0.24	at the bottom (of)	1,430	0.29
25	at once	110	0.23	at the age (of)	1,430	0.29
Total		12,237	25.77		113,603	23.12

involving preceding or following words with the adjective *fruitful* occur in the following rank orders:

Left collocates	Right collocates
potentially fruitful	fruitful collaboration
proves fruitful	fruitful source of . . .
extremely fruitful	fruitful talks
equally fruitful	fruitful relationship
particularly fruitful	fruitful approach
	fruitful discussion
	fruitful results
	fruitful ideas
	fruitful area

Collocations are sometimes still able to be recognised with other words in between. The collocation *potentially fruitful* could be found as it is or as the discontinuous collocation *potentially very fruitful*. Similarly, *fruitful collaboration* might occur as *a fruitful and, we hope, continuing collaboration*.

Analysis of the *BNC* shows many examples of collocational patterning with particular words, e.g.

- *abject* (which occurs 464 times in 100 million words) is particularly associated with *apology, misery, poverty, horror, failure*.

- *circumstances* (which occurs 10,380 times in 100 million words) is particularly associated with the occurrence of *in, under, extenuating, straitened, mitigating, exceptional, propitious, unforeseen, aggravating, suspicious, fortuitous, unfavourable, adverse, mysterious, certain, particular, normal, special, changing, different, difficult, similar, appropriate*.

- *terribly* (which occurs 1,252 times in 100 million words) is particularly associated with the following words: *homesick, sorry, excited, upset, unhappy, sad, embarrassing, boring, embarrassed, disappointed, painful, depressed, afraid, brave, worried, frightened, impressed, tired, expensive, hurt, complicated, ill, funny, glad, proud, helpful, busy, wrong, exciting, important, angry, guilty, difficult, dangerous, interested, keen, nice*.

- *pretty* (which occurs 7,941 times in 100 million words) is most commonly used as an intensifying adverb. The most frequent collocations including this use of *pretty* are: *horrendous, hefty, cute, hopeless, tame, boring, pathetic, awful, straightforward, plump, nasty, ghastly, dismal, depressing, hectic, feeble, dreadful, dull, shrewd, weird, grim, fed up, tough, miserable, horrible, impressive, confusing, rotten*. The most frequent collocates of *pretty* used as an adjective are: *vivacious, dark-haired, polly, frock, floral, blonde, dresses, flowered, villages, girl, slim, lace, looks, exceptionally*.

Task 2.10

Make lists of what you consider could be collocations that include the words *can't* (e.g. *you can't be too careful*), *never* (e.g. *I've never heard of that*), *don't* (e.g. *I don't want to know*), *think* (e.g. *what did you think of . . . ?*).

Task 2.11

From Text 2.4, list the sequences of words which you think have the 'feel' of being collocations. What implications do you think the phenomenon of collocation has for language teaching?

Leading learners' dictionaries now recognise the role of collocations in English and list important examples in various ways. Any software that can produce concordances can be used to identify collocations. A popular user-friendly program is WordSmith Tools. It is available through the Internet at http://www.hit.uib.no/wordsmith/. A useful website for information on corpora and software for corpus analysis is ICAME at http://www.hit.uib.no/icame.html.

2.6 Word distribution

Authoritative English dictionaries such as the 20-volume *Oxford English Dictionary* (2nd edn, 1989) list over 500,000 headwords. Many of these headwords have multiple senses. Whether we learn English as a first, second or foreign language, any individual learns or uses only a very small proportion of these words. Some words are rarely used and it is of no importance if a learner never learns them. On the other hand, some words (especially function words) are used very frequently and it is essential that learners understand their meanings and develop proficiency in their use. Three function word types (*the*, *of*, *and*) account for about 11 per cent of all the English words we ever hear, speak, read or write. To make most efficient use of the time available for learning, it is very important for learners of English to learn how to use the frequently used words in the language as soon as possible. Fortunately, the development of corpus linguistics has made it much easier to identify which are the most frequently used words in particular domains of use, or in the language as a whole.

2.6.1 High frequency words

High frequency words include all the 250 or so function words and up to about 2,000 content word lemmas or families. The most frequent 1,000 words account for about 70 per cent of all the words we use. The most frequent 2,000 words account for about 75 per cent of all the words we use. West (1953) provided the most famous and widely used list of high frequency words. More recent lists based on the computer analysis of a wider variety of spoken and written texts are now available (see 2.6.2).

2.6.2 Academic words

Academic words are a special group of up to about 600 word families which are used widely across many academic subject fields. Words such as *adjust, consist, establish, previous, series, underlie* typically contribute up to 10 per cent of the running words in textbooks used at high school or university. Any learner who wishes to use English as a medium of instruction needs to know these words. Coxhead (2000) has published an up-to-date Academic Word List (see 2.6.6 below). The list of the most frequent 2,000 lemmas in the *BNC* includes about 40 per cent of this Academic Word List. Together these two lists contain about 80 per cent of all the words in typical academic texts. It should be noted, however, that a learner who knows only high frequency and academic words will still be unfamiliar with at least two words in every ten on a page.

2.6.3 Technical words

According to Nation (2001: 12), about 5 per cent of the running words in a text are typically technical words. These may be quite frequent within a particular subject area or domain of use, they differ according to the subject area, and they tend not to be used outside particular domains of use. For example, for driving a car technical words would include *steering wheel*, *wipers*, *brake*, *indicator*, *oil pressure*, whereas in medicine technical words would include *cauterise*, *appendectomy*, *speculum*.

2.6.4 Low frequency words

The remaining 15 per cent of words in a text, including proper nouns, may be called low frequency words, although some proper nouns may be frequent in particular contexts. Most of the words in a large dictionary are low frequency words. Some could be classed as technical words in particular fields, others are simply not used very often in any context. (Examples include *revile*, *labyrinth*, *cogent*, *surmise*, *bullion*, *eponymous*.) As language users, native speakers of English continue to learn low frequency words throughout their lives, and develop strategies such as guessing from context and referring to dictionaries to deal with unfamiliar words. Teachers need to keep in mind that while 2,000 or so high frequency word lemmas must be a priority for language learning and teaching because of the coverage they give, knowledge of up to 10,000 word families is necessary for reasonably fluent comprehension of a good quality newspaper. As noted above, in very large corpora in which the texts are selected to represent the language as a whole, the most frequent 250 or so words are nearly all function words. In specific domains of use, however, some technical content words can be very frequent.

In an individual text or in a representative corpus of texts of English, the words are not evenly distributed. A few words occur many times, and as many as half the words occur only once. In the 1-million-word unlemmatised *Wellington Corpus of Written New Zealand English* (Bauer, 1993) there are 43,700 different word forms. The following distribution occurs and is typical of such corpora.

The 1,000th most frequent word occurs 108 times
2,000th	55
3,000th	35
4,000th	24
5,000th	18
6,000th	14

Research has shown that low listening and reading comprehension scores correlate highly with low vocabulary knowledge scores. Intensive English courses for learners should aim to teach 2,000 words in the first year, and up to the 6,000-word level by the end of the second year.

Word frequency should be only one of the factors that influence decisions as to what to teach and learn. While the most frequent words of English are important for all learners, once we get beyond the most frequent 2,000 words, then the **range** of use over a wide number of regional, social and situational contexts, and also areas of specialisation such as academic English, become increasingly important for curriculum planning and the preparation of teaching materials.

Task 2.12

Approximately what percentage of the words in Text 2.4 are function words?

2.6.5 Information on word frequency from the British National Corpus

There are many English corpora now available for studying how frequently particular words occur in different domains of use. These corpora range in size from 1 million words in, for example, the *Brown Corpus of Written American English* to the *Longman American Corpus* (50 million words of spoken and written US English), the *British National Corpus* (*BNC*) (100 million words), the *Bank of English Corpus* (400 million words) and even the Internet itself, where in 2002 it was estimated that it contained over 175 billion words of text in English.

The *BNC* is of particular interest because it is by far the largest structured representative sample of spoken and written English available. The *BNC* contains over 100 million running words from 4,000 texts, 90 per cent of which are from a wide variety of written sources, and 10 per cent from spoken English sampled from over 30 parts of the United Kingdom. Table 2.7 is a list of the 2,000 most frequent word lemmas in that corpus. This list covers almost 76 per cent of the word tokens in the corpus. It also shows how many times each lemma occurs per 1 million words, and their word class grammatical tag.

Table 2.7 Rank order of the most frequent 2,000 lemmas in the whole
British National Corpus (frequency per million words)

(*Note*: this list omits numerals and years but includes letters and proper nouns)

Lemma	Tag	Freq.	Lemma	Tag	Freq.	Lemma	Tag	Freq.
the	Det	61,847	one	Num	1,962	find	Verb	990
be	Verb	42,277	see	Verb	1,920	one	Pron	953
of	Prep	29,391	so	Adv	1,893	our	Det	950
and	Conj	26,817	know	Verb	1,882	want	Verb	945
a	Det	21,626	time	NoC	1,833	day	NoC	940
in	Prep	18,214	take	Verb	1,797	after	Prep	927
to	Inf	16,470	up	Adv	1,795	between	Prep	903
have	Verb	13,655	as	Prep	1,774	many	DetP	902
it	Pron	10,878	some	DetP	1,712	er	Uncl	896
I	Pron	10,241	when	Conj	1,712	those	DetP	888
to	Prep	9,343	could	VMod	1,683	because	Conj	852
he	Pron	8,469	year	NoC	1,639	down	Adv	845
for	Prep	8,412	into	Prep	1,634	yeah	Int	834
not	Neg	7,995	its	Det	1,632	three	Num	800
that	Conj	7,308	then	Adv	1,595	back	Adv	793
you	Pron	6,984	two	Num	1,563	thing	NoC	776
with	Prep	6,575	my	Det	1,549	tell	Verb	775
on	Prep	6,475	out	Adv	1,542	such	DetP	763
they	Pron	6,081	about	Prep	1,524	on	Adv	756
do	Verb	5,594	think	Verb	1,520	there	Adv	746
by	Prep	5,096	come	Verb	1,512	through	Prep	743
she	Pron	4,888	your	Det	1,391	over	Prep	735
at	Prep	4,790	now	Adv	1,382	must	VMod	723
this	DetP	4,623	no	Det	1,343	still	Adv	718
but	Conj	4,577	other	Adj	1,336	even	Adv	716
his	Det	4,287	only	Adv	1,298	child	NoC	710
we	Pron	4,202	give	Verb	1,284	too	Adv	701
from	Prep	4,134	just	Adv	1,277	put	Verb	700
that	DetP	3,792	good	Adj	1,276	more	DetP	699
which	DetP	3,719	more	Adv	1,275	here	Adv	699
or	Conj	3,707	people	NoC	1,256	own	DetP	695
an	Det	3,430	these	DetP	1,254	last	Ord	691
will	VMod	3,357	also	Adv	1,248	oh	Int	684
say	Verb	3,344	any	DetP	1,220	mean	Verb	677
as	Conj	3,006	first	Ord	1,193	become	Verb	675
would	VMod	2,904	very	Adv	1,165	Mr	NoC	673
can	VMod	2,672	new	Adj	1,154	government	NoC	670
their	Det	2,608	look	Verb	1,151	no	Int	662
there	Ex	2,532	may	VMod	1,135	work	NoC	653
what	DetP	2,493	well	Adv	1,119	old	Adj	648
all	DetP	2,436	should	VMod	1,112	leave	Verb	647
if	Conj	2,369	way	NoC	1,108	work	Verb	646
get	Verb	2,210	use	Verb	1,071	life	NoC	645
her	Det	2,183	like	Prep	1,064	great	Adj	635
make	Verb	2,165	than	Conj	1,033	woman	NoC	631
go	Verb	2,078	how	Adv	1,016	where	Adv	628
who	Pron	2,055	man	NoC	1,003	need	Verb	627

Table 2.7 (cont'd)

Lemma	Tag	Freq.	Lemma	Tag	Freq.	Lemma	Tag	Freq.
erm	Uncl	627	week	NoC	476	play	Verb	386
seem	Verb	624	large	Adj	471	power	NoC	385
feel	Verb	624	member	NoC	471	change	NoC	384
system	NoC	619	four	Num	465	per cent	NoC	384
same	DetP	615	turn	Verb	465	pay	Verb	381
might	VMod	614	always	Adv	462	young	Adj	379
case	NoC	613	follow	Verb	460	both	Adv	378
part	NoC	612	end	NoC	458	interest	NoC	376
ask	Verb	610	where	Conj	458	often	Adv	376
group	NoC	607	without	Prep	456	national	Adj	376
number	NoC	606	few	DetP	450	money	NoC	375
yes	Int	606	within	Prep	449	development	NoC	375
however	Adv	605	about	Adv	447	book	NoC	374
world	NoC	600	local	Adj	445	water	NoC	372
house	NoC	598	begin	Verb	440	away	Adv	371
show	Verb	598	during	Prep	440	other	NoC	367
area	NoC	585	state	NoC	440	hear	Verb	367
over	Adv	584	bring	Verb	439	form	NoC	365
another	DetP	581	word	NoC	438	room	NoC	364
company	NoC	579	although	Conj	436	level	NoC	360
high	Adj	574	before	Prep	434	second	Ord	358
in	Adv	573	when	Adv	431	British	Adj	357
as	Adv	567	next	Ord	431	right	Adj	354
most	Adv	565	family	NoC	428	early	Adj	353
problem	NoC	565	fact	NoC	426	car	NoC	353
against	Prep	562	like	Verb	424	include	Verb	353
again	Adv	561	most	DetP	422	London	NoP	351
never	Adv	559	social	Adj	422	perhaps	Adv	350
under	Prep	553	going (to)	Verb	417	policy	NoC	348
try	Verb	552	help	Verb	416	council	NoC	348
call	Verb	535	start	Verb	414	believe	Verb	347
place	NoC	534	quite	Adv	412	market	NoC	346
hand	NoC	532	five	Num	409	right	Adv	346
much	DetP	531	run	Verb	406	court	NoC	344
school	NoC	529	head	NoC	402	already	Adv	343
party	NoC	529	every	Det	401	allow	Verb	342
something	Pron	526	write	Verb	400	possible	Adj	342
small	Adj	518	side	NoC	398	nothing	Pron	341
why	Adv	509	set	Verb	398	meet	Verb	339
each	DetP	508	month	NoC	398	big	Adj	338
keep	Verb	505	business	NoC	394	yet	Adv	337
provide	Verb	505	night	NoC	393	effect	NoC	336
while	Conj	503	long	Adj	392	lead	Verb	334
out of	Prep	491	important	Adj	392	result	NoC	334
off	Adv	486	eye	NoC	392	whether	Conj	332
country	NoC	486	move	Verb	391	mm	Int	330
different	Adj	484	much	Adv	390	live	Verb	329
point	NoC	484	home	NoC	390	idea	NoC	328
hold	Verb	481	question	NoC	390	John	NoP	328
really	Adv	481	information	NoC	387	use	NoC	328

Table 2.7 (*cont'd*)

Lemma	Tag	Freq.	Lemma	Tag	Freq.	Lemma	Tag	Freq.
study	NoC	327	suggest	Verb	288	stop	Verb	255
name	NoC	326	anything	Pron	288	programme	NoC	255
job	NoC	326	term	NoC	288	girl	NoC	254
stand	Verb	326	towards	Prep	286	moment	NoC	254
body	NoC	325	low	Adj	286	age	NoC	252
happen	Verb	325	public	Adj	285	father	NoC	252
report	NoC	325	let	Verb	284	Britain	NoP	251
line	NoC	323	require	Verb	284	send	Verb	250
such as	Prep	321	read	Verb	284	value	NoC	250
law	NoC	318	continue	Verb	283	order	NoC	250
later	Adv	317	period	NoC	283	force	NoC	250
almost	Adv	316	figure	NoC	282	matter	NoC	248
friend	NoC	315	centre	NoC	282	act	NoC	248
face	NoC	315	society	NoC	282	receive	Verb	247
carry	Verb	313	police	NoC	278	health	NoC	246
road	NoC	313	lose	Verb	277	lot	NoC	246
authority	NoC	313	add	Verb	275	decide	Verb	245
himself	Pron	311	city	NoC	275	main	Adj	245
both	DetP	310	change	Verb	273	though	Conj	245
far	Adv	310	fall	Verb	273	enough	Adv	244
of course	Adv	310	need	NoC	273	less	Adv	243
together	Adv	308	probably	Adv	273	street	NoC	243
talk	Verb	308	available	Adj	272	decision	NoC	243
appear	Verb	307	community	NoC	272	until	Conj	242
little	Adj	306	million	NoC	272	industry	NoC	242
political	Adj	306	kind	NoC	271	patient	NoC	242
before	Conj	305	price	NoC	271	mind	NoC	241
six	Num	305	control	NoC	270	class	NoC	241
minister	NoC	305	action	NoC	269	sure	Adj	241
able	Adj	304	cost	NoC	269	win	Verb	241
produce	Verb	304	issue	NoC	269	several	DetP	240
rate	NoC	303	process	NoC	269	clear	Adj	239
late	Adj	302	position	NoC	268	for example	Adv	239
hour	NoC	302	remain	Verb	268	understand	Verb	238
door	NoC	302	A / a	Lett	268	major	Adj	238
general	Adj	301	remember	Verb	268	church	NoC	238
office	NoC	300	course	NoC	267	around	Prep	237
sit	Verb	300	minute	NoC	266	itself	Pron	237
right	NoC	299	bad	Adj	264	paper	NoC	237
war	NoC	297	today	Adv	263	themselves	Pron	237
since	Conj	295	buy	Verb	262	condition	NoC	237
mother	NoC	295	speak	Verb	261	describe	Verb	237
offer	Verb	293	education	NoC	260	develop	Verb	237
person	NoC	290	actually	Adv	260	agree	Verb	236
full	Adj	289	ever	Adv	259	economic	Adj	236
reason	NoC	289	type	NoC	259	open	Verb	235
view	NoC	289	so	Conj	258	reach	Verb	234
consider	Verb	289	research	NoC	258	upon	Prep	234
far	Adj	288	at least	Adv	257	bank	NoC	234
expect	Verb	288	subject	NoC	256	after	Conj	233

Table 2.7 *(cont'd)*

Lemma	Tag	Freq.	Lemma	Tag	Freq.	Lemma	Tag	Freq.
century	NoC	233	ground	NoC	215	situation	NoC	198
therefore	Adv	232	letter	NoC	215	ago	Adv	198
section	NoC	232	evidence	NoC	215	care	NoC	198
only	Adj	231	meeting	NoC	215	strong	Adj	197
table	NoC	231	walk	Verb	215	so that	Conj	197
England	NoP	231	off	Prep	214	record	NoC	197
activity	NoC	231	foot	NoC	214	manager	NoC	197
hundred	NoC	231	rather	Adv	213	project	NoC	197
build	Verb	230	sell	Verb	213	raise	Verb	196
death	NoC	230	boy	NoC	213	example	NoC	196
including	Prep	230	wait	Verb	213	European	Adj	195
among	Prep	229	back	NoC	212	yesterday	Adv	195
sense	NoC	229	game	NoC	212	base	Verb	194
building	NoC	229	third	Ord	211	home	Adv	194
involve	Verb	229	food	NoC	211	training	NoC	194
sort	NoC	229	union	NoC	211	window	NoC	194
likely	Adj	228	role	NoC	210	break	Verb	193
real	Adj	227	ten	Num	210	explain	Verb	193
spend	Verb	227	half	DetP	209	all	Adv	193
staff	NoC	227	else	Adv	209	learn	Verb	193
black	Adj	226	event	NoC	208	central	Adj	193
team	NoC	226	land	NoC	208	apply	Verb	193
return	Verb	225	shall	VMod	208	increase	Verb	192
draw	Verb	224	white	Adj	207	sale	NoC	192
experience	NoC	223	cause	Verb	206	cover	Verb	191
particular	Adj	223	art	NoC	206	grow	Verb	191
student	NoC	222	sometimes	Adv	205	air	NoC	191
town	NoC	221	thus	Adv	205	usually	Adv	191
Mrs	NoC	221	pass	Verb	204	difference	NoC	191
international	Adj	221	support	NoC	204	light	NoC	191
language	NoC	221	stage	NoC	203	university	NoC	191
either	Adv	220	range	NoC	203	wife	NoC	190
certain	Adj	220	trade	NoC	203	relationship	NoC	189
difficult	Adj	220	teacher	NoC	203	claim	Verb	189
special	Adj	220	voice	NoC	203	sir	NoC	189
particularly	Adv	220	accept	Verb	202	report	Verb	189
die	Verb	220	behind	Prep	202	indeed	Adv	188
plan	NoC	220	watch	Verb	202	quality	NoC	188
hope	Verb	219	arm	NoC	202	support	Verb	188
open	Adj	219	God	NoP	202	lie (/lay)	Verb	187
morning	NoC	219	club	NoC	202	everything	Pron	187
management	NoC	219	field	NoC	201	someone	Pron	187
department	NoC	219	parent	NoC	201	rule	NoC	187
across	Prep	217	history	NoC	201	certainly	Adv	186
create	Verb	217	free	Adj	200	cut	Verb	184
committee	NoC	217	account	NoC	200	story	NoC	184
product	NoC	217	material	NoC	199	form	Verb	184
whole	Adj	216	short	Adj	198	similar	Adj	184
practice	NoC	216	easy	Adj	198	worker	NoC	184
around	Adv	215	whose	DetP	198	tax	NoC	184

Table 2.7   (cont'd)

Lemma	Tag	Freq.	Lemma	Tag	Freq.	Lemma	Tag	Freq.
pound	NoC	184	achieve	Verb	169	American	Adj	157
true	Adj	183	rather than	Prep	169	David	NoP	157
little	DetP	183	seek	Verb	169	as if	Conj	157
once	Adv	183	chapter	NoC	169	election	NoC	157
stay	Verb	183	choose	Verb	168	drive	Verb	156
human	Adj	183	deal	Verb	168	future	NoC	156
model	NoC	183	theory	NoC	168	used (to)	Verb	156
data/datum	NoC	183	until	Prep	167	colour	NoC	156
common	Adj	182	property	NoC	167	various	Adj	155
nature	NoC	182	poor	Adj	166	rise	Verb	155
long	Adv	181	son	NoC	166	represent	Verb	155
necessary	Adj	181	wide	Adj	165	site	NoC	155
officer	NoC	181	south	NoC	165	close	Adj	154
Europe	NoP	181	director	NoC	165	shop	NoC	154
structure	NoC	181	financial	Adj	165	loss	NoC	154
contain	Verb	181	leader	NoC	165	clearly	Adv	153
unit	NoC	180	face	Verb	164	evening	NoC	153
method	NoC	180	twenty	Num	164	animal	NoC	153
hospital	NoC	180	north	NoC	163	up to	Prep	152
bed	NoC	180	firm	NoC	163	heart	NoC	152
movement	NoC	179	application	NoC	163	standard	NoC	152
B / b	Lett	179	cos/'cos	Conj	163	benefit	NoC	152
because of	Prep	178	board	NoC	162	purpose	NoC	152
detail	NoC	178	king	NoC	162	page	NoC	151
reduce	Verb	178	production	NoC	162	fine	Adj	150
since	Prep	178	secretary	NoC	162	place	Verb	150
simply	Adv	177	US	NoP	162	anyone	Pron	150
especially	Adv	177	fail	Verb	161	discuss	Verb	150
single	Adj	177	soon	Adv	161	English	Adj	150
date	NoC	177	chance	NoC	161	doctor	NoC	150
UK	NoP	177	opportunity	NoC	161	pick	Verb	150
hard	Adj	176	operation	NoC	161	factor	NoC	150
as well as	Prep	176	share	NoC	161	music	NoC	150
personal	Adj	176	foreign	Adj	161	hair	NoC	150
seven	Num	176	lord	NoC	160	May	NoP	150
establish	Verb	176	agreement	NoC	160	love	NoC	150
wall	NoC	175	picture	NoC	159	love	Verb	150
join	Verb	174	simple	Adj	159	prove	Verb	149
eight	Num	174	serve	Verb	159	wrong	Adj	149
computer	NoC	174	test	NoC	159	argue	Verb	149
private	Adj	173	contract	NoC	159	wear	Verb	149
herself	Pron	172	concerned	Adj	158	charge	NoC	149
approach	NoC	171	recent	Adj	158	pattern	NoC	149
amount	NoC	171	end	Verb	158	piece	NoC	148
bit	NoC	171	security	NoC	158	at all	Adv	148
wish	Verb	170	thousand	NoC	158	present	Adj	148
scheme	NoC	170	kill	Verb	157	basis	NoC	148
former	DetP	170	occur	Verb	157	more than	Adv	148
president	NoC	170	source	NoC	157	design	NoC	148
award	NoC	170	according to	Prep	157	p	NoC	148

Table 2.7 (cont'd)

Lemma	Tag	Freq.	Lemma	Tag	Freq.	Lemma	Tag	Freq.
tree	NoC	147	choice	NoC	138	growth	NoC	131
catch	Verb	147	couple	NoC	138	finally	Adv	130
royal	Adj	147	near	Prep	138	compare	Verb	130
population	NoC	147	refer	Verb	138	mile	NoC	130
C / c	Lett	147	capital	NoC	138	lady	NoC	130
April	NoP	147	round	Adv	138	final	Adj	129
enjoy	Verb	146	hotel	NoC	138	happy	Adj	129
despite	Prep	146	player	NoC	138	top	NoC	129
pressure	NoC	146	above	Prep	137	whom	Pron	129
performance	NoC	146	forward	Adv	137	task	NoC	129
knowledge	NoC	146	act	Verb	137	function	NoC	129
plant	NoC	146	village	NoC	137	risk	NoC	129
June	NoP	146	station	NoC	137	sound	NoC	129
fire	NoC	145	nine	Num	137	provision	NoC	129
news	NoC	145	individual	Adj	136	county	NoC	129
March	NoP	145	film	NoC	136	east	NoC	128
further	Adv	144	attempt	NoC	135	resource	NoC	128
introduce	Verb	144	association	NoC	135	behaviour	NoC	128
size	NoC	144	feature	NoC	135	defence	NoC	128
garden	NoC	144	individual	NoC	135	west	NoC	127
series	NoC	144	per	Prep	135	floor	NoC	127
eat	Verb	144	income	NoC	135	St	NoP-	127
environment	NoC	144	effort	NoC	134	style	NoC	127
rest	NoC	143	French	Adj	134	obtain	Verb	127
better	Adv	143	following	Adj	134	science	NoC	127
before	Adv	143	relate	Verb	134	announce	Verb	127
enter	Verb	143	cup	NoC	134	red	Adj	126
present	Verb	143	nice	Adj	134	feeling	NoC	126
success	NoC	143	organisation	NoC	134	hall	NoC	126
analysis	NoC	143	manage	Verb	133	note	Verb	126
point	Verb	142	affect	Verb	133	response	NoC	126
arrive	Verb	142	everyone	Pron	133	skill	NoC	126
natural	Adj	142	close	Verb	133	college	NoC	126
thought	NoC	142	current	Adj	133	horse	NoC	126
ensure	Verb	142	technology	NoC	133	character	NoC	125
plan	Verb	141	identify	Verb	133	myself	Pron	125
region	NoC	141	please	Adv	133	user	NoC	125
attention	NoC	140	whatever	DetP	132	serious	Adj	124
list	NoC	140	difficulty	NoC	132	answer	NoC	124
set	NoC	140	machine	NoC	132	nor	Conj	124
space	NoC	140	in order	ClO	131	quickly	Adv	124
pull	Verb	140	modern	Adj	131	forget	Verb	124
statement	NoC	140	degree	NoC	131	indicate	Verb	124
relation	NoC	140	legal	Adj	131	look	NoC	124
step	NoC	139	energy	NoC	131	normal	Adj	124
for	Conj	139	treatment	NoC	131	Peter	NoP	124
sea	NoC	139	Scotland	NoP	131	army	NoC	124
demand	NoC	139	labour	Adj	131	economy	NoC	124
principle	NoC	139	thank	Verb	131	investment	NoC	124
labour	NoC	139	cell	NoC	131	wonder	Verb	124

Table 2.7 (cont'd)

Lemma	Tag	Freq.	Lemma	Tag	Freq.	Lemma	Tag	Freq.
dog	NoC	124	discussion	NoC	116	circumstance	NoC	110
Dr	NoC	124	aspect	NoC	116	oil	NoC	110
along	Prep	123	generally	Adv	116	client	NoC	110
recently	Adv	123	industrial	Adj	116	obviously	Adv	110
suffer	Verb	123	chairman	NoC	116	sector	NoC	110
brother	NoC	123	nearly	Adv	115	direction	NoC	109
husband	NoC	123	remove	Verb	115	basic	Adj	109
maintain	Verb	123	throw	Verb	115	attack	NoC	109
previous	Adj	123	visit	Verb	115	seat	NoC	109
France	NoP	123	baby	NoC	115	Soviet	Adj	109
publish	Verb	123	round	Prep	115	each other	Pron	108
responsibility	NoC	122	daughter	NoC	115	fight	Verb	108
total	Adj	122	sorry	Adj	115	intend	Verb	108
argument	NoC	122	sun	NoC	115	successful	Adj	108
season	NoC	122	United	NoP-	115	attitude	NoC	108
anyway	Adv	122	box	NoC	114	miss	Verb	108
avoid	Verb	121	exist	Verb	114	original	Adj	108
concern	NoC	121	river	NoC	114	aware	Adj	108
bill	NoC	121	dead	Adj	114	military	Adj	108
prime	Adj	121	Paul	NoP	114	discover	Verb	107
express	Verb	121	customer	NoC	114	drop	Verb	107
suppose	Verb	121	institution	NoC	114	exactly	Adv	107
significant	Adj	121	force	Verb	113	push	Verb	107
away from	Prep	120	encourage	Verb	113	hit	Verb	107
finish	Verb	120	appropriate	Adj	113	de	NoP	107
element	NoC	120	specific	Adj	113	Germany	NoP	107
glass	NoC	120	profit	NoC	113	goal	NoC	107
determine	Verb	119	as well	Adv	113	disease	NoC	107
duty	NoC	119	reflect	Verb	113	yourself	Pron	107
increase	NoC	119	admit	Verb	112	employment	NoC	107
July	NoP	119	assume	Verb	112	hon	Adj	107
a bit	Adv	119	top	Adj	112	prevent	Verb	106
save	Verb	118	measure	NoC	112	refuse	Verb	106
design	Verb	118	stone	NoC	112	sign	NoC	106
tend	Verb	118	conference	NoC	112	popular	Adj	106
one	NoC	118	division	NoC	112	New	NoP	106
leg	NoC	118	smile	Verb	112	October	NoP	106
listen	Verb	118	prepare	Verb	111	affair	NoC	106
fund	NoC	118	George	NoP	111	appeal	NoC	106
claim	NoC	118	post	NoC	111	beyond	Prep	105
park	NoC	118	replace	Verb	111	heavy	Adj	105
suddenly	Adv	118	procedure	NoC	111	ability	NoC	105
title	NoC	118	commission	NoC	111	regard	Verb	105
note	NoC	117	proposal	NoC	111	holiday	NoC	105
treat	Verb	117	fill	Verb	110	professional	Adj	105
outside	Prep	116	help	NoC	110	item	NoC	105
share	Verb	116	mention	Verb	110	show	NoC	105
summer	NoC	116	unless	Conj	110	technique	NoC	105
control	Verb	116	improve	Verb	110	medium	NoC	105
throughout	Prep	116	image	NoC	110	pupil	NoC	105

Table 2.7 (cont'd)

Lemma	Tag	Freq.	Lemma	Tag	Freq.	Lemma	Tag	Freq.
fish	NoC	105	speaker	NoC	101	agency	NoC	96
version	NoC	105	check	Verb	100	planning	NoC	96
campaign	NoC	105	complete	Verb	100	collection	NoC	96
maybe	Adv	105	deal	NoC	100	communication	NoC	96
okay	Adv	105	cost	Verb	100	Ireland	NoP	96
lay	Verb	104	access	NoC	100	fifty	Num	96
direct	Adj	104	sound	Verb	100	considerable	Adj	96
teach	Verb	104	Richard	NoP	100	arise	Verb	96
advice	NoC	104	star	NoC	100	species	NoC	96
press	NoC	104	text	NoC	100	through	Adv	95
a little	Adv	104	thirty	Num	100	fit	Verb	95
drug	NoC	104	no	NoC	100	left	Adj	95
September	NoP	104	easily	Adv	99	physical	Adj	95
visit	NoC	104	trouble	NoC	99	sister	NoC	95
dark	Adj	104	cause	NoC	99	supply	NoC	95
library	NoC	104	effective	Adj	99	examine	Verb	95
reveal	Verb	104	traditional	Adj	99	Michael	NoP	95
advantage	NoC	103	western	Adj	99	document	NoC	95
operate	Verb	103	payment	NoC	99	define	Verb	95
answer	Verb	103	York	NoP	99	complete	Adj	94
cold	Adj	103	though	Adv	99	responsible	Adj	94
surface	NoC	103	mouth	NoC	99	hot	Adj	94
state	Verb	103	ah	Int	99	above	Adv	94
America	NoP	103	base	NoC	98	career	NoC	94
immediately	Adv	102	second	NoC	98	study	Verb	94
worth	Prep	102	down	Prep	98	weight	NoC	94
ready	Adj	102	facility	NoC	98	up to	Adv	94
blood	NoC	102	independent	Adj	98	November	NoP	94
James	NoP	102	reference	NoC	98	solution	NoC	94
memory	NoC	102	survey	NoC	98	December	NoP	94
return	NoC	102	German	Adj	98	influence	NoC	94
television	NoC	102	realise	Verb	98	budget	NoC	94
variety	NoC	102	context	NoC	98	existing	Adj	94
Island	NoC	102	Scottish	Adj	98	software	NoC	94
in terms of	Prep	102	laugh	Verb	98	bear	Verb	93
culture	NoC	102	earlier	Adv	97	fear	NoC	93
January	NoP	102	deep	Adj	97	opinion	NoC	93
less	DetP	101	extend	Verb	97	hang	Verb	93
green	Adj	101	earth	NoC	97	medical	Adj	93
depend	Verb	101	importance	NoC	97	rock	NoC	93
useful	Adj	101	article	NoC	97	bird	NoC	93
record	Verb	101	chair	NoC	97	district	NoC	93
Sunday	NoP	101	object	NoC	97	sign	Verb	93
bar	NoC	101	involved	Adj	96	Wales	NoP	93
competition	NoC	101	interesting	Adj	96	damage	NoC	93
extent	NoC	101	possibility	NoC	96	tomorrow	Adv	93
enable	Verb	101	means	NoC	96	shake	Verb	93
majority	NoC	101	public	NoC	96	recognise	Verb	93
parliament	NoC	101	card	NoC	96	requirement	NoC	93
talk	NoC	101	notice	Verb	96	organisation	NoC	93

Table 2.7 (cont'd)

Lemma	Tag	Freq.	Lemma	Tag	Freq.	Lemma	Tag	Freq.
call	NoC	92	male	Adj	89	file	NoC	86
extra	Adj	92	review	NoC	89	Oxford	NoP	86
whole	NoC	92	strategy	NoC	89	primary	Adj	86
edge	NoC	92	employee	NoC	89	I / i	Num	86
on to	Prep	92	II / ii	Num	89	obvious	Adj	85
blue	Adj	92	interested	Adj	88	length	NoC	85
stock	NoC	92	no longer	Adv	88	future	Adj	85
exchange	NoC	92	travel	Verb	88	balance	NoC	85
option	NoC	92	hill	NoC	88	copy	NoC	85
quarter	NoC	92	otherwise	Adv	88	branch	NoC	85
miss	NoC	92	below	Adv	88	nation	NoC	85
opposition	NoC	92	hardly	Adv	88	wind	NoC	85
eventually	Adv	91	result	Verb	88	States	NoP	85
occasion	NoC	91	expression	NoC	88	league	NoC	85
arrangement	NoC	91	perform	Verb	88	none	Pron	84
highly	Adv	91	status	NoC	88	demand	Verb	84
radio	NoC	91	West	NoP	88	doubt	NoC	84
executive	NoC	91	tea	NoC	88	front	NoC	84
aid	NoC	91	Christmas	NoC	88	move	NoC	84
target	NoC	91	partner	NoC	88	pain	NoC	84
Charles	NoP	91	band	NoC	88	accident	NoC	84
match	NoC	91	directly	Adv	88	train	NoC	84
railway	NoC	91	failure	NoC	88	February	NoP	84
attend	Verb	91	reader	NoC	88	spirit	NoC	84
concept	NoC	91	shoulder	NoC	88	William	NoP	84
network	NoC	91	like	Adv	88	studio	NoC	84
once	Conj	90	even if	Conj	87	let's	Verb	84
lack	NoC	90	fair	Adj	87	stare	Verb	84
corner	NoC	90	turn	NoC	87	environmental	Adj	83
fly	Verb	90	protect	Verb	87	strength	NoC	83
sex	NoC	90	truth	NoC	87	contact	NoC	83
race	NoC	90	adopt	Verb	87	normally	Adv	83
forest	NoC	90	confirm	Verb	87	imagine	Verb	83
finger	NoC	90	essential	Adj	87	positive	Adj	83
mum	NoC	90	marriage	NoC	87	up	Prep	83
gain	Verb	89	owner	NoC	87	official	NoC	83
fully	Adv	89	civil	Adj	87	enough	DetP	82
scene	NoC	89	Saturday	NoP	87	attempt	Verb	82
slightly	Adv	89	trust	NoC	87	shape	NoC	82
afternoon	NoC	89	beautiful	Adj	87	contribution	NoC	82
equipment	NoC	89	v	Prep	87	senior	Adj	82
past	Adj	89	completely	Adv	86	transport	NoC	82
scale	NoC	89	past	NoC	86	cash	NoC	82
ball	NoC	89	start	NoC	86	beat	Verb	82
message	NoC	89	newspaper	NoC	86	born	Verb	82
speech	NoC	89	safety	NoC	86	gas	NoC	82
sport	NoC	89	farm	NoC	86	works	NoC	82
kitchen	NoC	89	trial	NoC	86	museum	NoC	82
peace	NoC	89	sentence	NoC	86	debate	NoC	82
crime	NoC	89	Smith	NoP	86	reform	NoC	82

Table 2.7   (cont'd)

Lemma	Tag	Freq.	Lemma	Tag	Freq.	Lemma	Tag	Freq.
best	Adv	81	latter	DetP	78	ignore	Verb	74
agent	NoC	81	emerge	Verb	78	settle	Verb	74
pair	NoC	81	regional	Adj	78	strike	Verb	74
care	Verb	81	fig	NoC	78	link	Verb	74
annual	Adj	81	mark	Verb	77	reality	NoC	74
rise	NoC	81	separate	Adj	77	sight	NoC	74
no one	Pron	81	deny	Verb	77	boat	NoC	74
associate	Verb	81	shoot	Verb	77	for instance	Adv	74
English	NoC	81	practical	Adj	77	estate	NoC	74
marry	Verb	81	aim	Verb	77	inside	Prep	74
artist	NoC	81	understanding	NoC	77	winter	NoC	74
presence	NoC	81	official	Adj	77	ring	Verb	74
protection	NoC	81	credit	NoC	77	wine	NoC	74
nuclear	Adj	81	impact	NoC	77	prison	NoC	74
collect	Verb	80	early	Adv	76	S / s	Lett	74
hope	NoC	80	danger	NoC	76	Henry	NoP	74
master	NoC	80	half	NoC	76	propose	Verb	74
queen	NoC	80	order	Verb	76	additional	Adj	74
driver	NoC	80	progress	NoC	76	dad	NoC	74
meaning	NoC	80	key	Adj	76	possibly	Adv	73
candidate	NoC	80	path	NoC	76	respond	Verb	73
vote	NoC	80	supply	Verb	76	press	Verb	73
voice	Verb	80	reaction	NoC	76	writer	NoC	73
huge	Adj	79	track	NoC	76	active	Adj	73
rich	Adj	79	flower	NoC	76	clothes	NoC	73
employ	Verb	79	video	NoC	76	as to	Prep	73
play	NoC	79	appoint	Verb	76	employer	NoC	73
adult	NoC	79	merely	Adv	76	offer	NoC	73
commercial	Adj	79	distance	NoC	75	weekend	NoC	73
consequence	NoC	79	instead	Adv	75	vehicle	NoC	73
exercise	NoC	79	regular	Adj	75	debt	NoC	73
release	Verb	79	comment	NoC	75	somebody	Pron	73
relatively	Adv	79	gold	NoC	75	objective	NoC	73
issue	Verb	79	link	NoC	75	largely	Adv	73
August	NoP	79	conclusion	NoC	75	instead of	Prep	72
Robert	NoP	79	chief	Adj	75	arrange	Verb	72
slowly	Adv	79	content	NoC	75	powerful	Adj	72
relevant	Adj	79	due	Adj	75	survive	Verb	72
P / p	Lett	79	aim	NoC	75	carefully	Adv	72
beginning	NoC	78	drink	Verb	75	telephone	NoC	72
apparently	Adv	78	politics	NoC	75	battle	NoC	72
safe	Adj	78	reply	Verb	75	hole	NoC	72
due to	Prep	78	justice	NoC	75	Mary	NoP	72
speed	NoC	78	observe	Verb	75	standard	Adj	72
proportion	NoC	78	skin	NoC	75	D / d	Lett	72
route	NoC	78	belief	NoC	75	farmer	NoC	72
assessment	NoC	78	bag	NoC	75	injury	NoC	72
consideration	NoC	78	etc	Adv	75	expert	NoC	72
Africa	NoP	78	mhm	Int	75	package	NoC	72
mind	Verb	78	alone	Adv	74	colleague	NoC	72

Table 2.7 (cont'd)

Lemma	Tag	Freq.	Lemma	Tag	Freq.	Lemma	Tag	Freq.
nevertheless	Adv	72	cabinet	NoC	69	South	NoP-	67
complex	Adj	72	introduction	NoC	69	exhibition	NoC	67
concentrate	Verb	71	author	NoC	69	launch	Verb	67
impossible	Adj	71	domestic	Adj	69	consumer	NoC	67
confidence	NoC	71	previously	Adv	69	EC	NoP	67
light	Adj	71	administration	NoC	69	equally	Adv	66
generation	NoC	71	sexual	Adj	69	quick	Adj	66
mainly	Adv	71	smile	NoC	69	sheet	NoC	66
hard	Adv	71	tonight	Adv	69	appearance	NoC	66
lift	Verb	71	prefer	Verb	68	bridge	NoC	66
key	NoC	71	cheap	Adj	68	promote	Verb	66
phone	NoC	71	extremely	Adv	68	limit	Verb	66
insurance	NoC	71	ordinary	Adj	68	potential	Adj	66
painting	NoC	71	commit	Verb	68	quiet	Adj	66
sample	NoC	71	demonstrate	Verb	68	soft	Adj	66
forty	Num	71	relief	NoC	68	construction	NoC	66
e.g.	Adv	71	threaten	Verb	68	description	NoC	66
approach	Verb	70	actual	Adj	68	in front of	Prep	66
along	Adv	70	grant	Verb	68	improvement	NoC	66
cross	Verb	70	technical	Adj	68	session	NoC	66
test	Verb	70	bus	NoC	68	housing	NoC	66
commitment	NoC	70	repeat	Verb	68	northern	Adj	66
visitor	NoC	70	strange	Adj	68	religious	Adj	66
warm	Adj	70	investigation	NoC	68	flat	NoC	66
drink	NoC	70	mountain	NoC	68	Mark	NoP	66
plus	Prep	70	regulation	NoC	68	twelve	Num	66
ship	NoC	70	coffee	NoC	68	discipline	NoC	66
currently	Adv	70	song	NoC	68	contrast	NoC	66
middle	Adj	70	wage	NoC	68	lip	NoC	66
somewhere	Adv	70	row	NoC	68	increasingly	Adv	66
volume	NoC	70	acquire	Verb	68	existence	NoC	66
judge	NoC	70	sleep	Verb	68	gentleman	NoC	66
threat	NoC	70	Thomas	NoP	68	distribution	NoC	66
conflict	NoC	70	united	Adj	68	TV	NoC	66
legislation	NoC	70	insist	Verb	67	apart from	Prep	65
entirely	Adv	69	feed	Verb	67	own	Verb	65
manner	NoC	69	fairly	Adv	67	very	Adj	65
background	NoC	69	in particular	Adv	67	deliver	Verb	65
fresh	Adj	69	excellent	Adj	67	proper	Adj	65
charge	Verb	69	meal	NoC	67	audience	NoC	65
front	Adj	69	wood	NoC	67	broad	Adj	65
experience	Verb	69	category	NoC	67	famous	Adj	65
yard	NoC	69	internal	Adj	67	retain	Verb	65
entry	NoC	69	tradition	NoC	67	conversation	NoC	65
engine	NoC	69	dinner	NoC	67	theatre	NoC	65
touch	Verb	69	interview	NoC	67	prince	NoC	65
victim	NoC	69	tour	NoC	67	crisis	NoC	65
E / e	Lett	69	past	Prep	67	measure	Verb	65
stuff	NoC	69	traffic	NoC	67	code	NoC	65
Edward	NoP	69	football	NoC	67	loan	NoC	65

Table 2.7 (cont'd)

Lemma	Tag	Freq.	Lemma	Tag	Freq.	Lemma	Tag	Freq.
representative	NoC	65	impose	Verb	63	detailed	Adj	60
Japan	NoP	65	cry	Verb	63	murder	NoC	60
cultural	Adj	65	rural	Adj	63	weapon	NoC	60
belong	Verb	64	J	NoP	63	afraid	Adj	60
usual	Adj	64	address	Verb	62	tape	NoC	60
unable	Adj	64	destroy	Verb	62	female	Adj	60
attract	Verb	64	intention	NoC	62	concentration	NoC	60
respect	NoC	64	average	Adj	62	overall	Adj	60
freedom	NoC	64	bright	Adj	62	enterprise	NoC	60
magazine	NoC	64	initial	Adj	62	Edinburgh	NoP	60
limit	NoC	64	mark	NoC	62	T / t	Lett	60
promise	Verb	64	whereas	Conj	62	bedroom	NoC	60
contribute	Verb	64	nobody	Pron	62	neck	NoC	60
formal	Adj	64	thanks	NoC	62	recognise	Verb	60
limited	Adj	64	Christian	Adj	62	kid	NoC	60
flight	NoC	64	egg	NoC	62	nod	Verb	60
hide	Verb	64	definition	NoC	62	pp	NoC	60
reject	Verb	64	declare	Verb	62	even though	Conj	59
writing	NoC	64	examination	NoC	62	expensive	Adj	59
assess	Verb	64	notice	NoC	62	handle	Verb	59
joint	Adj	64	onto	Prep	62	spread	Verb	59
pension	NoC	64	substantial	Adj	62	clear	Verb	59
rain	NoC	64	worry	Verb	62	combine	Verb	59
consist	Verb	64	aircraft	NoC	62	correct	Adj	59
explanation	NoC	64	decade	NoC	62	growing	Adj	59
plate	NoC	64	output	NoC	62	recommend	Verb	59
unemployment	NoC	64	name	Verb	61	absence	NoC	59
lovely	Adj	64	will	NoC	61	attack	Verb	59
conservative	Adj	64	divide	Verb	61	bottle	NoC	59
asset	NoC	64	fourth	Ord	61	sufficient	Adj	59
all right	Adv	64	head	Verb	61	store	NoC	59
i.e.	Adv	64	immediate	Adj	61	influence	Verb	59
ltd	Adj	64	suitable	Adj	61	criticism	NoC	59
invite	Verb	63	equal	Adj	61	wave	NoC	59
twice	Adv	63	ought	VMod	61	eastern	Adj	59
ahead	Adv	63	stick	Verb	61	birth	NoC	59
spring	NoC	63	Paris	NoP	61	teaching	NoC	59
challenge	NoC	63	reasonable	Adj	61	Irish	Adj	59
capacity	NoC	63	offence	NoC	61	shout	Verb	59
factory	NoC	63	leading	Adj	61	transfer	NoC	59
sing	Verb	63	everybody	Pron	61	instruction	NoC	59
youth	NoC	63	X / x	Lett	61	error	NoC	59
selection	NoC	63	reduction	NoC	61	assembly	NoC	59
vary	Verb	63	middle	NoC	60	acid	NoC	59
while	NoC	63	train	Verb	60	straight	Adv	59
warn	Verb	63	address	NoC	60	ear	NoC	59
dream	NoC	63	bottom	NoC	60	settlement	NoC	59
victory	NoC	63	run	NoC	60	educational	Adj	59
finance	NoC	63	working	Adj	60	scientific	Adj	59
surely	Adv	63	appointment	NoC	60	realise	Verb	59

Table 2.7   (cont'd)

Lemma	Tag	Freq.	Lemma	Tag	Freq.	Lemma	Tag	Freq.
undertake	Verb	59	guide	NoC	57	widely	Adv	56
democratic	Adj	59	household	NoC	57	assumption	NoC	56
sort of	Adv	59	step	Verb	57	curriculum	NoC	56
module	NoC	59	guest	NoC	57	congress	NoC	56
Inc.	Adj	59	screen	NoC	57	Darlington	NoP	56
either	DetP	58	welcome	Verb	57	below	Prep	55
dangerous	Adj	58	experiment	NoC	57	escape	Verb	55
totally	Adv	58	nurse	NoC	57	direct	Verb	55
photograph	NoC	58	Jack	NoP	57	heat	NoC	55
weather	NoC	58	silence	NoC	57	wild	Adj	55
cut	NoC	58	secure	Verb	57	display	NoC	55
lead	NoC	58	sixty	Num	57	daily	Adj	55
pleasure	NoC	58	publication	NoC	57	focus	Verb	55
whilst	Conj	58	increased	Adj	57	reading	NoC	55
channel	NoC	58	expenditure	NoC	57	remind	Verb	55
critical	Adj	58	treaty	NoC	57	gate	NoC	55
lunch	NoC	58	program	NoC	57	gun	NoC	55
select	Verb	58	slow	Adj	56	location	NoC	55
absolutely	Adv	58	under	Adv	56	southern	Adj	55
account	Verb	58	disappear	Verb	56	theme	NoC	55
fee	NoC	58	journey	NoC	56	investigate	Verb	55
Friday	NoP	58	dry	Adj	56	instrument	NoC	55
mental	Adj	58	trip	NoC	56	Tom	NoP	55
temperature	NoC	58	connection	NoC	56	professor	NoC	55
beside	Prep	58	cover	NoC	56	cat	NoC	55
waste	NoC	58	metal	NoC	56	Liverpool	NoP	55
solicitor	NoC	58	noise	NoC	56	gallery	NoC	55
frequently	Adv	58	tiny	Adj	56	closely	Adv	55
implication	NoC	58	dress	Verb	56	generate	Verb	55
recognition	NoC	58	organise	Verb	56	ministry	NoC	55
desire	NoC	58	sum	NoC	56	Jesus	NoP	55
institute	NoC	58	thin	Adj	56	emphasis	NoC	55
component	NoC	58	illustrate	Verb	56	increasing	Adj	55
grant	NoC	58	imply	Verb	56	afford	Verb	54
republic	NoC	58	sky	NoC	56	neither	Adv	54
MP	NoC	58	captain	NoC	56	advise	Verb	54
seriously	Adv	57	Monday	NoP	56	earn	Verb	54
familiar	Adj	57	pool	NoC	56	inform	Verb	54
properly	Adv	57	violence	NoC	56	narrow	Adj	54
block	NoC	57	map	NoC	56	prospect	NoC	54
elsewhere	Adv	57	phase	NoC	56	spot	NoC	54
double	Adj	57	display	Verb	56	hand	Verb	54
partly	Adv	57	scientist	NoC	56	opening	NoC	54
recall	Verb	57	perfect	Adj	56	priority	NoC	54
unlikely	Adj	57	conclude	Verb	56	combination	NoC	54
brain	NoC	57	crowd	NoC	56	soldier	NoC	54
necessarily	Adv	57	initiative	NoC	56	alone	Adj	54
transfer	Verb	57	historical	Adj	56	drive	NoC	54
contact	Verb	57	search	NoC	56	rely	Verb	54
climb	Verb	57	sequence	NoC	56	supposed	Adj	54

Table 2.7 (cont'd)

Lemma	Tag	Freq.	Lemma	Tag	Freq.	Lemma	Tag	Freq.
empty	Adj	54	busy	Adj	53	motion	NoC	53
fifteen	Num	54	fear	Verb	53	breath	NoC	53
faith	NoC	54	Martin	NoP	53	R / r	Lett	53
liberal	Adj	54	outside	Adv	53	apparent	Adj	53
tool	NoC	54	wing	NoC	53	membership	NoC	53
troop	NoC	54	tall	Adj	53	revenue	NoC	53
succeed	Verb	54	lane	NoC	53	Ian	NoP	53
married	Adj	54	crown	NoC	53	Corp	NoC	53
upper	Adj	54	flow	NoC	53	last	Verb	52
interpretation	NoC	54	release	NoC	53	careful	Adj	52
as though	Conj	54	coal	NoC	53	match	Verb	52
learning	NoC	54	I / i	Lett	53	persuade	Verb	52
North	NoP-	54	vote	Verb	53	suggestion	NoC	52
tooth	NoC	54	approve	Verb	53	attractive	Adj	52
hell	NoC	54	bloody	Adj	53	clean	Adj	52
urban	Adj	54	total	NoC	53	cope	Verb	52
mistake	NoC	53	castle	NoC	53	gather	Verb	52
prepared	Adj	53	variation	NoC	53	ring	NoC	52
alternative	NoC	53	literature	NoC	53	incident	NoC	52
burn	Verb	53						
Total tokens per million								757,328

Key to word class categories used in the BNC:

Adj	adjective (e.g. good, old, fine, early, regional)
Adv	adverb (e.g. now, well, suddenly, early, further)
ClO	clause opener (in order [that/to], so as [to])
Conj	conjunction (e.g. and, but, if, because, so that)
Det	determiner (e.g. a, an, every, no, the)
DetP	determiner/pronoun (e.g. this, these, those, some, all)
Ex	existential particle (there in there is, there are, etc.)
Fore	foreign word (e.g. de, du, la)
Form	formula (e.g. $2x + z$)
Gen	genitive ('s,')
Inf	infinitive marker (to)
Int	interjection or discourse marker (e.g. oh, aha, oops, yep, no)
Lett	letter of the alphabet, treated as a word (e.g. p, P, Q, r, z)
Neg	negative marker (not, -n't)
NoC	common noun (e.g. wealth, walls, child, times, mission)
NoP	proper noun (e.g. Malaysia, Paris, Susan, Roberts, Tuesday)
NoP-	word which is normally part of a proper noun (e.g. San in San Diego)
Num	(cardinal) number (e.g. one, four, forty, viii, 8, 55, 1969)
Ord	ordinal (e.g. first, 1st, 9th, twenty-first, next, last)
Prep	preposition (e.g. of, in, without, up to, in charge of)
Pron	pronoun (e.g. I, you, she, him, theirs, none, something)
Uncl	unclassified (e.g. erm)
Verb	verb – excluding modal auxiliaries (e.g. tell, find, increase, realise)
VMod	modal auxiliary verb (e.g. can, will, would, could, may, must, should)

Table 2.8 lists the 50 most frequent word lemmas in each of the four major content word classes in the whole *BNC*, and the number of times they occur per 1 million words. It is often salutary for teachers to compare this information with their own intuitions about what the most frequent nouns, verbs, adjectives or adverbs might be.

Task 2.13

Discuss with colleagues which senses of the verbs *see, look, run* from Table 2.8 you would expect to be most useful for learners of English. Look at a learner's dictionary if necessary for analyses of senses.

Task 2.14

Discuss with colleagues how teachers of English might best provide learners with repeated opportunities to meet the words in Table 2.7 in use, and to have opportunities to use the words in speech and writing.

Table 2.9 summarises the distribution of words in the *BNC*. The three most frequent lemmas (*the, be, of*) make up 13.4 per cent of all the words in the corpus; the ten most frequent lemmas make up 25.1 per cent of all the words, and so on. Teachers should also note that the 1,000 most frequent words are not necessarily the 1,000 most useful for a particular group of learners, and word frequency is not the only thing to take account of in designing a syllabus for language learners. Nevertheless, Table 2.7 gives some idea of the 2,000 lemmas that were made most use of in the United Kingdom in the 1990s, and this information should be borne in mind in the teaching process.

Because of its size and the care taken to structure the corpus to be as representative as possible, the *BNC* is almost certainly the most reliable picture we have of the most frequent words in British English. Even so, it reflects the time and place in which it was compiled. For example, *computer, sir, Paul, John, George, lord, Soviet, environment, pounds, Scotland, London, EC, Liverpool, Edinburgh, Irish* are among the words occurring in the most frequent 2,000 words. That *Darlington* should have occurred as frequently as *Liverpool* is an unexpected consequence of the sampling process.

We would expect, of course, a similar corpus compiled in, say, the United States to have distinguishing features (such as the names of certain large cities) that would differ from those mentioned frequently in the *BNC*.

A degree of caution is called for in interpreting rank frequency lists such as the one in Table 2.7. The computer counts word **types** not **senses**. Thus

Table 2.8   Rank lists of the 50 most frequent nouns, verbs, adjectives and adverbs in the *British National Corpus* (frequency per million words)

Common nouns		Verbs		Adjectives		Adverbs	
time	1,833	be	42,277	other	1,336	so	1,893
year	1,639	have	13,655	good	1,276	up	1,795
people	1,256	do	5,594	new	1,154	then	1,595
way	1,108	will	3,357	old	648	out	1,542
man	1,003	say	3,344	great	635	now	1,382
day	940	would	2,904	high	574	only	1,298
thing	776	can	2,672	small	518	just	1,277
child	710	get	2,210	different	484	more	1,275
Mr	673	make	2,165	large	471	also	1,248
government	670	go	2,078	local	445	very	1,165
word	653	see	1,920	social	422	well	1,119
life	645	know	1,882	important	392	how	1,016
woman	631	take	1,797	long	392	down	845
system	619	could	1,683	young	379	back	793
case	613	think	1,520	national	376	on	756
part	612	come	1,512	British	357	there	746
group	607	give	1,284	right	354	still	718
number	606	look	1,151	early	353	even	716
world	600	may	1,135	possible	342	too	701
house	598	should	1,112	big	338	here	699
area	585	use	1,071	little	306	where	628
company	579	find	990	political	306	however	605
problem	565	want	945	able	304	over	584
service	549	tell	775	late	302	in	573
place	534	must	723	general	301	as	567
hand	532	put	700	full	289	most	565
party	529	mean	677	far	288	again	561
school	529	become	675	low	286	never	559
country	486	leave	647	public	285	why	509
point	484	work	646	available	272	off	486
week	476	need	627	bad	264	really	481
member	471	feel	624	main	245	always	462
end	458	seem	624	sure	241	about	447
state	440	might	614	clear	239	when	431
word	438	ask	610	major	238	quite	412
family	428	show	598	economic	236	much	390
fact	426	try	552	only	231	both	378
head	402	call	535	likely	228	often	376
month	398	provide	505	real	227	away	371
side	398	keep	505	black	226	perhaps	350
business	394	hold	481	particular	223	right	346
night	393	turn	465	international	221	already	343
eye	392	follow	460	special	220	yet	337
home	390	begin	440	difficult	220	later	317
question	390	bring	439	certain	220	almost	316
information	387	like	424	open	219	of course	310
power	385	going to	417	whole	216	far	310
change	384	help	416	white	207	together	308
per cent	384	start	414	free	200	probably	273
interest	376	run	406	short	198	today	263

Table 2.9   Distribution of the most frequent word lemmas in the
British National Corpus

Number of word lemmas	Proportion of word tokens in corpus
3	13.4
10	25.1
50	42.0
100	48.7
500	63.8
1,000	71.3
2,000	75.7

right, classed as an adjective, includes as the same word type *right* as in *right hand* and *right* as in *you were right*. Further, Table 2.7 is based on the whole *BNC*, combining both spoken and written texts, and thus important differences between speech and writing in the relative frequency of words are masked. For example, in spoken English *right* is often used as a discourse marker to begin an utterance, e.g. *Right, let's get going.* Teachers might also be surprised to find words such as *government* or *system* ranking so high in the list of common nouns. It is important to keep in mind that 90 per cent of the running words of text in the *BNC* is from written texts produced by British adults. The language tends to reflect fairly formal, informative prose. This is, of course, the target language of many adults who wish to learn English as a medium of instruction or for business and professional purposes. Unsurprisingly, the *BNC* is therefore probably not quite such a good basis for discovering the informal spoken English vocabulary needs of users of other varieties of English, or the language needs of young children.

Detailed information about the *BNC* is available on the Internet at http://info.ox.ac.uk/bnc. Leech et al. (2001) have produced a very useful volume of word lists based on an analysis of spoken and written texts in the *BNC*. Many of these lists can be downloaded from the Web for further analysis. (See http://www.comp.lancs.ac.uk/ucrel/bncfreq/lists/.)

2.6.6 An academic word list (AWL)

Table 2.10 is a modern academic word list compiled by Coxhead (2000). It contains headwords of 570 word families which account for approximately 10 per cent of the total words (tokens) in a corpus of 3,500,000 running words of written academic English. The corpus consists of texts from 28 disciplines within the four subject fields of Arts, Commerce, Law and Science. The word families were selected because they were not included in the first 2,000 words of English produced by West (1953), but occurred in all four general subject fields and in 15 or more of the 28 individual disciplines of the corpus. They each occurred at least 100 times in the corpus and at least 10 times in a subject field. It is interesting to note that about 90 per cent of the words in this academic word list are of Greek or Latin origin. Learners who are familiar with Greek and Latin roots and affixes may find it easier to learn these words.

Together with a list of the 2,000 most frequent words from a representative corpus, this academic word list gives coverage of over 80 per cent of the words in a wide variety of academic texts, excluding mainly technical or specialist words associated with particular disciplines.

There is some overlap between the words in the *BNC* most frequent lemmas list (Table 2.7) and those in the AWL (Table 2.10). About 225 of the AWL words are in the *BNC* top 2,000 words. But for learners of English as a medium of instruction we can be confident that the main pedagogical focus should be on the words in these lists before less frequent words receive attention. Words in the AWL which are also in the most frequent 2,000 *BNC* list are marked with an asterisk (*).

Table 2.10 An academic word list (Coxhead, 2000)

abandon	append	cease	comprise	convene
abstract	appreciate	*challenge	*compute	converse
academy	*approach	*channel	conceive	convert
*access	*appropriate	*chapter	*concentrate	convince
accommodate	approximate	chart	*concept	cooperate
accompany	arbitrary	chemical	*conclude	coordinate
accumulate	*area	*circumstance	concurrent	core
accurate	*aspect	cite	conduct	corporate
*achieve	*assemble	*civil	confer	correspond
acknowledge	assess	clarify	confine	*couple
*acquire	assign	classic	*confirm	*create
adapt	assist	clause	*conflict	*credit
adequate	*assume	*code	conform	criteria
adjacent	assure	coherent	consent	crucial
adjust	attach	coincide	*consequent	*culture
*administrate	attain	collapse	*considerable	currency
*adult	*attitude	*colleague	*consist	cycle
advocate	attribute	commence	constant	*data
*affect	*author	*comment	constitute	*debate
aggregate	*authority	*commission	constrain	*decade
*aid	automate	*commit	*construct	decline
albeit	*available	commodity	consult	deduce
allocate	*aware	*communicate	*consume	*define
alter	behalf	*community	*contact	definite
*alternative	*benefit	compatible	contemporary	*demonstrate
ambiguous	bias	compensate	*context	denote
amend	bond	compile	*contract	*deny
analogy	brief	complement	contradict	depress
*analyse	bulk	*complex	contrary	derive
*annual	capable	*component	*contrast	*design
anticipate	*capacity	compound	*contribute	*despite
*apparent	*category	comprehensive	controversy	detect

Table 2.10   (cont'd)

deviate	evolve	*image	*job	*objective
device	exceed	immigrate	journal	*obtain
devote	exclude	*impact	justify	*obvious
differentiate	*exhibit	implement	label	occupy
dimension	expand	*implicate	*labour	*occur
diminish	*expert	implicit	layer	odd
discrete	explicit	*imply	lecture	offset
discriminate	exploit	*impose	*legal	ongoing
displace	export	incentive	*legislate	*option
*display	expose	*incidence	levy	orient
dispose	external	incline	*liberal	outcome
distinct	extract	*income	licence	*output
distort	facilitate	incorporate	likewise	*overall
*distribute	*factor	index	*link	overlap
diverse	*feature	*indicate	*locate	overseas
*document	federal	*individual	logic	panel
domain	*fee	induce	*maintain	paradigm
*domestic	*file	inevitable	*major	paragraph
dominate	*final	infer	manipulate	parallel
draft	*finance	infrastructure	manual	parameter
drama	finite	inherent	margin	participate
duration	flexible	inhibit	mature	*partner
dynamic	fluctuate	*initial	maximise	passive
*economy	*focus	*initiate	mechanism	perceive
edit	format	*injure	media	*per cent
element	formula	innovate	mediate	*period
eliminate	forthcoming	input	*medical	persist
*emerge	foundation	insert	*medium	perspective
*emphasis	found	insight	*mental	*phase
empirical	framework	inspect	*method	phenomenon
*enable	*function	instance	migrate	philosophy
encounter	*fund	*institute	*military	*physical
*energy	fundamental	*instruct	minimal	*plus
enforce	furthermore	integral	minimise	*policy
enhance	gender	integrate	minimum	portion
enormous	*generate	integrity	*ministry	pose
*ensure	*generation	intelligence	minor	*positive
entity	globe	intense	mode	*potential
*environment	*goal	interact	modify	practitioner
equate	grade	intermediate	monitor	precede
equip	*grant	*internal	motive	precise
equivalent	guarantee	*interpret	mutual	predict
erode	guideline	interval	negate	predominant
*error	hence	intervene	*network	preliminary
*establish	hierarchy	intrinsic	neutral	presume
*estate	highlight	invest	*nevertheless	*previous
estimate	hypothesis	*investigate	nonetheless	*primary
ethic	identical	invoke	norm	*prime
ethnic	*identify	*involve	*normal	principal
evaluate	ideology	isolate	notion	*principle
*eventual	*ignorance	*issue	notwithstanding	*prior
*evident	*illustrate	*item	*nuclear	*priority

Table 2.10   (cont'd)

proceed	relax	*secure	substitute	transform
*process	*release	*seek	successor	transit
*professional	*relevant	*select	*sufficient	transmit
prohibit	reluctance	sequence	*sum	*transport
*project	*rely	*series	summary	trend
*promote	*remove	*sex	supplement	trigger
*proportion	require	shift	*survey	ultimate
*prospect	*research	*significant	*survive	undergo
protocol	reside	*similar	suspend	underlie
psychology	resolve	simulate	sustain	undertake
*publication	*resource	*site	symbol	uniform
*publish	*respond	so-called	*tape	unify
purchase	restore	sole	*target	unique
pursue	restrain	somewhat	*task	utilise
*qualitative	restrict	*source	*team	valid
quote	*retain	*specific	*technical	*vary
radical	*reveal	specify	technique	*vehicle
random	*revenue	sphere	*technology	*version
*range	reverse	stable	temporary	via
ratio	revise	statistic	tense	violate
rational	revolution	*status	terminate	virtual
*react	rigid	straightforward	*text	visible
recover	*role	*strategy	*theme	vision
refine	route	stress	*theory	visual
regime	scenario	*structure	thereby	*volume
*region	schedule	*style	thesis	voluntary
register	*scheme	submit	topic	welfare
*regulate	scope	subordinate	trace	*whereas
reinforce	*section	subsequent	*tradition	whereby
*reject	*sector	subsidy	*transfer	widespread

CHAPTER 3

Simple sentence parts, structures and functions

This chapter gives an overview of the parts and functions of the grammatical structures associated with 'simple' sentences. Simple sentences have only one lexical verb. These sentences form the basis of complex structures containing more than one clause, which are described in Chapter 7.

Objectives

When you have finished this chapter you should:

1 Be able to identify major differences between **spoken utterances** and **written sentences**.

2 Be able to identify the following word classes in simple sentences: **nouns, pronouns, verbs, adjectives, adverbs, prepositions, determiners**.

3 Be able to identify five main types of **phrase – noun phrases, verb phrases, adjective phrases, prepositional phrases, adverb phrases**, and their grammatical functions in simple sentences.

4 Know that a **simple sentence** contains a single **clause**.

5 Be able to identify the main constituents of **clauses – subjects, predicates, objects, complements, adverbials**.

6 Be able to identify **transitive verbs, intransitive verbs, copular verbs**.

7 Be able to identify the following **clause patterns: SV, SVO, SVA, SVC, SVOO, SVOC, SVOA, clauses which contain formal *there***.

8 Be able to identify the following sentence types and functions: **declarative, interrogative, imperative, exclamative**.

9 Be able to describe the structures that are used for asking **questions** and making **negative statements**.

3.1 Utterances and sentences

In Chapter 2 the word classes (nouns, verbs, etc.) were mentioned. In language use, words are grouped together in grammatical structures to express meaning. A sentence is one such unit of linguistic description. Most fluent speakers of a language have a sense of the 'unity' and 'completeness' of what is said or written and can identify when a string of words is not 'well formed' or 'grammatical'. For this reason it has sometimes been said that sentences have a psychological as well as a grammatical reality.

For example, in the following examples most people would agree that 1 has a sense of completeness while 2–5 seem incomplete. Sentence 2 has no **subject** (we don't know who has dinner). While 3, 4 and 5 have a subject, the rest (the **predicate**) seems incomplete. (* Shows structures that are not grammatical.)

1 *I have dinner about 7 o'clock most nights.*

2 **have dinner about 7 o'clock most nights.*

3 **I have about 7 o'clock most nights.*

4 **I have dinner 7 o'clock most nights.*

5 **I have dinner about 7 o'clock most.*

Sentences normally have at least a subject and a verb (but not always, especially when we speak). A **simple sentence** consists of a single **clause** containing one verb phrase. It can be joined to other clauses by means of conjunctions to make **complex sentences**. These are described in Chapter 7.

Before looking more closely at the parts of simple sentences, we need to be aware that in spoken English conversation, which is by far the most typical or frequent use of the language, the concept of 'sentence' is often rather different from that which is considered appropriate in written English. When we **speak**, our ideas usually flow in such a way that, in addition to saying what we intend, we also make false starts, change direction, leave things unfinished, and so on. When we speak, our **utterances** are often not grammatical when compared with written text, yet any ungrammaticality is rarely noticed.

Text 3.1, for example, is a transcription (without any attempt at punctuation) of part of a conversation between two young women, Emma and Hillary. On tape the conversation sounds clear and coherent, yet the participants interrupt each other; some utterances are incomplete; there are false starts, repetitions, fillers and hesitation phenomena; some utterances have no subject; and so on. Intonation and stress contribute to the meaning.

Text 3.1 Part of a conversation

EM> im going to have tea with john on sunday night he does did i tell you
     about the feed he cooked up last time

HI> oh did he

EM> oh it was about two weeks ago after i got home from church and he it
     was eight oclock and there was this note on my door emma ring john its
     urgent so i rang him in a big panic thinking what the hells going on you
     know he said oh ive cooked a roast of lamb ive cooked double you want
     to come round

HI> oh good one

EM> and he was just about cause he was hes never cooked in his life practically

HI> hes being did he

EM> yeah and anyway he was just about to have his first mouthful when i
     rang he was waiting for to ring hes so sweet and then i so i said yeah ill
     be round cos i hadnt eaten and i was starving hungry i was about to go
     down and raid the kitchen but i went went down went to his place and
     he had this great big he had two plates full of food

HI> yeah

EM> one plate was vegetables you know just steamed veggies and then the
     other plate was huge chunks of meat with hed done it really well with
     potato and kumara yeah

HI> guys are funny when they carve eh they put big chunks, not slices

---

Discussion topic

Text 3.1 is a transcription of the spontaneous spoken English of
two native speakers. Try to mark where the sentences begin and
end. How did you decide? Do you agree with each other on all the
sentence boundaries? Do you think the texts contain grammatical
errors? If so, are the errors similar to those made by second language
learners? Do all sentences have to have a subject and a verb? Is
there a difference between our grammatical **competence** (knowledge of how the language works) and our **performance** (what we
actually do)?

When we **write**, the texts we produce observe certain conventions,
such as divisions between words and the breaking of units into sentences
by means of capital letters and full stops. There is enormous variation in
the size of written sentences. In the 1-million-word *LOB Corpus of Written
British English* sentences range in length from 1 to 354 words, with a
mean of 19 words. In newspapers and fiction, sentence length tends to be
much shorter than in academic prose.

Table 3.1 Linguistic acceptability

No.	Test sentence	Group 1 judgement			Group 2 judgement		
		Yes	Not sure	No	Yes	Not sure	No
1	They always come here	28	0	0	47	1	0
2	Jack admired sincerity	26	2	0	42	5	1
3	I was sat opposite by a stranger	0	10	18	0	5	43
4	He wants some cake	28	0	0	48	0	0
5	He isn't much loved	15	10	3	7	31	10
6	It's in the front of the station	23	3	2	30	16	2
7	They aren't but they pretend to be	26	2	0	41	7	0
8	He dared to answer me back	26	2	0	44	3	1
9	Whom did you see	16	9	3	39	5	4
10	He is silly and crying	9	16	3	15	23	10
11	Neither he nor I knew the answer	26	1	1	42	4	2
12	He is regarded insane	9	10	9	11	22	15
13	Food was lacked by the children	6	9	13	9	20	19
14	Dusk was creeping up between the trees	21	4	3	20	14	14
15	The old man chose his son a wife	15	8	5	16	16	16
16	It's the man to whom I spoke	21	4	3	35	10	3
17	We provided the man a drink	7	9	12	8	19	21
18	I turn on the light for the room to look brighter	16	11	1	20	12	16
19	Neither I nor he felt a thing	20	4	4	36	8	4
20	They painted blue their door	4	4	20	0	10	38
21	A nice little car is had by me	1	1	26	0	1	47
22	He sits always there	2	6	20	0	1	47

Source: Adapted from Quirk, R. and Svartvik, J. (1996) *Investigating Linguistic Acceptability*, Table 1, pp. 106–9. Reprinted by permission of Mouton de Gruyter.

Even with written English it is not always easy to get native speakers to agree unanimously whether sentences are well formed. This is illustrated in a study by Quirk & Svartvik (1966: 106–109). Table 3.1 presents a summary of some of the results. Group 1 consisted of 28 undergraduates majoring in English. Group 2 consisted of 48 undergraduates majoring in Geography. All were native speakers of English. They were asked to judge whether or not each test sentence was a well-formed or 'possible' English sentence, or to indicate if they were not sure. What is surprising is that with the exception of Sentence 4 (*He wants some cake*) judgements were never unanimous.

> **Discussion topic**
>
> How might we account for the general lack of agreement about well-formedness among the 76 native speakers of English who took part in Quirk and Svartvik's study?

Text 3.2

post mortem reports show that four out of five fatal accident victims had alcohol in their systems it is not always the obviously intoxicated drunk that causes motorway collisions these highly inebriated individuals are often spotted by traffic officers or are seen first by other motorists and are carefully avoided the problem is the social drinker both male and female who looks normal and drives normally until the alcohol catches up even hangovers can render a person unfit to drive the hangover which is largely dependent on the amount of alcohol consumed previously will affect the central nervous system and the functions of the eyes.

Discussion topic

Text 3.2 has been reproduced without punctuation. Punctuate it and then compare the original, which is printed below, with what you have done. Why is punctuation necessary in written texts?

Post mortem reports show that four out of five fatal accident victims had alcohol in their systems. It is not always the obviously intoxicated drunk that causes motorway collisions. These highly inebriated individuals are often spotted by traffic officers or are seen first by other motorists and are carefully avoided. The problem is the social drinker (both male and female) who looks normal and drives normally until the alcohol catches up. Even hangovers can render a person unfit to drive. The hangover, which is largely dependent on the amount of alcohol consumed previously, will affect the central nervous system and the functions of the eyes.

3.2 Constituents and structures of simple sentences

3.2.1 Word order

Word order is important in most languages. English is no exception, as is illustrated with the following examples. Compare:

1 *My holidays begin at the end of next week.*

2 **The next end week holidays of begin my.*

3 **My holidays begin the next week end of.*

4 **Begin next week end my holidays.*

In English, there are many contrasting examples that can illustrate the important effect of word order on meaning, e.g.

5 *His dog chased my cat.*

6 *My cat chased his dog.*

7 *Did John ring you?*

8 *Did you ring John?*

Many learners have difficulty getting certain aspects of English word order right, especially in those parts of sentences that follow verbs, but word order errors have a surprisingly small effect on intelligibility. Compare, for example,

9 **I like very much James Bond movies.*

10 *I like James Bond movies very much.*

Of course, in Example 9, although the non-standard word order may be slightly ambiguous as to whether the speaker or writer is really wishing to say they like very many James Bond movies (but not all of them) or whether they like all of them a lot, the non-standard word order is unlikely to result in a catastrophic communication breakdown.

3.2.2 Phrases

A phrase is a unit of analysis smaller than a sentence and consisting of a single word or group of words. A phrase is associated with, or is an expansion of, the word class of its most important constituent (the **headword**). Five main types of phrase can be identified (the phrases are underlined).

1 **Noun phrases** consist of a noun (or pronoun) and any determiners, adjectives or other modifiers that are associated with it. The structure of noun phrases can be very complex because of modification by prepositional phrases.

> Cars are expensive.
>
> They are expensive.
>
> New cars are expensive.
>
> Some new cars are expensive.
>
> John's car is expensive.
>
> The car in my uncle's garage is expensive.
>
> The car that they bought last month was expensive.
>
> Cars at the top of the price range for imported vehicles without tax exemption can be very expensive.

2 **Adjective phrases** contain an adjective as headword with optional modifier.

> This information is useful.
>
> This information is very useful.
>
> This information is useful up to a point.
>
> This information is more useful than I expected.

3 **Adverb phrases**, which consist of an adverb as headword with optional modifiers, are able to be used to modify adjectives or adverbs, or whole clauses. They can take up various positions in sentences to highlight elements. Consider, for example,

> Max opened the door carefully.
>
> Carefully Max opened the door.
>
> Max drove carefully.
>
> Max drove very carefully.
>
> Max drove carefully enough.
>
> Max drove faster than he should have.

4 **Verb phrases** consist of a lexical verb and associated words which together form a **predicate**.

> Sara sings.
>
> Sara can sing.
>
> Sara has been singing all morning.
>
> Sara sings very well.
>
> Sara sings in the shower.
>
> Sara sings duets with Fred.

5 **Prepositional phrases** consist of a preposition and an **object** which is usually a noun phrase, e.g. *Sue was **in the room**.* The preposition *in* is followed by the noun phrase *the room* to form a prepositional phrase *in the room.*

> I saw my friends at the airport.
>
> The person at the airport was my neighbour.
>
> It was quite near your house.
>
> I was surprised at what you said.

Other phrase types include **determiner phrases** (e.g. *some of the* people) and number phrases (e.g. *a hundred and fifty* dollars).

Phrases can occur within phrases. The following sentence has seven phrases.

The teacher saw Sam at the back of the room.	noun phrase
The teacher saw Sam at the back of the room.	verb phrase
The teacher saw Sam at the back of the room.	noun phrase
The teacher saw Sam at the back of the room.	prepositional phrase
The teacher saw Sam at the back of the room.	noun phrase
The teacher saw Sam at the back of the room.	prepositional phrase
The teacher saw Sam at the back of the room.	noun phrase

The main phrase types are considered more fully in Chapters 4–6. A detailed linguistic description of phrase types and functions can also be found in Biber et al. (1999: 94–117).

Text 3.3

Water is the most important solvent on Earth. It makes up a large part of the bodies of all living things. Life would be impossible without water. Carbon dioxide and water are the two starting materials which green plants use to make sugars.

Task 3.1

List the noun phrases and prepositional phrases in Text 3.3. Underline the headword of each phrase.

3.2.3 Clause elements

A simple sentence consists of a single **clause**, which contains a verb phrase. A clause has various **constituents** which have different semantic roles. The major elements or constituents that can be found in clauses are **subject, predicate, object, complement, adverbial.**

3.2.3.1 Subject

The subject is the part of a clause that identifies the topic. It tells who or what the clause is about, who or what took an action or caused something to happen, or who is involved in a set of circumstances. The subject usually comes at the beginning of a clause and consists of a noun phrase. In each of the following sentences, the part underlined is the subject.

1 I know.
2 This doesn't work.
3 The new machine stopped.

Task 3.2

Underline the subjects of the verb phrases in Text 2.1.

The pro-subject *it* (sometimes called a 'dummy subject') frequently occurs in sentences referring to time, the weather or quantitative measures, e.g. ***It's my birthday tomorrow*** (cf. My birthday is tomorrow); ***It's going to rain***; ***It costs $10 to go to the movies*** (cf. To go to the movies costs $10).

3.2.3.2 Predicate

Everything in a sentence other than the subject is the predicate. The predicate tells us something about the subject. (The word comes from a Latin word which means 'to preach' or 'say in public'.) The predicate typically consists of a verb phrase including one or more of the following: verb, object, complement, adverbial. Together, a subject and predicate make up a **proposition**. Predicates can be short and simple or longer and complicated, including optional adverbials and other clauses forming complex sentences (see Chapter 7).

Task 3.3

In the following sentences, underline the **subject** and put brackets around the **predicate**.

1 I need a rest.

2 Fred is asleep.

3 You didn't recognise me yesterday.

4 The products sold here are imported from overseas.

5 The new computer is very fast.

6 It rarely rains in the Sahara desert.

7 In my opinion, that was a waste of time.

8 Before Christmas the price was much lower.

3.2.3.2.1 Verbs
Predicates must contain at least a finite verb (a verb which has a tense).

1 I agree.

2 The star exploded.   (*The star exploding.)

3 Sara is sleeping.   (*Sara sleep.)

Verbs such as *agree, explode, sleep*, which do not **require** any other words after them, are called **intransitive verbs**. Intransitive verbs, however, **can** (optionally) have adverbials after them, e.g.

1 I agree completely.   (how)

2 I slept without any difficulty.   (how)

3 The star exploded a million years ago. (when)

4 Sara is sleeping quietly in her bed,
  because she is tired.   (how) (where) (why)

Task 3.4

Agree, explode and *sleep* are used above as intransitive verbs. Make a list of ten other verbs which can be used intransitively. You can check your answers in a dictionary. (Intransitive verbs are usually labelled *intr.* or *intrans.* in a dictionary.)

3.2.3.2.2 Objects

Some verbs **require** an **object** after them. An object is a noun phrase (pronoun, noun or noun clause) which follows a verb and which usually answers the question 'what?' or 'whom?' after the verb, e.g.

1 I like <u>ice cream</u>.	(I like what?)
2 I asked <u>Sam</u>.	(I asked who or whom?)
3 I asked <u>a question</u>.	(I asked what?)
4 I know <u>Sue is a very good gardener</u>.	(I know what?)

Verbs which have an object after them are called **transitive verbs**. Sentence 4 shows that a whole sentence (*Sue is a very good gardener*) can be an object. Sometimes an object is followed by an optional adverbial, e.g. I bought some cheese *on Friday*. All the objects included in Sentences 1–4 are usually called **direct objects**. Some verbs require or permit two objects, e.g. *Sue gave Max a present*. Both *Max* and *a present* are objects. *Max* is an **indirect object**, and *a present* is a **direct object**.

Task 3.5

Here are some transitive verbs: *need, want, contain, make, avoid, enjoy, own*. Make a list of another ten transitive verbs.

Note that some verbs can be used both transitively and intransitively, e.g. *study, break, end*. List five others. Check your answers in a dictionary.

Task 3.6

In the following sentences, underline the **subject** and put brackets around the **object**.

1 Mary owns a hotel.
2 They appreciated your hospitality.
3 The new book contains a very good index.
4 Some people have big feet.

5 This bag holds all my books.

6 That new tie suits him.

7 For some reason, she wants a box of matches.

8 I really enjoy Mozart's piano sonatas.

9 You will like what I am going to tell you.

10 We need your help tomorrow morning.

Task 3.7

For each sentence below, decide whether the lexical verb is transitive (t) or intransitive (i) in that sentence. Remember, a transitive verb is followed by an object. Some of the sentences contain adverbials. Be careful to distinguish these adverbs from objects.

1 I don't watch TV very often.

2 These methods never fail.

3 I didn't see you at the weekend.

4 Max arrived early.

5 Our team won again.

6 We have completed our review of the department.

7 The price includes fares and accommodation.

8 I can swim.

9 My friend has a headache.

10 Sue enjoyed the concert.

3.2.3.2.3 Complements

Copular verbs are verbs (e.g. *be, seem*) which require a **complement** or an **adverbial** after them, e.g. She is *a dentist*; He seemed *angry*; She is *in Chicago*. The complement is a noun phrase or an adjective phrase which refers back to the subject.

3.2.3.2.4 Adverbials

Parts of the predicate that can answer the questions 'when?' or 'where?' or 'why?' or 'how?' are called **adverbials**. They can be

1 a single adverb ending in -*ly* (She left the room quickly)

2 a single adverb with no special ending (I'll meet you there)

3 a preposition phrase (We saw him on Friday)

4 a plain noun phrase (I met her that evening)

5 an adverbial clause (We'll ring you when we get home)

In this book the word **adverbial** is used to refer both to one-word adverbs and also to groups of words that function as adverbs. Adverbials are part of the predicate but they can come in many parts of the sentence, including before the subject. They are discussed in more detail in Chapters 6 and 7.

Task 3.8

In the following sentences, underline the subjects, put round brackets around the objects, and square brackets around the adverbials.

1 I go there at weekends.

2 She told me several times.

3 The day after tomorrow is my birthday.

4 In the morning we began the search.

5 He is retiring at the end of the year.

6 These things are not suitable.

7 I watch TV on Sunday nights.

8 For reasons of safety you can't enter that building.

9 They study how to cure headaches in that course.

10 Supplies of food are needed urgently in that region.

3.3 Clause patterns

The clause elements (e.g. verb, complement, object, etc.) combine to produce 'patterns' or 'structures'. **Clause patterns** are also called valency patterns (or verb patterns because they typically consist of a verb and the words that follow). Although word order constraints operate in all parts of the grammar of sentences, the overall structure of sentences is controlled or determined by verbs. The words that follow a verb can include a noun phrase, an adjective phrase, a prepositional phrase, an adverb phrase, or another clause.

Different verbs can have different 'patterns' of words after them. Compare, for example,

1 *I gave them an answer.*
   *I suggested them an answer.

2 *I wished her a rapid recovery.*
   *I hoped her a rapid recovery.

The ungrammatical sentences shown with an asterisk are typical errors made by learners of English. Part of the task of learning to construct sentences is learning what patterns of word classes can follow particular verbs.

3.3.1 Major clause patterns

There are a number of different possible clause patterns in English, including various sub-patterns of major patterns. Many of the patterns are not frequently used and do not need to be explicitly taught to learners. Many also involve patterns with more than one clause. These form **complex sentences** and are discussed in Section 7.5.2.

A traditional way of describing verb patterns is in terms of the grammatical functions of the words that follow the verb in a clause. Seven major patterns can be identified which occur with single word lexical verbs.

1 Subject + Verb (SV)

2 Subject + Verb + Object (SVO)

3 Subject + Verb + Complement (SVC)

4 Subject + Verb + Adverbial (SVA)

5 Subject + Verb + Object + Object (SVOO)

6 Subject + Verb + Object + Complement (SVOC)

7 Subject + Verb + Object + Adverbial (SVOA)

These clause patterns can also have an optional adverbial added in most cases. Patterns 1–4 are by far the most frequent in English. We will consider each of the patterns in turn.

3.3.1.1 Pattern 1: SV

This pattern involves the use of intransitive verbs which have no object and is usually straightforward for language learners, e.g. *Sue's cat died. I have retired.* Sometimes, however, there is an optional adverbial after the verb, e.g. *I waited outside. They left an hour ago.* This may make the pattern seem to be different. Compare, for example,

Our neighbours returned next day.	(SV)
Our neighbours returned our newspaper.	(SVO)

There are very few verbs which are typically only intransitive. Examples are *come, go, wait, sleep.* Even some of these can have transitive uses, e.g. *This bedroom can sleep three people.*

3.3.1.2 Pattern 2: SVO

Verbs which are used transitively with one **direct object** are said to be monotransitive. They take the SVO pattern, e.g.

I cooked lunch.

Max described his new job.

Sue didn't mention her worries.

Biber et al. (1999: 382) found that most high frequency lexical verbs in the *LSWE Corpus* occur in transitive patterns.

SVO patterns are sometimes able to be expressed as passive voice sentences, e.g.

Someone stole my keys.

My keys were stolen.

Many verbs (e.g. *break*) can be used both transitively and intransitively, sometimes with changes of meaning, e.g.

The glass broke.	(SV)	(intransitive)
I broke the glass.	(SVO)	(transitive)

Task 3.9

Label the following sentences appropriately as SVO or not SVO.

1 The team elected a new captain.

2 We had a good meal.

3 Copper can bend.

4 I didn't like that movie.

5 I went to the top of Mount Victoria last night.

6 We paint our house every six years.

7 He will resign from the end of next month or after a special general meeting.

8 The light shines through the curtains.

9 Sue paints whenever she gets the chance.

3.3.1.3 Pattern 3: SVC

The verb *be* is by far the most frequently used verb in English. In one study, it accounted for 31 per cent of all verb forms (Ota, 1963). In scientific texts *be* sometimes accounts for over 40 per cent of all the verbs used.

In some ways *be* is not like other verbs at all. It cannot be classified as either transitive or intransitive. In many languages there is no equivalent of the English verb *to be*. For example, in English we can say *I am a pilot* or *Fred is happy*, but in some other languages these sentences have the form *I (a) pilot* or *Fred happy*.

The verb *be* is sometimes called a **copular verb** because it links elements. The copula has almost no meaning of its own, but it functions as a link between the subject and the adjective or noun in the predicate. That is, something is needed after the copula to complete the predicate. Adjectives or nouns which complete the predicate are called **subject complements**. In the sentences *Fred is busy* or *Sue is the director*, the complements are *busy* and *the director*. Sentences with a complement are the most frequent of all English verb patterns, and account for up to a third of all the sentences we use.

In most sentences which contain the SVC pattern, the verb is a form of *be*. Other verbs which can occur in this pattern include *seem, feel, get, become, grow, smell, stay, taste, appear, sound, remain, look*. These verbs also need a complement, e.g. *She seems pleased. He became ill. He remained a bachelor.*

Some of the verbs that occur in the SVC pattern can also occur in other patterns, e.g.

Fred felt sick. (SVC)	*The customer felt the fabric.* (SVO)
The food tasted good. (SVC)	*Fred tasted the food.* (SVO)

Sentences such as *He is at work* resemble SVC sentences, but *at work* is an obligatory adverbial rather than a subject complement. Subject + verb + adverbial patterns (SVA) are Pattern 4 sentences (see below).

Task 3.10

Label the following sentences appropriately as SVC, SVO or SV.

1 The apple tasted sour.

2 The doctor felt my pulse.

3 My elderly aunt grows magnificent roses.

4 I get cold in this room.

5 Mary got first prize again.

6 The crowd remained calm after the explosion.

7 No more food remained after the party.

8 The people became angry because of economic conditions.

3.3.1.4 Pattern 4: SVA

In many sentences adverbials are optional. We can say *I opened the door quickly* or *I opened the door*. However, when adverbials occur after the verb *be*, they are usually obligatory, e.g. *Sam is on the committee*. Most adverbials which occur anywhere else except after part of the verb *be* are optional and can be moved to other positions in the sentence without changing the meaning, e.g. *The movie finished at 10.30* could be *At 10.30 the movie finished*.

Task 3.11

Label the following sentences appropriately as SVC or SVA.

1 These chairs are uncomfortable.

2 My friends weren't at the concert last night.

3 The next game will be at the end of the year.

4 This is one of the most important things you need to know.

5 Freda is on the committee.

6 Who are you?

7 My father was a trapeze artist in a circus.

8 You will be sorry about this.

9 Our new neighbour is a very interesting person.

10 London is south of Edinburgh.

Note: It is not always easy to distinguish SVA from SVC patterns.

In the following sentences (1–3) the verb pattern is unambiguous.

1 *I broke the cup.*	SVO
2 *The rain stopped.*	SV
3 *The work was very tedious.*	SVC

Sometimes there are alternative ways of describing the structure of a sentence, as the following examples show.

4 *Sue/looked/at the scenery.*	SVA
5 *Sue/looked at/the scenery.*	SVO
6 *The passengers/got/out.*	SVA
7 *The passengers/got out.*	SV

The alternatives depend on whether we think the adverb (or preposition) has a close relationship with the verb, or a close relationship with the noun, or should stand by itself.

3.3.1.5 Pattern 5: SVOO

The SVOO pattern has two object noun phrases, and is said to have ditransitive or double transitive verbs.

S	V	O	O
I	gave	them	our address.
I	bought	Fred	a ticket.

The first object (*them, Fred*) is sometimes called an **indirect object** preceding the direct object. The SVOO pattern can usually be changed into an SVOA pattern (Pattern 7) in the following way:

S	V	O	O
He	gave	them	our address.
He	bought	Fred	a ticket.

S	V	O	A
He	gave	our address	to them.
He	bought	a ticket	for Fred.

3.3.1.6 Pattern 6: SVOC

The SVOC pattern is not common. The relationship between the two nouns that come after the verb is like the relationship between the nouns that come before and after the verb *to be*, e.g.

S	V	O	C	S	V	C

They elected **Adams President** = Adams was **President**.

Sometimes the last item is an **adjective** instead of a **noun**, e.g.

S	V	O	C	S V	C

The ride made **me dizzy** = I was **dizzy**.

3.3.1.7 Pattern 7: SVOA

In this pattern some verbs have an obligatory adverbial. The most frequent verb taking this pattern is *put*, e.g. *I put the book on the shelf* (cf. **I put the book*). For some verbs which take this pattern, however, the adverbial is not obligatory, e.g. *hold, leave, keep, send, bring, take. I sent a letter (to my aunt); I left my phone number (with the receptionist)*.

Task 3.12

The sentences below are all either SVOO or SVOA. Identify the parts of each sentence and label them.

1 I saw them last Friday.

2 We read stories to the children.

3 I sold her my ski boots.

4 I lent her my lecture notes.

5 My aunt bought me a new pen.

6 This book shows the parts of the body in colour.

7 I paid $10 for it.

8 Will you give me a ride?

9 Save me a seat.

10 Don't tell me what to do.

Task 3.13

Label the following sentences as being SV, SVO, SVC, SVA, SVOO, SVOC or SVOA.

1 He gave them a donation.

2 He painted the fence white.

3 We watch TV every Sunday evening.

4 He bought her an ice cream.

5 He did not regret his decision.

6 Fred completed the job quickly.

7 Several of us told them the results.

8 They thought him unreasonable.

9 He smiled cheerfully.

10 He was not very sophisticated.

When verbs can occur in more than one pattern, there is often a slight change of meaning.

1 *Smith led the other runners.*	(SVO)	(Smith *led* whom?)
2 *The track led into the forest.*	(SVA)	(The track *led* where?)

3 *We have eaten.*   (SV)
  We have eaten very well.   (SVA)
  We have eaten an apple pie.   (SVO)

4 *She gave him a red rose.*   (SVOO)
  They gave several presents.   (SVO)
  They gave generously.   (SVA)

Task 3.14

Work out whether the items underlined in the following sentences are grammatically **obligatory** or **optional**. Explain the reason for your answer.

1 It made her <u>happy.</u>

2 I can't sleep <u>very well on hot nights.</u>

3 Would you like <u>a cup of tea</u>?

4 Keeping fit can be <u>costly.</u>

5 This course provides <u>an opportunity to learn about grammar.</u>

6 Please send me <u>a postcard.</u>

3.3.1.8 Formal *there*

A variant of Pattern 4 (SVA) occurs in sentences containing unstressed *there* followed usually by a form of *be*.

There was water all over the floor.

There is not very much damage.

There must be some matches somewhere.

Formal *there* behaves rather as an 'empty' word to enable the speaker to avoid beginning a sentence with an indefinite noun phrase, or a number.

Water was all over the floor   → *There was water all over the floor.*

A book is on the table.   → *There's a book on the table.*

Three people are in the building. → *There are three people in the building.*

Formal *there* is used in the *LOB Corpus* 2,794 times in about 1 million running words. It is thus quite a frequent item. It is unstressed and is thus pronounced differently from the adverb of place *there*. Compare:

There's only one left.   /ðəz/

I saw you there.   /ðeə/

Over two-thirds of the sentences in which formal *there* occurs have the following patterns:

> *There* + *be* + noun phrase + prepositional phrase (e.g. *There's bad weather on the way.*)
>
> *There* + *be* + noun phrase (e.g. *There was no answer.*)

3.3.2 Frequency information on the use of clause patterns

Altenberg (1993) reports an investigation of the relative frequency of use of clause patterns in 5,004 examples of recurrent word sequences extracted from the *London–Lund Corpus of Spoken British English* (Svartvik, 1990). As Table 3.2 shows, in Altenberg's study SVC and SVO were by far the most frequent patterns, while the other patterns were comparatively rare. The most common pattern, accounting for 46 per cent of the 5,004 examples, was SVC when the complement was an adjective. The study shows the importance of SVC and SVO patterns and the relative infrequency of other patterns. Of course, the relative proportions of the patterns obviously

Table 3.2 Distribution of clause patterns in spoken English

Clause patterns	No. of tokens	%
Copula		
SVC (adj.)	2,282	45.6
SVC (nom)	674	13.5
SVA	274	5.5
Monotransitive (one object)		
SVO	1,048	20.9
SVO (V = *have*)	374	7.5
Complex transitive		
SVOC (adj.)	74	1.5
SVOC (nom)	9	0.2
SVOA	141	2.8
SVO + *to* infinitive	2	0.0
SVO + bare infinitive	2	0.0
SVO + *-ing* clause	4	0.1
SVO + *-ed* clause	5	0.1
Ditransitive		
SVOO	50	1.0
SVO + prep. + O	65	1.3
Total	5,004	100.0

Source: Adapted from Altenberg, B. (1993) 'Recurrent verb complement constructions in the London-Lund Corpus' in J. Aarts, P. de Haan and N. Oostdijk (eds) *English Language Corpora: Design, Analysis and Exploration. Papers from the Thirteenth International Conference on English Language Research on Computerized Corpora, Nijmegen 1992*, Table 1, p. 230. Reprinted by permission of Rodopi BV.

reflect certain characteristics of spoken discourse (e.g. a large number of interactive expressions such as *that's right, that's true, that's all right, I'm sorry*) which are not necessarily as common in written uses of English.

3.3.3 Subject–verb concord

There is a very important grammatical relationship called **concord** or **agreement** between the subject and the verb in English sentences. In clauses where there is a pronoun subject *he, she* or *it* or there is a singular noun that could be replaced by *he, she* or *it*, then an *-s* ending is put on the stem of the verb if it is present tense, e.g. *I like chocolate. They like chocolate. He/she/it likes chocolate.* Many learners of English find it difficult to apply this concord rule, especially if their first language does not have similar concord rules. Learners may say or write constructions such as **He like New York; *My father go to work every morning.* If the subject is plural, then the plural form of the verb is used, e.g.

> *The plates are in the cupboard.*　　*Mary and Sara live in the same house.*

There are a few English nouns (including collective nouns – see Section 4.1.10) where both singular or plural forms are acceptable, e.g.

> *Australia has won the World Cup.*　　*Australia have won the World Cup.*
> *The government is changing*　　　　*The government are changing*
> 　*those laws.*　　　　　　　　　　　　*those laws.*

3.4 Sentence types and functions

Clauses or sentences that make statements are called **declaratives**. The clause patterns described in Section 3.3 were shown in their **declarative** forms. In Section 3.4, we mainly consider **interrogative** and **imperative** sentence types, which function especially as ways of **asking questions** and ways of **directing** other people.

Sentence types	Examples	Main functions
declarative	*Sue reads poetry.*	making statements
interrogative	*Does Sue read poetry?*	asking questions
imperative	*Read this poem by Tuesday, please.*	directing others

A fourth sentence type, exclamatives, which function to express attitude, are not frequent, e.g. *What a film!*

Sentence types can have more than one function. For example, an interrogative can sometimes function as a way of directing others (a directive) rather than asking a question, e.g.

> *Can you be quiet?*
>
> *Is anyone else feeling cold?* (A request for someone to close the window)

An interrogative can make a statement, e.g.

> *How can anyone trust this administration?*
> *How many times do I have to tell you not to touch wet paint?*
> *Who do you think you are!*

Similarly, a declarative can sometimes function as a question or a directive, e.g.

> *I don't know your name.* (question)
> *I really find it disruptive when you come late to class.* (directive)

According to Fries (1957), the main sentence types occur in **spoken** English in roughly the following proportions. In written English, the proportion of interrogatives is usually much smaller.

Sentence types	%
declaratives	60
interrogatives	28
imperatives	7
exclamatives, greetings, calls	5

3.4.1 Interrogatives

There are two main types of interrogative sentences: Yes–No questions and *wh-* questions. There are also some less important subclasses of each. Particular intonation patterns are associated with each type (see 1.6.2.5).

3.4.1.1 Yes–No questions (these are sometimes called verbal questions because the verb is used to make the interrogative form).

Yes–No questions are used if we want or expect only *yes* or *no* or *I don't know* for an answer. To form them we reverse the order of the subject and the auxiliary verb (or the verb *to be* if it is the main verb), and usually use a rising intonation, e.g.

> *He is reading.*　　*Is he reading?*
> *She can sing.*　　*Can she sing?*
> *He is in the office.*　　*Is he in the office?*

Twenty-four English verb forms (*am, is, are, was, were, has, have, had, do, does, did, can, could, will, would, may, might, shall, should, must, ought, need, dare, used*) can exchange position with the subject in this way. The auxiliary verb is sometimes called an **operator**. If there is no auxiliary verb, we insert *do, does* or *did* as operator.

> *He likes chocolate cake.*　　*Does he like chocolate cake?*
> 　　　　*Not *Likes he chocolate cake?*

Task 3.15

Make up yes–no questions which ask whether the following state-ments are true or not. Note that only one verb in each sentence is used to make the question, and that quite complex changes are sometimes required in verb forms.

1 He has often had to go to the doctor about it.

2 These shirts were cheaper than the ones I got last time.

3 They are likely to tell me about it.

4 She can prove that she was there.

5 He threw the old papers away.

6 You could argue that it was his fault.

7 Your aunt sold the car that she won.

8 The polls are showing declining support for the government.

9 Someone spoke to her as she walked through the park.

3.4.1.2 Tag questions

Tag questions are short questions which can be put at the end of a statement, often to seek agreement or confirmation from a listener. Tag questions are formed by 'copying' (and reversing the order of) the subject and the auxiliary verb or verb *to be*. In most cases the tag question is made negative if the statement is positive. If the statement is negative, the tag is positive, e.g.

You have read this book, haven't you?

You haven't read this book, have you?

She can speak Spanish, can't she?

The children aren't ready to go, are they?

If there is no auxiliary verb in the statement, we use *do, does* or *did* in the tag, e.g.

You like pumpkin soup, don't you?

Liz doesn't eat nuts, does she?

Tag questions can be used with a number of subtle differences in intona-tion to express doubt and certainty, and the speaker's attitude to the truth of a statement. Learners of English often find it takes a long time to acquire proficiency in their use. One typical learning difficulty with tags is remembering to replace the subject of the statement with an appropriate pronoun, e.g. *All the staff members were at that meeting, weren't they?* Learners sometimes use *is it* or *isn't it* as a tag for all subjects and auxiliaries, e.g. *He's not on his own, is it? *They got wet when it rained, isn't it?*

3.4.1.3 *Wh*-questions

Wh-questions are sometimes called 'open questions' or 'pronominal questions' because an **interrogative** (*who, whom, whose, what, which, why, when, where, how,* etc.) stands in place of the information we want in the answer. Interrogative pronouns can ask a question about any part of a sentence, and typically have a falling intonation, e.g.

> *Susan Smythe enthusiastically addressed a large crowd for over an hour at the meeting last night to persuade them to support energy conservation.*

Subject: *Who* addressed a large crowd . . .

Predicate: *What* did Susan Smythe do . . .

Object: *Who* (or *whom*) did Susan Smythe address . . .

Adverbial: *When* did Susan Smythe address the large crowd . . .

Adverbial: *Where* did Susan Smythe address the large crowd . . .

Adverbial: *How long* did Susan Smythe address the large crowd for . . .

Adverbial: *Why* did Susan Smythe address the large crowd . . .

Adverbial: *How* did Susan Smythe address the large crowd . . .

For *wh*-questions we usually use the interrogative **plus** the yes–no question form:

> *He is going there.*
> *Is he going there?*   – Yes.
> *Where is he going?*   – Home.

> *She went to Sydney.*
> *Did she go to Sydney?*   – Yes.
> *Where did she go?*   – To Sydney.

> *You asked Fred to dinner.*
> *Did you ask Fred to dinner?*   – Yes.
> *Who did you ask to dinner?*   – Fred.

Who is more common nowadays than *whom* when asking a question about the object of a verb. It is not worth bothering your students with the extra learning burden of using *whom* in such sentences.

The interrogative word must always come first in a *wh*-question, so when we ask a question about the subject we do not need to reverse the subject and the verb. Because the word order is not changed, we do not have to use an auxiliary: *Fred was the winner. – Who was the winner?*

Wh-questions can also use *how, what . . . like, what happened.* For example, we use *how* or *how* + adjective or adverb in questions which ask about

    a someone's health (e.g. *How are you feeling?*)

    b an amount of something (*How big was it? How much rice is left?*)

    c a recent experience (e.g. *How was your trip? What was it like?*)

    d the manner in which something happened or is done (*What happened?*)

Discussion topic

Make questions using *how, how* + adjective or adverb or *what . . . like* to ask for the information underlined in the answers below.

1 There are 50 millilitres of medicine in this bottle.

2 The light in the library is not very good.

3 He learned the language by living in a foreign country.

4 She was very helpful.

5 I enjoyed my holiday very much.

6 She visits her brother once a week.

7 The steps to the university are very steep.

8 My suitcase weighs 15 kilos.

9 The television set in the flat is old and doesn't work well.

10 Thirteen extra chairs are required for the concert.

11 I'm feeling fine, thank you.

12 The party was great, thank you.

Task 3.16

Make up *wh*-questions that ask for the information underlined in the following sentences.

1 Her car is outside the Post Office.

2 His aunt lives in Scotland.

3 You can read the newspaper while you are waiting.

4 She left New Zealand to see the world.

5 He took the news of his defeat in the election very badly.

6 Their son works for an airline.

7 They sell most of the strawberries before Christmas.

8 Their youngest daughter is a brain surgeon.

9 His leg has swelled up quite a lot since he hurt it playing football.

> **Task 3.17**
>
> Make up *wh*-questions that could elicit the following short answers:
>
> 1 Jane Austen.
>
> 2 All over the place.
>
> 3 With a hammer.
>
> 4 Money.
>
> 5 I don't know.
>
> 6 Whether she wanted a job or not.

3.4.1.4 Alternative questions

These question types differ from Yes–No and *wh-* questions in the type of answer expected and in intonation. In the following sentences, *yes* or *no* would be inappropriate answers to Questions 1 and 2. The appropriate response to Question 1 would be to name *cherries* or *nectarines*, or perhaps to say *neither*. Sentence 3 is ambiguous, and an appropriate response could be *cherries* or *yes/no*.

1 *Do you like cherries or nectarines best?*	(Alternative)
2 *Did you buy it or was it a present?*	(Alternative)
3 *Do you sell cherries or nectarines?*	(Alternative or Yes–No)
4 *Do you have any cherries or nectarines?*	(Yes–No)

In alternative questions there is typically rising intonation on the first of the alternatives.

3.4.1.5 Indirect questions

When a speaker or writer reports a previously asked question, there are changes in the sentence that learners of English typically find difficult. Compare the following:

1 *Can you tell me where the station is?*	*She asked if I could tell her where the station is.*
2 *What is she doing?*	*He wondered what she was doing.*

3.4.2 Imperatives

Imperatives are mainly used to influence other people, to make suggestions and give directions, e.g. *Go away; Please tell me what happened; Wait a minute; Don't touch; Take a pill twice a day.* Imperatives use the stem form of the verb without a subject (which is assumed to be *you*). Imperatives are probably the most common way of expressing directives. However, appropriate politeness, the status of speaker and hearer, how well they know each other, and so on, all influence the item we choose in order to express directives. Sometimes we use statements, questions or just hints rather than imperatives to express directives. For example, instead of using an imperative *Please get the box from the top shelf for me*, a speaker might use a statement as in 1 below.

1 *I don't think I can reach the top shelf.*

2 *Would you like me to ring Tom to say you'll be late?*

3 *Does anyone drive past the post office on the way home?*

3.5 Negation

In the preceding section, the sentence types were described in their positive (or **affirmative**) mode. It is also possible to express declarative, interrogative and imperative sentences with a **negative** function to reject or deny a statement.

3.5.1 Meaning

Negative meaning is commonly expressed by negating the verb in a declarative sentence.

a If there is an auxiliary verb (or operator) we simply add *not* (or *never*) after the auxiliary or operator. The same 24 auxiliary verb forms mentioned in 3.4.1.1 for forming Yes–No questions form negatives by adding *not*, e.g.

> *Max is   a good listener.*
> *Max is not a good listener.*   (*Max isn't a good listener.*)
> *He will   leave.*
> *He will not leave.*   (*He won't leave.*)

b If there is no auxiliary verb or operator we must put one in. We use *do, does* or *did*.

> *He   owns a bookshop.*
> *He does not own a bookshop.*   (*He doesn't own a bookshop.*)
> *He   arrived home on Friday.*
> *He did not arrive   home on Friday.*   (*He didn't arrive home on Friday.*)

It is also possible to make other parts of the sentence negative and, indeed, negation by means of *no* rather than *not* is quite common in written

English. In the following sentences the *no* in the noun group carries the negation: *It can reflect identity in a way that no other speech variety can; That was no accident; We have no time.*

3.5.2 Affixes

Affixes such as *un-, il-, im-, in-, ir-* occur especially in written English to express negation , e.g. *unhappy, illogical, immature, inadequate, irrelevant*).

3.5.3 Other ways of expressing negation

Other ways of expressing negation include items such as *nothing, nobody, rarely, never, hardly, any* and various constructions with *have*, e.g.

Nobody came.

Nothing unusual happened that day.

He is rarely late.

We never believed him.

I hardly knew him (and neither did my sister).

Interrogative sentences can be negated as follows:

Isn't he ready yet?

Doesn't he want to come with us?

Learners (and native speakers) sometimes have difficulty knowing whether to answer *Yes* or *No* to negative Yes–No questions, e.g. *Didn't he ring?*

Similar learning problems occur with tag questions as to whether to answer *Yes* or *No* to the following:

You didn't ring me, did you?

You left a message, didn't you?

Sometimes negative interrogatives are not questions but function as exclamations, e.g.

Didn't she do well.

Wasn't that a great concert.

Negative imperatives include the use of *don't*, e.g.

Don't move.

Don't tell anyone (will you).

Negative imperatives are sometimes expressed with positive lexical verbs, e.g.

Keep off the grass.

Refrain from drinking alcohol while on this medication.

3.5.4 The use of negatives

Tottie (1991) found that in British English there are twice as many negatives in speech (2.67 per 100 words) as in writing (1.28 per 100 words). She also found that a third of written negatives are affixal (*unnecessary*, *impolite*) while only 8 per cent of spoken negatives are affixal. Evidence by Biber at al. (1999) from the *LSWE* corpus shows that *no*-negation is used in about 30 per cent of written negatives and in only about 10 per cent of spoken negatives.

3.5.5 Focus and scope of negation

Learners of English sometimes find it difficult to be sure what it is that is being negated. Compare, for example, the effect of primary stress in the following:

I didn't ring 'Mary today.   (I rang Fred.)

I didn't 'ring Mary today.   (I went to see her instead.)

I didn't ring Mary to 'day.   (I rang her yesterday.)

Consider which verb is really being negated in the following:

I don't believe he knows.   (I believe he doesn't know.)

I don't think you're right.   (I think you're not right.)

Task 3.18

Underline the negated items in Text 3.4.

Text 3.4

Keeping warm is vital in winter. Not many people like cold weather, but for elderly people it can be particularly uncomfortable and even dangerous. The right food and drink are vitally important to keeping warm and healthy in the long winter days. During cold weather, hot meals and plenty of hot drinks will make you feel warmer inside. Don't miss breakfast, have plenty of hot drinks and at least one hot main meal each day. It's also a good idea to have a hot drink before going to bed. As we get older our bodies are not as good at keeping warm as they once were. Try if possible to keep as active as you safely can and avoid being inactive for long periods. Do not underestimate just how cold it can be outside. If you have to go out always wear a cap or hat and several layers of light clothing, and don't just wear one layer of heavy clothing. You can take a few simple steps to help keep your home warmer in wintertime by not leaving doors and windows open, remembering, of course, to ensure there is enough ventilation to keep the air fresh in rooms where heating appliances are in use.

3.6 Learning about clause patterns

To learn to write well-formed sentences and paragraphs, learners usually need help by means of focusing tasks and editing procedures to develop the necessary skills. There are many commercially available books of tasks for learners, and teachers may also need to compile additional tasks. The following points should be kept in mind.

1 Encourage learners to check their own work, and especially to check whether each sentence has a subject and a verb. Some learners of English may find it hard to remember to always use a subject. Learners with other language backgrounds may omit the verb *to be*, and write **It good.*

2 Learners need to know that the normal order for English sentences is **Subject Verb**. Learners need to know that the additional parts of the simple sentence such as object or complement usually come **after** the verb. If the order in the learner's first language is SVC or SVO like English, they may have few problems with English word order. Although the most frequently used sentence pattern is SVC, learners need to know how to use the 'formal *there*' pattern for stating the existence or position of a thing. That is, they will usually need practice to encourage them to write *There is a fly in my soup* rather than *A fly is in my soup*.

3 Learners need to know that many verbs (especially the most frequently used ones) can be used in more than one pattern, and that part of learning each English verb is to learn what, if anything, must follow it. When we learn the verb *take*, we have to learn that it can be followed by one or two objects, e.g. *I took her temperature* (SVO) or *I took him a drink* (SVOO), but that it never occurs in the SV pattern. Learning what words can come after verbs is usually more difficult than learning the meaning of the verbs.

4 Although it is usually relatively easy for learners of English to identify the pattern of short sentences such as *The treasurer banked the money*, they often find it harder to identify the pattern in a simple sentence where items have been modified, e.g. *The new treasurer, Fred Blades, banked the subscription money last Friday after the annual general meeting of the Clevedon Golf Club.*

5 Teachers may find it useful to consider these additional ways of developing learners' skills in using clause patterns.

   a Get students to copy accurately from a written text and to write down material that is dictated to them.

   b Get students to read a sentence and then to write another one with the same pattern but on a different topic (e.g. with different nouns and verbs).

c Get students to make corrections in simple sentences in which a word or words have been omitted.

d Get students to identify subjects, objects, complements, main verbs and adverbials in sentences.

e Get students to edit their own and each other's work.

6 When helping students to ask questions, teachers sometimes may be tempted to spend a lot of time covering all the various difficulties. It is worth remembering that in written English questions are not very frequent. Even in classrooms, teachers tend to use interrogatives as directives (*What are you doing?*) or for feedback and testing (e.g. *What's the capital of France?*) rather than for asking questions where the speaker does not know the answer.

Children learning their first language usually ask most of the questions. Because teachers sometimes use too many question forms, learners of English as a second language often get little chance to practise questions themselves. Pair activities where learners must work together to complete a task are one way to give learners practice in asking questions.

CHAPTER 4

Nouns and noun phrases

This chapter gives an overview of the constituents and structure of noun phrases, and especially of those aspects that are often the source of problems for learners of English.

Objectives

By the end of this chapter you should be able to:

1 Identify **nouns** in texts.

2 Describe the main **categories of nouns**.

3 Classify frequent nouns into five categories.

4 Decide whether particular nouns used in texts are used **countably** or **uncountably**.

5 Identify **noun phrases** in texts.

6 Analyse the **structure of noun phrases** in texts.

7 Describe the main categories of English **determiners** and their functions.

8 Identify and classify determiners in texts.

9 Identify the **concord** between particular determiners and classes of nouns.

10 Describe possible **sequences of determiners**.

11 Describe what **articles** are, and how they are used.

12 Describe the system of English **personal, possessive** and **reflexive** pronouns.

13 Describe the main uses of **interrogative, demonstrative** and **indefinite pronouns**.

14 Describe typical learning and teaching problems in noun phrases.

4.1 Noun identification and classification

Nouns form the head (or core) of very frequent and important parts of sentences called **noun phrases**. In the following noun phrases, the nouns are in bold type.

food

my **lunch**

a good **meal**

the **meal** that I had last **night**

Nouns are an important word class because they specify or show what an utterance or text is about. The difficulty of written texts has been shown to depend on nouns more than other parts of speech. For example, Elley & Croft (1989) found that nouns were the most difficult class of words to guess correctly when every sixth word had been struck out of a text, as is shown in Table 4.1, which shows the proportions correctly guessed for the various word classes.

Table 4.1 Word class predictability

Word class	Nouns	Verbs	Pronouns	Adjectives	Adverbs	Conjunctions	Prepositions
% correct	28.6	72.4	72.6	52.1	38.9	59.4	74.4

The reason it is harder to guess a missing noun correctly may be that nouns have less redundancy associated with them than other word classes. If this is correct, then nouns may be particularly important for comprehension because they carry more unpredictable information than other word classes.

About a third of all the words in spoken or written texts are nouns or pronouns. In spoken English, nouns and pronouns are of equal frequency. In written non-fiction, nouns are about six or seven times more frequent than pronouns (see Table 2.1). Nouns tend to be especially more frequent than pronouns when they function as objects or complements which typically contain the new or less predictable information in the sentence.

Nouns have sometimes been defined on the basis of their meaning as the name of a person, place or thing. This works for some nouns, such as *driver, church* or *spoon*, but not very well for nouns such as *idea, problem, running, democracy*. It is almost certainly better to use other criteria based on **form** and **position** to help learners identify an unknown word.

4.1.1 The forms of nouns

Many nouns have two forms, **stem** and **stem+s**, e.g. *a chair, some chairs.* However, some nouns like *mathematics* or *suds* always have a final *-s*, and others, like *music* or *salt*, do not usually have a final *-s*. In the sentence *Those cyclists ride their bikes very fast*, the words *cyclists* and *bikes* are nouns and could occur in a different sentence without a final *-s*. *Ride* can also occur with a final *-s*, but in the sentence above it is a verb. Because most verbs also have a 'stem' and a 'stem+s' form (e.g. *I ride, he* or *she rides*), ability to change form is usually not enough to identify a noun. Many nouns can also end in *-ing* (e.g. *teaching*) and thus are not easy to distinguish from verbs that end in *-ing*. (Compare *Teaching can be stressful* with *I am teaching five classes today.*) In both spoken and written English about 80 per cent of nouns have the stem form without *-s*, i.e. the singular form. Proper nouns (see Section 4.1.11) can be identified because they begin with a capital (upper case) letter. As we saw in Section 2.4.2.2, various derivational affixes such as *-ation* and *-ness* can also identify nouns.

4.1.2 The positions of nouns in sentences

Nouns can often be identified because they follow a determiner or adjective, e.g.

a, the, Mary's, that

first, three, latest

big, heavy, pleasant, mathematical

Nouns also frequently follow a preposition, e.g.

in <u>time</u>

on <u>account</u> of <u>sickness</u>

Nouns can appear in several positions in a sentence, e.g.

in the **subject** position: The <u>wind</u> damaged our house.

in the **object** position: The wind damaged our <u>house</u>.

in a **complement** position after *be*: My new neighbour is a <u>teacher</u>.

In a statement, the subject of the sentence usually comes before the verb. The verb usually comes before any object or complement.

Task 4.1

In Text 4.1, identify the nouns. Write out each noun in a list and mark it as follows:

1 If identified as a noun by its **changeable ending**, write 1.

2 If identified by **preceding items**, write 2.

3 If identified by **sentence position**, write 3.

4 If identified by its **position after a preposition**, write 4.

5 If identified by its **form** as a proper noun, write 5.

Sometimes you may write more than one number to show that there is more than one clue which helped you identify the word as a noun.

Task 4.2

Count the nouns in Text 4.1 and Text 4.2 and calculate the approximate proportion of nouns in the total number of words in each text.

Text 4.1

Volcanoes

Volcanoes are not scattered randomly around the world. If you were asked to name countries in which volcanoes occur, you would probably think of places such as Japan, Iceland, Hawaii, Italy, New Zealand, and so on. At first, these areas may seem quite unrelated, but no matter what countries you think of, the volcanoes in them have one rather odd thing in common – they are all very near the sea. This isn't such an irrelevant statement as it may sound – it is a fact that almost all the volcanoes in the world are within a couple of hundred kilometres of the sea. There are remarkably few active volcanoes in the centres of continents – none at all in the Americas, away from the central mountain belt, none in central Asia or Australia, and only one away from the coast in Antarctica. There are some important exceptions in Africa, and also some recently dead volcanoes in France and Germany, but these form a rather specialised, distinct group. Volcanoes mainly occur where huge tectonic plates meet on the surface of the Earth.

Text 4.2

On Work – by Bertrand Russell

I want to say, in all seriousness, that a great deal of harm is being done in the modern world by belief in the virtuousness of work, and that the road to happiness and prosperity lies in an organized diminution of work. First of all: what is work? Work is of two kinds: first, altering the position of matter at or near the Earth's surface relatively to other such matter; second, telling other people to do so. The first kind is unpleasant and ill paid; the second is pleasant and highly paid. The second kind is capable of indefinite extension: there are not only those who give orders, but those who give advice as to what orders should be given. Usually two opposite kinds of advice are given simultaneously by two organized bodies of men; this is called politics. The skill required for this kind of work is not knowledge of the subjects as to which advice is given, but knowledge of the art of persuasive speaking and writing, i.e. of advertising.

from In Praise of Idleness

4.1.3 Learning noun identification

Identifying nouns is not normally a special problem for learners of English, but learning how to use nouns with other words (especially determiners) in noun phrases is an important source of difficulty. Learners of English need to recognise nouns and to know what other words they go with, e.g. they need to know they can say *this pen* and not *this write*. They need to know that nouns can occur in the subject, object and complement positions in sentences and after prepositions. Class activities for mature learners that teachers can use to help establish confident noun identification include substitution tables, cloze exercises, and other exercises in which the use of a word as a noun can be recognised because of its position.

4.1.4 Categories of nouns

The category that a particular noun belongs to has very important consequences for using English. English nouns can be classified in several ways, on semantic, grammatical and even phonological grounds (e.g. *rope*, *hope*, *soap* are nouns that have similar diphthongs). Not all of these classifications are of equal importance for learning English, however. For example, the distinction between common and proper nouns affects the use of capital letters (used in proper nouns); most nouns can be classified on semantic grounds as 'concrete' or 'abstract'. Concrete nouns are things that can be seen or touched (e.g. *a bottle, water, the moon, grass*). Abstract nouns are non-material or are not able to be seen or touched (e.g. *safety, problem, warmth, idea, education*). However, the distinction between concrete and abstract nouns is not important for learning English. Similarly, *apples, oranges* and *pears* are all nouns that belong to the class of *fruit*, but this is also not grammatically important.

The most important categories of nouns for learners are those that affect the grammar of sentences. There are five main categories of nouns that affect the grammar of sentences.

1 common nouns which are always countable

2 common nouns which are always uncountable

3 common nouns which can be countable or uncountable

4 common nouns which are collective nouns

5 proper nouns

A further group of nouns ('quantifying nouns') is used for specifying quantity in English (see Section 4.2.12).

4.1.5 Countable nouns and uncountable nouns

The most important grammatical distinction for English nouns is between

1 nouns we can count (e.g. *chairs, books, ideas, years, problems*)

2 nouns we cannot count (e.g. *furniture, water, ice, safety, time*)

Consider this example of how the class of noun affects other words:

a *There **aren't** as **many** chairs here as we need, **are** there?*

b *There **isn't** as **much** furniture here as we need, **is** there?*

The form of the verb (*aren't* or *isn't*), the determiner (*many* or *much*) and the tag (*are, is*) are all affected by whether the noun is countable (*chair*) or uncountable (*furniture*).

We perceive some nouns as individual countable units or things, each separate and distinct – *a spider, a toothbrush, a pen, a headache, an idea, a name, a meeting, an appointment*. We can count them – *three spiders, many new ideas, six meetings*, etc. Nouns that can be counted are called **countable nouns** (some grammar books call them 'count nouns').

We perceive some nouns as continuous masses, substances or abstract qualities which cannot be counted. They do not seem to exist as separate, distinct units – *milk, sugar, advice, research, weather, snow, homework*. These nouns are called **uncountable nouns** (they are sometimes called 'mass nouns' or 'non-count nouns'). We cannot count them, and we have to measure them in other ways. Uncountable nouns are measured in quantities, containers and units – a litre of *milk*, a can of *soup*, three pieces of *paper*, a lot of *snow*. In most texts, countable nouns are about four times more frequent than uncountable nouns.

Learning to use countable and uncountable nouns correctly is one of the most difficult learning problems for users of English as a second language. Learners may think that logically some uncountable nouns should be countable – e.g. *vocabulary, news, information, advice, luggage, furniture, money* (cf. *coins*), *research, knowledge, pasta, traffic, progress, machinery* (cf. *machine*). However, unfortunately for learners, logic does not always determine whether a noun is countable or uncountable, so we have to say *a lot of vocabulary, a piece of information, an item of news, a piece of advice, an item of luggage*, etc.

Task 4.3

Underline the nouns in this list that can be **countable**: *egg, milk, apple, pudding, jam, plate, wine, glass, chocolate, rice, tomato, flour, pepper, herb, ice cream, potato, bottle, ice, rubbish, information, luggage, problem, banana, spoon, tea, coffee, cup, thing, heat, number, volume, unit, weight, list, bravery, pride, virtue, poverty, feeling, time, ink, despair, name.*

Check your answers in a learners' dictionary. You will notice that some of the nouns can sometimes be countable and sometimes uncountable, usually with a change in meaning.

4.1.6 Grammatical number

English makes a distinction between the **singular** and **plural** forms of countable nouns. This distinction is called 'grammatical number', and it has important consequences for the choice of words that can go with such nouns. When a noun represents something **countable**, we use it in two forms, (a) the singular or 'stem form' (e.g. *apple, banana*) and (b) the plural or the 'stem+*s*' form (e.g. *apples, bananas*).

When a noun represents something **uncountable**, it is used only in the stem form. There is no plural form of a noun that represents something uncountable. We often find an uncountable noun without a preceding word: *Meat is expensive. Unemployment is increasing.* A singular countable noun is not found without a preceding word known as a **determiner**. Often the preceding word is *a*, but it may be another word such as *the, that, which, your, her, our, whose, Tom's, every, any, no, one, the other, another, either, many a*. When learners speak or write the singular form of a countable noun without a determiner preceding it they are almost certainly making a grammatical mistake.

4.1.7 Grammatical case

Case is a formal way of marking the grammatical functions of nouns. In modern English nouns, case inflections have disappeared except for the genitive case (e.g. *The **girl's** brother; the **cats'** owners; **Sue's** friends*), and even the genitive case is quite rarely used (Biber et al., 1999: 293). The genitive case on nouns is greatly outnumbered by the use of *of*-phrases. That is, *the top of the building* is more frequent than *the building's top*, although in some contexts where the noun or pronoun refers to a person, the *s*-genitive is more frequent (e.g. *Sam's head* or *his* head rather than *the head of Sam* or *the head of him*).

Task 4.4

Classify the nouns in Text 4.3 into countable (C), uncountable (UC) **according to the way they are used in the text.**

Text 4.3

A bad start

An item in a newspaper recently reported a most unfortunate way to start a marriage. A bridegroom had an accident on the way to his wedding and he broke an arm and a leg. He was taken to the local hospital but refused to stay. Doctors gave him injections to reduce the pain and help him get through the ceremony. The bridegroom arrived at the registry office in a wheelchair, with blood on his clothes and without his trousers, which had been cut off at the hospital. After the ceremony, at the reception the anaesthetic wore off and the bridegroom passed out.

4.1.8 Irregular nouns

Most countable nouns are **regular**. That is, they express singular by the stem form and the plural by stem+*s*. However, some high frequency nouns are not regular and have to be learned individually, e.g.

> *a child* – *some children*; *a man* – *some men*; *a woman* – *some women*;
> *a tooth* – *some teeth*; *a sheep* – *some sheep*; *a leaf* – *some leaves*;
> *a foot* – *some feet*; *a fish* – *some fish*; *an analysis* – *some analyses*;
> *a phenomenon* – *some phenomena*; *this data* – *these data*; *a stimulus* –
> *some stimuli*; *a mouse* – *some mice*; *a knife* – *some knives*

Some nouns always have the stem+*s* form, e.g. *news, measles, shingles, linguistics, mathematics, darts, scissors, tweezers, glasses, clothes, knickers, pants, pyjamas, shorts, trousers, arms* (guns), *oats, savings, suds, thanks, wages, tropics, guts, insides, innards, noodles, surroundings.* Some other nouns usually have the stem+*s* form, e.g. *circumstances, socks, parents.* Some stem+*s* nouns such as *news* have a singular verb (*The news is good*). Others, such as *clothes*, take a plural verb (*My clothes are clean*). Some nouns are only plural but do not have a stem+*s* form, e.g. *police, cattle.* That is, we do not say **The police is coming; *The cattle is thirsty.* Sometimes, uncountable nouns are used as if they are countable nouns in order to categorise things, e.g. *several French wines* (= several kinds of French wine).

4.1.9 Nouns which are sometimes countable and sometimes uncountable

Many English nouns can be used as both countable nouns and uncountable nouns, e.g. *Sue likes coffee; She ordered two coffees.* We understand that *coffees* refers to *cups of coffee*. In a text we can tell from the words preceding or following a noun whether it is being used as a countable noun or as an uncountable noun in that particular text. Thus the distinction between countable and uncountable is partly natural and partly a consequence of how we cognitively view that noun.

Usually there is some difference in meaning in nouns which can be both countable or uncountable. Sometimes the difference is between a substance and an object, e.g. *cloth* and *a cloth*, *egg* (the food inside an egg) and *an egg*. Sometimes the difference is between a general phenomenon and a particular example, e.g. *liquid* and *a liquid*, *language* and *a language*.

Here are some nouns which can be countable or uncountable.

breakfast	breath	brick	business	cake	carpet
cloth	coffee	colour	company	danger	dinner
doubt	exercise	fear	fire	forest	hair
height	history	honour	hope	interest	iron
language	law	light	liquid	lunch	medicine
metal	noise	pain	paper	pity	pleasure
profit	rest	rope	rubber	seed	service
shade	shame	shelter	skin	smoke	sound
speed	stone	string	success	tea	thread
time	tin	trouble	use	value	war
waste	wind	wire			

Task 4.5

Classify these nouns into the five classes listed in 4.1.4.

music	honesty	theatre	Oxford University
job	equipment	moonlight	crew
scenery	water	happiness	disease
airport	truth	lecture	television
poet	pen	road	business
sugar	permission	cake	Telecom

Task 4.6

Write two sentences for each of the following words: *medicine, time, sight, interest, glass, skill, study.* The first sentence should show the word clearly used as a **countable** noun and the second sentence should show the word clearly used as an **uncountable** noun, e.g.

coffee: I would like three black coffees please. (C)
There's not much coffee left in the pot. (UC)

Task 4.7

Collect sentences produced by learners of English which contain errors resulting from incorrect use of countable or uncountable nouns, and see if you can explain the basis for the errors.

4.1.10 Collective nouns

A few nouns can be considered to be singular or plural without changing the form of the noun, e.g.

The committee has met.
           have

This government is always making new policy.
                are

These **collective nouns** can have a singular verb or a plural verb with their singular (stem) noun form.

Some collective nouns are: *audience, class, club, committee, crew, crowd, family, government, group, jury, majority, minority, the public, Parliament, staff, team.* Many proper nouns are collective nouns, e.g. *the United Nations, CNN, the Senate, Manchester United.*

The **attitude** of the speaker or writer determines whether a collective noun has singular or plural concord with the verb in the sentence; that is, whether the thing referred to is considered as a group of individuals or as a single entity.

4.1.11 Proper nouns

Nouns which begin with a capital letter form a separate class of nouns. Names of people, places, countries, days, months, institutions (e.g. *the British* Museum), commercial products (e.g. *a Cadillac*), and holidays are among the most frequent proper nouns. Most personal and locational nouns are not preceded by a determiner, e.g. *Fred, Sue, Mars, Asia, Everest.* Sometimes, however, proper nouns are preceded by a determiner, e.g. *The Guardian; a Toyota; I'm looking for a Mary Smith; the Himalayas; the Pacific.*

4.1.12 Quantifying nouns

Entities that are considered to be uncountable can be broken up into parts or grouped together and 'counted' by means of **quantifying nouns**, e.g. *a piece of cake, a bit of trouble, a piece of advice, a scrap of paper.* Some quantifying nouns are very specialised and are used with only one (or a few) nouns, e.g. *a rasher of bacon, a stack of books, a loaf of bread.*

4.1.13 Noun equivalents

Other word classes or grammatical structures, including pronouns, verb forms, and even whole sentences, can sometimes occupy the position of a noun in a sentence, e.g.

*Sue likes **books**.*	(*book* is a noun)
*Sue likes **them**.*	(*them* is a pronoun)
*Sue likes **to read**.*	(*to read* is a verb form)
*Sue likes **reading**.*	(*reading* is a verb form)
*Sue likes **what you said to her last Friday**.*	(a clause)

These noun equivalents are discussed in Chapter 7 of this book.

Task 4.8

Look in a learners' dictionary to see how the following nouns are classified. Make sure you understand any abbreviations used in the classifications.

    obligation   presidency   retirement   superciliousness

4.1.14 A teaching order for noun classes

It is not easy to decide how to teach learners to classify English nouns in such a way that they avoid confusion. Teachers need to decide whether to start with familiar items or unfamiliar items; items like first language items or items unlike first language items; high frequency countable items or high frequency uncountable items; concrete or abstract items. It is almost certainly a good idea to establish a teaching order with a number of steps such as the following to assist learners:

Step	Examples
1	*My name is Siri.*
2	*I have a cat.*
3	*These are floppy disks.*
4	*Here is some water.*
5	*I ordered two coffees.*
6	*The police are coming.*
7	*My trousers are torn.*

Research by Ljung (1991) on curricula and textbooks for teaching English has shown that there is a strong tendency to teach nouns and other words that denote simple concrete objects and physical actions at the expense of words which corpus analysis shows are often much more frequent, denoting abstraction, mental processes and social phenomena. That is, in English courses there is typically over-representation of words like *boat, desk, ticket, ball* and under-representation of words like *activity, attempt, detail, evidence, source, benefit*.

4.2 The structure of noun phrases

A noun phrase (sometimes called a 'noun group') normally has a noun or pronoun as its most important word or headword to identify what kind of entity is being referred to. The headword in a noun phrase can occur alone, e.g.

Noun phrase		Noun phrase
Scientists	conduct	*experiments.*
They	conduct	*experiments.*

When there is more than just the headword in a noun phrase, the other words are called **modifiers**. The headwords are underlined in the following examples of noun phrases.

a *scientist*

the young *scientist*

every *scientist*

a *scientist* from our laboratory

the *scientist* who won the Nobel Prize

Note that some modifiers come before a headword (premodifiers) and other modifiers come after (postmodifiers).

Task 4.9

Put brackets around the noun phrases in the following sentences and underline the headwords.

1 George's father gave him some money to go to a lecture on electricity.

2 He saw a person put something inside a coil of wire.

3 It was a piece of iron.

4 The iron became a magnet when an electric current was passed through the coil.

5 A simple method of making electricity was demonstrated by moving a magnet inside a coil of wire.

4.2.1 Premodifiers

Modifiers that come before noun headwords are usually **determiners** or **adjectives**. Most of the items that come before headwords in noun phrases occur in a fixed order or certain special positions. For example, in *the old car*, the determiner (*the*) precedes the adjective (*old*). Nouns can also occur as modifiers of noun headwords. In this case the modifying noun will occur after any adjective in the noun phrase. Here are some other examples:

every single day	(not **single every day*)
such a happy person	(not **a such happy person*)
the troubled coal industry	(not **the coal troubled industry*)

It is not common for a noun phrase to have more than two premodifiers in a sequence before the headword. The most frequent noun phrase structures (excluding postmodifiers) consist of the following four types in approximate order of frequency. They cover about 80 per cent of noun phrases.

1 determiner + headword, e.g. *the council, every person*

2 a noun alone (or a pronoun), e.g. *Churchill, Los Angeles, students, they*

3 determiner + adjective + headword, e.g *their personal files, all new cars*

4 adjective + headword, e.g. *private houses, Scottish law*

In conversation, about 65 per cent of noun phrases consist of a noun or pronoun alone, or *a* or *the* plus a noun.

Other structures include:

5 determiner + determiner + headword, e.g. *all the books*

6 determiner + determiner + determiner + headword, e.g. *her first three exams*

7 determiner + adjective + adjective + headword, e.g. *a narrow crooked path*

Adjectives can be modified with adverbs such as *very, rather, quite*, e.g. *a very narrow crooked path, a rather small foot*. Adjectives are considered in more detail in Chapter 6.

Task 4.10

Put brackets around all the noun phrases in Text 4.4 and underline the headwords.

Text 4.4

Earthquakes

An earthquake destroys buildings by shaking them to pieces. Engineers are finding ways to keep them standing when the ground moves. As an engineer in California observed in the aftermath of the 1989 quake: 'Earthquakes don't kill people. Buildings do.' Nobody wants to spend extra money to prepare for something that may never happen, and earthquake engineering has long been neglected. That attitude is now changing. Earthquake engineers may not have needed to be reminded that building design can make all the difference between life and death, but recent quakes have increased public interest in earthquake-resistant designs. These range from reinforcing masonry walls with steel beams to strengthen them, to supporting an entire building on rubber so that the structure can float in isolation.

4.2.2 Postmodifiers

Postmodifers, which occur **after** noun headwords, are sometimes known as 'qualifiers'. They are very frequent and include the following types. They may be:

a single word	*this boy* **here**; *trouble* **enough**
a determiner + noun	*Frederick* **the Great**
a prepositional phrase	*a slice* **of that bread**
a clause	*the man* **who is sitting next to her**
	the man **sitting next to her**
	the painting **described in this book**

Modifiers that follow headwords often consist of many words. This can make it hard for learners to realise that the modifier is related to the headword as part of a noun phrase.

Prepositional phrases are the most frequent postmodifiers of nouns, accounting for about 70 per cent of postmodifiers. However, because prepositional phrases can also modify verbs, learners may sometimes find it is difficult to decide whether a prepositional phrase belongs with a noun or with a verb, e.g.

1 The books *on the table* are mine.
On the table modifies the noun subject *books*, and shows **which** books.

2 He put the books *on the table*.
On the table functions as an adverbial, showing **where** he put the books.

3 She shut the door *in my face*.
In this case, knowledge of the world (or 'commonsense') makes it likely that *in my face* does not modify *door*, but rather is an adverbial.

Postmodifiers are discussed further in Chapters 6 and 7.

4.2.3 Functions of noun phrases

A noun phrase can occur as the subject, object or complement in a sentence, and it can also follow a preposition. Here are some examples:

Subject:	The police brought them news of the accident.
	John told me about the problems you have had.
Object:	We need clean water.
Complement:	This is the best answer.
	There isn't enough time.
Object of a preposition:	He glanced at Mary.
	Everyone who was born in this country has citizenship.

4.3 Determiners

Determiners are function words which occur before nouns to specify which instance of a noun is being referred to, e.g. ***this*** *person*, ***some*** *people*. There are about 50 determiners and most of them are high frequency words which, if not used correctly, are a major source of difficulty for learners of English. About 14 per cent of the words in a spoken or written text are determiners. The most frequent determiners are articles (*a, the, Ø* (zero)). Because of their importance, articles are discussed separately, in Section 4.3.2.

4.3.1 The main English determiners

The main English determiners are: *a, an, all, a lot of, another, any, both, certain, double, each, either, enough, entire, every, few, a few, half, less, little, a little, many, more, most, much, my, your, her, his, its, our, their, neither, no, not many, not much, other, own, one third/a third* (etc.), *same, several, single, some, such, the, this, that, these, those, twice, various, what, which, whole, whose, Mary's* (etc.), *first* (etc.), *last, one, two* (etc.), *Ø*. Among these, *other, another, same, certain* are sometimes classified as adjectives rather than determiners, even though they do not have descriptive meaning in the same way as other adjectives do.

Task 4.11

In Text 4.5, highlight or underline all the determiners (except *Ø*).

Text 4.5

Some people argue that everyone who claims to have seen or to have photographed the Loch Ness monster has been either drunk, deceived by a log or interested in promoting the Scottish tourist industry. On the other hand, many people are quite prepared to concede that some animal or group of animals has been seen in the loch. The issue is whether this animal can be identified as the 'monster'. There is (to date) only one photograph of the creature. It has been studied carefully by experts, and the general consensus is that the picture reveals a row of playful otters. For this reason, arguments for the existence of the monster based on visual evidence have met with a good deal of scepticism. Another approach has been to consider how monsters might be able to survive in a freshwater environment. Could they obtain enough food to sustain themselves? Those that believe that they could, point out that Loch Ness is very deep, and moreover that it may be connected by a series of subterranean passages with the sea, allowing the monster to feed. Some say that the animal will be a whale or a basking shark which has lost its way or even come inland to die, and that this could explain the rare sightings.

4.3.1.1 Functions of determiners

Determiners have two main functions.

1 To act as signposts which point to or add specificity to nouns. This is sometimes called the deictic function, e.g. ***that*** house, ***the*** government.

2 To quantify. English has a strong tendency to specify 'how many' or 'how much' when nouns are used, e.g. ***three*** weeks, ***some*** food, ***a lot of*** trouble, ***several*** friends, ***more*** time.

Learners of English can usually learn the **meanings** of the determiners without difficulty, but learning to use determiners often requires a lot of practice.

4.3.1.2 Position of determiners

Which individual determiners can be used directly before particular nouns is a major learning problem. This is called **concord**. Certain determiners go before **countable nouns in the singular form**, others go before **countable nouns in the plural form**, and others go before **uncountable nouns**. Unfortunately for the learner, many determiners can go with more than one of these three kinds of nouns. Some idea of the scope of the learning task can be seen in Task 4.12, which shows the concord patterning for many of the determiners.

4.3.1.3 Categories of determiners

Determiners can be classified according to their position in a sequence when there is more than one. There are three main categories or positions.

1 Pre-determiners

2 Central determiners (articles, demonstratives, possessives)

3 Postdeterminers

   a Ordinal numbers
   b Quantifiers

For teaching, matters are complicated because a few determiners can occur in more than one category.

1 Pre-determiners (*all, both, half, double, once, twice, three times* (etc.), *a third* (etc.))
Pre-determiners can occur before:

> *the*
>
> *this, that, these, those* (demonstratives)
>
> *my, your, her, his, its, our, their* (possessives)

e.g.   *Half* these apples are rotten.

       Both her parents are still alive.

       All the staff members in that department are under 40.

If a personal pronoun follows a predeterminer then *of* is usually obligatory.

e.g.	*All of* it.	(* all it)	cf.	all books
	Both of you	(*both you)	cf.	both cars

Task 4.12

Complete the table below. Place a tick (✓) in the column next to each determiner if it can be used before the noun at the top of the column.

Determiners	A singular countable noun, e.g. *tree*	A plural countable noun, e.g. *trees*	An uncountable noun, e.g. *music*
a/an			
another			
each			
every			
one			
both			
a few			
a little			
many			
these/those			
much			
two, three, etc.			
my, their, etc.			
no			
the			
some			
any			
Ø (no determiner)			
other			
this/that			
several			
all			
a lot of			
either			
less/more			

2 Central determiners (articles, demonstratives, possessives)
The main ones are:

> a (an), another, the, no, either, neither, each, every, more, most, such,
>
> this, that, these, those (demonstratives), some, *any
>
> my, your, her, his, its, our, their, Mary's (etc.) (possessives)
>
> what, which, whose
>
> Ø (zero)
>
> *Any often replaces some in questions and after negatives, e.g. I want
> some bananas. Have you got any? We haven't any bananas today.

3 Postdeterminers

a **Ordinal numbers:** The main ordinals are *first, second* (etc.), *next, last, other.*

b **Quantifiers:** Quantifiers are an important way of telling us *how many* or
how much there is of what a noun refers to. There are two main groups
of quantifiers and they come last in a sequence after other determiners.
Some quantifiers can come before ordinals (e.g. *There are few second
chances; Several other people sent flowers*).

> i Cardinal numbers: one, two, three (etc.)
>
> ii Quantifying determiners: many, much, more, most
>   few, fewer, fewest
>   little, less, least
>   a few, a little, several

4.3.1.4 Phrasal quantifiers

Many determiners or nouns can be followed by *of* to form **phrasal quantifiers**, which can occupy the predeterminer position in a sequence. This
is an open class which is very important in English for quantifying (e.g.
***all** of the books*).

all of	a lot of	plenty of
both of	lots of	enough of
each of	the rest of	more of
some of	few of	less of
several of	little of	a number of
half of		a few of
many of		a little of
much of		a great deal of
any of		a large amount of
another of		a small quantity of

Not all determiners can be followed by *of* (e.g. **every of, *no of. All* is by far the most frequent quantifying determiner in spoken and written English, followed by *no, some, any* and *more*. Teachers should be aware that quantifying determiners (such as *all, each, few*) have a strong tendency to occur directly before nouns (e.g. *all books*), rather than in the other possible patterns (e.g. *all of the books, all of her books*).

Quantifying nouns are used for 'measuring' quantities of countable and uncountable nouns, and act like determiners. Examples include:

a box of (chocolates)	*a kilo of (cheese)*	*a piece of (paper)*
a pack of lies	*a packet of (biscuits)*	*a litre of (oil)*
a bit of (string)	*a heap of rubbish*	*a bag of (rice)*
a tonne of (steel)	*a group of (people)*	*a lump of wood*
a cup of (tea)	*20 gallons of (petrol)*	*a series of (problems)*
an item of news		

4.3.1.5 Sequences of determiners

Sometimes (but not often) more than one determiner occurs before a noun. Their ordering is important, and not all sequences are possible, e.g.

both my *feet feel cold* (**my both feet*)

all the *examples in this book are clear* (**the all examples*)

some of the last few *films I've seen have been boring* (**the few last some films*)

both the next two *examples* (**both two next examples*)

each of the other three *contestants*

the rest of my last few *dollars*

However, the relationships between determiners are complicated and the rules underlying their use are not always well understood by linguists. The categories of determiners overlap and some determiners can be classified in more than one position.

Because most sequences of determiners are no longer than two items (e.g *three more, all the*), it should only rarely be necessary to teach sequences of more than two items.

4.3.2 Articles

The **articles** *the, a (an), Ø (zero)* are the most frequent determiners in English and in fact *the* is the most frequently used of all English words. Many English language teachers consider articles to be among the hardest words to use correctly in English, and even advanced learners often make many errors in their use, e.g.

*I saw car have accident.

*Therefore English language is not really used much by students in
   my country.

*I spilt milk on floor.

In texts, *the* usually accounts for a little over 50 per cent of all the occurrences of determiners. *The* is much more frequent than *a*, which accounts
for only about 20 per cent of determiners. All the other determiners,
excluding the zero determiner, make up the remaining 30 per cent of
determiner use.

   The article system in English has the following main forms:

   a (or *an* if the following word begins with a vowel)

   the /ðə/ (or /ðiː/ if the following word begins with a vowel)

   Ø (nothing before the noun)

Whenever we use a noun in English without another preceding determiner (such as *all, each, my, which, another*, etc.), we must use one of the
three forms of the article system (*a, the,* Ø) before that noun.

   In Sentence 1 below, both *a* and *the* are possible in both spaces but Ø is
not possible.

   1 _____ tree we planted is outside _____ window.

In Sentence 2, only *the* is possible.

   2 _____ music that you played was very beautiful.

In Sentence 3, Ø fits the first space. Only *a* is possible in the second space.
In some contexts (e.g. in response to the question *What do you think of
these drinks?*) *the* can occur in the first space.

   3 _____ coffee is _____ stimulating drink.

Learners need to know that

   The can be used before all nouns.

   A (or *an*) may only be used before countable, singular nouns.

   Ø may be used before uncountable nouns or countable plural nouns.

For learners of English it is important to keep in mind that countable
nouns in the singular form must have an article or another determiner
before them, but not Ø.

   Proper nouns usually do not have any article, e.g. *Mary, Wellington*.
Exceptions include some geographical entities and political or social
institutions, e.g. *The Times, the Sudan, the United Nations, the Netherlands,
the Amazon*.

A few idiomatic uses of countable nouns, including institutions, places of work, times, means of transport and seasons, can occur without articles, e.g.

I'm going to work, school, university, hospital, church, ballet, gym, gaol.

I'm going by bus, train, plane, ferry, taxi.

I went there on Tuesday, at Christmas, in winter.

But note that not all institutions etc. occur without articles, e.g. *I'm going to **the** airport (station, supermarket, dentist).*

Nouns which are sometimes countable and sometimes uncountable (e.g. *glass*) can cause learners problems because the same noun can occur in the singular form with *a* or with *Ø*. Compare: *I saw glass on the ground* and *I saw a glass on the ground*. At an early stage when the countable/ uncountable distinction and the use of articles are just being learned, both uses of nouns like *glass* represent a heavy learning burden and they should not be introduced together.

In a series of countable nouns, the articles after the first can (optionally) be omitted, e.g.

I bought a pen, eraser, ruler and packet of stamps.

The fields, hills and trees were all covered with snow.

Task 4.13

Underline or highlight the nouns in Text 4.5.

1 Approximately what proportion are preceded by *the*?

2 Approximately what proportion are preceded by *a* (or *an*)?

3 Approximately what proportion are preceded by *Ø*?

4 Approximately what proportion are preceded by another determiner?

Discussion topic: Article use

Learners of English sometimes seem to use articles randomly. Paragraph (a) below is an example of a text where articles have been randomly placed before nouns. Remove, add or change the articles **only where necessary** to make the text well formed. How does what you have done compare with the original text, which is printed in Paragraph (b)? What conclusions do you draw about article use? What would the effect be if you simply omitted all articles?

a Articles used randomly

There is an evidence that there is the serious problem with the engines used by the airlines whose the planes have been grounded by a Civil Aviation Board. It seems that a problem is not limited to the high-powered variant of a new engine. According to the documents released last week, the problem with the cracked engine blades probably caused by the poor design was identified in the earlier models over the year ago. A latest suspect engine is the specially modified version designed to provide the extra thrust. The experts believe that the design fault in the modifications causes the vibration, and this led to a crash on an M1 motorway in January.

b Original text

There is evidence that there is a serious problem with the engines used by the airlines whose planes have been grounded by the Civil Aviation Board. It seems that the problem is not limited to a high-powered variant of the new engine. According to documents released last week, a problem with cracked engine blades probably caused by poor design was identified in earlier models over a year ago. The latest suspect engine is a specially modified version designed to provide extra thrust. Experts believe that a design fault in the modifications causes vibration, and this led to the crash on the M1 motorway in January.

Task 4.14

In the paragraph below, find the nouns that occur with a zero article (Ø). Explain why no article is needed. Your answers will be one or more of the following:

1 Because the noun is a plural countable form.

2 Because the noun is uncountable.

3 Because the noun is a proper noun.

4 Because the noun is preceded by another determiner.

From reports received from nearby villages where unsuccessful attempts had been made to break into houses, and from evidence I had seen on the roads, I knew that a dangerous leopard was still in the area. Then, some days after the arrival of my friends, news was brought that a cow had been killed in a village several kilometres from Prayag and near the village where I lived. We found that a leopard had broken down the door of a small building and had killed one of the cows inside.

4.3.2.1 The meaning and use of articles

Articles have the following functions:

1 They can direct our attention towards a following noun, e.g. *Don't look at the **light**.*

2 They can remind us that something has been previously mentioned, e.g. *I heard a **bird** . . . **The** bird was a grey warbler.*

3 They can alert us to look for more information, e.g. ***The** book I'm reading is interesting* (which book).

4 They can tell us there is only one of the following noun, e.g. ***The** moon looks pale.*

5 They can show whether the speaker or writer is making a generalisation, using a noun to refer to all of a class of things (**generic** or **general reference**), or referring to a particular thing (**specific reference**), e.g.

The wasp is a threat to young birds.	(generic)
Books are expensive.	(generic)
The book I'm reading is interesting.	(specific but definite)
Would you lend me a book?	(specific but indefinite)

4.3.2.2 General reference

Table 4.2 shows that *a, the, Ø* can all be used to show general reference. However, they are not all correct in all contexts. Most learners will find it easiest to learn to produce only one of the forms initially, namely the *Ø* form, because the *Ø* form can be used with both countable and uncountable nouns for general reference. Also, because the *Ø* form goes with the plural form of the noun (*whales*), it may seem more logical to refer to the whole group of things by using the plural than by using the singular. Further, the *Ø* form + plural noun is always correct for general reference, whereas *a* and *the* are sometimes incorrect, e.g. **The volcano is dangerous*, or **The school is important for all children* are not acceptable ways of generalising.

Table 4.2   General reference

Countable nouns	Uncountable nouns
Ø article e.g. *Whales are huge animals.* indefinite article *a* e.g. *A whale is a huge animal.* definite article *the* e.g. *The whale is a huge animal.*	*Ø* article e.g. *Music is food for love.*

Table 4.3 Specific reference

	Countable nouns	Uncountable nouns
Definite	*the whale* (singular) *the whales* (plural)	*the music*
Indefinite	*a whale* (singular) *some whales* (plural) *whales* (plural)	*some music* *music*

Although learners may initially learn to produce only the *Ø* article for general reference, in reading and listening they are sure to meet *a* and *the* used to refer to whole classes of things, especially in scientific or journalistic contexts.

4.3.2.3 Specific reference

When nouns are used to refer to specific members of a class of things and are not generalising about whole classes, they usually have a determiner (especially an article) before them. Specific reference can be definite or indefinite. The choices are shown in Table 4.3.

4.3.2.3.1 Specific reference: definite

The **definite article** *the* can be used with both countable and uncountable nouns to **specify**. **Specifying** *the* occurs before singular and plural countable nouns and uncountable nouns to show that the following noun refers to someone or something that is known or identified to the reader or listener. Listeners can get irritated if the speaker uses *the* for something that is not specified, e.g.

Did you see *the* notice? – (What notice!)

Specifying *the* is used to show that the following noun refers to one particular member of a class which is identifiable through any of the following ways:

1 Situation or contextual reference

If the noun can refer to only one thing in a given context or situation, it can be preceded by *the*, e.g.

the moon (we normally only refer to our own)

the Prime Minister
For citizens of a particular country, this normally means the Prime Minister of that country.

Fred has a new house. **The** *walls are white and* **the** *doors are red.*
In the context of these sentences, *walls* and *doors* must refer to the walls and doors of Fred's new house.

2 Anaphoric reference

If the noun has been used before and it is repeated with *the*, this shows that the noun refers to the same one that was mentioned before, e.g.

> I saw an old man and his dog. **The** man was tall and thin.
> The second time *man* is mentioned it refers to the same person as the first time.

3 Cataphoric reference

If the noun is identified by subsequent elaboration within a noun phrase, then the reference is **cataphoric**, e.g.

> The box **on your doorstep** is for you. (tells which box)

Biber et al. (1999: 260–70) show that anaphoric reference accounts for less than a third of the uses of *the* in all registers, whereas situational reference of *the* is especially important in conversation, and cataphoric reference is especially important in news and academic prose (i.e. non-fiction). Overall, teachers should bear in mind that corpus analysis shows that specific reference accounts for over 90 per cent of uses of the definite article, whereas the use of *the* for general reference is not frequent.

Task 4.15

Write *the* where it is required.

It was one of most magnificent buildings I had ever seen. Walls were painted white and where they joined roof there was a carved border. Floor was covered with a thick, soft carpet and pattern on it was extremely beautiful. Lights were made of many round pieces of glass which made a pleasant noise in wind. Windows were large and could be opened to allow smell of flowers in surrounding garden to come in. Roof was very steep and outside it came out over walls to protect them from rain. Because of this doors could always be kept open.

4.3.2.3.2 Specific reference: indefinite

The **indefinite article** *a* (*an*), *some* or *Ø* can refer to one or more particular items which the speaker does not, or cannot, specify, or where the listener cannot be expected to exactly identify a particular one. There are five subcategories of indefinite specific reference.

1 Indefinite *a* or *some*

In this case neither the listener nor the speaker (reader or writer) can necessarily identify or wants to identify exactly the things referred to. It often has the meaning **any one(s) at all** or **it doesn't matter which one(s)**, e.g.

Please pass me a match.

Would you like an orange?

I'll go and buy a bottle of wine.

Have some grapes.

Please play us some music.

Make sure there's some paper there.

2 Individualising *a* or *some*

In this case, the speaker or writer is thinking of a particular thing or things, but the listener or reader does not yet know exactly which one(s). This use of *a* is often found for the first mention of something in a story, e.g.

*I saw **an** old friend of yours.*

*There was **a** bottle of beer in the fridge.*

*I heard **some** wonderful music last night.*

The indefinite article *a* often occurs before a countable noun which appears for the first time, and *the* often occurs before a noun which was first mentioned in a previous sentence. Thus, *a* often appears in noun phrases in the object or complement position of a sentence, whereas *the* often appears in the sentence subject position, e.g.

*I saw **a** child with a kite.*

***The** child was very happy.*

*Then **the** kite crashed.*

In some varieties of English, the word *this* is used as an individualising indefinite article, e.g.

*I met **this** girl and she said she knew you.*

3 Classifying *a*

The indefinite article is also used for classifying, e.g. *Sue is **a** gymnast. This is **a** Boeing 747.* This use typically occurs after *be*.

The **plural** of classifying *a* is Ø – *They are teachers* (not *some teachers*). With uncountable nouns we use the zero article (Ø) – *This is gold.*

4 Numerical *a* (= *one*)

Here *a* means **one, not two** e.g. *I owe you **a** dollar. I would like to say **a** word or two about the club finances.*

5 Distributive *a* (= *per* or *every*)

This use of *a* is the equivalent of *per*, e.g. *He is paid $1,000 **a** week. I wasn't driving over 100 km **an** hour.*

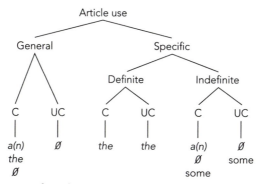

Figure 4.1 Summary of article use

Task 4.16

Insert *a* where it is required and work out which of uses 1–5 of the indefinite article discussed above is required in each case.

The street contained small drinking shops where visitors could get drunk for the equivalent of dollar. On Saturday nights about third of the male population of the town seemed to be drunk. I found hotel and spoke to man standing outside. He said that the local people who had jobs worked very hard. One woman worked twelve hours day as tailor mending clothes for franc item. Some people managed to earn hundred francs week. This is not much when you remember that potatoes cost three francs kilo. I lived in the area for about year and half. I could earn only 36 francs week by giving English lessons. I realised I had to get better paying job.

Task 4.17

Insert *a* and *the* where they are needed. Explain why they are needed.

According to old story, man killed crane and gave it to his cook. Cook roasted it and ate one of its legs. Then he put it on plate on dinner table. Man came and sat down at dinner table. He turned bird upside down and asked, 'Where is other leg?' Cook replied, 'Crane has only one leg, sir.' Next morning man and cook went together to river-bank. Crane was standing there in water on one leg. Man clapped his hands and bird lowered its other leg and flew away. Man turned to cook and said, 'Look at that crane! It has two legs.' Cook replied, 'That is true, but you did not clap your hands yesterday and so crane on plate did not lower its other leg.'

4.4 Learning the structure and use of noun phrases

Probably the hardest aspect of the noun phrase for many learners of English is learning when to use the articles *a* and *the* (and when not to use them), and remembering to add *-s* for the countable noun plural form when it is appropriate.

Long sequences of items in noun phrases, although theoretically possible, are normally very infrequent and therefore should not receive much attention from teachers, e.g. ***Every one of the first eight runners*** *will receive a prize*. The important exceptions are modifiers which follow the noun headword. For example, consider the noun phrase *the person described in this book*. When the modifier has a non-finite verb (such as *described* above), learners may think that the non-finite verb is the main verb of the sentence, and interpret it **not** as '*which is described*' but as a finite verb, 'The person described something'. Teachers should find ways to make the structure of the noun group clear to their learners. This is important because such post-modifying items occur frequently.

Remembering how to use the more than 50 different determiners and several different patterns of occurrence before nouns is a big learning task. Teachers sometimes find it is useful to have a table or wall chart like the one in Task 4.12. You can give it to a class in its finished form, or you can build it up gradually with the class as they meet different determiners. This means that they can monitor their own written work. A simple check will show that **these book* is not well formed.

Exercises should concentrate on correct **forms** and on the **meaning** of determiners because most determiners give important information about how many occurrences a particular statement applies to. There is a big difference between the meaning of the following sentences.

All of these cakes are delicious.

Some of these cakes are delicious.

Several of these cakes are delicious.

Learners can be helped to use determiners appropriately by means of gap-filling exercises before nouns, and by exercises which require the learners to put the correct form of a noun after each determiner in a text, e.g. *I saw several old* _____ *(tree). We didn't have much* _____ *(food).*

Comprehension exercises based on understanding determiners are also useful, e.g. in a text containing the sentence *There are many different sizes and shapes of cells, most of which are much too small to be seen without a microscope*, the teacher can ask learners whether statements are true or false, e.g.

There are about four different cell shapes. There are cells which you can see without a microscope.

Even if we exclude articles, at least 14 per cent of all the words in a text are typically used to express ideas of quantity (Kennedy, 1987). Determiners are a very important way in which quantification is expressed in English.

There are several reasons why correct use of articles is often hard for learners of English to acquire.

1 Different articles can sometimes have the same function, thus resulting in overlapping of use, e.g. *a (an)*, *the*, *Ø* + nouns can all be used to make general statements.

2 The same form can sometimes have different functions, e.g.

> *the* can be used for general or specific reference
>
> *a (an)* can classify or specify (with several meanings)

3 In many languages, distinctions which are important in English noun phrases are not relevant. That is, apart from the meaning of the headword,

> there is no countable–uncountable marking
>
> there is no singular–plural marking
>
> there is no definite–indefinite marking
>
> there is no capital letter and non-capital letter marking
>
> there is no general–specific marking
>
> there are no articles.

In English, information which is given partly through form and partly through context helps a listener know whether the speaker is placing an item in its class (*This is a dog*, meaning, *This is one individual belonging to the class of things called 'dogs'*) or is speaking of it as a particular example of its class (*Fred has a dog*), or is thinking of the whole class (*Dogs are intelligent animals*), and so on.

Other languages express such ideas in different ways than by obligatory marking of the noun or the use of preceding articles. Even in English, native speakers do not always mark the ideas in the same way. In all languages, context and the listener or reader's previous knowledge contribute to successful communication. Part of the teacher's task is to help learners realise that articles in English are not redundant and they often convey important information. For example, when a reader meets *the* in a text this is nearly always a sign that he or she is expected to know the thing referred to, or there is information in the text to enable the reader to identify it. Science and social studies texts often provide good material for studying the use of plural nouns or uncountable nouns without articles to make general statements. Learners may find some rules on a wall chart help them to use articles correctly.

- A singular countable noun **must** have *a*, *the* or *another determiner* before it.
- *A* can only go with singular countable nouns.
- *The* can go with all types of nouns.
- Only **uncountable** nouns and **plural countable** nouns can occur alone, without an article or other determiner.

Modified cloze exercises are often used to practise articles. These are exercises where the articles are removed and the learners must put them in. Sometimes no spaces are left to show where the articles go. You can make it a little easier by marking the places where the articles have been removed.

4.5 Pronouns

Pronouns are function words which stand in place of nouns or noun phrases. Pronouns enable us to refer to things or people succinctly, or when we do not know the referent, e.g.

Mary is only 30 years old.

The new Member of Parliament is only 30 years old.

She is only 30 years old.

Pronouns are also very important in the structure of texts, especially in conversation, by helping avoid repetition. In the sentence *John told Mary that John had lost Mary's keys and John was sorry*, the use of pronouns would enable us to avoid repetition and achieve cohesion.

The various classes of pronouns include:

personal pronouns	*I, me, you, we, us, she, him, he, her, it, they, them*
possessive pronouns	*my, your, his, her, its, their, our*
reflexive pronouns	*myself, yourself, himself, herself, itself, ourselves, themselves*
demonstrative pronouns	*this, that, these, those*
indefinite pronouns	*everyone, none, nobody, something, anyone, etc.*
interrogative pronouns	*who, what, which, whose*
relative pronouns	*that, who, which*

In language learning, the most difficult pronouns for learners are usually the personal, possessive and indefinite pronouns. Personal pronouns are about ten times more frequent than all the other pronouns together, especially in conversation. *I, me, it* and *you* are particularly frequent. Learning to use pronouns is usually not easy because the structure of the system is not the same in all languages, and some pronouns have more than one function in English.

Table 4.4 Personal, possessive and reflexive pronouns

Functions	Singular				Singular and plural	Plural	
	First person	Third person			Second person	First person	Third person
Subject	I	he	she	**it**	**you**	we	they
Object	me	him	**her**	**it**	**you**	us	them
Possessive	my	**his**	**her**	its	your	our	their
Independent possessive	mine	**his**	hers	–	yours	ours	theirs
Reflexive	myself	himself	herself	itself	yourself/yourselves	ourselves	themselves

Note: The bold type shows where two forms are the same but have more than one function.

4.5.1 Personal, possessive and reflexive pronouns

The system of English personal, possessive and reflexive pronouns, the complexity of the learning task and the potential confusion for learners can be illustrated by Table 4.4.

Teachers need to be familiar with the information in Table 4.4 because this system can seem to be very illogical and unsystematic for learners. For example, in English there can be different pronoun forms for:

● **Person** (first, second and third) *I, you, he, she, it, we, you, they*

● **Gender** (male, female, non-personal) is distinguished by means of different forms for third person singular (*he, she, it*) but not for third person plural (*they*). Gender is not distinguished at all for first or second persons, singular or plural.

● **Case**

the **subject** and **object** functions
(but only for first and third person)

I saw the film. Tom saw *me*.
They saw me. I saw *them*.
He saw me. I saw *him*.
She saw me. I saw *her*.

● **Number** (singular or plural) is distinguished by means of different forms for **first** person (*I – we*) and for **third** person (*he/she/it – they*), but not for **second** person (*you – you*).

Sometimes one form can have two functions, e.g. *her* can be an object pronoun for third person singular, feminine (e.g. John saw *her*); *her* can also be a possessive pronoun (e.g. John saw *her* car). This does not apply to the masculine, where there are two different forms: *him/his*.

There can be potential difficulties in the use of pronouns. Compare

1 *Mary saw her friend.*

2 *John saw her friend.*

In Sentence 1 *her* can stand for the subject, *Mary,* **or** for some other (female) person, depending on the context. In Sentence 2, *her* cannot stand for the subject.

Compare the referent of *he* in

3 *John told Fred he looked sick.*

4 *John told Fred he felt sick.*

In 3, it is Fred who looks unwell, whereas in 4 *he* refers to John.

Sometimes native speakers of English do not use the standard pronoun system, and in some varieties of English there are variations leading to sentences such as *I like them apples. He took me book. John and myself went. Me and John were there.* The *-s* ending is a feature of most of the independent possessive forms (*mine, hers, yours,* etc.). Children learning English as their first language sometimes overgeneralise this regularity and add *-s* to the exception in this group and say *mines* for *mine.* Sometimes an object pronoun like *me* gets used by young children for subject position (*Me want it*).

Learners of English often avoid using reflexive pronouns, saying, for example, (*You*) *Look in the mirror* rather than *Look at yourself in the mirror.* Reflexive pronouns are rarely a major source of error for learners, however, even though some native speakers of English seem to have trouble using them correctly. In some varieties of English, *myself* is used as a first person personal pronoun, e.g. *John and myself went there last year. She told John and myself about her award.* Corpus analysis suggests that learners are most likely to need to use reflexive pronouns when they refer back to an identical noun phrase in the same clause in the subject position, e.g.

*I saw **myself** in the mirror.*

*She hurt **herself** when she fell off her horse.*

Discussion topic

Compare the pronoun system in English with the pronoun system of one or more other languages you know. In the other language:

1 Are there different forms for the subject and object positions (e.g. *I/me*)?

2 Is there a special possessive form for use with nouns (e.g. *my* book)?

3 Is there a different independent possessive form (e.g. *mine*)?

4 How many words are there for *we*?

5 Is there a distinction between male and female (*he* and *she*)? If so, is it in both the singular and plural?

6 Is there a distinction between humans (*he/she*) and non-humans (*it*)? If so, is it in both singular and plural?

7 Are there special pronouns for two people or things (e.g. *you two, we two*)?

8 How many words are there for *you*?

9 Are there different words for *you* (singular) and *you* (plural)?

10 Are there distinctions that do not exist in English, e.g. special pronouns for older or more respected people, special pronouns for different family members?

Task 4.18

Underline the personal and possessive pronouns in the sentences below and describe their form and function, e.g. *I* (first person singular, subject).

1 He didn't want to go out last night.

2 The smell of rotten food made them feel sick.

3 The man noticed a drop of blood on his leg.

4 The dentist saw her yesterday.

5 The news made me aware of the risks.

6 First, we must get permission to go inside.

7 Give us the tools.

8 She said she had done it to the best of her ability.

4.5.2 Demonstrative pronouns

The demonstrative pronouns *this, that, these, those* are used for showing that an entity is known or has been referred to, and also for showing whether the entity referred to is near or more distant from the speaker or addressee, e.g. *This* is the book I told you about; *Those* are mine; What's wrong with *these*?

Demonstrative pronouns can be used as determiners as well as pronouns. That is, they can occur before a noun as well as alone in place of a noun or noun phrase. Compare, e.g.

This book is a novel. (determiner)

This is a novel. (pronoun)

Table 4.5 Demonstrative pronouns

		Countable		Uncountable
		Human	Non-human	
Singular	Pronoun	1 this that	5 this that	9 this that
Singular	Determiner	2 this that	6 this that	10 this that
Plural	Pronoun	3 these those	7 these those	
Plural	Determiner	4 these those	8 these those	

Table 4.5 shows how they are used.

Task 4.19

In the following sentences, indicate which of the numbered functions of the demonstratives (the words in italics) is being used.

1 *That* is the thing I was referring to.

2 *This* is Mere.

3 *These* problems are greater than *this* report indicates.

4 She painted all of *those* pictures last year.

5 Have you seen *these* before?

6 *This* is only one of the issues.

7 I think that *that* is enough for today.

4.5.3 Indefinite pronouns

Indefinite pronouns are used when the speaker or writer is not able or
does not want to be more specific. There are four main groups of indefinite pronouns:

1 *everybody, everyone, everything*

2 *somebody, someone, something*

3 *anybody, anyone, anything*

4 *nobody, no-one, nothing, none*

Indefinite pronouns are part of the system in English for expressing quantification, which, as we noted earlier, is a major semantic category expressed in English. Indefinite pronouns can cause comprehension difficulties in listening and reading, because their meaning is sometimes vague, especially with negation, e.g.

5 There were *many* in the park.

6 There weren't *many* in the park.

Sentence 6 does not mean simply that *many* is negated. It also asserts indirectly that there were few people in the park.

4.5.4 Interrogatives and relative pronouns

Corresponding to the personal pronouns there is a system of interrogatives and relative pronouns. As Table 4.6 shows, they make no distinction

Table 4.6 Interrogative and relative pronouns

	Interrogative		Relative	
Functions	Human	Non-human	Human	Non-human
Subject	1 who e.g. *Who told you?*	5 what e.g. *What caused the accident?*	9 who that	12 which that
Object (after verbs and prepositions)	2 who whom e.g. *Who(m) did they invite?* *To whom did she refer?*	6 what e.g. *What did they decide?* *On what did he base his decision?*	10 who whom that Ø	13 which that Ø
Determiner	3 what which whose e.g. *What author do you recommend?* *Which student got the prize?* *Whose father works at night?*	7 what which whose e.g. *What colour do you like?* *Which house is yours? Whose work did you read?*	11 whose	14 whose
Independent possessive	4 whose e.g. *Whose are those?*	8 whose which e.g. *Whose are those? Which does he want?*	–	–

between singular and plural. Relative pronouns are discussed in more detail in Chapter 7 in association with the structure of relative clauses.

Task 4.20

In Table 4.6 each set of interrogative and relative pronouns has a number, from 1 to 14. In the following sentences, indicate which of these numbers the underlined pronoun corresponds to.

1 Who broke the jug?

2 Whose book is this?

3 She is a person whose honesty can be relied on.

4 I'd like to meet the person who wrote that poem.

5 What did he say?

6 The report that caused the most discussion was written by Max.

7 Those who believe everything they hear are usually disappointed.

8 She sent me a letter in the course of which she apologised for what she had said.

9 What caused the landslide?

10 The threat of another interruption which might cause us to miss our flight was a worry.

Task 4.21

In the sentences below, certain words have been underlined. Decide whether they are pronouns or determiners. If they are pronouns, decide what they refer to if possible.

1 I looked out across the lawn at the students – some were stretched out under the trees, while others had gone out strolling.

2 You've had enough fun for today.

3 No-one has got anything done yet.

4 A voice rang out from the back of the group and everybody burst out laughing.

5 A swarm of bats took fright and some flew out into the light.

6 Someone offered to reimburse him for any expenses involved in the trip, but nothing came of it.

Learners of English as a second language can begin with a small number of pronouns which are appropriate to their uses of English. It is not necessary to learn the complete system at one time. It can be built up gradually. Personal pronouns are usually the most useful ones to start with because of their frequency of use.

The personal and possessive pronouns and some other pronouns and determiners (especially *this, that, these, those*) are very important in reading. These words help to link the sentences of a text together. The text cannot be understood easily if the reference of the pronouns and determiners is not understood. In addition to gap-filling exercises, another common exercise is to leave the pronouns in the passage and ask the learners to say what they refer to, e.g. *Cool rainwater falls on the ground. It seeps slowly down through the cracks and faults in the mudstone.* What does *it* refer to? Task 4.22 contains a text which tells part of an Indonesian legend. The deletion of the pronouns reveals how frequent and important pronouns can be in text, and how complex the selection of appropriate pronouns can be for learners of English.

Task 4.22

Put an appropriate pronoun in the spaces provided.

Long ago an old woman and ___(1)___ young son, who was called Malin Kundang, lived in a little village. ___(2)___ were very poor. Malin and ___(3)___ mother loved each other very much. ___(4)___ could not bear to be away from each other even for a short time. When Malin Kundang grew older ___(5)___ wanted to earn some money. ___(6)___ wanted to leave ___(7)___ small village and go to trade in a big town. One day ___(8)___ told ___(9)___ mother about ___(10)___ plans. When ___(11)___ heard this, ___(12)___ began to cry and could not say anything. ___(13)___ didn't know what to do. The next day, early in the morning, ___(14)___ asked ___(15)___ mother again to allow ___(16)___ to go away. At first ___(17)___ would not let ___(18)___ go because ___(19)___ was afraid that ___(20)___ would not come back to ___(21)___. But Malin Kundang would not let ___(22)___ stop ___(23)___. When ___(24)___ told ___(25)___ that ___(26)___ would come back soon and bring money with ___(27)___ ___(28)___ reluctantly let ___(29)___ go.

CHAPTER 5

Verbs and verb phrases

This chapter gives an overview of the structure and function of verb phrases and especially of those aspects which learners of English often find hard.

Objectives

By the end of this chapter you should be able to:

1 Identify **verbs** in texts.

2 Know whether a particular verb in a text is **finite** or **non-finite**.

3 Know the difference between **lexical (or full) verbs, primary verbs** and **modal auxiliary verbs**.

4 Identify **phrasal** verbs.

5 Know the forms of **regular** English verbs and the most common **irregular** verbs.

6 Know the distribution of **frequent lexical verbs** in different genres.

7 Identify and describe the structure of **finite** and **non-finite verb phrases**.

8 Describe the structure of **simple** and **complex** verb phrases.

9 Identify and describe the structure and use of **infinitive** constructions.

10 Know which uses of infinitive constructions are most frequent.

11 Identify **-*ing* participle** functions in texts.

12 Identify **-*ed* participle** functions in texts.

13 Know which uses of -*ing* participle and -*ed* participle constructions are most frequent.

14 Identify and describe the main uses of the **passive voice**.

15 Know the difference between **tense, aspect, voice** and **mood**.

---

16 Know how **simple present** and **simple past** tenses are used in spoken and written texts.

17 Know the structure and use of verb forms that express **perfect aspect**.

18 Know the structure and use of verb forms that express **progressive aspect**.

19 Know the difference between **stative** and **dynamic** verbs.

20 Know how **future time** is expressed in English.

21 Know how **modal verbs** and their main meanings are used in texts.

5.1 Verb identification and classification

Verbs typically describe states, actions or events, e.g.

I *like* chocolate.

He *left* the room.

I *found* my keys.

I *think* you *are* right.

Verbs have sometimes been characterised as 'doing words' or 'words of action' in some grammars. However, because many verb occurrences do not involve action (e.g. *is, have, know, believe, think, hope*), it is probably better to recognise verbs on the basis of their form. There are three main classes of verbs: **lexical verbs** (e.g. *think, find, replace*), **primary verbs** (*be, have, do*) and **modal verbs** (e.g. *will, can, might*). They have different functions and grammatical characteristics. We will consider these classes of verbs in turn.

Verbs are very frequent. In the *Brown Corpus* of 1 million words of written American English (Francis & Kučera, 1982) verbs make up over 17 per cent of the words in 'informational' (non-fiction) writing, about 22 per cent of the words in texts of 'imaginative writing' (fiction), and over 18 per cent of the words overall. Corpus-based research on written British English gives similar results (see Table 2.1.). About 10 per cent of words in a corpus are typically lexical verbs, about 7 per cent are primary verbs, and about 1.5 per cent are modal verbs.

5.1.1 Lexical verbs

The vast majority of the different verbs in English are lexical verbs. Lexical verbs, like other word classes, have a small number of very frequent items and huge numbers of rare items. In a corpus analysis of about 150,000 words of US English texts taken from unrehearsed radio interviews, TV

Table 5.1 Most frequent lexical verbs with their tense and aspect use
(adapted from Ota, 1963: 66–71)

Most frequent verbs	% of the 17,166 finite verbs in Ota's corpus	Verb-form use (%)				
		Simple present	Present progressive	SImple past	Past progressive	All other verb-form uses
think	5.0	87.8	1.3	9.7	0.3	1.0
know	3.6	88.7	0.0	8.2	0.0	3.1
say	2.6	37.4	2.5	50.0	0.7	9.4
want	2.4	81.1	0.0	17.7	0.2	1.0
go	1.7	32.1	27.5	26.5	2.4	11.5
get	1.5	47.7	9.2	36.6	1.1	5.4
come	1.4	33.6	11.2	39.0	3.3	12.9
see	1.3	65.0	0.9	23.0	0.0	11.1
make	1.3	36.6	8.8	29.2	0.9	24.5
mean	1.2	82.6	0.0	15.4	0.0	2.0
feel	0.9	68.7	3.3	22.7	0.7	4.6
take	0.9	27.5	9.4	38.9	2.0	22.2
Total	23.8					

plays and academic writing, Ota (1963) found that 12 lexical verbs accounted for 23.8 per cent of the 17,166 occurrences of verbs in his corpus. The 12 most frequent lexical verbs in Ota's corpus are listed in Table 5.1, which also shows that these frequent verbs are not used with equal frequency with different tenses.

In a much more comprehensive analysis based on the 40-million-word *LSWE Corpus*, Biber et al. (1999: 358) found almost 40 years later that over 10 per cent of the words in the corpus were lexical verbs, and that the 12 most frequent lexical verbs in English were substantially the same as Ota found – *say, get, go, know, think, see, make, come, take, want, give, mean* (each occurring at least once every 1,000 words of text). *Give* was not among Ota's 12 most frequent (it was 15th), while *feel* from Ota's list was not among the 12 most frequent in Biber et al. The 12 most frequent lexical verbs in the list of Biber et al. accounted for 45 per cent of all lexical verbs in spoken English conversation but only 11 per cent of all lexical verbs in academic writing. The similarity between Ota's and Biber et al.'s analysis illustrates the remarkable stability of language use.

Many lexical verbs are associated with particular registers or fields of use. For example, Johansson (1981) compared the way particular verbs were associated with either written academic British English or British fiction in the 1-million-word *LOB* corpus. The verbs most distinctively associated with each of these categories are listed in Table 5.2.

Table 5.2 Most distinctive verb forms in two genres of the *LOB* Corpus
(from Johannson, 1981)

Verbs	
Academic	Fiction
measured	kissed
assuming	heaved
calculated	leaned
occurs	glanced
assigned	smiled
emphasised	hesitated
obtained	exclaimed
executed	murmured
tested	gasped
corresponding	hurried
vary	flushed
bending	cried
varying	eyed
loading	staring
measuring	paused
determine	whispered
isolated	waved
dissolved	nodded
resulting	frowned
defined	shivered
occur	muttered
stressed	shared
illustrates	flung

Biber et al. (1999: 360ff.) classify lexical verbs into seven major semantic groups based on core meanings. (Some verbs belong to more than one group, e.g. *contact* = 'activity' or 'communication'.) The most frequent verbs in each group, occurring more than 300 times per million words in at least one of four genres, are shown in Table 5.3. The four genres are conversation, news, fiction and academic writing.

In Biber et al.'s analysis the 280 most frequent verbs are distributed approximately as follows:

	%
activity verbs	49
mental verbs	19
communication verbs	13
existence verbs	8
occurrence verbs	5
causative verbs	4
aspectual verbs	3

Table 5.3 Semantic groups of verbs

Activity verbs	Communication verbs	Mental verbs	Causative verbs	Simple occurrence verbs	Existence/ relationship verbs	Aspectual verbs
make	say	see	help	become	seem	start
get	tell	know	let	happen	look	keep
go	call	think	allow	change	stand	stop
give	ask	find	require	die	stay	begin
take	write	want		grow	live	continue
come	talk	mean		develop	appear	
use	speak	need		occur	include	
leave	thank	feel			involve	
show	describe	like			contain	
try	claim	hear			exist	
buy	offer	remember			indicate	
work	suggest	believe			represent	
move		read				
follow		consider				
put		suppose				
pay		listen				
bring		love				
meet		wonder				
play		understand				
run		expect				
hold		hope				
turn		assume				
send		determine				
sit						
wait						
walk						
carry						

Source: Adapted from Biber, D. et al. (1999) *Longman Grammar of Spoken and Written English*, Table 5.1, p. 365. Reprinted by permission of Pearson Education Ltd.

In spoken English, fiction and news genres there tends to be more use of 'activity verbs', while in academic English there tends to be greater use of 'existence verbs'.

5.1.1.1 Regular verbs

Regular lexical verbs have four forms: **stem** (or base), **stem+s**, **stem+ed** and **stem+ing** (e.g. *want, wants, wanted, wanting*).

5.1.1.2 Irregular verb forms

Irregular verbs typically have a different past tense or *-ed* participle than regular verbs (e.g. *make, made, have made*, not *make,*maked, *have maked*). Because some of these irregular verbs are among the most frequent lexical verbs in English, they can be a major source of errors for second language learners.

There are about 200 irregular lexical verbs in English. Some have a vowel change for the past tense or -ed participle (e.g. *feed, fed, fed*), or different past tense and -ed participle forms, e.g. *rang, rung*. About 80 of these 200 irregular verbs are rare and probably not worth teaching, e.g. *beseech, smite*).

Grabowski and Mindt (1995) analysed the use of the 160 different irregular verbs which occur in the *Brown* and *LOB* corpora. If we include the very frequent primary verbs *be, have, do*, which are also irregular and which account for 60 per cent of the irregular verb tokens, then the 20 most frequent irregular verbs account for 84 per cent of all irregular verb tokens in these written corpora. The rank order of the 20 most frequent irregular verbs in the corpora is: *be, have, do, say, make, go, take, come, see, know, get, give, find, think, tell, become, show, leave, feel, put*. It is worth noting that in the two corpora, in addition to the 160 irregular verbs, 4,240 different **regular** lexical verb types occur (96 per cent of the lexical verb types). These **regular** verbs, however, account for only 42 per cent of the verb tokens, while 58 per cent of verb tokens in the corpus come from irregular verbs. Thus, learning the small number of high frequency irregular verbs is very cost-effective for learners of English. Language change can be observed in the use of some irregular verbs. For example, some native speakers of English say *I rung him, We swum about 500 metres, The boat sunk, She sung it very well*, using the -ed participle form instead of the past tense (*I rang him, We swam about 500 metres*, etc.). Table 5.4 contains a list in alphabetical order of 84 irregular verbs which occur with relatively high frequency in English.

5.1.1.3 Other sub-classes of lexical verbs

In addition to the distinction between **transitive** and **intransitive** verbs described in Section 3.2.3.2.1, other sub-classes of lexical verbs include:

1 A distinction between **dynamic** and **stative** verbs. Dynamic verbs include *follow, change*, e.g. *I* **can't** *follow these instructions, I'm following your instructions, I changed my mind, We* **are** *changing our* address. Stative verbs such as *know, mean, seem, want, like, think* describe 'states' and rarely occur with progressive aspect, e.g.

I know the answer.	*I **am knowing** the answer.
This word means 'enough'.	*This word **is meaning** 'enough'.
You seem unhappy.	*You **are seeming** unhappy.
I want some fresh mushrooms.	?I'm **wanting** some fresh mushrooms.

2 **Multiword verbs.** Some verbs consist of two or more words. The two main types are **phrasal verbs** and **prepositional verbs**. Whole books have been written for learners of English on multi-word verbs. These

Table 5.4 High frequency irregular English verbs

Infinitive	Simple past	-ed participle	Infinitive	Simple past	-ed participle
be	was/were	been	leave	left	left
become	became	become	let	let	let
begin	began	begun	lie	lay	lain
bend	bent	bent	lose	lost	lost
bite	bit	bitten	make	made	made
blow	blew	blown	mean	meant	meant
break	broke	broken	meet	met	met
bring	brought	brought	pay	paid	paid
broadcast	broadcast	broadcast	put	put	put
build	built	built	read	read	read
burn	burnt/burned	burnt/burned	ride	rode	ridden
buy	bought	bought	ring	rang	rung
catch	caught	caught	rise	rose	risen
choose	chose	chosen	run	ran	run
come	came	come	say	said	said
cut	cut	cut	see	saw	seen
deal	dealt	dealt	sell	sold	sold
do	did	done	send	sent	sent
draw	drew	drawn	set	set	set
drink	drank	drunk	shake	shook	shaken
drive	drove	driven	show	showed	shown
eat	ate	eaten	sing	sang	sung
fall	fell	fallen	sink	sank	sunk
feed	fed	fed	sit	sat	sat
feel	felt	felt	sleep	slept	slept
fight	fought	fought	speak	spoke	spoken
find	found	found	spend	spent	spent
fly	flew	flown	stand	stood	stood
forget	forgot	forgotten	steal	stole	stolen
freeze	froze	frozen	strike	struck	struck
get	got	got	swim	swam	swum
give	gave	given	swing	swung	swung
go	went	gone	take	took	taken
grow	grew	grown	teach	taught	taught
hang	hung	hung	tell	told	told
have	had	had	think	thought	thought
hear	heard	heard	throw	threw	thrown
hide	hid	hidden	understand	understood	understood
hold	held	held	wake	woke	woken
keep	kept	kept	wear	wore	worn
know	knew	known	win	won	won
lead	led	led	write	wrote	written

consist of a lexical verb plus a particle. If the particle is an **adverb**, then the construction is usually called a **phrasal verb**. If the particle is a **preposition**, the construction is called a **prepositional verb**. It is often not easy to distinguish them.

a **Phrasal verbs**. The most frequent adverbial particles include *up, out, on, in, off, down* (e.g. *get up, carry out, come on, move in, take off, put down*). Phrasal verbs can be transitive or intransitive.

> The plane **took off**; He **gave in**. **Come on**! (intransitive)
>
> I **cleaned up** the mess; They **brought up** four children. (transitive)

b **Prepositional verbs**. These two-part verbs have a lexical verb followed by a preposition.

> I **looked at** the screen.
>
> We **talked about** the weather.
>
> They **put up with** many complaints.

An important grammatical characteristic of phrasal verbs is that they are normally able to have the adverbial particle separated from the verb, and indeed it must be separated if there is an object that is a pronoun, e.g.

1 She *brought up* her children.   *She *brought up* them.

2 She *brought* her children *up*.   She *brought* them *up*.

Compare 1 and 2 with the following example of a **prepositional verb** where the verb and particle cannot be separated:

3 He *looked after* his elderly mother.   He *looked after* her.

4 *He *looked* his elderly mother *after*.   *He *looked* her *after*.

Phrasal verbs are a very productive and frequently used part of English vocabulary and new ones continually come into spoken use in particular. Recent additions include *chill out, stress out, stuff up, blob out*. Prepositional verb use is described in more detail in Section 6.3.3.

5.1.2 Auxiliary verbs

A total of about 24 auxiliary verb forms can function as part of complex verb phrases (with a lexical verb) by taking the tense marking and contributing to how aspect and voice are expressed (e.g. *I **have been** sitting here for an hour*). Auxiliary verbs (including primary verbs and modal verbs) typically account for about 8 per cent of all the verb tokens in corpora of spoken or written English, and they are an important focus of attention for learners of English.

5.1.2.1 Primary auxiliary verbs

There are three **primary auxiliary verbs** (*be, have, do*) which, like modal auxiliary verbs (see 5.1.2.2), are often unstressed in spoken English, or written in contracted forms (e.g. *She's, I've*).

As we saw in Sections 3.4.1 and 3.5.1, *do* (*does*, *did*) is also important for forming interrogative and negative clauses which lack another auxiliary (***Do** you speak Spanish?*). *Do* can also be used in place of a lexical verb (*Yes, I do/No, I don't*), and for emphasis (e.g. *Do tell us*). *Have* and *do* can also be used as lexical verbs, e.g.

He has a headache.

I did my homework.

In addition to its use as a primary auxiliary verb (e.g. *He is leaving* tomorrow), *be* also has a very important use as a copular verb (Section 3.2.3.2.1), e.g.

Fred is a teacher.

Sue was unhappy.

She's in my class.

In Ota's (1963) study of verb form use, the verb *be* (both as an auxiliary verb and as a copular verb) accounted for over 30 per cent of all the verb forms used in his corpus. This high use of *be* reflects, in part, the high frequency of SVC and SVA clause patterns in English.

5.1.2.2 Modal auxiliary verbs

Modal auxiliary verbs introduce additional meaning into a verb phrase. There are nine modal verbs in English (*will, would, can, could, may, might, shall, should, must*) and several other verbs which behave in some ways like modals (*need, dare, ought to, used to*) and which are called **marginal modals**. Marginal modals are not frequent. A further group of words know as **semi-modals** is semantically related to modals (*have to, have got to, be supposed to, be to*). For learners, difficulties arise from the structures that modals occur in, as well as from their meanings.

Typical errors made by learners include:

*If I was suddenly very rich, I visit many countries.

*This is may be difficult.

*Learners can be able to get hold of the order of the story.

*She must have another one staying with her. She can not alone.

*Finally I could found my passport.

5.1.2.2.1 Distribution of modals

Modals do not have a third person singular (stem+s) form, nor an *-ing* or *-ed* participle. They come before *not* in negative constructions (e.g. *He cannot drive*) and before the subject in Yes–No questions (e.g. *Can Max drive?*). They can occur alone in the verb phrase in shortened sentences, often in response to a question, e.g. *Who is willing to go? – I will.* If there is a modal in a verb phrase, it always comes first.

Table 5.5 Distribution of modal verbs in the *BNC*

	All BNC texts (100m words) %	All BNC spoken texts (10m words) %	All BNC written texts (90m words) %
will	22.9	26.5	22.2
would	19.9	21.5	19.6
can	18.3	23.1	17.4
could	11.6	9.4	11.9
may	7.8	2.3	8.7
might	4.2	3.9	4.3
shall	1.4	1.4	1.4
should	7.6	5.7	8.0
must	5.0	2.8	5.3
ought to	0.4	0.6	0.4
need to	0.2	0.1	0.3
dare	0.1	0.1	0.1
used to	0.8	2.8	0.4
Modals per 1,000 words	14.6	21.5	13.8

Various frequency counts of written and spoken English show an overall frequency of about 15 modals per 1,000 words – roughly five per typical magazine page. Modals occur more often in spoken English than in written English, as shown in Table 5.5. The four most frequent modal verbs (*will, would, can, could*) account for over 72 per cent of all modal occurrences. The least frequent modal is *shall*. From a language learner's point of view, Table 5.5 shows that some modals are much more frequent than others and are probably worth learning sooner than the less frequent ones.

Modal verbs can occur in nine verb phrase structures, as shown in Table 5.6, which uses the modal verb *must* as an example. The relative frequency of the modal verb phrase structures shows that by far the most frequent structure for most modals is the **modal + infinitive** verb phrase (e.g. *They must tell us*). In fact for all modals about 90 per cent of uses occur in the **modal + infinitive** or the **modal + *be* + -*ed* participle**

Table 5.6 Distribution of modal verbs in verb phrase structures of the *BNC*

Modal verb structures	% of all modals in the *BNC*
1 Modal alone (e.g. *They won't go! – They must.*)	1.9
2 Modal + infinitive (e.g. *They must tell us.*)	76.0
3 Modal + *be* + *-ed* participle (e.g. *We must be told.*)	14.6
4 Modal + *be* + *-ing* participle (e.g. *They must be fixing it.*)	1.5
5 Modal + *have* + *-ed* participle (e.g. *They must have told him.*)	5.1
6 Modal + *be* + *being* + *-ed* participle (e.g. *It must be being fixed.*)	0.1
7 Modal + *have* + *been* + *-ed* participle (e.g. *They must have been told.*)	0.6
8 Modal + *have* + *been* + *-ing* participle (e.g. *He must have been following us.*)	0.1
9 Modal + *have* + *been* + *being* + *-ed* participle (e.g. *We must have been being followed.*)	0.1
	100.0

structures. Several of the structures in which modals can occur (Numbers 6–9) are so rarely found in the *BNC* that they are unlikely to justify inclusion in a language course even at advanced levels.

5.1.2.2.2 The meanings of modals

Many types of modal meaning have been identified by linguists, including **possibility, certainty, ability, habit, inference, obligation, desirability, intention, necessity, politeness, consent, willingness, permission.** Greenbaum and Quirk (1990) describe these 'core meanings' of modals and, in addition, they show that all the modal verbs except *can* sometimes express how 'certain' a speaker is about the truth of an utterance. This is called the epistemic use of modal verbs, e.g.

You *must* be home before dark.	(core use = obligation)
You *must* be joking.	(epistemic use = *I am almost certain you are joking.*)

Core meanings

Each modal has a core meaning or meanings.

must	You *must* be careful when you cross the road. (obligation)
can	He *can* read. (ability) You *can* go. (permission)
	Tomatoes *can* give you indigestion. (possibility)
may	You *may* leave now. (permission) They *may* call. (possibility)

will	I'll ring you tonight. (intention) I'll do it. (willingness)
should	You *should* ask for help. (obligation)
shall	*Shall* I make you some coffee? (willingness) I *shall* never forget this. (intention)
might	He said you *might* know about it. (possibility)
could	We *could* leave it here. (possibility/permission)
would	*Would* you help them? (willingness)
ought to	I *ought to* clean the stove, but I can't be bothered. (obligation)
have to	I *have to* be home by 6 p.m. (obligation)
have got to	I've *got to* go now. (obligation)
be to	He *is to* report to the police every day while on bail. (obligation)

In spoken English, *have to* is about three times as frequent as *must* for expressing obligation. *Should* is also typically more frequent than *must* in written English to express obligation.

Epistemic meanings

Epistemic modality is the expression of degrees of certainty. The main modals are listed as follows, approximately from most certain to least certain.

must	You *must* be our new neighbour. You were born in 1960. It's 2003 now, so you *must* be 43 this year.
will	Ask Sam, he *will* know the answer. (The speaker is certain *now*, not at some time in the future.)
would	It *would* cost thousands of dollars to repair it.
should	I'll post the letter on Monday and it *should* arrive on Wednesday.
ought to	He *ought to* be home by now.
might	Don't do that, you *might* hurt yourself.
may	You *may* like this.
could	Don't wait for us, we *could* be late. That flooded river *could* be dangerous.

The modals that express the strongest certainty are *must, will, would,* followed by *should. Ought to, might, may, could* express the possibility of something happening (including of course the possibility of it **not** happening), and have a lower degree of certainty. These epistemic meanings which tell us about how certain we are of our statements are frequent for some modals, as Table 5.7 shows.

Table 5.7 Use of modal auxiliaries in the *London–Lund* (spoken) and *LOB* (written) corpora based on Coates (1983) (percentages)

	Core use					Epistemic use		Other uses	
	Obligation–necessity								
must	53			(65)		46	(31)	1	(4)
need	87					13			
should	42			(51)		18	(12)	40	(37)
ought	84			(84)		9	(13)	7	(3)
	Possibility		Ability		Permission				
can	65	(64)	21	(25)	5	(3)		9	(8)
could	25	(30)	12	(29)	2	(2)	4	(7)	56	(32)
may	4	(22)			16	(6)	74	(61)	6	(11)
might	1				1		54		44	
	Willingness		Obligation		Intention				
will	13	(8)			23	(14)	58	(71)	6	(7)
shall	19	(9)	2	(34)	18	(19)	61	(35)	1	(3)
would	4	(6)			1	(3)	83	(83)	12	(8)

Note: Percentages from the *LOB Corpus* of written British English are in parentheses.

Modal meaning can also be expressed in other ways without using modal verbs (e.g. *you have **permission to** . . .* ; *You are **obliged to** . . .* ; *He is **certain to be** . . .* ; *I **doubt that** . . .* ; *It is **likely that** . . .* ; *We are **allowed to** . . .* ; **perhaps**; **obviously**; **poison**; **fragile**; **tend to** . . .* ; *It's **a good idea to** . . .* ; **ensure**; **essential**; **optional***) (see Holmes, 1988). Some users of English (especially as a second or foreign langage) tend to 'overuse' modal verbs instead of using some of the alternatives. For example, the speaker who says *I won't help you* instead of *I'm not able to help you* may leave an unintended meaning of refusal.

In Table 5.8, a corpus-based analysis by George (1963) of the use of different meanings of the modal verb *would* per thousand words illustrates the semantic complexity of modals, and the challenge for learners of English.

Task 5.1

Underline or highlight the verb forms in Text 5.1.

i What is the most frequent verb you have underlined?

ii What proportion of the verb phrases contain a modal verb?

Table 5.8 Uses of *would* with their frequencies in written English
(adapted from George, 1963)

	Use	Example	Occurrences per 1,000 verbs
1	reported *will* referring to future time	He thought there *would be* no need for him to go.	4.0
2	indicating probability of an assumption (epistemic)	(a knock on the door) That *would be* Henry. It *would seem* that he knows.	3.4
3	indicating wish of speaker	*Would* you open the window, please?	1.8
4	emphatic, indicating wish or insistence in the past	I didn't want him to, but he *would* come.	1.4
5	in the main clause of a hypothetical statement, indicating non-fulfilment of the condition, + *have* + *-ed*	I *would have gone* if I'd known. (I didn't know)	1.2
6	reported *will*, intention	He said he *would* go later.	1.0
7	characteristic repetition	He *would* practise for hours.	1.0
8	indicating refusal	He *wouldn't* do it.	1.0
9	*would have been* + *-ing*	If I'd gone, I'd *have been* relaxing on the beach.	0.1
10	*would rather*	I'd *rather* come with you.	0.1
11	*would rather have* + *-ed*	I *would rather have seen* the other film!	0.1
12	after *would sooner*	I'd *sooner* teach French than History.	0.1
		Total	15.2

Text 5.1

Nuclear energy

At a time when scientific advance was seen as universally beneficial, the nuclear industry was judged to be at the cutting edge of technology. It was crucial to a country's status as an advanced nation. But there is a second powerful strategic argument which propelled nuclear power forward in Britain, as in other countries. This is the fact that it is based on what has appeared to be a uniquely simple fuel, and one whose exploitation could avoid dependence on a variety of other uncertain choices. One of the arguments for the development of nuclear energy in the immediate aftermath of the Second World War was a predicted shortage of coal. Coal provided the fuel for much the greater part of the country's electricity. There were power cuts over the winter of 1947 because the industry could not cope with the demand. Worse was expected to come as industrial and domestic consumption of electricity picked up after the attrition of the war years. Now, however, there was an alternative. A single pound of uranium, it was claimed, would produce the same energy as a thousand tons of coal, whilst a hundred tons of uranium could provide all the electricity that the country could possibly need. In fact, apart from industrial disputes, the nuclear industry's pessimistic predictions about supplies of fossil fuels have been proved wrong in practice. Fossil fuels came to be a problem, not because of shortages, but because they cause pollution. Similarly, after the Chernobyl disaster, nuclear energy was seen to bring dangers of a different kind.

Task 5.2

All animals (1) *can catch* diseases. Some of these diseases are only slightly harmful, like the common cold. Others (2) *can cause* serious deformities, like polio or foot-and-mouth disease. Others, like rabies, (3) *can kill*. Many of these animal diseases are caused by tiny particles called viruses. These particles are so small that we (4) *cannot see* them with our eyes alone; we (5) *must look* at them through an electron microscope, which magnifies them to over a million times their normal size. There are many different types of virus. The virus which causes sore throats and runny noses invades only the cells lining our throats and noses. It (6) *will not be found* in other parts of the body. Viruses which attack insects are different from the ones which attack other animals and ourselves.

Which meaning do the modals have in the text?

1 *can catch*	a	permission	4 *cannot see*	a	permission
	b	ability		b	ability
	c	possibility		c	possibility
2 *can cause*	a	permission	5 *must look at*	a	obligation
	b	ability		b	certainty
	c	possibility	6 *will not be found*		
3 *can kill*	a	permission		a	willingness
	b	ability		b	predictability
	c	possibility		c	intention

Task 5.3

Underline each verb phrase that contains a modal. Decide whether each modal expresses a core meaning (C) or an epistemic meaning (E) (about the certainty of knowledge).

1 You dream every night, even though you may not remember anything when you wake up.
2 Yawning is a reflex action we can't control and usually means we need more sleep.
3 If you eat enough carbohydrates and fats the protein will be saved for more useful, body-building work.
4 The information may be about how to do something.
5 Roy said it was a shame to waste it, but even he didn't see what they could do with it.
6 We musn't let them out of our sight for a moment.
7 If we're not quick about it, they'll get away from us.
8 I wonder where they are? They must have seen us.

5.1.2.2.3 Learning how to use modal verbs

Because modal meanings and structures are complex, learners will only gradually build up to using the whole system productively. Table 5.7 shows that epistemic meanings are very frequent for many of the modals – especially *will, would, must, may, might*. It can be helpful to the learners if sentences that contain these modals are linked initially with meanings of certainty and possibility rather than futurity.

For production, learners do not need all the forms and meanings until a very advanced level. As we have seen, some meanings are expressed by two or three modals. Learners can get by with only one of them, e.g.

	might	
It	*could*	*rain.*
	may	

Could seems to be the most frequent of these in spoken English, and therefore it is perhaps sensible to teach it before *might* or *may*. Similarly, *should* can cover *ought to*. *Would, could, should, might* are all used to express hypothetical statements or conditions, e.g. *It **would/might/could/should** be better to go this way.* *Would* is the most frequent and can be chosen for learners to use. Choosing only one form out of several that can express the same meaning reduces the learning burden by removing a source of confusion. In hypothetical statements, the presence or absence of *not* with modals can be especially difficult, e.g. *I would go if I had time* means *I won't be going,* even though there is no negative with *would*.

Discussion topic

This task is intended to help teachers focus on some of the criteria which may be used to decide on a teaching order for modals.

A For the seven modals given below, rank each one on three scales:

Frequency: Use 1–7. Give 1 to the most frequent, 7 to the least frequent and the numbers 2–6 to the others. (See Table 5.5.)

Needs: Use 1, 2 or 3. Give 1 to the uses you think are most essential for production, 3 to the least needed uses for production, and 2 to those which are in between.

Learnability: Use 1, 2 or 3. Give 1 to the modal uses which you think are easiest to learn, 2 to those uses which are neither very easy nor very difficult, and 3 to the uses which you think are least learnable.

Modal uses	**Frequency**	**Needs**	**Learnability**
a A vacancy will be available shortly.			
b An obvious example of a cultural difference might be how elderly people are treated.			
c Using the native language of one student would only estrange the other students.			
d Anyone interested should contact me.			
e A house is available from 1 May to 31 August if the owner may use it for the last half of June.			
f Twenty-four hours' notice ensures that the equipment can be delivered on time.			
g A background in physics could be useful.			

There is no single 'correct' answer. Your answer will be a matter of judgement.

B Consider your rankings across the columns and decide on a sensible teaching order for these seven modal uses.

5.2 Finite verb forms and verb phrases

5.2.1 Finite verbs

English sentences typically have a lexical verb or a primary verb as the main verb, on their own or preceded by one or more auxiliary verbs. Sentences require at least one **finite verb**. A finite verb is a verb which can be marked for tense (**present** or **past**) or third person singular. All forms of a verb except infinitives and -ed or -ing participles are finite verbs. Lexical verbs and primary verbs have both finite and non-finite forms. All modal verbs are finite, although they do not have a third person singular form.

Table 5.9 shows the finite and non-finite forms of three lexical verbs (*mend, give, put*) and the primary verb *be*. *Mend* is a regular verb; the other three are all irregular.

As we saw in Section 5.1, most English verbs are 'regular'. That is, they have four forms, like those of *mend* (*mend, mends, mended, mending*). *Mend* is the form common to *mend, mends, mended* and *mending*, and is called the 'stem' (or 'base') form. With lexical verbs, we can tell whether a stem form is finite or non-finite if the form has to change to stem + -s when the subject is third person singular, e.g. *I mend shoes; He mends electronic equipment*. We can also tell whether a verb is finite if it changes to the stem + -ed form when the time referred to is past, e.g. *He mends electronic equipment; He mended my stereo*.

With regular lexical verbs, the stem form is finite on some occasions and non-finite on some occasions; therefore we can speak of the 'finite

Table 5.9 Forms of English verbs

Form	*mend* (regular)	*give* (irregular)	*put* (irregular)	*be* (irregular)
finite stem	*mend*	*give*	*put*	*am* *are*
stem + -s	*mends*	*gives*	*puts*	*is*
stem + -ed	*mended*	*gave*	*put*	*was* *were*
non-finite stem (infinitive)	*mend*	*give*	*put*	*be*
stem + -ed	*mended*	*given*	*put*	*been*
stem + -ing	*mending*	*giving*	*putting*	*being*

stem form' and the 'non-finite stem form' (or **infinitive**). The stem + -*ed* form is also finite on some occasions and non-finite on others. We can speak of the 'finite stem + -*ed* form' (past tense) and the 'non-finite stem + -*ed* form' (-*ed* participle). The stem + -*s* form is always **finite**. The stem + -*ing* form is always **non-finite**. In Table 5.9, whereas the verb *mend* like all regular verbs has four forms, the verb *be* has eight forms, the verb *give* has five forms, and the verb *put* has three forms.

On the basis of a verb form frequency count in a corpus of half a million words of written British English, George (1963) found the following distribution of verb forms:

	%
Finite stem (including stem + -*s*)	21
Non-finite stem (infinitive)	21
Finite stem + -*ed* (past tense)	27
Non-finite stem + -*ed* (-*ed* participle)	20
Stem + -*ing* (-*ing* participle)	11
	100

Task 5.4

Underline or highlight the finite verbs in Text 5.2.

Text 5.2

Dinosaur eggs

A collection of 80-million-year-old eggs has shed new light on the parenting style of dinosaurs, suggesting that some of them built nests and cared for their young much as birds do today. The ancient Troodons, whose nearly intact nests were discovered in Montana, were in some ways closer to modern birds than to crocodiles and other reptiles, according to a report in *Nature*. Many scientists believe birds are evolutionary descendants of dinosaurs. Troodons were fast, slender-limbed creatures about the size of adult humans, and may have been among the most intelligent of dinosaurs. Several nests of fossilized Troodon eggs were discovered on Montana's Egg Mountain, in Teton County. Researchers studying the nests concluded, based on their positions, that the eggs were laid two at a time in a bird-like pattern that suggests parental incubation of the eggs. The eggs also are relatively large with thick, tough shells. By contrast, crocodiles lay a large number of smaller eggs in a single batch. The eggs are buried under sediment and the offspring are left to fend for themselves after hatching.

Task 5.5

Complete this table of irregular verbs.

Stem form	Finite stem + -*ed* form (past tense)	Non-finite stem + -*ed* form (-*ed* participle)
1	cost	
2 spread		
3		fed
4		bought
5	made	
6	got	
7 draw		
8	gave	
9	swam	
10 grow		
11		put
12		sung
13	understood	
14 fall		
15 ring		
16 steal		

Many learners of English have difficulty using verb forms correctly, and make errors such as the following:

*This chocolate, it good.

*Yesterday he go to school.

*I going soon.

*He have been drive a taxi.

In some languages it is possible to say *This good*, but not in English. Learners need to know that, with few exceptions, an English clause is not complete without a finite verb. It is important to establish the finite–non-finite distinction so that learners do not think that *He reading a book* is a well-formed sentence. It is a good idea to get learners to check their written work to see that each clause has a verb in the present or past tense, and that present tense verbs in the third person singular are in the stem + -*s* form. Learners can be given the responsibility for correcting errors of this kind in their own written work. The teacher can underline the word to show there is an error and put C (for Concord) in the margin. The learners then do their own correction, e.g.

C   Usually the adult bird <u>stay</u> in the nest.

5.2.2 Finite verb phrases

Finite verb phrases consist of one finite verb, plus sometimes one or more other verb forms. Finite verb phrases can be **simple** (i.e. have only one verb form) or **complex** (i.e. have one or more non-finite forms after the finite verb). In the following examples, the verb forms are underlined, with the finite verb form in parentheses.

Simple verb phrases, e.g.

She Margaret Drabble (<u>is</u>) a novelist.

She (<u>writes</u>) novels.

She (<u>wrote</u>) *A Natural Curiosity*.

Complex verb phrases, e.g.

She (<u>can</u>) <u>write</u> novels.

She (<u>could</u>) <u>have written</u> more novels.

She (<u>must</u>) <u>have been writing</u> novels all her life.

She (<u>might</u>) <u>be writing</u> another novel soon.

She (<u>has</u>) <u>written</u> several novels already.

Most of her novels (<u>have</u>) <u>been published</u> in London.

She (<u>is</u>) <u>writing</u> a reference book too.

According to Joos (1964) there are 222 possible **complex** verb phrase structures in English for every transitive lexical verb. They are typically a major source of difficulty for learners. Some complex verb phrase structures are very rare (e.g. *You **must have been being followed***) and it is unlikely that they are worth including in a teaching curriculum.

The verb forms which can come before a lexical verb always follow a particular order (Greenbaum & Quirk, 1990: 42). There are potentially up to five positions for a sequence of verb forms. Only the first item of a sequence of verb forms is finite. All the other items are non-finite forms. A complex verb phrase always ends with an item from Position 1 (see Table 5.10).

The order of the items in a complex verb phrase can be summarised as follows:

● If a **complex** verb phrase with two items begins with *am/is/are/was/ were* then it must be followed **either** by the -*ed* participle of a lexical

Table 5.10 The order of items in complex verb phrases

Auxiliary verb forms		Lexical verb forms 'Position 1'	Position of items	Examples
First (finite) item in the verb phrase	Possible subsequent (non-finite) items in the verb phrase			
'Position 2' am/is/are/was/were		-ed participle	2–1	is followed
'Position 3' am/is/are/was/were	being	-ing participle -ed participle	3–1 3–2–1	is following is being followed
'Position 4' has/have/had	been been been + being	-ed participle -ed participle -ing participle -ed participle	4–1 4–2–1 4–3–1 4–3–2–1	has followed has been followed has been following has been being followed
'Position 5' modal verb, e.g. will/would/can/could/ may/might/shall/should/ must	be be be + being have have + been have + been have + been + being	infinitive -ed participle -ing participle -ed participle -ed participle -ed participle -ing participle -ed participle	5–1 5–2–1 5–3–1 5–3–2–1 5–4–1 5–4–2–1 5–4–3–1 5–4–3–2–1	will follow will be followed will be following will be being followed will have followed will have been followed will have been following will have been being followed

verb, e.g. *was followed,* **or** by the *-ing* participle of a lexical verb, e.g. *was following.*

● If a complex verb phrase with **three** items begins with *am/is/are/was/ were,* then it must be followed by *being* + the *-ed* participle of a lexical verb, e.g. *was being followed.*

● If a complex verb phrase begins with *have, has* or *had* then it must be followed by an *-ed* participle, e.g. *have followed.* If the *-ed* participle following *has/have/had* is *been,* then it is followed **either** by an *-ed* participle, e.g. *have been followed,* **or** by an *-ing* participle, e.g. *has been following.* If the *-ing* participle form is *being,* then it must be followed by an *-ed* participle of a lexical verb, e.g. *has been being followed.*

● If a complex verb phrase begins with a modal verb, then the modal can only be followed by an infinitive, e.g. *can go.*

If the infinitive which follows a modal is *be* then it can be followed **either** by an *-ed* participle, e.g. *can be done,* **or** by an *-ing* participle, e.g. *can be doing.* If the *-ing* participle which is selected to follow **modal** + *be* is *being,* then it must be followed by an *-ed* participle, e.g. *must be being done.*

If the infinitive which follows a modal is *have*, then it must be followed by an *-ed* participle, e.g. *must have finished*. If the *-ed* participle following the modal + *have* is *been*, then it is followed **either** by another *-ed* participle, e.g. *must have been told*, **or** by an *-ing* participle, e.g. *must have been sleeping*.

If the *-ing* participle is *being* then it must be followed by an *-ed* participle, e.g. *must have been being followed*.

These verb phrases that are made up of various sequences of the five positions are usually given names such as:

the perfect	(4 + 1)
the progressive	(3 + 1)
the perfect in the passive voice	(4 + 2 + 1)

Sometimes two lexical verbs can be found together e.g. *stopped working, want to go, likes eating*. These are not like the structures in Table 5.10, but are discussed as part of the grammar of verb complementation in Chapter 7. Learning to use complex verb phrases is typically one of the biggest challenges for learners of English, who produce sentences such as the following:

*Using gesture **is depend** on people's education.*

*The earthquake **was occurred** in Iran.*

*The government **was welcomed** this development.*

*I **have living** here three years.*

*They **can driving** taxi every night.*

The information in Table 5.10 can be used for teaching purposes. However, it is vital that teachers remember that verb phrases with three or more items are not common, and should not be a primary focus of pedagogy. More advanced students can be encouraged to monitor their own use of complex verb phrases to see that they conform to the structures in Table 5.10.

Task 5.6

Consider these verb phrase errors made by learners. Work out what sequences of items should be used to make these sentences correct.

1 He has finish his work.

2 I was biting by a mosquito.

3 We will going to the dance tomorrow.

4 They have help their friends.

5 Are you go with me?

6 Were you being follow?

Text 5.3

Flu shots

Nobody knows how many people in San Diego County get flu shots each year, but health officials are sure there should be more. With the annual flu season looming, hospitals throughout the region have teamed up with the county health department in their first consolidated effort to get the vaccine into more arms. A publicity blitz begins today, and a centralised telephone line has been set up to help people in the county find the most convenient among more than 400 places and times to get the shot. The vaccine is recommended for anyone over 60 and anyone whose disease-fighting ability is weakened by a chronic medical condition. According to national estimates, only about half the elderly and fewer than a third of younger people with chronic diseases in the United States get flu shots each year, although flu, which causes many deaths, can often be prevented by means of a simple vaccination.

Task 5.7

From Text 5.3 list the finite complex verb phrases and mark their structure (2–1, 3–2–1, etc. as in Table 5.10).

Task 5.8

Complete the complex verb phrases in the following sentences using the lexical verb provided.

1 It can _____ that they were aware of what had happened. (*show* 5–2–1)

2 In some places, people _____ all their crops. (*lose* 4–1)

3 The car he _____ is not his. (*drive* 3–1)

4 What surprised me were the number of people who said that they _____ by wasps. (*sting* 4–2–1)

5 There are many things which _____.
(*improve* 5–2–1)

6 I heard that the water level _____.
(*check* 3–2–1)

7 The distance between Earth and the moon _____.
(*calculated* 4–2–1)

8 You _____ not _____ what will happen. (*predict* 5–1)

9 Something _____ about the potholes in our street. (*do* 5–2–1)

Discussion topic

Names such as 'the present perfect progressive' are sometimes given to the various verb forms. What are the names given to the 15 verb phrase examples in Table 5.10?

5.3 Non-finite verb forms and verb phrases

In Table 5.9, three non-finite verb forms are listed. These are verb forms which do not take tense.

1 infinitive (or non-finite stem)

2 *-ing* participle (or stem + *-ing*)

3 *-ed* participle (or non-finite stem + *-ed*)

5.3.1 The infinitive (or non-finite stem)

Stem forms of English verbs account for over 40 per cent of verb uses, and we have already seen that these stem forms can be finite or non-finite, as the following examples using the stem form *drink* show:

I **drink** two cups of coffee a day.	(finite use)
Sam **drinks** two cups of coffee a day.	(finite use)
I like to **drink** five cups of tea a day.	(infinitive use)
Sam likes to **drink** a couple of cups of tea a day.	(infinitive use)
I saw him **drink** several cups of tea.	(infinitive use)

Non-finite stems are usually called **infinitives**. They make up about 20 per cent of verb forms used in written English.

The infinitive has two forms:

i	non-finite stem	(*drink*)
ii	*to* + non-finite stem	(*to drink*)

These forms have several functions. One important function is to join 'propositions' or 'ideas', e.g. *Sue asked me to leave the room* can be thought of as having two underlying sentences:

i *Sue asked me something.*

ii *I leave the room.*

In *Sue asked me to leave the room*, the *to* of the infinitive (*to leave*) acts as if it carries or replaces the subject and the tense of *leave*. Part of learners' difficulty is caused by the fact that the subject and tense may not be explicit or clear with non-finite verbs. English complex sentences in particular tend to have many more infinitives than shorter simple sentences such as those used by children. Understanding how to use the differences between finite forms and infinitives is usually difficult for students to learn. The difficulty may lead to the production of stem + -s forms where they are not needed (e.g. *I swims every day*), the omission of stem + -s forms where they are needed (e.g. *He swim every day*), or to the omission of *to* when it is needed (e.g *I like eat chocolate*).

Typical errors:

I want him repair it by Friday.

She made the class to stay in late.

Sam want to goes.

Sad movies make him cries.

He can't plays tennis.

Sue want leave soon.

In addition to problems arising from confusing finite stem forms with infinitives, learners' difficulties can arise from not being sure about the subjects of infinitives.

Sam asked to **leave** the meeting.	(who leaves?)
Sam asked me to **leave** the meeting.	(who leaves?)
Sue asked her sister to **cut** some firewood.	(who cuts the wood?)
Sue promised her sister to **cut** some firewood.	(who cuts the wood?)

Text 5.4

An ageing population

Life expectancy in Britain has increased dramatically in the last century. Men and women born between 1910 and 1912 could expect to live an average 53 years. Those born between 1987 and 1988 can expect to live an additional 20 years. Life expectancy at birth is now an average 72 years for males and 78 years for females, but many people can be expected to live much longer. It is anticipated that life expectancy at birth will rise by 2–3 years over the next 40 years and possibly increase further. Increases in the elderly population, in both absolute and proportionate terms, have resulted from long-term downward trends in the birth rate coinciding with decreased mortality at all ages. The elderly population is expected to continue growing, in the foreseeable future, but at a slower rate than in the recent past. However, by 2031 the number of people aged at least 65 will have reached over 12 million, a rise of 38 per cent since 1991. Between 1981 and the turn of the century the proportion of the population aged over 65 remained fairly steady at 15–16 per cent. Thereafter, the ageing of the post-war baby boom generation becomes apparent, and by 2031 over one-fifth of the population is expected to be over 65.

Task 5.9

a Underline or highlight all the infinitives in Text 5.4.

b Note what proportion of the infinitives are:

  i non-finite stem

  ii *to* + non-finite stem

5.3.1.1 Structures, functions and distribution of infinitives

Table 5.11 shows that infinitives occur most often (about 75 per cent of the time) after a modal verb or after another lexical verb. George (1963) based his analysis on a written corpus of about half a million words of British English. It should be noted that although the infinitive without *to* was more frequent than the infinitive with *to* in George's study, both forms are used a lot.

Table 5.11   Uses of infinitives (adapted from George, 1963)

	% of infinitive uses	
A Infinitives without *to*		
i Imperatives	12	
Stop. Don't *listen* to him.		
ii After a modal verb	45	
You should *go.* We can't *do* it.		
iii After a noun or pronoun	1	
I heard them *go.*		58
B Infinitive with *to*		
i After a verb (+ noun)	29	
She wants *to leave.* He wants me *to go.*		
ii After a noun	6	
your refusal *to help* a place *to live*		
iii After an adjective	5	
He's easy *to please.* She's certain *to know.*		
iv Others, e.g.	2	
To refuse would offend them. I don't know what *to do.*		42
		100

In Table 5.11, B(iii), the adjective + *to* + stem, occurs as the complement in the SVC pattern, and accounts for about 5 per cent of infinitive uses. We can say: *The child was **brave to do that**, but not **The brave to do that child was . . .* nor **The brave child to do that was. . . .* Even though this structure is not frequent, it is quite complex, having a number of sub-groups:

1 Adjectives which behave like *kind*

> You are *kind to say* that.
>
> It is *kind* of you *to say* that.
>
> How *kind* of you *to say* that.

Other adjectives which are like this are: *absurd, brave, clever, cruel, good, honest, naughty, nice, polite, right, rude, silly, stupid, thoughtful, thoughtless, wicked, wise, wrong.*

2 Adjectives which behave like *sorry*, e.g.

> I was *sorry to hear* that.

Other adjectives like this, which express emotion or feeling, are: *amazed, delighted, pleased, disappointed, shocked, surprised, horrified, excited, anxious, impatient, happy, content, afraid, eager, glad.*

3 Adjectives which behave like *certain*, e.g.

> I am *certain to need* help.

Other adjectives like this are: *ready, sure, unfit, fit, slow, prompt, willing, quick, bound, likely, liable, lucky, able, unable, fortunate, first, last, apt.*

5.3.1.2 Meanings of *to* + infinitive

Because infinitives are not marked for tense or person, listeners or readers have to work out some of the grammatical meaning from context. Infinitives can express several different grammatical meanings, e.g.

> He took out a pen *to write* down my address.
> = so that he could write down my address (the infinitive here expresses purpose)
>
> Before anything could be done *to warn* her, she was hit by the train.
> = Before anything could be done *which would warn her.*
> (The construction containing the infinitive *to warn* is interpreted as if it were a relative clause.)
>
> Seeming not *to need* help, Harry got back into the car.
> = Because it seemed that Harry did not need help. . . .

Constructions which include infinitives sometimes have a formulaic quality, e.g.

I want to go.

I'm going to ring.

She seems to like going out.

I'm sorry to hear about your mother.

I'm pleased to be able to help.

etc.

Task 5.10

Make a list of ten common formulaic expressions like *I want to . . .* , *I've got to . . .* , which contain infinitives.

Task 5.11

Write five sentences with different verbs which have the pattern **verb + *to* + infinitive**.

Task 5.12

Write five sentences with different verbs which have the pattern **verb + noun + *to* + infinitive**.

5.3.1.3 Learning to use infinitives

The high frequency of infinitives and the finite stem, which have the same form, create a learning and teaching problem. It is necessary for learners to distinguish between two items of equal frequency, of the same form, but with different behaviour in different contexts. Learners need to distinguish between the finite stem and the non-finite stem for production and comprehension. For production, learners need to learn: *They want to go*, *He wants to go*, but not **He want to goes . . .* or **He wants to going*.

For comprehension, learners need to be aware that if a stem form is finite it conveys information through its tense, e.g. habitual actions. An infinitive with the same form as the finite stem may be associated with present, future, past, or no time at all, e.g. *They persuaded her to go. Go* here may mean that *she went* (a past event) or it may refer to the present or future.

Learners have to get enough practice in comprehension and production for verb form use to become largely automatic. Until it does so, in some cases through learning collocations and formulaic expressions, many learners will have difficulty avoiding errors. Thus teachers should encourage listening and reading activities which provide the massive exposure to input which helps learners consolidate the explicit rules they have been taught about verb form use.

5.3.2 *-ing* participles (or stem + *-ing*)

The *-ing* participle (e.g. *writing, eating, seeing*) is sometimes called the **present participle**, but this can be a misleading term because, in a sentence such as *I saw him riding his bike*, the time reference is past, not present. **Stem + -ing** forms make up about 10 per cent of all verb forms. There are many uses and functions of **stem + -ing** in a wide range of constructions. These can be sources of error for learners of English, e.g.

1 **He is knowing anything you are wanting to ask.*
2 **According to my situation, it would be more interested if they start do their work individually by write down their ideas.*
3 **Incomplete pictures are needed to complete after describe each item.*

One cause of learners' difficulties is that **-ing participles** are sometimes used as nouns or adjectives. The major uses identified in a corpus-based study by George (1963) are shown in Table 5.12.

Task 5.13

Which categories of Table 5.12 do the *-ing* forms in the following sentences belong to?

1 These statistics are alarming.
2 Sue is reading *Hamlet*. Don't disturb her.
3 I like reading.
4 The pleasures of reading are well known.
5 I saw her reading *Hamlet*.
6 While reading I went to sleep.
7 The man reading in the bath dropped his book.
8 A reading course is available for $20.
9 I started reading *Oliver Twist* last year but I lost interest.
10 Reading is one of life's many pleasures.

Table 5.12 Main uses of -ing participles (adapted from George, 1963)

		% of stem + -ing forms
1	**Adjective** a *floating* island These pictures are *interesting*.	22.1
2	**Verb (+ noun) + -ing participle** I saw her *leaving*. I like *eating*.	17.6
3	**Noun** You have forgotten your *knitting*. the cost of *living*	16.6
4	**Non-finite use** While *eating*, I felt sick.	13.4
5	**Present progressive** What are you *doing*? (now) I'm *writing* a cheque. What are you *doing* tomorrow? (future) She is *seeing* her doctor once a week. (habit)	7.8
6	**Past progressive** They were *talking* when I left. (at the moment) He was always *getting* into trouble. (habitual)	7.0
7	**Verb + preposition + -ing** I hadn't thought of *leaving*.	3.8
8	**All other progressives**, e.g. He had been *working*. (past perfect progressive) She has been *living* here for years. (present perf. prog.)	1.6
9	**All other constructions**, e.g. It's no use *worrying*. *having* been allowed to enter There's someone *waiting*. worried at there *being* no solution	7.4
		100.0

Task 5.14

Look at the positions and functions of the *-ing* forms in Text 5.5 and work out which of the categories in Table 5.12 they should be assigned to.

Text 5.5

Public transport

Statistics show that far more people are riding bicycles these days than driving cars, yet many are put off by the dangers of urban traffic. Cycling has been ignored in transport planning for years. Even today, little effort is made to cater for the growing demand for safe cycling routes. Environmental groups are campaigning for more money and importance to be placed on the needs of cyclists, with a target of doubling cycle use over the next five years. The greatest incentive, however, for reducing car use is to provide an efficient and popular public transport service. In many European cities, and more recently in the USA, it has been accepted that the only efficient and cost-effective way of moving people in and out of cities is by rail. In Britain delays, strikes and overcrowding on trains make this public service an undesirable option. Environmentalists call for priority to be given to providing a frequent, reliable and cheap railway network which will encourage more people to leave their cars at home.

5.3.2.1 Learning to use -*ing* participles

In many English courses, it is typical for -*ing* participle forms to be introduced to learners as forms associated with progressive aspect. However, as Table 5.12 shows, a frequent use of -*ing* participle forms is as adjectives. Some teachers therefore introduce -*ing* participle forms **first** as adjectives in noun phrases. Most ordinary adjectives can be used predicatively (i.e. after the verb *be*). At a later stage, the first introduction to progressives can be the predicative use of -*ing* participle forms, which learners have already encountered as adjectives in noun groups, e.g.

She suffered increasing pain.   *The pain is increasing.*

The **verb (+ noun) + -*ing* participle** construction in Table 5.12 involves complex constructions with two verbs. The first verb is usually a finite verb and the second has the -*ing* participle form. The verbs which take an -*ing* form after them are best learned as part of the learning of verb complements (see Chapter 7). Some of these verbs also take *to* + infinitive complements with the same meaning, e.g.

I like		*I like*	
I began	*to eat.*	*I began*	*eating.*
I will start		*I will start*	

Where a verb can have either *to* + infinitive or an -*ing* participle after it, it is probably worth establishing **one** pattern firmly with each verb before introducing the second pattern.

In some cases the meaning is different. Compare these examples:

She stopped to do it.   *She stopped doing it.*

We remembered to do it.   *We remembered doing it.*

Many verbs occur with **to** + **infinitive** after them and not **stem** + **-ing**, e.g.

I hope to go there.   **I hope going there.*

I want to go there.   **I want going there.*

I wished to go there.   **I wished going there.*

The use of an *-ing* participle as a noun does not normally cause problems for learners (e.g. *Swimming is good for you*). Some of the other *-ing* participle uses are like nouns in some ways but like verbs in other ways. Some of these are rather difficult and will usually come later in an English course, e.g.

I don't like *gardening.*

I don't like you/your *smoking* here.

I remember *leaving* it here.

Don't rely on *receiving* them this week.

She was fond of *going* to concerts.

-ing participles in non-finite clauses

While eating I felt sick includes the non-finite clause *while eating.*

Such uses are quite frequent items but they are probably harder to understand than complete clauses, e.g. *while I was eating.* . . . The teaching of **stem** + **-ing** in non-finite clauses is best left until advanced levels.

5.3.3 *-ed* participles (non-finite stem + *-ed*)

The *-ed* **participle** is sometimes called the **past participle**, but this can be a misleading term because the time reference is not necessarily past (e.g. *The job will be **finished** soon*). About 20 per cent of verb forms are the *-ed* participle. They are thus about as frequent as finite stems and infinitives. For learners of English, the *-ed* participle can cause major problems for comprehension because it has the same form as **finite stem** + **-ed** (past tense) and the verb *be* is frequently omitted if the passive voice form is part of a reduced relative clause (see Chapter 7).

Compare:

1 The cyclist *injured* his back.

2 The cyclist *injured* by the rock fall later died.

In Sentence 1 *injured* is **finite stem** + **-ed** (past tense). Although in Sentence 2 *injured* is **non-finite stem** + **-ed**, and is a reduced form of the relative clause *who was injured*, it is easy for learners of English to start interpreting the sentence by thinking that the cyclist injured someone or something. The *-ed* participle is also used as part of perfect aspect (e.g. *He has finished the job*) (see 5.4.2) and as part of the passive voice (see 5.4.3).

Typical errors in using *-ed* participles:

1 **I am very interesting in chess.*

2 **The output can be vary.*

3 **It would be interested that one from each group reads aloud what they have written.*

4 **Make each group do a presentation which is base on their report.*

5 **Twenty witnesses had to be interviewed, many of whom were shaken.*

The main constructions in which the *-ed* participle occurs are shown in Table 5.13.

When the *-ed* participle is a participle of occurrence, the focus is usually on the action of the verb, and the agent *by*-phrase is often omitted.

He was injured (by an explosion) last Friday.

She was given $2,000 (by the Council).

Table 5.13 Main uses of *-ed* participles (adapted from George, 1963)

		% of non-finite stem + *-ed*
1	**As a participle of occurrence** (passive voice) He was *injured* by falling debris. The letter was *opened*. The letter *opened* by mistake was for you. We weren't *allowed* to leave. They were *taught* Latin at school.	41.6
2	**As a participle of state used predicatively** I was *delighted* to hear it. We found our friends *excited* about it.	16.7
3	**Perfect aspect** He *has finished* his work. They *had gone* home.	27.0
4	**As an attributive adjective** the yellow *varnished* walls a *determined* person	11.7
5	**In a non-finite clause** Her bag *clutched* under her arm, Anna rose to speak. She stopped, her eyes *fixed* on the animal.	3.0
		100.0

Reduced relative clauses are discussed in Chapter 7. Sentences such as *The letter (which was) opened by mistake was for you* occur frequently, and use *-ed* participles of occurrence.

The use of *-ed* participles as **participles of state** resembles predicative adjective use, and is not as frequent as their use as participles of occurrence. Participles of state also resemble adjectives in that they can usually take *very* before them (whereas participles of occurrence cannot), e.g.

-ed participle	adjective	
We are (very) *pleased*	(happy)	that . . .
We are (very) *satisfied*	(happy)	with . . .
We are (very) *depressed*	(sad)	about . . .
We are (very) *tired*	(weary)	of . . .

The use of the *-ed* participle for expressing perfect aspect is discussed in Section 5.4.2 of this chapter. The use of *-ed* participles in non-finite clauses is learned at more advanced levels of the acquisition process and is described in Chapter 7.

Task 5.15

Identify and list the *-ed* **participle** forms in Text 5.6. Put a number (1–5) beside each participle to show which of the categories from Table 5.13 is being used.

Text 5.6

Population growth

An independent report prepared for the UN's World Health Organization (WHO) claims that environmental destruction resulting from over-population has killed millions of people every year, largely as a result of the contamination of water, soil and air. The report says that unless population growth can be drastically reduced, the resources needed to support the human race will be overwhelmed. The birth rate will only be cut, however, if the health prospects of poor families are improved. At present, 3.2 million children die every year from diarrhoeal diseases associated with polluted water supplies, a further 2 million die from malaria, while hundreds of millions are infested with intestinal parasites. Respiratory and other complaints triggered by air pollution affect hundreds of millions in both rich and poor countries, the report adds. It argues that major efforts to improve the health and education of poor people, coupled with family planning programmes, are necessary to reduce fertility rates and thus population size.

5.4 Verb phrase functions

In addition to carrying the meaning of lexical verbs, verb phrases express several kinds of grammatical meaning. We have already considered one of these, the basic distinction between finite and non-finite verb phrases. Other parts of the meaning of verb phrases are associated with **tense**, **aspect**, **voice** and **modality** (or **mood**). It is common for all these grammatical forms or processes to be loosely referred to by teachers and learners as **tenses**. However, some of the difficulties in learning and teaching verb form use come from not recognising that verb forms express contrasts of meaning associated with **tense, aspect, voice** and **mood**.

5.4.1 Tense

English has two tenses: **present** and **past**. That is, verbs have different forms or inflections for present and past. The verb forms are called **simple** when they are the only verb in a verb phrase, and **complex** when there is more than one word in the verb phrase. The tense of the finite verb determines whether the complex form is 'present' or 'past'.

Simple verb phrases:

This *is* enough.	(simple present)
Max *cleans* his car every Saturday.	(simple present)
The weather *was* terrible last year.	(simple past)
Sue *cleaned* her car last weekend.	(simple past)

Complex verb phrases:

e.g. *is talking, are talking, am talking, has moved, has been moved, has been moving, is moved* (complex present)

e.g. *was talking, were talking, had moved, had been moved, had been moving, was moved* (complex past)

The only inflection for marking present tense is the third person singular suffix (*-s*) on the verb, e.g. *I like chocolate, She likes chocolate.* Past tense regular verbs have an *-ed* suffix, e.g. *He **wanted** some chocolate.*

The terms 'simple present' and 'simple past' refer to the form of the verb, not its meaning. These tense **forms** can have several **meanings**. While the present tense forms typically refer to **present time**, and the past tense forms typically refer to **past time**, they do not always do so. For example, in conversation, the simple present is sometimes used to refer to past time (historic present tense use) – *We met this man, and he asks where we are going. . . .*

Past tense is frequently used to report 'direct' speech, e.g.

'I'm studying Spanish in the evenings.'

Harry said he was studying Spanish in the evenings.

Table 5.14 Uses of simple present

		% of simple present uses
Present actual	e.g. *I'm hungry.*	59
Neutral (no time reference)	*I like Wellington.*	31
Habitual or repeated states or events	*I leave for work at 8 a.m.*	6
Others (including future reference)		4
		100

Table 5.15 Uses of simple past

		% of simple past uses
Past actual	e.g. *I got wet last night.*	31
Neutral	*I liked my schooldays.*	6
Habitual past	*For years I went hiking every summer.*	5
Narrative past	*He opened the door and walked out.*	58
		100

In both spoken and written English, the simple present and the simple past are by far the most frequently used verb forms. George (1963) found that simple present and simple past together accounted for about half of the verb forms used. A substantial number of these occurrences are of the verb *be* (*am, is, are, was, were*). Each of these two verb tenses (the simple present and the simple past) has different uses or functions, as Tables 5.14 and 5.15 show.

Learners of English are sometimes taught that the simple present and simple past are mainly used for expressing habit. Tables 5.14 and 5.15 show clearly that this is not the case. The main functions of the simple present and simple past in written English are associated with different kinds of writing. The simple present is used especially for **description**. The simple past is used especially for **narrative** or **reporting**.

Studies of verb form use carried out on both British and American English since the 1960s have repeatedly found that about 80 per cent of finite verb forms in spoken and written texts come from simple present and simple past tense use, whereas only about 10 per cent of verb form use is derived from the use of perfect and progressive aspect, with all other verb forms contributing the remaining 10 per cent (see Kennedy, 1998: 126).

Discussion activity

Underline the finite verbs in Text 5.7. How is the use of present or past tense related to the function of the text?

Text 5.7

Caffeine

The world's fondness for caffeine gets greater every year. Huge amounts are consumed all over the world. The discovery and use of caffeine-containing plants is associated with various legends and myths about the discovery of tea and coffee. The discovery of tea is attributed to the Chinese emperor Shen Nung. According to legend, in 2737 BC, one evening the emperor was boiling water in an open kettle over a campfire built from the branches of a nearby shrub. Some scorched leaves from these branches swirled up in the column of hot air and fell back into the water. Rather than discarding the contaminated water, the emperor tasted it and was intrigued by the astringent taste and refreshing aroma. Further experimentation with more leaves of the same tree convinced Shen Nung of the value of the plant as a health-giving medicine. Over the centuries, the use of tea expanded from its initial role as a medicinal herb to that of a ubiquitous social beverage.

The discovery of coffee has a different origin. In one of the common legends about coffee, a sharp-eyed Arabian goatherd named Kaldi noticed his goats munching the bright red, cherry-like fruit of a shrub native to north-eastern Africa. Soon after the goats ate the berries, they began prancing around with unusual gusto. Kaldi tried the berries himself and was so refreshed and invigorated that he danced along with his goats. This frolicsome behaviour was noticed by a monk who was passing by on his way from Mecca. Impressed, the monk asked Kaldi the secret of his energy. Kaldi showed him the berries. The monk was delighted to find that he could now pray longer and with more attention. He spread the word to his fellow monks, who experimented with other ways to consume the berries. Eventually, people found that roasting the seeds, grinding them up, and soaking them in hot water produced a beverage that was tasty and gave a greater kick than could be achieved by merely chewing the caffeine-containing fruit and seeds.

5.4.1.1 Expressing future time

There is no formally marked future tense in English, although some teachers tell their learners that *will* and *shall* + infinitive are the future tense, e.g. I **will ring** *you tomorrow*. *Will* and *shall* do not always refer to the future. They both have several other meanings and functions, e.g. *I assume you will already know about this.*

Many other modal verbs besides *will* and *shall* refer to the future. This is usually because they refer to things which have not yet happened, but which may happen (at some future time), e.g.

You can go soon.

It would be stupid to do that.

We could try to do it.

We might stay at home tomorrow.

You must stop talking.

You should finish this by Friday.

You may not be able to find him.

The major difference between *We will stay at home tomorrow* and *We might stay at home tomorrow* is the amount of certainty we feel about it.

Futurity is also expressed in several other ways. For example, some lexical verbs, adverbials, adjectives and nouns also imply a future activity or state.

We *decided to* go.

I *want to* try it.

I *hope to* meet him there.

At the *forthcoming* election, the restriction on advertising applies.

They *are likely to* be an important factor in our lives.

In the future we ought to try to spend less.

Future time is, of course, also expressed through context, and 'knowledge of the world', e.g. *To get to the airport, take the train* (said to a person planning to take a plane from London Airport).

Quirk et al. (1985: 217) suggested that the order of frequency for expressing future time with verb forms is as follows:

1 *will, shall* or *'ll* + infinitive

2 Simple present

3 *be going to* + infinitive

4 Present progressive

Will, shall, 'll + infinitive account for about 40 per cent of verb form use for referring to future time, the simple present also accounts for about 40 per cent, *be going to* + infinitive and the present progressive account for 10 per cent, and all other verb forms account for the remaining 10 per cent.

5.4.1.2 Learning to use tenses

To a considerable extent, time relationships are primarily marked in English and most languages through context and adverbials. Tense changes to the verb 'agree with' the adverbial or contextual marking. Many textbooks use single sentences to show tense use, but this is not a good idea. It is context in text that determines tense use, and learners need to be shown this association. Tense use may show a change in function from an account of **a particular observed example** (in the past tense) to **a general rule or principle** (in the present tense). It can be useful to get learners to mark the place in a text where tense change shows a change in function.

Stories (narratives) are typically set in the past. However, novels and children's stories often contain a lot of direct speech. In children's stories and readers, the actual narrative in the past tense may be only about 50 per cent of the total. All the rest is direct speech. Direct speech may refer to past, present or future time, so that there is a considerable mixture of verb forms. For this reason, stories and novels with a lot of direct speech may not provide the best model for a consistent use of tenses. Different topics tend to 'invite' the use of present or past tense. To help give learners practice focusing on a particular use of a tense in writing exercises, it is important to select topics with care. Topics which tend to be associated with use of the simple present include generalised description (e.g. how a car engine works, what I like to do on Sundays, the ozone layer); opinion (e.g. a book review); instruction and procedures (e.g. how to make muesli, what to do in case of fire).

Topics which tend to be associated with the use of the simple past include narrative (e.g. what I did in the holidays, my most dangerous experience, a fishing trip); historical description (e.g. primary education in the 1930s, sixteenth-century English theatre, food preferences 100 years ago); reports (e.g. minutes of a meeting, report of a press conference).

5.4.2 Aspect

In addition to marking verbs for tense (present or past), English marks verbs for **aspect**. Aspect is a grammatical term for describing how the speaker or writer regards an action or state or process from the point of view of the passing of time.

English verb forms can mark **two aspects**, **perfect aspect** and **progressive aspect**. Perfect aspect is formed by the auxiliary verb *have* + *-ed* **participle**, e.g. *I have finished my latest painting*. Progressive aspect is formed by the auxiliary verb *be* + *-ing* **participle**, e.g. *He is waiting for you outside*.

Perfect aspect is mainly a way of associating with the verb whether the state or action is or was complete ('perfected') or not at the present moment or at a particular point in the past.

Progressive aspect is a way of associating with the verb whether the state or action is or was continuing. Sometimes verbs express both perfect and progressive aspect (see 4 and 8 below).

Most verbs can have the following active (non-modal) structures:

1 Present tense with non-perfect, non-progressive aspect
   (Zoë washes her car on Fridays.)

2 Present tense with perfect, non-progressive aspect
   (Zoë has washed her car.)

3 Present tense with non-perfect, progressive aspect
   (Zoë is washing her car.)

4 Present tense with perfect and progressive aspect
   (Zoë has been washing her car.)

5 Past tense with non-perfect, non-progressive aspect
(Zoë washed her car last weekend.)

6 Past tense with perfect, non-progressive aspect
(Zoë had washed her car when she sold it.)

7 Past tense with non-perfect, progressive aspect
(Zoë was washing her car when I saw her.)

8 Past tense with perfect and progressive aspect
(Zoë had been washing her car for hours when I saw her.)

The examples given above for each of these eight structures are in the active voice. Each of them can, of course, also have a passive voice version, e.g. (1) *Zoë's car **is washed** on Fridays*; (3) *Zoë's car **is being washed***; (6) *Zoë's car **had been washed** when it was sold*, etc.

About 90 per cent of verbs in spoken or written English are not marked for aspect. About 5 per cent of verbs are marked for perfect aspect, with slightly higher frequency of use in spoken English. Progressive aspect is marked in about 5 per cent of verbs. We will now consider perfect and progressive aspect more closely.

5.4.2.1 Perfect aspect

Perfect aspect is not frequent in English, and some of the possible forms are very rare indeed. Analysis of written corpora suggests that in every 100 verb forms about five consist of ***has**, **have** or **had** + -**ed** participle*, e.g. *She has told me already.*

Structures containing a **modal verb** + ***have** + -**ed** participle* (e.g. *You should have told me*) typically occur less than once in every 200 verb forms. Structures containing ***has**, **have** or **had** + **been** + -**ing** participle* occur only once in about 500 verb forms, e.g. *I **have been living** here for over a year.*

While verbs marked for perfect aspect are not very frequent, they can have many uses, meanings or functions. The most frequent use of perfect verb forms is typically the past perfect in narrative texts to show that the order of events has changed. Past perfect aspect places an event or state chronologically before another and indicates the current relevance of that information. The order of mention in the text and the actual order of occurrence are often not the same, e.g.

> *Suda's parents gave her a camera for her birthday. The next day at school Suda told her friends about her present. She wanted to show the new camera to her friend. She opened her bag to get the camera, but she couldn't find it. She **had left** it at home.*

Another important use of perfect aspect is to indicate a focus on result (up to the present or up to a point in the past). Table 5.16 summarises the distribution of uses of perfect aspect in a large-scale verb-form frequency count by George (1963).

Table 5.16   Most frequent uses of perfect aspect forms (based on George, 1963)

		% of perfect aspect forms
1	In past narrative *Before I could move he* **had reached** *the door.*	28
2	Present result *She* **has bought** *a new car.*	23
3	Result at a time in the past *As a result of his accident he* **had bought** *a new car.*	9
4	Continuity *I* **have lived** *here since 1970.*	6
5	Experience *I* **have** *never* **tasted** *caviar.*	6
6	Continuity *I* **had lived** *there since 1970.*	4
7	Non-fulfilment after *could, might,* etc. *No one* **could have expected** *that.*	4
8	Experience *I* **had** *never* **tasted** *caviar before then.*	4
9	Non-fulfilment after *would* *I* **would have gone** *if I had known.*	2
10	Non-fulfilment (perfect infinitive) *You were* **to have seen** *him (but didn't).*	2
11	In hypothetical conditional clauses *If we* **had gone**, *we would have seen her.*	2
12	Past perfect progressive *I learned that he* **had been working** *on it for years.*	2
13	Present perfect progressive *He* **has been seeing** *her every Friday.*	1
14	All others, e.g. *You* **will have heard** *of this.*	7
	Total	100

Text 5.8

Feeding modern cities

Since the 1940s, food in Britain has undergone a remarkable revolution – new foods, new processes, new substitutes for food, new markets, new means of transportation have become available. With it has come greater variety and choice, as well as convenience and speed of preparation. And, like any other revolution, there have been advantages and disadvantages for the unsuspecting and often vulnerable consumer. Knowledge of organic chemistry was much less before the Second World War and the subsequent introduction of chemical nitrates, pesticides and hormones to promote intensive farming of both land and livestock has since then led to immense environmental difficulties. Most people today live in towns or cities and hence rarely buy food that is fresh from the farm. Most of it is preserved in some way; it is transported and various methods are employed to change and enhance its appearance; it may be prepared or pre-cooked for convenience and finally packaged for maximum appeal. Some of these methods are extremely useful. They ensure we have nutritious and appealing food all year round. Others are superfluous and, while enhancing the appeal of food, may lessen its nutritional value and increase its price. They may even introduce elements into the food which are detrimental to health or pollute the environment.

Task 5.16

In Text 5.8, identify the verb phrases which have perfect aspect.

Task 5.17

The following sentences contain perfect aspect verb phrases. Identify these and classify them into the following categories:

a Present perfect (describes a recent past event. It often goes with adverbs such as *yet, not, already, recently*) and resultative present or past perfect

b Present or past perfect progressive (describes something which continues right up to the time of speaking – it usually goes with *for* or *since*)

c Present or past perfect of experience (it often goes with an adverb of frequency, such as *ever, never, once, usually, several times, often, rarely, always*)

Also consider whether you could replace the perfect aspect verb forms with simple past or simple present. If you could replace the perfect, label it **optional**. If you cannot replace it, label it **obligatory**.

1 The largest balloon I have ever seen rose slowly into the still air.

2 The safety regulations remind the passengers to stay in their places until the balloon has landed.

3 The same thing has been happening every morning since we arrived in the district.

4 The animals on the farm were, as I have already mentioned, quite a sight.

5 It was the worst drink I have ever tasted.

6 Since he was elected President many of the claims which were made about him have been shown to be true.

7 I have taken out a year's subscription to the *Evening Post*.

Discussion topic

Check for yourself (or your learners) that you understand that a notion of non-fulfilment can be implied in some of the following perfect aspect verb phrases.

1 They should have asked her (but they didn't).

2 She could have stayed.

3 He ought to have said he was sorry.

4 You shouldn't have gone to all that trouble (but you did).

5 He couldn't have avoided going there.

6 She needn't have stopped to help them.

7 He must have known she needed help.

8 They might have been there when it happened.

9 She wouldn't have asked them for help if she hadn't needed it.

10 If he had gone, he would have seen her.

5.4.2.1.1 Learning the use of perfect aspect

As we have seen, the present and past perfect verb forms are not nearly as frequent as simple present or simple past. However, perfect aspect is a source of error for learners of English, as the following examples show:

Yesterday, we have finished this chapter.

I am living here since three weeks.

You should asked them last night.

I would asked them but I wasn't there.

He would had do it again but no time.

The uses of present perfect (*have lived*) and present perfect progressive (*have been living*) described in Table 5.16 are often optional and rarely obligatory. Teachers should concentrate initially on one obligatory use for productive purposes *for* or *since* + something going on right up to the moment of speaking, e.g.

I have been waiting *for* the last 30 minutes.

I have been waiting *since* ten o'clock.

Other uses can often be expressed by the simple present or the simple past, e.g.

Have you heard about it?	=	*Did you hear about it?*
I have never tasted octopus.	=	*I never tasted octopus.*
I have rarely seen her smile.	=	*I rarely see her smile.*
Wait until you have been told.	=	*Wait until you are told.*

The past perfect should also initially be practised only in obligatory uses. Although in narratives the past perfect sometimes occurs with time conjunctions such as *when* or *before* (e.g. *When I got to the station, the train **had already left***), the most frequent obligatory use of the past perfect is when there is no time expression in the text to show the sequence of events.

Exercise types for learning the use of the past perfect need to focus on the sequencing of events. For example, students can be asked to read the following sentences aloud in the order they are written. This builds up a story. The final sentence contains a *had* + stem + *-ed* form. It tells an event which happened earlier in the sequence of events.

Jane	opened the door.
She	looked outside.
She	climbed up the steps at the end of the path.
She	opened the gate.
She	walked to a local shop.
She	asked for a newspaper.
She	looked for her purse, but couldn't find it.
She	had left her house without any money.

5.4.2.2 Progressive aspect

Progressive aspect is marked on verbs to indicate that an event or action is in progress. The **present progressive** marks actions or events that are currently in progress or will be in progress at some future time, e.g.

This year I *am studying* Roman history.

You *are sitting* in my seat.

She *is leaving* tomorrow on the early flight.

We *are going* to spend a week in Paris next spring.

The **past progressive** marks events or actions that were in progress at a time in the past, e.g.

She *was living* in New York when I last saw her.

As shown in Table 5.1, certain verbs tend to occur more or less frequently with progressive aspect. Many verbs associated with cognition or communication tend to be rarely used with progressive aspect, e.g. *think, know, want, mean, say*. Other verbs, especially associated with activity, e.g. *talk, play, drive, work*, tend to have a larger proportion of their uses marked for progressive aspect, but there are no simple rules for characterising which semantic groups of verbs are associated with progressive aspect, as Biber et al. (1999: 470) have noted.

From a teaching perspective, it is important to keep in mind that progressive aspect has not been found to be frequent in most verb form frequency counts. For example, the *Brown Corpus* (Francis & Kučera, 1982) of 1 million words of written US English contained only 3.06 per cent of verbs marked for progressive aspect. Progressive aspect tends to be used more frequently than this, however, in conversation.

Learners of English are sometimes introduced to the progressive aspect in sentences like

> Lee is *walking* to the door.
>
> Now he is *opening* the door.

Such English courses suggest that use of the present progressive is for 'now', whereas the simple present is used for 'habit'. Students are given practice with pairs of sentences such as *I am writing **now**. I write **every day**.* Learners can get the idea that the simple present does not refer to 'now' and that the present progressive does not refer to 'habit'. In fact, this is quite incorrect. Corpus analysis suggests that, although habit is typically expressed by the simple present, the present progressive is used with about 10 per cent of verb tokens that express habit. Similarly, past habit is typically expressed by the past progressive or ***would*** + **infinitive** for about 25 per cent of verb tokens that express habit.

5.4.3 Voice

Voice is a grammatical term which refers to whether the focus of a sentence is on the subject or the object. About 90 per cent of sentences with transitive verbs focus on the subject and are said to be **active** voice. The remaining 10 per cent focus on the object and are said to be in the **passive** voice.

The passive voice enables us to focus on the object of a verb by bringing it to the front of the sentence. It is also used when we do not wish to (or cannot) specify the subject, e.g. *Fred broke a cup* is active voice. *A cup was broken* is passive voice.

The passive voice is formed by use of the verb *be* + *-ed* participle of transitive verbs, e.g.

	Active	Passive
simple present	*They call their dog 'Jackson'.*	*Their dog is called 'Jackson'.*
simple past	*They called their dog 'Jackson'.*	*Their dog was called 'Jackson'.*
modal	*Someone will drive you home.*	*You will be driven home.*
present perfect	*They have sold their house.*	*Their house has been sold.*
past perfect	*Someone had stolen my bike.*	*My bike had been stolen.*
present progressive	*They are painting their house.*	*Their house is being painted.*
past progressive	*They were painting their house.*	*Their house was being painted.*
modal perfect	*The officer could have asked you for your passport.*	*You could have been asked for your passport.*

Although passive voice is possible with most transitive verbs, some verbs occur particularly frequently with passive voice use, e.g. *be associated with, be based on, be charged with, be designed to, be arrested, be revealed, be sold.* On the other hand, other transitive verbs are rarely found in the passive, e.g. *like, survive, want.*

As we have seen, the simple present and simple past are overwhelmingly the most frequent verb forms in English. Of verb forms that include the passive voice, the simple present and simple past passive are the most frequent. All other verb phrases which contain the passive are rarely found in representative corpora, except for the present and past perfect passive, which, while not frequent, occur often enough to be worth learning to use.

The structure of the passive voice was mentioned in Section 5.3.3 in connection with the use of **non-finite -ed participles.** Although the active voice is often recommended as being simpler and more stylistically desirable for users of English (and the passive is discouraged by some computer grammar checkers), the passive is used quite a lot in academic, technical, more formal and especially written uses of English. Francis & Kučera (1982) in their analysis of written American English (the 1-million-word *Brown Corpus*) found that about 11 per cent of verb tokens were passive, but that there was considerable variation among genres. It can be seen in Table 5.17 that

Table 5.17   Active and passive predications in the *Brown Corpus* (based on Francis & Kučera, 1982: 554) (percentages)

		%	%
	Genre	Actives	Passives
I	**Informative prose**		
	A. Press: reportage	87.34	12.66
	B. Press: editorial	88.83	11.17
	C. Press: reviews	90.72	9.28
	D. Religion	88.23	11.77
	E. Skills and hobbies	85.75	14.25
	F. Popular lore	87.49	12.51
	G. Belles-lettres	89.43	10.57
	H. Miscellaneous (e.g. government documents)	75.85	24.15
	J. Academic	78.05	21.95
	Mean		14.60
II	**Imaginative prose**		
	K. General fiction	95.21	4.79
	L. Mystery and detective	96.19	3.81
	M. Science fiction	93.40	6.60
	N. Adventure and western	98.41	3.59
	P. Romance and love story	96.68	3.32
	R. Humour	93.13	6.87
	Mean		4.20
	Mean for whole corpus		11.07

all informative genres had a higher proportion of passives than any of the imaginative prose genres.

5.4.3.1 Learning to use the passive voice

The passive voice is sometimes taught as a variation or transformation of the active voice verb forms: *Harry broke a cup* → *A cup was broken by Harry.* However, most passive sentences are not simply alternative stylistic versions of active sentences. They are written as passive sentences for particular reasons, often because the subject of the active sentence (i.e. the agent of the verb) is not important or not known. In this case there is usually no *by* + **agent**, e.g.

> The metal *was heated* to 200°C.
>
> When salt *is added* to water, it dissolves.
>
> A suspect *was arrested* last evening.

About 80 per cent of passive sentences have no *by*-agent explicitly stated.

Further, if students are taught to change an active sentence into a passive one, it may involve several difficult steps which could lead to error, e.g. *A stranger attacked him* → *He was attacked by a stranger.*

> Move the object to the subject position and change the form of the pronouns, e.g. *him* → *he.*
>
> Move the subject to the final position.
>
> Add *by* before the subject.
>
> Add the appropriate form of *be* in the same tense as the finite verb.
>
> Change the finite verb to the *-ed* participle.

Some learners may find it easier to approach passives through the already known SVC construction.

	S	V	C
Beginners	I	am	cold.
	I	am	tired.
Intermediate	It	was	damaged.
	She	was	injured by broken glass.
Advanced	It	is	heated to 200°C under pressure.

Because the active and passive voice involve major word order changes, learners often pay little attention to the grammatical forms, but concentrate on the lexical items and their positions. They may be shown that *rice absorbs water* is roughly similar in meaning to *water is absorbed by rice*, but then they confuse the form and produce sentences such as *water absorbs rice, *rice absorb water, *water is absorb rice, *rice is absorb by water*, etc. (George, 1972: 105).

Another source of difficulty with the passive voice for learners of English is the use of reduced relative clauses which lead learners to interpret the passive non-finite *-ed* participle as if it were the finite past tense in the active voice, e.g.

People injured in an accident should not be moved until a doctor arrives.

Learners may think that *injured* is an active finite verb (*People injured someone...*) instead of a reduced relative clause in the passive voice (*People who are injured...*). (This difficulty is discussed further in Section 7.5.2.)

Task 5.18

In Text 5.9 identify the passive voice verb phrases by underlining or highlighting them. Note which of the passive voice constructions have a *by*-agent.

Text 5.9

Food preservation

The days are over when fruit and vegetables were eaten only in the area and season in which they were harvested, and a few were put aside for home pickling or preserving. Today, most fruits and vegetables are sold every month of the year, if we are willing to pay the price of importing and employing the latest methods of food preservation. Canning, freezing, drying, irradiation and the addition of preservatives, both natural and chemical, are just some of the methods that have been developed by food technologists to ensure availability of food. Each method has its advantages and disadvantages both to health and the preservation of the planet. Firstly, the large-scale transportation of food comes up against environmental difficulties. While it may be very pleasant to eat strawberries all year, it is perhaps worth remembering the energy that is used to transport these luxuries, the extra fungicides and pesticides that have been added to ensure that during the journey they do not deteriorate, and the fact that though the strawberries may appear fresh, they may have been shipped thousands of miles and kept in cold storage for months. Such delays will reduce their food value and result in the loss of vitamins and minerals.

5.4.4 Mood

Mood is a grammatical term which is used to refer to the 'truth condition' (factual or imaginary) meaning of a verb. The usual finite verb form expresses the **indicative mood**, e.g. *He **likes** chocolate; I **liked** chocolate when I was young.* When we imagine something that is not actual, we can use the **subjunctive mood**, e.g. *If I **were** you (but I'm not you) I would stay* at home; *If you* **went** *to the concert tomorrow, you'd enjoy it (but I don't know whether you'll go)*; *I wish I* **were** *going with you (but I'm not going).* Note that while *wish* is followed by the subjunctive, *hope* is not, e.g. *I* **hope** *I am going with you. Hope* takes the indicative mood because it describes an actual (not imaginary) situation. Nowadays many users of English say or write *If I* **was** *you* rather than *If I* **were** *you.*

The subjunctive mood uses the same verb form as the past tense, and this makes it potentially confusing for learners, i.e. *If I were you* refers to the present, not the past, whereas *If I had been you . . .* refers to the past. Where the subjunctive is used, e.g. after *wish* or in *if*-clauses, it tends to occur in formulaic expressions, e.g. *If I were you . . .* ; *I wish I didn't have to. . . .* Fortunately, the subjunctive mood expressed through verb forms is not frequent in English and is used particularly in formal written genres.

Imperative expressions are sometimes called **imperative mood**, e.g. *Leave the room immediately*; *Don't touch it.*

Task 5.19

Write the tense, aspect, voice and mood meanings associated with the following verb phrases.

Verb form	Tense	Aspect	Voice	Mood
1 She watches them.				
2 She watched them.				
3 She is watching them.				
4 She has watched them.				
5 She has been watching them.				
6 They had been watched.				
7 They had been being watched.				
8 (She insists that) he watch them.				
9 It shouldn't have happened.				
10 Don't move your fingers.				

5.5 Distribution of simple and complex verb phrase structures

Joos (1964) carried out a corpus study of verb phrase use in British English. He studied a single work (Bedford's *The Trial of Dr. Adams*), the account of a courtroom trial. He found 8,038 finite verb phrases plus almost 1,100 non-finite. Of 224 types of possible simple and complex finite verb phrases, only 79 occurred in the corpus, and 10 of these occurred only once.

Table 5.18   Order of frequency of simple and complex finite verb phrases
(based on Joos, 1964)

Type	Example	% of finite forms
1	I always *say* no good *comes* of these cases	35.5
2	When the doctor *went* away *did he leave*	26.7
3	the defence *have decided* not to call the doctor	4.0
4	Morphia and heroin *were* commonly *used*	3.6
5	both morphia and heroin *are administered* to people	3.1
6	If there were, I *would take* them and *destroy* them	2.7
7	the answers sound as colourless as one *can make* them	2.6
8	the period when he *was prescribing* for her	2.2
9	*are* you *standing* there and *saying* as a trained nurse	2.2
10	*had* you *made* any inquiries before giving evidence	2.0
11	I *will* certainly *help* you	1.4
12	asks if he *may put* a further question to the witness	1.1
13	And you still say so? I *do*	1.0
14	did the doctor ask you for anything? He *did*	1.0
15	*would* you *have expected* the doses to have a fatal result	1.0
16	you *must believe* me	0.8
17	whether he *might say*	0.8
18	cases where this amount *has been given*	0.8
19	he told me I *should prepare* a codicil	0.7
20	I did not think you *could prove* murder	0.7
21	He *might have given* hyoscine	0.4
22	the only way in which justice *can be done*	0.4
23	you *could have asked* this very helpful person	0.3
		95.0

Table 5.18 shows the 23 that occurred most frequently. Types 1–15 accounted for 90 per cent of the tokens, and Types 1–23 accounted for 95 per cent. The remaining 56 types accounted for just 5 per cent of the tokens. While the distribution of verb forms varies according to register and text, for learners of English it is clear that it is worthwhile, in the initial stages at least, to concentrate on a small number of verb form types.

Table 5.18 lists the most frequent finite verb phrases based on Joos (1964). A frequency count of finite and non-finite uses of verb forms reported in George (1963) analysed the relative frequency of verb forms and functions in written British English. Table 5.19 summarises the most frequent occurrences.

Table 5.19   Order of frequency of verb forms and functions in written English (based on George, 1963)

		% of verb form occurrences
1	simple past narrative	15.6
2	simple present actual	12.0
3	simple past actual	8.3
4	simple present neutral	7.0
5	-ed participle of occurrence	5.9
6	verb to + infinitive	3.8
7	-ed participle of state	3.3
8	-ing participle = adjective in noun groups	2.5
9	-ed participle = adjective in noun groups	2.3
10	past perfect narrative	1.9
11	imperative don't + infinitive	1.7
12	-ed participle + prepositional object	1.5
13	simple past neutral	1.5
14	stem + -ing in free adjuncts	1.5
15	simple past habitual	1.4
16	noun + to + infinitive	1.3
17	present perfect	1.2
18	simple present iterative	1.1
19	verb + -ing participle	1.1
20	verb + to + infinitive	1.0
21	verb + noun/pronoun + to + infinitive	1.0
22	stem + -ing = noun	1.0
23	imperative	1.0
24	noun + preposition + -ing participle	0.9
25	verb + noun/pronoun + -ing participle	0.9
26	will + infinitive	0.8
27	can + infinitive	0.8
28	would + infinitive	0.8
29	present progressive 'now'	0.6
30	-ed participle + to + infinitive	0.6
31	past progressive	0.5
32	to have + to + infinitive	0.5
33	could + infinitive	0.5
34	simple present (future)	0.4
35	must + infinitive	0.4
36	adjective + to + infinitive	0.4
37	all other verb forms	13.0
		100.0

In Table 5.19, the six most frequent items account for over half of all verb form occurrences in the corpus, the most frequent 10 verb forms account for almost 63 per cent of the verb forms, and the most frequent 30 verb forms account for over 83 per cent of the verb forms. It should be clear from Tables 5.18 and 5.19 that in verb form use (as we have found in many other aspects of English grammar) the various items and processes are not used with equal frequency, and this has implications for language teaching. Where learning time is limited, it is usually essential to ensure that high frequency items are not overlooked. Use in the language is typically a reasonably good indication of usefulness.

Discussion topic

Consider how the information in Table 5.19 might influence a curriculum for the teaching of English.

CHAPTER 6

Modification of noun phrases, verb phrases and sentences

This chapter is designed to show how **adjectives, adverbials** and **prepositions** are used, and the difficulties that learners of English are faced with in using them.

Objectives

By the end of this chapter you should be able to:

1 Identify **adjectives**.

2 Explain the **functions of adjectives**.

3 Identify the various **forms of adjectives**.

4 Describe the **positions adjectives are found in**.

5 Explain the functions of **comparative** and **superlative** adjective and adverb forms.

6 Distinguish **adjectives** from **participles**.

7 Identify **adverbs** and **adverbials**.

8 Distinguish **adjectives** from **adverbs**.

9 Describe the main structures that can be used as **adverbials**.

10 Explain the main **semantic functions of adverbials**.

11 Distinguish between **adjuncts, subjuncts, disjuncts** and **conjuncts**.

12 Identify **prepositions**.

13 Explain the main **functions of prepositions** and **prepositional phrases**.

14 Know which **prepositions** are most frequently used.

15 Distinguish between **prepositional verbs** and **phrasal verbs**.

6.1 Adjectives

We have already seen in Chapter 4 that determiners can modify nouns. Nouns can also be modified in other ways as part of noun phrases, e.g.

1 a *successful* athlete

2 an *outstanding* athlete

3 an athlete *from Spain*

4 an athlete *who was successful in the Olympics*

5 an athlete *known all over the world*

These five examples show that nouns can be modified by single words, phrases, or whole clauses. Some modifiers occur before the nouns they modify; others occur after. One of the classes of noun modifiers consists of single words called **adjectives** which associate certain characteristics such as colour, size or shape to nouns, e.g. *a red car*. This section describes the use of adjectives. The modification of nouns by phrases or clauses is described in Chapter 7.

6.1.1 Adjective forms

Some words can be identified as adjectives by their suffixes, such as *-able* (*commendable*), *-ful* (*careful*), *-ish* (*selfish*), *-ous* (*precious*), *-al* (*mental*), *-ic* (*scientific*), *-less* (*hopeless*), *-y* (*crafty*), *-ive* (*attractive*). Many adjectives, however, especially frequent ones, do not seem to have formal clues to identify them, e.g. *clean, unique, fast*. Unlike adjectives in some other languages, English adjectives do not have plural forms.

6.1.2 Adjective types

6.1.2.1 Attributive and predicative adjectives

When adjectives occur before a noun, they are called **attributive adjectives**, e.g. *an **old** car*. When adjectives occur in a predicate as complement of a copular verb, they are said to be used as **predicative adjectives**, e.g. *That car is **old***. While most adjectives can occur with an attributive function before a noun and with a predicative function after the verb *be*, some high frequency adjectives do not occur in both positions, e.g.

the main road　　(*the road is main)

the child is asleep　(*an asleep child)　See also *awake, afraid, alone, alive*.

this is utter rubbish　(*this rubbish is utter)

Although some textbooks have lists of adjectives that do not occur with both attributive and predicative functions, learners of English probably best learn them in context. Adjective use is typically more frequent in written genres than in spoken English, and attributive uses of adjectives are much more frequent than predicative uses. When nouns are modified by determiners, adjectives or other nouns, adjectives always follow determiners and come before nouns functioning like adjectives, e.g.

> *an old country house*
> det adj   noun   noun (headword)

6.1.2.2 Postpositional adjectives

Adjectives can sometimes be found postpositionally, i.e. they follow a noun or pronoun, e.g.

> a house *big* enough for our family
> a person *eager* to please
> a man *known* for his generosity

These constructions may be considered to be reduced relative clauses (e.g. *A house that is big enough for our family*). (See Section 7.4.2.2.)

6.1.2.3 Compounds

Adjective compounds have been identified by Biber et al. (1999: 533) as very productive noun modifiers. They often involve *-ed* or *-ing* participles, and are often hyphenated. The main categories of adjective compounds are:

Adverb + adjective	e.g. *critically ill, highly sensitive*
Adverb + -ed participle	e.g. *carefully planned, widely held, recently elected*
Adverb + -ing participle	e.g. *slow-moving, rapidly expanding*
Adjective + -ed participle	e.g. *ready-made, open-ended*
Adjective + -ing participle	e.g. *free-standing, long-serving*
Noun + adjective	e.g. *smoke-free, life-long*
Noun + -ed participle	e.g. *king-sized, poverty-stricken*
Noun + -ing participle	e.g. *peace-keeping, nerve-wracking*
Adjective + noun	e.g. *full-time, large-scale, long-distance*

Nouns are also used frequently in modern English to modify other nouns. In these **compound nouns** the modifying nouns function like adjectives but are not adjectives, in that they do not have comparative forms and cannot themselves be modified by degree adverbs such as *very*. Examples of compound nouns include the following:

a *killer* asteroid

the *NASA* team

a *motorbike* race

bathroom water supply replacement parts

refrigerator level adjustment screw

6.1.2.4 Stative and dynamic adjectives

There are differences between **stative** and **dynamic** adjectives in their grammatical behaviour. Stative adjectives include the majority of adjectives, e.g. *tall, happy, red, famous*. Stative adjectives do not usually take the **progressive** aspect of the verb or the **imperative**, e.g.

*He's being tall.

*Be tall.

*Don't be tall.

Dynamic adjectives, e.g. *careful, jealous, obstinate, brave*, can occur with progressive aspect or the imperative, e.g.

You're being stupid again.

Don't be shy.

6.1.3 Ordering of adjectives

Some teachers of English think it necessary to give learners practice in arranging the order of adjectives when more than one adjective comes before a noun.

a poor old black cat

*a black old poor cat

a huge old smelly leather-bound encyclopaedia

*a leather-bound old smelly huge encyclopaedia

However, as we saw in Chapter 4, sequences of adjectives are not frequent in English, and it is likely that any ordering of adjectives is based on collocational structures (habitual sequences) rather than on supposedly 'logical' semantic criteria ('shape' before 'colour', etc.).

Task 6.1

In Text 6.1, identify and list the following modifiers of nouns:

a attributive adjectives

b predicative adjectives

c nouns

Text 6.1

Compulsory education

Compulsory state education for all children is a recent phenomenon. In most European countries education for all children dates from the nineteenth century. In England and Wales, the year 1870 was the effective beginning of a state system. They were not the first in Europe, however, to realise that a literate workforce would be needed to meet the complex demands of industry. Provision of elementary schooling was essential for economic reasons. A pool of people who could read and calculate was essential if the world of commerce were to expand. Expenditure on education was not regarded as a means of giving opportunity to the masses. It made economic sense. The Victorian period was one of tremendous economic and social change. The old values that had underpinned Britain when it was an agrarian society were threatened by a new urban poor. The ruling classes, and the traditions that they represented, had no power or influence in the squalid housing estates that grew up near each new factory and mill. To avoid revolution, it was necessary for the largely illiterate workforce to believe that their welfare would be protected by the powerful middle class. This goal could be achieved through expanding educational opportunities.

Task 6.2

Classify these adjectives according to whether they can occur (i) only attributively, (ii) only predicatively, or (iii) both:

sensible, afraid, main, giant, resulting, leading, alone, certain (as in *a certain smile*), *last, annual, scientific, due, awake, unpayable, actual, urgent, overdue, asleep, old* (as in *He's an old friend*)

6.1.4 Adjectives and verb participles

In the following sentence, *fervent* and *sustained* modify the noun *criticism*.

This has aroused the fervent and sustained criticism of the opposing groups.

Fervent is an adjective. The word *sustained* has the form of a verb (*-ed* participle) but behaves as a noun modifier. It is a **participial** adjective which parallels the adjective *fervent* and can be preceded by *very*. *Opposing* has the form of an *-ing* participle. It is used here as a participial adjective which modifies 'groups'. Participial adjectives are used frequently, especially in academic and journalistic written genres. Learners of English often find participial adjectives confusing and sometimes interpret them as verbs. Compare these sentences:

1 *This rule is **amazing**.*	4 *Sue is **amazing** her doctors.*
2 *I was **relieved**.*	5 *I was **relieved** by another teacher.*
(= stopped worrying)	(= replaced)
3 *Grammar is **interesting**.*	6 *This problem is **interesting** all of us.*

In Sentences 1–3, the words in bold type are participial adjectives. In Sentences 4–6, the words in bold type are participles in complex verb phrases.

The confusion between some adjectives and verbs is not surprising because in some languages there is no difference. For example, while English has *The red cloth* or *The cloth is red*, some other languages can say the equivalent of *The cloth reds*, i.e. what is an adjective in English can be a verb in some other languages. This relationship between verbs and adjectives is also sometimes seen in English. Compare:

Her head is sore.	*Her sore head.*
Her head is aching.	*Her aching head.*

Some grammarians have suggested that English attributive adjectives can be derived from predicative adjectives or participles by means of **reduced relative clauses**, e.g.

1 *The animal [The animal was captured by the trap] was frightened.*
2 ⇒ *The animal which was captured by the trap was frightened.*
3 ⇒ *The animal captured by the trap was frightened.*
4 ⇒ *The animal captured was frightened.*
5 ⇒ *The captured animal was frightened.*

Note also that *frightened* can behave as an adjective or a participle. Compare:

*a very **frightened** animal*	(adjective)
*an animal which was **frightened** by the trap*	(participle)

Greenbaum & Quirk (1990) refer to 'verbal force' as helping determine whether to interpret an *-ed* or *-ing* form as an adjective or a participle. It is nevertheless sometimes still difficult to tell the difference between a participial adjective and a participle.

Task 6.3

Identify the participial adjectives in Texts 6.2 and 6.3.

Text 6.2

Change

Most offices, by the very nature of their structure and function, are geared to stability or slowly modified processes. Accelerated change of the kind that computers bring is disrupting and disturbing. This is because people in stable organisations tend to expect a steady continuation of existing arrangements, and because departments unaccustomed to change frequently find they have become too inflexible to assimilate it without increasing stress. Social as well as technical factors are therefore highly relevant for successful adaptation to new techniques and processes.

Text 6.3

Menacing asteroids

In June 2002 an asteroid about 100 m in diameter passed within 120,000 km of the Earth. This was described by experts to have been a 'close shave'. Some scientists have urged their governments to fund special telescopes to detect incoming asteroids. There is growing agreement that about 65 million years ago an asteroid about 8 km in diameter hit the Caribbean. The resulting dust cloud blotted out the sun and changed the climate. Affected species included the dinosaurs, which became extinct. Increasing research in many parts of the world is revealing that devastating asteroid hits have occurred quite often in the past, most recently in Siberia in 1908, when 2,000 sq km of forest were destroyed. Menacing asteroids are thought to number at least 1,000 and there is apparently no known method of protecting the Earth from the possibility of a direct hit.

6.1.5 Adjective complementation (i.e. elaboration of an adjective)

Some adjectives bond with one or more words that follow (e.g. *good at*, *fond of*, *close to*) to produce an extended or complementised use.

There are four ways in which adjectives may be complementised:

1 by a prepositional phrase, e.g.

I'm grateful *for your help.*

They're dependent *on each other.*

I'm tired *of hearing her complaints.*

Many adjectives are characteristically followed by particular prepositions to produce adjectival complements. Some adjectives can be followed by several prepositions which each produce different meanings. These combinations should be learned together as collocations, e.g.

good at	pleased at	happy to	different from
good for	pleased for	happy with	new to
good to	pleased with	happy for	suitable for
good with	pleased about		

2 **by a clause which contains a finite verb**, e.g.

We were sure *that you would ring.*

I'm sorry *that you left early.*

3 **by a non-finite clause which contains a to-infinitive**, e.g.

The food is ready *to eat.*

I was sorry *to hear of your mother's illness.*

4 **by a clause which contains an -*ing* participle**, e.g.

I'm happy *living here.*

She's busy *typing her assignment.*

6.1.6 Comparative and superlative

Many adjectives are 'gradable', which means that they can have comparative and superlative forms and functions. Some take the suffix -*er/-est*. The others are preceded by *more/most, less/least*, e.g.

-er/-est:	strong	stronger	strongest
more/most:	intense	more intense	most intense
less/least	intense	less intense	least intense

Adjectives of three or more syllables usually have *more/most* forms rather than -*er/-est* suffixes.

Gradable adjectives can be modified by degree adverbs, e.g. *very good, terribly helpful*. Many adjectives however are not gradable and do not have comparative or superlative forms or degree modification, e.g. *atomic, nuclear, giant, leading, actual, due, annual, monthly*.

From a learner's point of view it is important that the gradability of the **form** of the adjective (*tall, taller, tallest*) is not confused with the meaning of the comparison. The word *tall* is already semantically comparative. When we say *That person is tall* we mean *tall* when compared with the average person. On the other hand, when we say *Tom is taller than Bill*, we do **not** mean that Tom is necessarily *tall*. Both Tom and Bill could be short people but Tom could nevertheless be taller than Bill. Thus, it is not a good idea to teach *Tom is tall, Mary is taller, Sam is the tallest*. It is simply confusing. (Sam, for example, is also *taller than Mary or Tom*.)

In a small study of 947 comparisons using comparative forms, Quirk et al. (1985: 463) found:

- **Comparatives** are more frequent than **superlatives**.
- Only 25 per cent of comparatives are accompanied by an explicit statement of what they are compared with (e.g. *Mary is taller than Max*).
- *-er* is more frequent than *more* + adjective (because the most frequent adjectives take *-er/-est*).
- *More* + adjective is more frequent than *less* + adjective.
- *-est* is more frequent than *most* + adjective.
- *Most* + adjective is much more frequent than *least* + adjective.
- Comparative adjectives with *-er* have few **types** but many **tokens**:

	-er/-est	more/most	less/least	Total
Types	56	246	42	344
Tokens	553	345	49	947

In other corpora, over 75 per cent of comparatives typically occur in constructions such as *Make the line longer* or *This one is heavier*, without explicit comparison of what they are being compared with using *than*.

6.1.7 Other ways of making comparisons

In addition to learning about **comparatives**, learners of English need to learn about how to make **comparisons**. As well as the use of *-er*, *more* and *less*, we find other linguistic devices are used for making comparisons.

Mitchell (1990) has noted that some adjectives seem to have 'positive' meaning (e.g. *good, wise, confident, high*) whereas others have 'negative' meaning (e.g. *bad, angry, low*), and the interaction of particular adjectives, positive or negative, *more . . .* or *less . . .* , can produce a range of ways of comparing things. Also, words or phrases such as *superior, in comparison with, when compared with* are sometimes used, e.g.

Australian wine is cheaper this year.

Australian wine is less expensive than it was last year.

Australian wine is not as expensive as Californian.

The price of Australian wine isn't as high as Californian.

Sam thinks Californian wine is better.

Californian wine is more expensive at our supermarket.

Sue thinks Australian wine is superior to Californian.

In comparison with other wines, Chilean wine is good value.

> **Discussion topic**
>
> Identify all examples of comparison in any newspaper article. What proportion of the comparisons use comparative or superlative forms, and what proportion use other ways of making comparisons? What significance might this distribution have for teaching?

6.1.8 Adjectives and adverbs

Many adverbs are systematically derived from adjectives through the addition of -*ly*, e.g.

quick	*quickly*
happy	*happily*
steady	*steadily*
unique	*uniquely*

Not all -*ly* words are adverbs (e.g. *friendly, lovely, miserly, unseemly, elderly*). Similarly, constructions containing adjectives often have a parallel **adverbial** construction.

She is a consistent worker.	*She works consistently.*
reliable	*reliably*
creative	*creatively*
quick	*quickly*
fast	*fast*

The last example illustrates a problem for learners of English. Because some words have identical adjective and adverb forms, e.g. *fast*, it is wrongly assumed that there are other parallels, and this leads to errors such as:

*I did it good.

*She helped him quick.

*She is a very creatively person.

It should be noted, however, that in informal use, native speakers of English sometimes use adjectives instead of adverbs, e.g. *He played awesome.*

6.2 Adverbs and adverbials

Adverbs and **adverbials** are words or groups of words that can modify sentences, verbs, adjectives or other adverbs. Adverbs are usually single words. The term 'adverbial' is used to include both single-word adverbs and also phrases or clauses that modify adverbially.

6.2.1 Forms of adverbs

There are three main classes of adverbs based on their form.

1 **Simple adverbs** (e.g. *well, only, down, rather, quite, today*); many of these mark spatial location (e.g. *near, far, there, back, close*) or time (e.g. *now, then, never, next*).

2 **Compound adverbs** (e.g. *somehow, somewhere*, etc.).

3 **Derivational adverbs**: many of these are derived from adjectives by adding *-ly*, e.g. *quick–quickly, abrupt–abruptly*.

Learners of English do not usually have difficulty with the form of adverbs, except where adverbs have the same form as adjectives (see 6.1.8).

6.2.2 Forms of adverbials

Adverbials are expressed in five main ways:

1 Single-word adverbs, e.g. *never, there, soon*.

2 Noun phrases, e.g. *I get paid **every week***.

3 Prepositional phrases, e.g. *I saw her **on Friday**, He's waiting **in the office***.

4 Finite subordinate clauses, e.g. *I'll ring you **when I get home**, I sent flowers **because it was her birthday***.

5 Non-finite subordinate clauses, e.g. *I broke my leg **when skiing**, He rang **to tell us the news***.

The use of prepositional phrases as adverbials is the most frequent way in which adverbials are expressed in all major genres of English. (See further examples in Section 6.3.) More detailed description of finite and non-finite subordinate clauses used as adverbials occurs in Sections 7.4.2.3 and 7.5.5.3.

Adverbials can occur at the beginning, middle or end of sentences, e.g.

1 ***On Friday***, I went to a movie.

2 I *still* can't believe it.

3 We could see them ***through the open window***.

Adverbials occur most frequently at the end of sentences. Some adverbials can be moved without changing meaning between initial and final positions in a sentence (Examples 1 and 3 above). It is less common for adverbials which can occupy medial positions (e.g. *still, never*) to have such freedom to move.

6.2.3 Grammatical functions of adverbs

Adverbs can modify other word classes (including other adverbs). The main kinds of modification are as follows:

1 Adverbs as premodifiers of adjectives ('adverbs of degree') e.g.

very early	*quite* pleasant	*fully* clothed
completely clear	*somewhat* reserved	*perfectly* intelligible
really enjoyable	*absolutely* essential	*totally* untrue
just right	*rather* loud	*fairly* well-off
easily identifiable	*terribly* nice	*entirely* coincidental
pretty bad	*highly* publicised	*utterly* unsuitable
too loud	*so* tired	*particularly* important

Adverbs of degree can be sub-categorised into:

Amplifiers:

Maximisers, e.g. *completely, totally, utterly, quite*

Boosters, e.g. *highly, terribly, really, very*

Approximators, e.g. *almost, nearly, virtually*

Downtoners, e.g. *fairly, quite, rather, partly, hardly*

The most frequent adverbs of degree include *very, so, really, too, completely*. In conversation, 'swear words' such as *bloody* or *damn* also often occur as amplifiers. In academic writing, *extremely, highly, particularly, fully, quite, significantly* tend to be frequent. There are also preferred degree words in different regional varieties of English. In US spoken English, for example, *real* is often found (e.g. *real good*) where *really* might be used in UK English.

What is particularly noticeable, however, in the use of degree adverbs is that, although in theory many of them are interchangeable (e.g. *totally clear/completely clear*), in practice they collocate strongly with particular adjectives. Analysis of the relationships occurring between degree adverbs and adjectives in the 100-million-word *BNC* shows that particular degree adverbs collocate strongly with particular adjectives, as the following examples show.

absolutely	totally	clearly	pretty	highly	terribly
diabolical	unsuited	demarcated	horrendous	sexed	upset
knackered	unprepared	delineated	hopeless	manoeuvrable	sorry
gorgeous	illegible	signposted	disgusting	esteemed	excited
livid	unsuitable	articulated	boring	politicised	embarrassing
thrilled	impractical	identifiable	straightforward	commended	unhappy
devastated	uncharacteristic	visible	dull	flammable	sad
frightful	illogical	defined	awful	ritualised	boring
ludicrous	unacceptable	distinguishable	depressing	prized	painful
immaculate	unconnected	audible	sure	inflammable	brave
disgraceful	devoid	definable	slim	acclaimed	afraid

2 Adverbs as premodifiers of other adverbs

Degree adverbs can also modify other adverbs, as in the following examples:

very carefully	*pretty* badly
extremely slowly	*rather* slowly
quite clearly	*too* quickly

3 Adverbs as premodifiers of quantity words or phrases

Some adverbs have a very important role as approximators which can be used before quantifying determiners, e.g.

almost all	*about* a thousand
approximately half	*nearly* every
over 300	

4 Adverbs as premodifiers of noun phrases

A small number of frequent adverbs can occur before noun phrases, e.g.

quite a shock	*such* a disaster
rather a lot	

5 Adverbs as modifiers of verbs, e.g.

The news travelled *quickly*.

They spoke *quietly*.

Adverbs of frequency are used to show how often something happens. With lexical verbs, adverbs of frequency usually precede the verb; with the copular verb *be* and with auxiliary verbs, adverbs of frequency usually follow the verb, e.g.

I *often* drive to work.

They *usually* finish their work on time.

They are *always* late.

They were *sometimes* at work late at night.

You should *always* let them know.

In the *BNC*, the 20 most frequent adverbs of frequency (from the most frequent to the least) are: *never, always, often, ever, sometimes, usually, once, generally, hardly, no longer, normally, increasingly, twice, frequently, rarely, in general, occasionally, mostly, regularly, constantly.*

Task 6.4

In Text 6.4 underline all the adverbials (including single-word adverbs).

Text 6.4

Dolphins

Dolphins have always fascinated humans, and the fascination may be mutual. Our cousins who live in the sea seem to have created a society far closer to human ideals of Utopia than anything we have managed to achieve on land, and their social behaviour and lifestyle embody many of the virtues and qualities we humans value. Their movement in the oceans speaks to us of freedom, grace and beauty. Their society is co-operative, with many examples of seemingly altruistic behaviour, and dolphins are always ready to come to the assistance of those in distress, both their own species and humans. Apart from a few minor displays, they are free of aggression towards their own kind. We see them communicating easily with one another, trying to communicate with us and solving problems. The ancient Mediterranean cultures believed that the dolphin represented the vital power of the sea. The dolphin was a guardian of the sea and a guide to other worlds. In those times, killing a dolphin was tantamount to killing a person, and both crimes were punished with the death penalty.

Task 6.5

Change the following sentences so that they contain an adverb form which corresponds to the underlined adjective.

1 Her writing is legible.
  She ....

2 He is a brilliant runner.
  He ....

3 They made a careful study of the play.
  They ....

4 She is a persuasive speaker.
  She ....

5 There has been very heavy rain.
  It ....

6 They rang us on frequent occasions.
  They ....

7 The rain was quite light during the night.
  It ....

8 She is a fast worker.
  She ....

6.2.4 Semantic functions of adverbials

Adverbials have four major functions according to the kind of semantic role they have in sentences. These functions are **adjuncts**, **subjuncts**, **disjuncts** and **conjuncts**.

1 Adjuncts

Adjuncts are the most frequent of all adverbial types. They can occur in initial, medial or end parts of sentences, and typically express information about such notions as where, when, how often, how, why, under what circumstances something occurs. Many sentences at least give information about **where** and **when** events occur, e.g.

> I saw Tom (*in the library*) (*last night*).

Adjuncts are usually optional, but with some verbs an adverbial adjunct is obligatory, e.g.

> Mary put the letter *into the fire.*

It is sometimes hard to tell whether the adjunct is modifying the verb, the predicate or the whole sentence. The main semantic categories of adjuncts are:

- **space** (position, direction), e.g.

> I like it *here.*
> The bus arrived *from Leeds.*
> She threw the ball *through the window.*
> *In Christchurch* there are beautiful parks.
> He is *in a state of confusion.* (figurative)

- **time**, e.g.

> I saw her *recently.*
> *Every week* I ring my mother.
> Max fixed his car *in a couple of hours.*
> He was born *before World War II.*
> Sue has worked here *for over thirty years.*
> Don't get up *until you feel better.*
> I *often* read novels.

- **manner**, e.g.

> Max looked at Sue *nervously.*
> He walks *with a limp.*
> Don't talk to them *like that!*
> They did *well.*

- **means, instrument, agency**, e.g.

> Sam was hit on the head *by a golf ball.*
> Sue inspires her class *by her example.*
> Someone broke open the door *with an axe.*

- **contingency**, e.g.

> He cried out *in pain.*
> He cried out *because he was injured.*
> She stayed home *to avoid the traffic.*
> Tom made a speech *despite his cold.*

2 Subjuncts

Subjuncts are not always easy to distinguish from adjuncts, and may seem to behave as if they are in parenthesis. Subjuncts function to add emphasis, to intensify and to focus attention. Some also express viewpoint, degree of probability, attitude or courtesy.

> I *simply* haven't enough time to help you.
> Tom *completely* ignored the problem.
> It happened *very* quickly.
> She *sort of* laughed at the idea.
> This is *certainly* faster.
> I was *only* joking.
> She won't mind *in the slightest.*
> I'll *probably* be late.
> They *definitely* knew about it.
> You are *cordially* invited to stay behind for a drink.
> Will you *please* take your seats.

3 Disjuncts

Disjuncts are adverbials that are sometimes known as 'sentence modifiers', because they may seem to be outside the rest of the sentence. They are sometimes used in a formulaic manner especially in conversation. They can act as fillers in discourse to give the speaker time to plan, or as a way of taking the floor, e.g.

> *Frankly,* I don't want to hear about it.
> *To be perfectly honest,* I don't understand him.
> *If you don't mind me saying so,* I like your choice of colours.

Other disjuncts include: *actually, as a matter of fact, in all honesty, speaking personally, in a word, naturally, strangely enough, fortunately, in all sincerity, at the end of the day.*

4 Conjuncts

Conjuncts are adverbials that join utterances and at the same time express a semantic relation between them. They are important markers of cohesion, especially in written English, e.g.

in the first place, secondly, furthermore, and above all, in addition, therefore, namely, in other words, eventually, moreover, nevertheless, even so, consequently, however

---

Task 6.6

In Text 6.5 identify the adverbials and classify them according to whether they are adjuncts, subjuncts, disjuncts or conjuncts.

Text 6.5

Diamonds

Humans have valued diamonds for at least 2000 years. Some natural diamonds are found as perfect octahedrons, with considerable visual appeal. Stones like these began to be highly valued in India, the earliest source of diamonds. Merchants carried diamonds from India along trade routes through the Middle East. They sold the best diamonds en route, so that by the time the eastern goods reached the Mediterranean only the most uninspiring of the diamonds were left. Consequently in the western world diamonds were at first not regarded as objects of beauty – other stones such as emeralds and red garnets were preferred. Even so, in Roman days diamonds had a far greater monetary value than gold, because they were reputed to be indestructible, and, more importantly, it was believed that they would safeguard their wearer against a whole range of misfortunes, from poison to madness. These magical attributes persisted through the ages and died out only with the rise of scientific investigations in the sixteenth century. By this time diamonds were well known in western Europe, and were worn as jewels, but it was not until 1796 that the chemical nature of diamond was finally established. In that year a London chemist, Smithson Tennant, burned diamonds and found that carbon dioxide was the end product; the same amount of carbon dioxide was produced by burning equal weights of diamond and charcoal. Evidently diamond was just another form of carbon. However, despite an enormous amount of effort, it was not until the 1950s that diamonds were successfully synthesised.

Task 6.7

Classify the adjuncts in Text 6.5 into the semantic functions of space, time, manner, means and contingency.

6.3 Prepositions and prepositional phrases

Prepositions are by common consent one of the hardest parts of English to learn how to use. There are about 100 prepositions. They make up about 8 per cent of all the words we use in spoken English, and about 12 per cent of the words we use in written genres. The main prepositions are shown in Table 6.1. Some are listed in more than one semantic category.

Table 6.1 The main English prepositions

	Simple forms	Complex forms
space/ direction	about, above, across, after, against, along, amid(st), among(st), around, at, before, behind, below, beneath, beside, between, beyond, by, down, for, from, in, into, inside, near, off, on, onto, opposite, out, outside, over, past, round, through, throughout, to, towards, under, underneath, up, upon, via, with, within	along with, away from, by the side of, close to, down at, down by, down from, down in, down on, down to, from among, from above, in front of, inside of, near to, next to, off from, off to, on board, on top of, out at, out from, out of, out on, out to, outside of, over to, to within
time	about, after, around, at, before, between, beyond, by, during, following, for, from, in, on, over, past, pending, since, through, throughout, till, to, until, within	in the course of, in time of, previous to, prior to, subsequent to
relationship/ association	about, among, as, at, barring, between, beyond, concerning, considering, despite, except, excepting, excluding, failing, for, given, in, including, like, of, on, notwithstanding, regarding, respecting, to, unlike, within, without	accompanied by, according to, apart from, as a result of, as for, as opposed to, as to, as well as, because of, by way of, contrary to, due to, except for, in accordance with, in addition to, in case of, in charge of, in common with, in comparison with, in connection with, in contrast to, in favour of, in keeping with, in lieu of, in line with, in place of, in regard to, in return for, instead of, in spite of, in light of, in view of, on account of, on behalf of, owing to, rather than, regardless of, relative to, save for, together with, with reference to, with regard to, with respect to
agency	by, from, through, with	by agency of, by dint of, by means of, by way of, out of

Table 6.2 Distribution of the most frequent prepositions in the *British National Corpus* (written texts only)

Preposition	%	Preposition	%
of	26.1	behind	0.2
in	16.1	including	0.2
to	8.1	rather than	0.2
for	7.3	since	0.2
on	5.7	up	0.2
with	5.7	upon	0.2
by	4.6	up to	0.2
at	4.1	above	0.1
like	3.8	according to	0.1
from	3.7	along	0.1
as	1.9	as to	0.1
into	1.4	apart from	0.1
about	1.1	away from	0.1
after	1.0	because of	0.1
between	0.8	below	0.1
over	0.8	beside	0.1
through	0.7	beyond	0.1
before	0.6	despite	0.1
against	0.5	down	0.1
under	0.5	due to	0.1
during	0.4	inside	0.1
out of	0.4	in terms of	0.1
within	0.4	near	0.1
without	0.4	on to	0.1
off	0.3	onto	0.1
such as	0.3	outside	0.1
towards	0.3	per	0.1
across	0.2	round	0.1
among	0.2	throughout	0.1
around	0.2	until	0.1

Simple prepositions consist of one word. **Complex** prepositions consist of two or three words.

Research on large corpora has shown that a small number of prepositions account for most occurrences of prepositions. The distribution of the most frequently used prepositions in the 90 million words of written texts in the *BNC* is shown in Table 6.2. Over a quarter of the preposition tokens in the corpus are accounted for by *of;* half of the preposition tokens are accounted for by *of, in, to.* The most frequent 14 prepositions account for over 90 per cent of prepositional tokens in the corpus.

Task 6.8

In Text 6.5 identify the prepositions by underlining them. Be careful not to underline *to* when it is part of an infinitive.

6.3.1 Functions of prepositions

Prepositions function as linguistic glue to bind other linguistic units together and to show the relationship between them. Most commonly, prepositions come before a noun phrase to form a **prepositional phrase**, e.g.

> I'll meet you at your house.
>
> They visited us for an hour or two.
>
> There's no difference between these results.

Of tends to be used especially to relate two nouns, as in *the cost of a meal*, where a possessive (genitive) construction would be used in some other languages.

Prepositional structures can function to modify noun phrases, verb phrases and clauses.

a To postmodify noun phrases (i.e. to function as adjectivals), a prepositional phrase is the most common way, especially using *of*, e.g.

> The people at the airport checked our tickets.
>
> She ran the race of her life.
>
> He had no hope of winning.
>
> She gave me a book on gardens.
>
> That's the road to Auckland.

b To function as adverbials by modifying verb phrases, e.g.

> I will meet you at the airport.
>
> I saw them on Friday.

c To function as the complement of a verb, e.g.

> We looked at her paintings.
>
> She laughed at me.
>
> She laughed with me.

Prepositions can sometimes get separated from their complements ('deferred prepositions'), e.g.

> She is worth listening to.
>
> What are you looking at?
>
> Has the meal been paid for?
>
> Who did you give it to?

d To function as the complement of an adjective, e.g.

> We were angry at the decision.

6.3.2 Prepositional structures

The complement of a preposition can be:

a noun phrase	(at *the airport*)
a *wh*-clause	(from *what you told me*)
an *-ing* clause	(by *signing this cheque*)

Task 6.9

In Text 6.6 identify:

a The prepositional phrases that postmodify nouns or noun phrases and therefore function adjectivally;

b The prepositional phrases that function adverbially.

Text 6.6

Wind power

In many countries there are plans to build wind farms for the production of electricity without the disadvantages of carbon emissions. Off the coast of Denmark, 80 wind turbines in the Horns Rev wind farm generate power for 150,000 homes. Some of the turbines built at sea are in water that is over 30 metres deep, but the extra cost of construction is justified because of the strength and consistency of the wind offshore. Large wind farms are also under construction on land in several parts of Europe. In Spain it has been recognised for some time that there is enough wind to make it economical to generate electricity by means of wind turbines. There are plans to expand installations in many countries, including Germany, the Netherlands, Ireland, New Zealand and the United Kingdom. In the United States there are many wind farms in operation, and the world's largest is ironically in Texas, which is also a centre of the oil industry. Wind power has moved to centre stage as a new, environmentally acceptable technology. By 2020, 12 per cent of the world's electricity could be generated from wind if the threat of climate change is taken seriously.

6.3.3 Prepositional verbs

We have already introduced the grammatical distinction between phrasal verbs and prepositional verbs in Section 5.1.1.3.

Prepositional verbs have a lexical verb followed by a preposition, e.g.

look at

look after

sympathise with

complain about

put up with

Some prepositional verbs have two noun phrases after them. The first noun phrase often refers to a person or persons. Kreidler (1966) described some common prepositional verbs of this type (see Table 6.3). Learners of English should learn as collocations the prepositional constructions associated with such verbs.

Table 6.3 **Prepositional verb structures** (based on Kriedler, 1966)

to _____ somebody *about* something
advise, ask, caution, consult, inform, question, see, tease, tell, warn

to _____ *to* somebody *about* something
complain, speak, talk

to _____ *with* somebody *about* something
(dis)agree, argue, confer, consult, communicate, debate, differ, discourse, dispute, expostulate, joke, quarrel, sympathise

to _____ somebody *for* something
ask, blame, denounce, esteem, excuse, forgive, petition, prepare, press, punish, (dis)qualify, reproach, reprimand, reward, send, thank, value

to _____ *on* somebody *for* something
count, depend, rely

to _____ *to* somebody *for* something
apologise, appeal, apply

to _____ somebody *from* something
deter, discourage, dissuade, distract, exclude, excuse, exempt, hinder, prohibit, protect, release, rescue, restrain, stop

to _____ somebody *of* something
accuse, acquit, convict, convince, cure, defraud, dispossess, relieve, remind, strip, suspect

to _____ somebody *on* something
compliment, congratulate

to _____ somebody *with* something
acquaint, afflict, assist, bother, burden, credit, encourage, familiarise, furnish, help, impress, infect, inspire, ply, provide, reward, supply, threaten, trouble

to _____ something *at* somebody
aim, point, shoot, throw

to _____ something *for* somebody
do, preserve, reserve, save

to _____ something *from* somebody
borrow, collect, conceal, exact, expect, get, hide, obtain, order, purchase, secure, steal

to _____ something *to* somebody
admit, ascribe, attribute, concede, confess, credit, declare, dedicate, delegate, describe, devote, dictate, do, entrust, explain, impart, justify, mention, present, propose, point out, report, reveal, say, submit, suggest, supply, throw

to _____ something *with* somebody
discuss, dispute, share

There are alternative analyses possible for some prepositional verb constructions, e.g.

Sue	*looked*	*after her mother*	or	*Sue*	*looked after*	*her mother*
Subj	Verb	Adverbial		Subj	Verb	Object

In the examples *She looked up*, *He walked away*, many speakers of English consider the sentences to be SVA.

These examples can have another adverb like *slowly* between the verb and the preposition (*He walked slowly away*).

In the following examples, however, many speakers consider the sentences to be SV rather than SVA:

The deal *fell through.*

In the end he *gave in.*

Phrasal verbs and prepositional verbs cause major problems for learners of English, not only because it is sometimes hard to analyse the grammatical relationship between the verb and the particle or preposition, as the examples above illustrate, but also because the meaning of the whole is not always obvious from the meaning of the parts (e.g. *to hold out*). In addition, since many verbs occur with several different adverbial particles or prepositions, they can be confusing for learners, e.g.

to set out	(= to begin a journey)	*to bring off*		(= succeed)
to set up	(= to establish)		*about*	(= cause)
to set to	(= to begin)		*up*	(= raise)
to hold up	(= to delay)		*to*	(= revive)
to hold out	(= to last, endure)		*in*	(= introduce)
to hold over	(= to postpone)		*on*	(= instigate or cause)

Multi-word verbs can be so difficult and confusing that it may be easiest for some learners to learn the productive use of the words in brackets, and some successful learners say they do this. However, for receptive use, it is necessary to understand the phrasal verbs or prepositional verbs.

6.3.4 Meanings of prepositions

Part of the learning difficulty of prepositions arises from the fact that most of them have many meanings or uses. The most frequent, *of* and *in*, each have over 40 senses given in comprehensive dictionaries.

It is often hard for learners of English to know which preposition to use with particular nouns or verbs. It is not easy, for example, to see why some of the following are not always acceptable or equivalent to each other.

I'll wait for you *at/on/by/in/*with* the corner

Similarly, it is not obvious why we should say **under** (or **in**) *these circumstances* rather than *at/from/on/by/with these circumstances*.

Many prepositions are said to have a **locative** (spatial) core meaning, with other uses **derived** from the core meaning as **extended** (**transferred** or **figurative**) uses, e.g.

under the table	*under* discussion
on the table	*on* trial
beneath the waves	*beneath* contempt

Unfortunately it is not always clear what the core spatial meaning is. Consider, for example, these spatial meanings of *on*:

a book on the table	*a smile on my face*
a ring on my finger	*the apples on the tree*
a fly on the ceiling	*You're on my list.*
a switch on the wall	*The box is on its side.*

Some extended uses of *on* include:

on Sunday	*on a trip*
on 10 June	*on the committee*
on time	*on principle*
on the premises	*on your recommendation*
on the brink of tears	*on guard*
on friendly terms	*on approval*

Although prepositions are hard, most courses do not give them enough attention, and learners are often left to learn how to use them as best they can. Too much attention is usually given to literal, physical uses, whereas most prepositions are used with extended meanings that are abstract and figurative.

Discussion topic

Discuss which of the following examples might represent core uses of the prepositions to be learned first by your students, and which examples represent transferred uses to be learned later.

1 **On**

1 a mat **on** the floor; 2 float **on** the water; 3 a book **on** loan; 4 **on** holiday for three weeks; 5 **on** a bicycle; 6 **on** a bus; 7 a blister **on** the sole of my foot; 8 **on** the last day of the year; 9 **on** Christmas Eve; 10 a house **on** fire; 11 a kite **on** a string; 12 hang your coat **on** a peg; 13 **on** the sunny side of the hill; 14 **on** the side of my

---

friends; 15 these goods are **on** sale; 16 **on** his farm; 17 **on** the morning of 1 June; 18 **on** his best behaviour; 19 a tutorial **on** prepositions; 20 **on** holiday today

2 **In**

1 put it **in** her basket; 2 a chair **in** the corner; 3 **in** 1984; 4 breathe **in**; 5 stand **in** line; 6 **in** my experience; 7 **in** circumstances like this; 8 **in** June; 9 **in** ten years' time; 10 **in** a field; 11 **in** the middle of the park; 12 **in** the afternoon; 13 **in** bed; 14 **in** his bath; 15 **in** time for lunch; 16 **in** the middle of next week; 17 **in** a moment; 18 **in** general; 19 **in** particular; 20 **in** case

3 **At**

1 **at** sunset; 2 **at** a depth of five feet; 3 sit **at** the window; 4 point **at**; 5 seven weeks **at** sea; 6 **at** once; 7 **at** the end of the year; 8 **at** the end of the road; 9 **at** the station; 10 We stop **at** Singapore; 11 Children start school **at** five years of age; 12 growl **at** the class; 13 to be amused **at** her difficulty; 14 **at** the bottom of the class; 15 **at** the bottom of the sea; 16 **at** the edge of the pond; 17 Who is **at** fault? 18 **at** the back of the house; 19 wonder **at** his knowledge; 20 **at** work

4 **Under**

1 **under** a blanket; 2 walk **under** a ladder; 3 **under** the doctor; 4 **under** control; 5 **under** repair; 6 **under** a new leader; 7 **under** a bucket; 8 **under** age; 9 **under** half an acre; 11 **under** observation; 12 **under** attack; 13 speak **under** your breath; 14 to write **under** another name; 15 classified **under** primary meanings; 16 work **under** difficult conditions; 17 stand **under** a castle wall; 18 the village nestles **under** a hill

5 **Between**

1 the wall **between** two rooms; 2 the cupboard **between** the windows; 3 **between** the wars; 4 this ship sails **between** Sydney and Auckland; 5 an argument **between** them; 6 to push **between** the spectators; 7 **between** Monday and Friday; 8 **between** 90 and 100 dollars; 9 a comparison **between** two systems of education; 10 share this cake **between** you; 11 to choose **between** two courses; 12 stop **between** stations

The main meanings derived from the core **spatial** uses of prepositions usually have something to do with **time, cause, purpose, means, accompaniment** or **concession**.

Computer corpus analyses can provide information on the relative frequency of use of the meanings of some of the main prepositions. By

Table 6.4   Major functions of *at* in the *LOB Corpus*

At occurs 5,951 times in the 1-million-word *LOB Corpus*, with the following distribution of uses:

	% of *at* tokens
Place	
at showing position e.g. He is *at* the office.	37.8
at showing direction e.g. She glanced *at* her watch.	11.6
Time	
at showing a point in time e.g. *at* 11 o'clock; *at* that moment	12.6
at showing a period of time e.g. *at* that time; *at* night	10.2
Event/activity	
e.g. *at* the coronation; *at* this conference	6.4
Quantity/degree	
e.g. *at* 120°F; *at* least	15.9
State/manner	
e.g. *at* loggerheads with; *at* ease	1.0
Cause	
e.g. dismay *at* the amount of damage	1.0
Miscellaneous	
e.g. *at* any rate; leave it *at* that	3.6
Total	100.0

way of illustration, Tables 6.4 and 6.5 show analyses of the use of *at* and *between* in the 1-million-word *LOB Corpus* of written British English.

It should be clear, however, that such information as is contained in Tables 6.4 and 6.5 does not necessarily make it easy to decide what meanings of a preposition are the core meanings to be taught first.

Discussion topic

What are the core meanings of *in, for, by*? You may need to consult a modern dictionary for ideas.

Table 6.5 Major semantic functions of *between* in the *LOB Corpus*

Between occurs 867 times in the 1-million-word *LOB Corpus*, with the following distribution of uses:

Location	% of between tokens

a Between two or more places, entities or states
    e.g.   the channel *between* Africa and Sicily
    Let nothing get *between* her and her ambition.
	24.9

b Between points on a scale or range
    e.g.   temperatures *between* 1000° and 1450°C
    earnings *between* £5 and £6 a week
	6.6

Movement	

a Going from one place or state to another
    e.g.   She ran *between* the dining room and the kitchen.
    signals passing *between* them in free space
	2.8

b Going between entities
    e.g.   The lane curled off *between* its high hawthorns.
    He was observed . . . walking *between* the metals.
	1.6

Time	

a Occurring at some time between two events or points in time
    e.g.   anytime *between* November and late February
    98 changes of Cabinet *between* 1834 and 1912
	4.6

b Duration, occupying a period between two events or points in time
    e.g.   the time *between* pouring and knock out
    to keep myself going *between* terms at college
	5.0

Other relationships	

a Bond between entities, states or places
    e.g.   it had forged a bond *between* them
    an alliance *between* the Castilian and Leonese nobility
	11.1

b Interaction between entities or states
    e.g.   a row *between* Lawrence and Frieda
    communication *between* management and employees
	16.7

c Similarity
    e.g.   the resemblances *between* Lawrence's inner life and his own
    the important parallel *between* Handel and Beethoven
	2.1

d Difference
    e.g.   the distinction *between* ancient and modern
    the discrepancy *between* expected and observed scores
	17.7

e Comparison
    e.g.   a comparison *between* different car manufacturers' guarantees
    There is little to choose *between* the two.
	2.1

Dividing or sharing
e.g.   the division of the world *between* two ideological camps
    a balance has to be kept *between* the various denominations
    between them, fantasy and science have gobbled up the remainder
	4.8

Total	100.0

6.3.5 Prepositional collocations

Prepositions often occur before or after particular words. Table 2.6 in Chapter 2 lists the 25 most frequent collocates of *at* in spoken or written texts of the *BNC*.

Discussion topic

1 Discuss the advantages and disadvantages of teaching *at* as part of collocations such as those listed in Table 2.6.

2 List collocations with *in* which you think might be frequent and worth teaching to intermediate or advanced learners of English. If possible, check your intuitions with the evidence from a corpus.

Analysis of the collocations in which prepositions typically occur can be useful in planning teaching strategies. Table 6.6 contains the words

Table 6.6 Words occurring four or more times immediately before *between* or *through* in the *LOB Corpus*

		No. of tokens			No. of tokens
*difference	between	59	go	through	36
*relationship		25	pass		33
*distinction		19	come		20
*relation		16	be		15
*gap		12	and		13
*agreement		11	get		12
*contrast		11	break		10
*distance		11	*him		10
*place		11	run		10
be		10	*way		9
*comparison		9	*it		8
exist		9	fall		7
*meeting		9	lead		7
*contact		8	look		7
*link		8	out		7
and		7	in		6
in		7	live		6
as		6	only		6
*conflict		6	*them		6
*correlation		6			
*gulf		6			
lie		6			
that		6			
*time		6			

Note: Nouns are recorded in their singular form, verbs in their stem form.
*= noun or pronoun

that occur six or more times immediately before *between* or *through* in the *LOB Corpus*. It is clear that *between* is typically preceded by a noun, whereas *through* is typically preceded by a verb. In the case of *between*, any core spatial use is not the most frequent use for that preposition.

6.3.6 Learning to use prepositions

Analysis of learners' errors in using prepositions suggests that about two-thirds of the errors are typically the use of a 'wrong' preposition, e.g. **I am satisfied on these* results (instead of *satisfied with*). About 20 per cent of errors arise from the omission of a preposition, e.g. **I am satisfied these results*. The remaining errors tend to be the result of overuse of prepositions where they are not necessary, or in the wrong part of the sentence (e.g. **I am satisfied these results with*).

As noted earlier, prepositions are very frequent and the core meanings are not necessarily the main learning difficulty. The large number of extended uses of prepositions are probably best learned by encouraging extensive reading. Learners typically take a long time to become aware of subtle differences in verb–preposition meanings, e.g. compare *look at/look after/look for* or *concerned about/concerned with*. Adding to the difficulty is the way in which different word classes of the same root word sometimes go with different prepositions, e.g.

fond of	*sympathy for*
fondness for	*sympathise with*
	sympathetic to

Some idea of the complexity of prepositional use and the dimensions of the learner's task is captured in this perhaps apocryphal report of a child's question:

> *Upon seeing a book his mother had brought upstairs, he complained:*
> *'What did you bring that book that I didn't want to be read to out of*
> *up for?'*

CHAPTER 7

Beyond the simple sentence

This chapter is designed to show the structure and use of sentences which contain more than one clause or lexical verb, and the difficulties such sentences can cause for learners of English.

Objectives

By the end of this chapter you should:

1 Know the difference between a **simple sentence** and a **complex sentence**.

2 Be able to identify **co-ordinated constructions**.

3 Be able to identify **co-ordinating conjunctions**, and know their main meanings and functions.

4 Be able to identify where **ellipsis** has occurred in a sentence and suggest what has been ellipted.

5 Be able to identify **nominal clauses** in texts.

6 Understand the **functions of nominal clauses**.

7 Understand how **indirect speech** is structured.

8 Be able to identify **relative clauses** in texts.

9 Know the difference between **restrictive** and **non-restrictive relative clauses**.

10 Be able to identify **subordinating conjunctions**.

11 Be able to identify **adverbial clauses** in texts.

12 Know the functions of the main **adverbial clause types**.

13 Be able to identify **non-finite clauses** in texts.

14 Be able to describe the main **structures and functions of non-finite clauses**.

7.1 Sentences and clauses

In Section 3.1 we noted that a sentence may be thought of as a string of words which has a sense of completeness and unity, and which typically has certain elements such as a subject, a verb and sometimes an object or complement, and perhaps one or more adverbials, e.g.

1 *My father snores.*
2 *Sara likes Athens on fine days.*
3 *This coffee is excellent.*
4 *Your keys are on the table in the kitchen.*
5 *I borrowed some money.*

Sentences are built out of clauses. A clause is a string of words which typically has a subject and a finite verb.

A **simple sentence** consists of one clause. Often, however, sentences contain more than one clause. Sentences 1–5 above are examples of simple sentences consisting of one clause. Sentences which consist of more than one clause are called **complex sentences**, e.g.

6 *I borrowed some money.*
7 *I borrowed some money and (I) took a taxi.*
8 *I borrowed some money because I couldn't find my wallet.*
9 *I borrowed some money when I got to work because I couldn't find my wallet and I needed a taxi so that I could get home before my friend left for the airport.*

Sentence 6 is a simple sentence consisting of one clause. Sentences 7–9 are complex. Sentence 7 consists of two clauses (*I borrowed some money. I took a taxi.*) Sentence 8 consists of two clauses (*I borrowed some money* (because) *I couldn't find my wallet.*) Sentence 9 consists of six clauses:

	I borrowed some money
(when)	I got to work
(because)	I couldn't find my wallet
(and)	I needed a taxi
(so that)	I could get home
(before)	My friend left for the airport

In theory there is no upper limit to the number of clauses that can make up a complex sentence. In practice, sentences which have too many clauses are hard to understand, or are considered to be awkward.

In complex sentences, the clauses can be in different relationships to each other. In Sentence 7 the two clauses are of equal status but are linked together. They are said to be **co-ordinated clauses**. In Sentence 8, the **main clause** is considered to be *I borrowed some money*. The other clause (*because I couldn't find my wallet*) is considered to be **subordinate** to the main clause. This **subordinate clause** works as an adverbial which tells us why I borrowed some money.

Some clauses do not have finite verbs or subjects. The italicised clauses in Sentences 10 and 11 are without subjects or verbs. In 12 the italicised clause does not have a finite verb.

10 *Where possible* you should avoid eating too much fat.

11 *Although one of the leading authorities in her field* she was not a confident speaker.

12 *Opening the exhibition* the Prime Minister thanked the organisers.

Clauses without finite verbs or subjects are considered in Section 7.3.

Text 7.1

Village railway stations

The railway station was one of the hubs of English village life. It was a centre of news, gossip and advice, and the home of a bookstall and telegraph office. Its disappearance has been followed in many cases by that of the village shop, the village post office and the village pub. It has been part of the slow, inexorable process of rural decay that became inevitable when economic viability replaced communal need, and left whole areas more isolated than they had been at any time since the eighteenth century. The country railways, of course, never made a profit. But they provided a vital social service and their closure marked the end of an era. What was it about the station that was so fascinating? The station was truly a gateway which people passed through in endless profusion on a variety of missions. It was a place of motion and emotion, arrival and departure, joy and sorrow, parting and reunion. Here are some boys and girls going away to school, their fathers and mothers filling up the moments of waiting with many last-minute instructions, in order to shut out their anxieties which their children must not see. At another place a wife is saying good-bye to a husband. Elsewhere a son or daughter is setting out into the great world to win a name and place. In the corner of a carriage a lonely soul sits, his face screened by a magazine, with no one to say goodbye to him at this end of his journey or welcome him at the other.

Task 7.1

In Text 7.1, identify each clause and indicate whether they are finite (i.e. they have a finite verb) or non-finite (i.e. they have a non-finite verb). For clarity, list each clause on a separate line. In doing so, you should be aware, however, that this oversimplifies the relationship between some of the clauses. For example, as we will see in the later sections, some relative clauses occur inside other clauses.

7.2 Co-ordination

Co-ordination is a linguistic process that involves the linking of units which belong to the same word class or the same grammatical level, e.g.

nouns	I grow *grapes and kiwifruit.*
adjectives	I bought some *old and dusty* books.
	The weather was *warm but windy.*
main verbs	They could have been *killed or injured.*
modal verbs	We *can and must* help them.
adverbs	She spoke *quickly but clearly.*
noun phrases	I bought *some fresh apples and some yoghurt.*
verb phrases	He *can revise but not rewrite* his assignment.
preposition phrases	He voted *for the government and against the opposition.*

When clauses are co-ordinated they form a **compound sentence** (e.g. *He talked slowly but wasn't understood; They practised hard, played well at the trial, and should get into the team*).

Co-ordinated clauses are usually linked by a **co-ordinating conjunction** (co-ordinators). The most common co-ordinating conjunctions are *and, but, or*. These are used to indicate addition, contrast or choice.

Addition	Contrast	Choice
and	*but*	*or*
both . . . and	*yet*	*either . . . or*
as well as	*still*	*nor*
not only . . . but also	*nevertheless*	*neither . . . nor*

In the *British National Corpus*, the word *and* accounts for 74 per cent of co-ordinating conjunctions, *but* accounts for 12 per cent, and *or* for 10 per cent. Co-ordinators of clauses have certain grammatical characteristics and functions including the following:

1 Co-ordinators occur only at the beginning of a clause.

2 Clauses beginning with a co-ordinator cannot be moved to the beginning of a sentence:

> *I boiled some water and made a cup of tea.*
>
> **And made a cup of tea, I boiled some water.*

3 If the subject of two compound clauses is the same, then the subject does not have to be repeated, e.g.

> *I rang him and (I) asked him to dinner.*

4 *And, or* (not *but*) can link more than two clauses, e.g.

> *I visited my aunt, (I) cleaned the car and (I) went to the supermarket, all on the same day.*

Task 7.2

In the following sentences, underline the co-ordinated items and put the conjunctions in brackets. What is the word class or grammatical function of the co-ordinated items?

1 Sue greeted Max and Fred.

2 Max and Fred waved back.

3 The long and boring flight took 11 hours.

4 My cat used to come inside and sit beside the fire in the evening.

5 She worked very hard and late into the night.

6 Empty beer cans and heaps of paper covered the floor.

7 We went onwards and upwards until we reached the top of the hill.

8 Apples and pears are both cheap at present.

Text 7.2

Humans take to the air

About 200 years ago, the occupants of a rural French village looked up one morning and saw an unusual object overhead. It was huge, silent and spherical and seemed to float out of the sky. After it landed in a field the villagers were afraid but they nevertheless attacked the monster with sticks and farm implements. Burning fabric added to the confusion. The object was, of course, a hot air balloon. Apparently someone tied it to a horse or other farm animal, which ran through the fields and caused further damage. Since those early attempts at flying, there have been amazing developments, and we now tend to take air travel for granted.

Task 7.3

Identify the occurrences of co-ordination in Text 7.2. Underline the co-ordinated items and put brackets around the co-ordinating conjunctions.

7.2.1 Functions of co-ordinators

And can mark or express the following relations:

addition ('also')	He works in an office during the week *and* goes sailing at the weekend.
sequence ('then')	I boiled the water *and* made a cup of tea.
result ('so')	It's been raining *and* my washing is still wet.
contrast ('yet')	I've been working all day *and* I still haven't finished.
condition ('if')	Give us the tools *and* we'll finish the job.

The use of *and* to express sequence, result or condition is not reversible, e.g. **I made a cup of tea and boiled the water.*

For co-ordination with *and*, some kind of perceived connection or relevance seems to be needed. Compare, for example,

1 **Eggs cost $3 a dozen and I think it's going to rain.*
2 *Lend me a dollar and I'll get a timetable.*
3 *I worked all weekend and I met the deadline.*

But can mark or express the following relations:

unexpected contrast (yet)	He's over 60 *but* still runs 10 km a day.
contradiction (but rather)	I don't mind what he said *but* it's the way he said it.
exception (except)	They had never caught anything *but* herring in the harbour.

Or can mark or express the following relations:

exclusion (one or the other)	I have enough money for a ticket *or* a pair of jeans.
inclusion (both are possible)	You can go to the Red Series *or* the Blue Series, *or* both.
correction	He works for the government, *or*, more correctly, he's on the payroll.
negative condition (if)	Don't touch that *or* you'll get burned. Hurry up *or* we'll be late.

Task 7.4

In Text 7.2, work out the function of each of the co-ordinators.

Discussion topic

Which of the following co-ordinated sentences can have the clause order reversed? Is there any common pattern or rule which allows for reversibility of clauses?

1 He walked over to the table and sat down.

2 She asked when the train left and bought a ticket.

3 She turned out the light and went to sleep.

4 He put out the cat and read the paper.

5 She sold her house and moved to Wellington.

6 On holiday we visited my aunt and spent a few days at the beach.

Discussion topic

The following sentences written by learners of English contain faulty co-ordination. Identify the problems and correct them.

1 *The person has short hair and bald.

2 *This year I am proud of and gives me many things I'll never forget.

3 *They've met these words before but not been looked at more deeply.

4 *In this piece of writing, I describe what the problem is, what the causes of this problem and what the steps and techniques I should use to deal with the problem.

5 *She divides them into small groups and ask them to discuss the problems.

6 *Looking at colourful pictures will make the learners interested and will eager to learn.

7.2.2 Learning about co-ordination

For learners of English, sentences that include co-ordination can be difficult to comprehend because learners are not sure of what is being co-ordinated, e.g.

The volume of the music and the heat gave him a headache and soon made him feel sick.

What gave him a headache? What made him feel sick? What did the volume of the music do? Did the heat give him a headache? Did the volume of the music make him feel sick?

The river rose above the lake and flooded the farm.

Did the lake or the river flood the farm?

In summer the ground hardened like concrete and had to be chipped out in chunks.

It was the *ground*, not the *concrete*, that had to be chipped out.

Where there is co-ordination it is useful for teachers to check that their students are clearly aware of who or what is doing what to what. A major cause of problems in using co-ordination is ellipsis (see Section 7.3).

7.3 Ellipsis

In Chapter 4, we saw that pronouns are devices that help us avoid repetition and excessive redundancy, e.g. *Mary bought a car and **she** really enjoys driving it.* (Cf. **Mary bought a car and Mary really enjoys driving it.*) Other pro-forms can also help us avoid unnecessary repetition, e.g. *I like Mozart and **so does** Fred.* (Cf. **I like Mozart and Fred likes Mozart.*) *He told me to leave and I **did**.* Sometimes, words or phrases are omitted completely, e.g. *Mary bought a car and [] really enjoys driving it.*

Where words are deliberately omitted to avoid repetition (but can be recovered) the process is known as **ellipsis**. Ellipsis is very important, especially in complex sentences. In both spoken and written English in co-ordinated constructions we tend to reduce or abbreviate wherever possible, especially to avoid repetition. In ellipsis, even though words or phrases can be omitted, they must be able to be recovered. Subjects, complements, objects, verbs, noun phrases and verb phrases are among the parts of sentences that can be ellipted. For learners of English, ellipsis can take time to get used to.

In the following examples, part of the sentence has been ellipted.

My friend owns, enjoys and profits from his collection of paintings.

I'll see you tomorrow or later in the week.

When a verb is ellipted in a co-ordinated sentence, the phenomenon is called **gapping**, e.g.

Max is looking after the visitors and Fred the rest of the family.

Noun phrase ellipsis is especially frequent, e.g.

1 *This bread is as good as my own.* (bread)
2 *There was a loud bang followed by another.* (bang)
3 *New Zealand kiwifruit are the best in the world.* (kiwifruit)
4 *That speech was the last he made as Prime Minister.* (speech)
5 *I like rye bread but the kids prefer white.* (bread)
6 *Take as much as you want.* (?)

Corpus analysis shows that ellipsis of the subject of a clause is the most frequent kind, e.g.

The government knows it doesn't have the support of most of the electorate but continues nevertheless to try to enact its legislative programme.

In addition to noun phrase ellipsis, other parts of sentences can be ellipted, e.g.

1 *I would have gone if I could.* (have gone)

2 *He was at university at the same time I was.* (at university)

3 *More people are enrolled this year than there were last year.* (enrolled)

4 *You can tell her if you like.* (to tell her)

5 *I want to refuse but I don't know how to.* (refuse)

6 *Has she been told? – No, but she will be.* (told)

7 *He said he'd ring as soon as he got home and he did.* (ring)

Task 7.5

In the following sentences, identify what has been ellipted.

1 I'm happy to go if you are.

2 John went to the movies but Freda didn't want to.

3 Has Sue found her keys? She ought to have by now.

4 Got a match?

5 I like Beethoven. Do you?

6 Want a drink?

7 Good to see you.

8 I'll play the piano if you will.

9 My friends own, pay the expenses on but don't use their beach cottage.

10 I'll see you tomorrow or later in the week.

11 I wanted him to do it today but he can't.

12 The wind dropped and switched to the south.

13 She used to sit after dinner and drop off.

14 John washed the dishes and Bob the clothes.

15 I'm going to the movies tonight and Fred tomorrow.

16 I like avocados but Max doesn't.

17 Looks like rain.

18 The people injured in the crash gradually recovered.

Task 7.6

Which of the following elements should be ellipted or replaced by a pro-form?

1 John likes rugby league and Fred likes rugby league.
2 Sarah buys the food, Sarah cooks the dinner and Sarah does the dishes on Thursdays.
3 I earned $2,000 and Sally earned $3,000 during the university vacation.
4 One storm front passed slowly through the district on Tuesday and another storm front passed quickly through the district on Friday.
5 One storm front passed quickly through the district on Tuesday and another storm front passed quickly through the district on Friday.

Task 7.7

In Text 7.3, identify where ellipsis may have taken place and suggest what has been ellipted.

Text 7.3

Malaria

Every year there are at least 500 million cases of malaria worldwide, and at least one million deaths from the disease, many of them children. The majority of cases are in sub-Saharan Africa. The mosquitoes carrying the disease are increasingly resistant to insecticides, and malaria itself has become increasingly drug resistant. Malaria has been around for a long time, ravaging Roman armies 2000 years ago in Europe and, later, Genghis Khan's soldiers in Asia. It also had a profound effect in slowing the rate of European colonial expansion in the nineteenth century. During the Second World War, DDT was used effectively to control mosquitoes in tropical climates, but later it was discovered there were unacceptable ecological consequences, as well as resistance from the insects to the chemicals and drugs used to control them.

We are able to recover ellipted elements from sentences by several means. These include:

1 The context or situation in which a sentence is produced, e.g.

Want another one?
Did they win?
Serves them right.

2 The grammatical context, e.g.

> *Interest charges fall* (headline)
> *Bull charges man* (headline)
> *The person (that) I told you about rang (?me).*

3 Copying an item that comes before (anaphoric ellipsis), e.g.

> *I'll go if you will (go).*
> *I went to town but Fred didn't want to (go).*

4 Copying an item that comes after (cataphoric ellipsis), e.g.

> *If you want to (have the day off) you can have the day off.*

7.4 Subordination

We have defined a **complex** sentence as one that has more than one clause. As we have seen in Section 7.2, if these clauses are of equal status they are said to be **co-ordinated**. If one of the clauses does not begin with a conjunction, then it is the **main clause** (or matrix clause), and the other (or others) are considered to be **subordinate** to the main clause. Consider these examples of subordination:

1 Simple sentence, e.g.

> *He will help her.* (one clause)

2 Complex sentence, e.g.

> (i) *He will help her* (main clause)
>
>   *if she asks him.* (subordinate clause)
>
> (ii) *Max said Δ* (main clause)
>
>   *that he will help her* (subordinate clause)
>
>   *if she asks him.* (subordinate clause)

Sometimes a complex sentence contains several clauses, as in the following example:

> *Sue hopes that the person who took the bike which was outside her house returns it because she needs it so that she can ride to work.*

> (iii) *Sue hopes Δ_1* (main clause)
>
>   *Δ_1 that the person Δ_2 returns it Δ_4* (subordinate clause)
>
>   *Δ_2 (who = the person) took the bike Δ_3* (subordinate clause)
>
>   *Δ_3 (which = the bike) was outside her house* (subordinate clause)
>
>   *Δ_4 because she needs it Δ_5* (subordinate clause)
>
>   *Δ_5 so that she can ride to work.* (subordinate clause)

The relationship between main and subordinate clauses is sometimes called **embedding** – one or more clauses can be said to be 'embedded' in, or attached to, a main clause. Embedding is one of the most important processes in English because it makes possible a gigantic number of sentences (maybe an infinite number) from a finite set of words and thus it is one of the ways in which we can be creative in our use of language, saying or writing things that have never been said before. In theory there is no limit to the number of embeddings in a sentence. In practice, our attention span and the need for stylistic elegance and clarity limit the number of embeddings in a single sentence.

7.4.1 The marking of subordination

Most subordinate clauses begin with a word or words (a 'complementiser') which can mark the fact that the clause has subordinate status. These complementisers include:

1 Subordinating conjunctions

The main ones are *after, although, as, because, before, if, like, once, since, so that, that, though, unless, until, when, whenever, where, whereas, wherever, while, except for, as long as, as soon as, in case, no sooner than,* e.g.

I went to the movie *after I went shopping.*
She thinks *that* I lost her keys.

2 Wh- elements

what, which, who, why, what time, how, that, e.g.

I know *what* I have to do.
The novel *that* I like best was written by E. M. Forster.

3 Subordination can also be marked by subject verb inversion, e.g.

Had I the time, I would visit them.
Were she here, she'd be able to tell us.

4 Non-finite verbs or no verb, e.g.

To get the right answer you should use a calculator.
Where necessary, replace the rotten wood.

Sometimes subordination is not marked with a linguistic item, e.g.

I hope *(that) you are feeling better.*
I didn't know *(that) you had sold your house.*
The book *(that) you asked for wasn't available.*

7.4.2 Functions of subordinate clauses

Subordinate clauses can have several different **functions**. If a subordinate clause functions in place of a noun or noun phrase it is called a **nominal clause or noun clause**. If a subordinate clause functions as an adjective or adjective phrase it is called a **relative clause**. If a subordinate clause functions as an adverbial it is called an **adverbial clause**. If a subordinate clause is used for making a comparison it is called a **comparative clause**. In the following notes, each of these kinds of subordinate clause will be considered separately. Here are examples of each. Note that some subordinate clauses have non-finite verbs.

1 **Nominal clause** (functions as a noun phrase)

That she got better was a miracle.   (finite nominal clause – subject)

I heard *that you were there.*   (finite nominal clause – object)

I liked *what he said.*   (finite nominal clause – object)

She said *that Max should be home by five o'clock.*   (finite nominal clause – object)

This is *what he asked for.*   (finite nominal clause – subject complement)

I wanted *you to know.*   (non-finite nominal clause – object)

He likes *playing rugby.*   (non-finite nominal clause – object)

2 **Relative clause** (functions like a postnominal adjective to modify a noun)

The person *who rang me* was my uncle.

They've repaired the dam *that was wrecked by the earthquake.*

The cyclist *injured in the crash* is in hospital.

The person *to ask* is the manager.

3 **Adverbial clause** (functions as a modifier of a verb phrase or sentence)

I went home *after I had finished work.*

If you want some help please let me know.

She can't speak to you *because she is busy.*

4 **Comparative clause** (functions to make comparisons)

Sue is taller *than her sister.*

I like eating nectarines *more than (I like) apricots.*

Task 7.8

Underline the subordinate clauses in the following sentences.

1 I don't know what he's talking about.
2 Although we didn't have any rain this week, you can hardly say the weather has been fine.
3 Feilding is the town which he told us about.
4 If the phone goes, take a message.
5 Since we're in agreement, we may as well sign the papers.
6 The person who rang me last night wanted to sell insurance.
7 How can we help if they won't let us?
8 I changed courses because I didn't find the other one to be relevant.
9 I didn't know that you had retired.
10 If possible, I'd like to have a few days off.
11 He works longer hours than he did last year.

Task 7.9

In Texts 7.4 and 7.5, identify each subordinate clause. Some have a finite verb, others have a non-finite verb. Work out whether each subordinate clause is functioning as a noun phrase (nominal clause), an adjective (relative clause) or an adverbial (adverbial clause).

Text 7.4

A rescue at sea

A fisherman saved the lives of three young people yesterday when they were found near death after spending four days in shark-prone waters. The fisherman who rescued them was leaving the area when he saw a fishing buoy in the water. As he got closer he saw a young man and woman clinging to it. The two could barely speak and had to be lifted into the boat. The fisherman said that five minutes later the young woman asked him to look for her boyfriend, who had gone missing. About half a kilometre away, they found the young man delirious in the water. The trio had apparently been on a fishing boat that sank four days previously after it had been hit by a freak wave.

Text 7.5

A mountain rescue

A climber who suffered a heart attack on the slopes of Mount Everest was saved after a rescue operation involving his friend's wife in Hong Kong and a solar-powered mobile phone. The climber collapsed on the world's highest peak as temperatures began falling with only two hours' remaining daylight. His climbing partner called a relative in Hong Kong by mobile phone, after failing to get a land line to nearby Kathmandu. He said they needed help urgently. His relative, who was a doctor in Hong Kong, telephoned the Nepalese army and asked whether it could send a helicopter to rescue the climber. The army had a small helicopter available which could hover at high altitude for only 15 minutes with room for a patient and oxygen cylinder. After being treated by two doctors in the climbing party and surviving temperatures of –15°C, the climber was flown to Kathmandu Hospital. The rest of the party continued the expedition and hoped to reach the summit of Everest before the weather deteriorated.

7.4.2.1 Nominal clauses

Nominal clauses, functioning like nouns or noun phrases, are very frequent and can occur wherever nouns can occur as subjects, objects or complements, etc. You can usually test whether a subordinate clause is a nominal clause by seeing whether you can replace the clause with *it* or *something*, e.g.

> He thinks *you will be surprised.* (He thinks *something.*)
>
> I saw *the car hit the barrier.* (I saw *it* or *something.*)

There are four main structures or types of nominal clause.

7.4.2.1.1 *That*-clauses

That-clauses can behave like nouns, with the following main functions:

a Subject:

> *That Max likes milk on fruit* amazes me.
>
> *That you don't like yoghurt* surprises me.

When a *that*-clause functions as a subject, it is often moved to the end of the sentence, and a 'dummy' subject (*it*) put in its original place. This is called **extraposition**, e.g.

> It amazes me *that Max likes milk on fruit.*
>
> It surprises me *that you don't like yoghurt.*

b Object:

> I saw *that she had injured her arm.*
>
> Most people know *that the world is round.*
>
> He said *that he loves me.*

c Subject complement:

> Their policy is *that tuition fees should be lower*.
>
> The point was *that she made the best case*.

d Apposition:

> The rumour *that the government will reduce taxes* was denied by the politician.

e Adjective complement:

> I am sure *that things will get better*.
>
> I am pleased *that you will be there*.

That is often omitted in nominal clauses, especially in spoken English, following the verbs *think* or *say* (e.g. *I think you are right; I said I'd had enough*).

Biber et al. (1999: 662) have listed the most frequent verbs that have nominal clauses as objects. These include: *think, say, know, see, find, believe, feel, suggest, show* and many other 'speech act verbs' such as *admit, agree, announce, argue, insist, complain, acknowledge, deny, confess, hint, grant*.

Some adjectives can also be followed by *that*-clauses, e.g.

> It's good that we'll both be there.
>
> I was amazed that they hadn't heard about it.

certain	appropriate	afraid	true	horrible	unfair
glad	sad	good	shocked	amazed	confident

7.4.2.1.2 *Wh*-clauses

Wh-clauses can behave as if they are nouns, with the following main functions:

a Subject:

> *What she told us* was very useful.

b Object:

> I heard *what you said*.
>
> I wonder *when the plane is due*.
>
> I don't know *how to get in touch with her*.
>
> Do you know *what to do*?

c Subject complement:

> This is *what he gave me*.
>
> This is *how I found out*.
>
> That is *why I came here*.

d Object complement:

> The training made him *what he is today.*

e Adjective complement:

> We weren't certain *who was coming to the meeting.*

f Prepositional complement:

> I was looking for *where I had left my keys.*
>
> They asked her about *who they should appoint.*
>
> The news of *what had happened* reached us at 8 p.m.

The interrogative pronouns and adverbs that introduce *wh*-interrogative clauses include: *what, who, which, where, when, why, how.* The most frequent verbs complemented by a *wh*-clause are *know, wonder, understand, tell, ask, see, look at* (Biber et al., 1999: 689).

Noun clauses may be introduced by certain other conjunctions besides *that* or *a wh*-word, e.g.

> She asked him *if he was tired.*
>
> *Whether he goes or not* doesn't bother me.

That-clauses and *wh*-clauses are finite nominal clauses. That is, they contain finite verbs. In the section on non-finite clauses (7.5), we will consider examples of nominal clauses that are non-finite because they have *to*-infinitives or *-ing* complementisers, e.g.

> We like *to swim in the sea.*
>
> I like *eating kiwifruit and oranges.*

7.4.2.1.3 Nominal clauses in apposition

Sometimes certain abstract nouns such as *fact, reply, claim, news, idea, hope, rumour, theory, statement, discovery, suggestion, proposal, assumption, belief, remark, story* are followed by a nominal clause. The clause is said to be **in apposition to** the head noun, e.g.

> The idea *that I would go* is ridiculous.
>
> The rumour *that he is getting married* is completely false.
>
> The fact *that she knows how to read music* makes her the ideal candidate.
>
> He expressed the hope *that I would arrive safely.*
>
> The story *that I'm going to retire next year* is completely unfounded.

These clauses in apposition may look like relative clauses but they are interpreted differently. Compare:

1 Aristotle believed the story *that Plato had died.*

(nominal clause in apposition)

2 Aristotle believed the story *that Plato had told.*   (relative clause)

In the relative clause, *that* is a relative pronoun and can be replaced by *which*. In the appositive clause, *that* is a conjunction and it cannot be replaced by *which*.

Task 7.10

Underline the finite nominal clauses and identify their functions (subject, object, subject complement, apposition, complement of an adjective, complement of a preposition).

1 It seems clear that they are committed to the present policy.

2 It was likely that they wouldn't believe him.

3 They can do what they like.

4 'What I really wanted to know was this,' he said.

5 You could be certain that your visits were carefully recorded.

6 Many people are simply not aware that we do not have unlimited funds.

7 The fact that the joke has to be explained prevents it from being funny.

8 In this article, we will show that some fundamental problems of cognitive psychology can be accounted for in terms of macro-processing.

Text 7.6

A tale from Iran

When Nasreddin was young, he often didn't do what he was told, so his father started to tell him to do the opposite of what he wanted him to do. One day, when the two were bringing sacks of flour home on their donkeys, they had to cross a shallow river. When they were in the middle of it, one of the sacks on Nasreddin's donkey began to slip, so his father said, 'That sack is nearly in the water! Press down hard on it!' His father of course expected that he would do the opposite, but this time Nasreddin did what his father had told him to do. He pressed down on the sack and it went under the water. Of course, the flour was lost. When his father asked him why he had pushed down on the sack, Nasreddin said that he wanted to show his father that he now thought he should obey him.

Task 7.11

In Text 7.6, identify the finite and non-finite nominal clauses. In the margin, write the function of each nominal clause (subject, object, complement of preposition, etc.).

7.4.2.1.4 Indirect speech

As we saw in 7.4.2.1.1, a frequent use of nominal clauses is as objects after 'reporting' verbs such as *say, tell, think, hear, ask, wonder, complain*. This is sometimes called **indirect speech** or **reported speech**, e.g.

I agree with you.	→	He said *that he agreed with us.*
Do you want to go?	→	He asked *whether I wanted to go.*
You're right.	→	She thinks *I'm right.*
I am never consulted.	→	He complained *that he was never consulted.*
I was there.	→	She admitted *that she had been there.*
We don't know about it.	→	They denied *that they knew about it.*

Indirect speech is often hard for language learners, partly because of tense and word order changes, e.g.

Do you want to go?	→	He asked me *whether I wanted to go.*

Suggested 'rules' such as 'backshifting' from present to past tense can be quite hard to apply in practice, e.g.

Sue will meet you at 5 p.m.	→	He said *Sue would meet me at 5 p.m.*

However, we could also find *He said Sue will meet me at 5 p.m.*, especially if that time is still in the future.

Other linguistic changes in indirect speech sometimes include:

1 Pronoun changes, e.g.

I want some chocolate.	→	He said *he* wanted some chocolate. You said *you* wanted some chocolate.

2 *This* can change to *that*, e.g.

We like this style.	→	He said they liked *that* style.

3 *These* can change to *those*, e.g.

Dan took these photos.	→	He said Dan took *those* photos.

4 *Here* can change to *there*, e.g.

I'll come here tomorrow.	→	She said she'd go *there* tomorrow.

7.4.2.1.5 Learning how to use nominal clauses

1 Nominal clauses can make a sentence hard to understand (especially when they function as the subject of the sentence) because they can make it more difficult to work out the overall structure of the sentence, e.g.

What he said after you had made your speech was interesting.

This does not mean 'Your speech was interesting'.

Fortunately, only a small proportion of nominal clauses (possibly less than 5 per cent) function as subjects. Most nominal clauses (about 75 per cent) function as objects in indirect speech, e.g.

She said *that she agreed with me.*

2 Sentences containing a subject nominal clause with an introductory subject *it* (e.g. *It is likely that Fred will be there*) are especially difficult. In this sentence, *that Fred will be there* is the subject.

3 Sometimes the introductory verb affects the truth of the object nominal clause and this may confuse learners of English. Compare these sentences:

   a *Sue knew that Fred was sick.* (it is almost certain that Fred was sick)

   b *Sue thought that Fred was sick.* (we don't know whether Fred was sick or not)

   c *Sue doubted that Fred was sick.* (it is likely that Fred was not sick)

Other verbs like *know* include *realise, prove, mention*
Other verbs like *think* include *say, believe, assume*
Other verbs like *doubt* include *deny.*

Some students will need help to recognise the implications of noun clauses of this kind. Their attention can be drawn to them by comprehension questions and by training them to distinguish between facts and people's opinions.

4 In learning to produce sentences with nominal clauses, learners sometimes have word order difficulties, especially with indirect speech, e.g.

*He asked where do I live.

instead of   *He asked where I live.*

This difficulty may arise because reported statements are sometimes taught as being linked to direct questions (which have a different word order) instead of being linked to reported questions or direct statements, e.g.

Where are you going?	(direct question)
He asked me where I was going.	(reported question)
I am going shopping.	(direct statement)
He said he is going shopping.	(reported statement)

7.4.2.2 Relative clauses

A relative clause is a subordinate clause which functions like an adjective to postmodify a noun. For this reason relative clauses are sometimes called 'adjective clauses'. In the following sentences, a headword noun is modified by a following relative clause:

1 The <u>person</u> *who rang me* wanted to sell something.

2 The <u>person</u> *that rang me* sounded like you.

Relative clauses are typically introduced or linked to the headword they modify with a relative pronoun or relative adverb. These 'relative words' ('relativisers') include *who, whom, which, that, whose, where, when, how, why* and *Ø*, and they occur in place of a noun phrase that is the same as the preceding ('antecedent') noun phrase in the main clause.

Biber et al. (1999: 610) have shown that in newspapers and academic written English the relative word *that* is typically not as frequent as *which*, but in conversation and fiction *that* is the most frequent relative word. Overall, *that, which* and *who* are the most frequent.

That is the most flexible because it can be used with human or non-human antecedent nouns, e.g.

The person that we saw didn't seem to be well.

The boy that's playing the piano tomorrow is only seven years old.

The piano that we bought needed repairing.

Who, whom and *which* do not have the same flexibility.

7.4.2.2.1 Functions of relative clauses

Relative clauses can modify noun phrases which are subjects, objects, complements or objects of prepositions. For example:

Subject	:	The man *who arrived at the school* was a painter.
		The child *that you saw* is only six.
		The man *who(m) I saw* was a painter.
Object	:	I rang the teacher *who is in charge of the library*.
		I know the person *you met last night*.
Complement	:	That was the man *who(m) I saw at the school*.
Object of preposition	:	The man *that he shouted to* ran to help him.
		The man *he shouted to* ran to help him.
		The man *to whom he shouted* ran to help him.

In continuous spoken or written English it is common to find about one sentence out of every four containing a relative clause. It is not unusual to find over ten relative clauses per page of text in a novel. Learners of English sometimes make errors like the following when they produce relative clauses. The errors often involve the redundant use of pronouns or the mistaken omission of a relative pronoun.

1 *This is a procedure which we can follow it at a suitable time.

2 *This is not easy for the learners who they are being taught.

3 *He changed the programme which they listened.

4 *She returned to the place where she belonged to.

5 *The learners should find words and phrases could be used in the picture.

6 *In English we know some words which we are familiar with their usage.

7 *They learned to pass the exams which I think it is not good enough.

Discussion topic

In each of the above sentences, identify the problem which you think contributes to or results in the error.

The most frequent structure in which relative clauses occur is when the relative clause modifies an object, e.g.

I rang *the woman* **who** advertised her piano.
     object   subject of
              relative clause

I saw *the girl* **that** you told me about.
    object   object of
             relative clause

It is less common to find a relative clause which modifies a subject, e.g.

The man **who** lives next door is my uncle.
subject   subject of
            relative clause

The teachers **that** I prefer are not too strict.
subject   object of
            relative clause

7.4.2.2.2 Restrictive and non-restrictive relative clauses

The modification of a noun by a relative clause can be **restrictive** (defining) or **non-restrictive** (non-defining). A **restrictive relative clause** defines or identifies a particular noun antecedent and shows **which** one is being referred to, e.g.

The cafe *that opened last week* has good food.	(which cafe?)
The book *which you recommended* was useful.	(which book?)
The house *we would like to buy* is too expensive.	(which house?)
The man *who came to dinner* didn't stay long.	(which man?)

Note: A restrictive relative clause is usually not separated from its antecedent head noun with a comma in written English (or a pause in spoken English).

Computer grammar checkers often indicate that *which* is undesirable as a relativiser (e.g. The book *which you recommended* was useful). However, there are not good grounds for following this advice, either in theory or in actual use as shown in corpora.

A **non-restrictive relative clause**, on the other hand, simply gives further information about the headword or comments on the headword. We can assume that the headword is already identifiable or defined, e.g.

> Fred Jones, *who owns the new cafe*, is a good cook.

> The third example, *which is quite hard*, can be left until last.

Note: There is usually a comma (or pause) between an antecedent noun and a non-restrictive relative clause. Non-restrictive relative clauses usually do not have *that* as their relative pronoun, but it is possible, because some native speakers of English will accept the following:

> Fred Jones, *that owns the new cafe*, is a good cook.

Non-restrictive relative clauses are rather similar semantically to co-ordinated sentences, although the relative clause may be preferred stylistically, cf.

> He met Freda, *who invited him to a party*.

> He met Freda *and she invited him to a party*.

Sometimes a whole sentence acts as the head of a relative clause. These are called **sentential relative clauses**, e.g.

> John continues to respect his boss, *which is unusual*.

Table 7.1 summarises the appropriate forms of the most frequent relative pronouns, which go with headwords in different grammatical contexts in restrictive relative clauses.

Table 7.1 Relative pronouns in restricted relative clauses

Function	Person (human)	Non-personal (non-human)
Subject	who that	which that
Object	who(m) that	which that Ø
Complement of a preposition	at whom to whom in whom of whom etc.	at which to which in which of which etc.
Possessive	whose	whose of which

Table 7.2 Non-restrictive relative pronouns

Function	Personal (human)	Non-personal (non-human)
Subject	who	which
Object	who(m)	which
Complement of a preposition	at whom to whom in whom of whom etc.	at which to which in which of which etc.
Possessive	whose	whose of which

For non-restrictive relative clauses, the appropriate pronouns are shown in Table 7.2.

7.4.2.2.3 Relative clauses and adjectives
As we noted in Chapter 6, some linguists have suggested that adjectives (which usually come before nouns in English) can be seen as being related to embedded relative clauses. For example:

1	The woman (The woman is tall) is my neighbour.
⇒	The woman who is tall is my neighbour.
⇒	*The woman tall is my neighbour.
⇒	The tall woman is my neighbour.
2	Max drove the car. The car was rusty.
⇒	Max drove the car which was rusty.
⇒	*Max drove the car rusty.
⇒	Max drove the rusty car.
3	The police found the bike. Someone stole the bike.
⇒	The police found the bike. The bike was stolen (by someone).
⇒	The police found the bike which was stolen (by someone).
⇒	*The police found the bike stolen.
⇒	The police found the stolen bike.

In sentences such as 3, which contain a participial adjective (*stolen*), the possible derivation of the adjective from an embedded predicate is reasonably transparent.

7.4.2.2.4 Reduced relative clauses
Relative clauses can be 'reduced' in several ways which make them less explicit (and therefore potentially less easy for learners to follow), e.g. Sentence 1 can be reduced to the form in Sentence 2.

1 The car *which was parked outside my house* belonged to a friend of mine.

2 The car *parked outside my house* belonged to a friend of mine.

Types of reduction

1 In restrictive relative clauses, the relative pronoun is often omitted (except when it stands for a subject), e.g.

> The man *that Mary likes* is a musician.
>
> The man *Mary likes* is a musician.

cf.

> The person *who arrived last night* was my brother.
>
> *The person *arrived last night* was my brother.

2 The relative clause may be reduced to include a non-finite verb, e.g.

> The person *who was waiting outside* was a friend.
>
> ⇒ The person *waiting outside* was a friend.

Other non-finite verbs which occur frequently in reduced clauses include: *mentioned, given, used, caused, made, taken, produced, containing, using, involving, being,* e.g.

> The person *who was mentioned in the report* arrives tonight.
>
> ⇒ The person *mentioned in the report* arrives tonight.

In this last example, learners may wrongly interpret 'the person' as the subject of a finite verb 'mentioned', as in *The person mentioned your problems.*
Other examples of reduced relative clauses:

> I spoke to the person *standing alongside me.*
>
> The tree had leaves *falling off all over.*
>
> I've got friends *to help me.*
>
> The last person *to leave* should turn off the lights.
>
> They demanded the right *to run for President.*

3 The relative clause may be verbless and function as a prepositional phrase postmodifier, e.g.

> Give your paper to the person *who is on your right.*
>
> ⇒ Give your paper to the person *on your right.*

Task 7.12

In the following sentences:

a Underline the relative clauses.

b Put brackets around the antecedent noun phrase of each relative clause.

c Indicate whether the relative clause is restrictive (R) or non-restrictive (NR).

1 He showed me a small room which I could sleep in if necessary.

2 Later I spoke to the people that owned the house.

3 The proposal would have to be supported by all the owners, who could not easily be located.

4 The yacht he bought was made of fibreglass.

5 He was past the age at which he could easily get these things himself.

6 The earthworm can bend its body in any direction it wants.

7 That was the most famous picture Rembrandt had painted.

8 His attention was attracted towards a sound he couldn't identify.

Text 7.7

A mouse on a plane

According to a news report that I saw on TV, a mouse which was discovered on an aircraft scheduled to leave for London caused panic among passengers, who jumped out of their seats and ran to one end of the aircraft to escape. Airport workers and cleaners who were called in unfortunately failed to catch the mouse. Passengers were therefore transferred to another aircraft, which took off three hours late. It is hard to believe that adult passengers could be afraid of a mouse which couldn't possibly hurt them.

Text 7.8

Influenza

Influenza remains a serious and debilitating disease that is often underrated. Additional deaths which are above the normal winter increase are recorded regularly in association with influenza epidemics. Over the past decade in the US up to 47,000 deaths per influenza season have been observed with 80–90 per cent occurring in persons who are 65 years and older. Influenza is caused by a number of different viruses which are classified by structure as Influenza A, B or C. Influenza A causes less extensive epidemics of disease mainly in children and occasionally in adults but is rarely associated with additional deaths. The influenza virus has the ability to undergo major changes called 'shifts'. These usually occur at intervals of ten years or more and result in serious epidemics. Minor changes, which are called 'drifts', can also occur each year, which can result in new strains of the virus involved. Vaccination, which can offer 60–80 per cent protection in normal healthy adults when the vaccine and epidemic strains are closely related, can reduce the number of deaths which are normally caused by influenza.

Task 7.13

In Texts 7.7 and 7.8:

1 Underline all the relative clauses, including 'reduced' relative clauses.

2 Put the antecedent headword in brackets.

3 Note whether the relative clauses are restrictive (R) or non-restrictive (NR).

Task 7.14

Join up the following simple sentences to make a single sentence which contains a relative clause or clauses.

1 I saw a person. The person was waiting to use a phone.

2 The ferry crosses the Channel in about two hours. It is quite a big ship.

3 Some people get quite sick. Some people cross the Channel each year on the ferry.

4 My holiday begins on 3 June. I plan to take my holiday in Italy. I think the weather will be better in Italy.

5 I finished my assignment last Friday. My assignment took me several days to complete.

Task 7.15

Write examples which contain the following:

1 A restrictive relative clause which modifies the object of the main clause.

2 A restrictive relative clause which does not have a relativiser (relative pronoun).

---

3 A non-restrictive relative clause which modifies the subject of the main clause.

4 A restrictive relative clause which has been 'reduced' so that it contains a non-finite verb and no finite verb.

Check your answers with a colleague if possible.

7.4.2.2.5 Learning how to use relative clauses

Learners of English quite often misunderstand sentences which contain relative clauses. Where appropriate, teachers should check that learners can identify both the main and subordinate clauses. There are several possible reasons why sentences which contain relative clauses can be hard for learners to understand.

1 A relative clause adds another verb (finite or non-finite) to a sentence, e.g.

> I *saw* some of the pictures which Picasso *painted* in 1938.

Very often, sentences contain more than one relative clause, and there are therefore several verbs. This can make it hard to work out which subjects go with which verbs, e.g.

> I *saw* some of the pictures which Picasso *painted* during the period which he later *described* as one of the most difficult times he had *experienced* before he *settled* in Paris.

2 Where a relative clause is 'reduced', the verb is often a non-finite *-ed* or *-ing* participle.

> The woman (who was) *sitting* in the car looked unhappy.
> Some of the buildings (which were) *damaged* by the earthquake were not insured.

With reduced relative clauses, learners sometimes misinterpret the non-finite verb as being finite. Sometimes they misinterpret the time reference of non-finite verbs, or think that the preceding noun is the subject of the verb. (see Section 7.4.2.2.4). Non-finite clauses are discussed further in Section 7.5 of this book.

3 Relative clauses are sometimes not 'marked' by a relative word. Although some researchers have suggested that sentences with unmarked relative clauses are not necessarily harder to understand, some learners seem to fail to recognise a relative clause that is unmarked, e.g.

> I saw a man standing on the corner.

Teachers should check who the learners think was standing on the corner.

4 If a relative clause modifies a subject, it breaks up the main clause and thus adds complexity and potential confusion, e.g.

> The woman *who was speaking to Fred* owns a red car.

The principle of minimal distance claims that we normally expect the noun which immediately precedes a verb to be the subject of that verb. Thus, in the example above, *Fred* rather than *the woman* may wrongly be interpreted as the subject of *owns a red car.*

5 If the antecedent headword is the same as the object of the relative clause, then the relative clause can be much harder to understand because of the abnormal word order (OSV), e.g.

O   S   V

> I saw the person *(who) you described.*

(O)   S V

> He struggled against the apathy of the people *(whom) he employed.*

6 Sometimes two or three of these factors which may make comprehension difficult occur together, e.g.

> The person I met was friendly.

(no relative marker; interrupted main clause; abnormal (O)SV word order)

Discussion topic

Discuss possible sources of difficulty for learners in the following sentence:

> One of the things I want to discuss before we leave is whether the price they are asking for the house is too high.

It has been found that some learners of English avoid using relative clauses and thus make fewer errors in producing them than other learners. However, relative clauses cannot always be avoided in speech or writing and learners do produce sentences containing errors. Production problems with relative clauses seem to arise particularly from:

1 The misuse of relative pronouns

2 The repetition of direct objects, e.g.

> The question which we didn't know about it before was hard.

3 Not knowing how to cope with the object of a preposition, e.g.

> He changed the programme which they listened.
>
> She returned to the place where she belonged to.

7.4.2.3 Adverbial clauses

Adverbial clauses modify or add meaning to a main clause. They are very frequent in English. The clauses are linked by means of a subordinating conjunction, e.g.

Main clause	Conjunction	Adverbial clause
I had lunch	before	I went to the bank.
Sue doesn't eat chocolate	because	it gives her headaches.
Give me a call	if	you're going to be late.

The order of the clauses can be reversed:

I had lunch before I went to the bank.	(main clause – adverbial clause)
Before I went to the bank I had lunch.	(adverbial clause – main clause)
Cf. Before I had lunch I went to the bank.	(adverbial clause – main clause)

Although adverbial clauses can come before or after the main clause in a sentence, they come **after** the main clause in about 66 per cent of cases.

7.4.2.3.1 Semantic functions of adverbial clauses
The main semantic functions of adverbial clauses are:

Adverbial clause type	Main clause	Adverbial clause
	e.g.	
place	We took care	wherever we saw that sign.
time	I played soccer	when I lived in Auckland.
condition	She said she would go	if she had time.
concession	I went to work	although I wasn't feeling well.
cause/reason	He hurt his leg	because he fell off his bike.
purpose	We worked late	so we could get the job done.
result	She studied hard	so she passed her exam.
contrast	I like oysters	whereas none of my family do.
exception	I would give you a hand	except that I'm running late.

7.4.2.3.2 Main conjunctions used in adverbial clauses

Adverbial clause type	Main conjunctions
place	where, wherever
time	after, as, as soon as, before, once, since, until, when, whenever, while
condition	as long as, if, provided that, unless, on condition that
concession	although, as, even if, though, whereas, while
cause/reason	as, because, for, in case, seeing that, since, so that
purpose	in order that, in order to, so as to, so that
result	so, so that
contrast	whereas, while
exception	except that, only

Table 7.3 Distribution of the most frequent subordinating conjunctions in the *British National Corpus*

Conjunction	Total per 1 million words	Percentage
as	3,006	21.7
if	2,369	17.1
when	1,712	12.3
than	1,033	7.5
because	852	6.1
while	503	3.6
where	458	3.3
although	436	3.1
whether	332	2.4
before	305	2.2
since	295	2.1
so	258	1.9
though	245	1.8
until	242	1.7
after	233	1.7
so that	197	1.4
'cos	163	1.2
as if	157	1.1
for	139	1.0
unless	110	0.8
All others	818	5.9
Total	13,863	100.0

Note: The other major subordinating conjunction is *that*, but this word is mainly used for introducing nominal and relative clauses.

Overall frequency figures alone, however, are not enough to guide teaching. For example, *as*, *since* and *while* can all be used to introduce **time**, **reason** or **concession** adverbial clauses, and these are not equally frequent. For teaching purposes, it is worth noting that adverbial clauses of time, condition and cause/reason occur most frequently in texts. Adverbial clauses of time typically account for up to 50 per cent of all adverbial clauses in spoken and written English. If we leave aside adverbial clauses introduced by *that* (see note above), over 90 per cent of the adverbial clauses in written British English are clauses of time, condition or cause/reason.

It is important to note that adverbial clauses are sometimes non-finite. That is, they have no finite verb, and sometimes no subordinating conjunction, e.g.

1 *To help with the clean-up* the council hired extra staff.

2 *The exams over*, they went out and celebrated.

3 *Going through the doorway*, he caught sight of Amanda.

Non-finite adverbial clauses are discussed in Section 7.5.

Text 7.9

A missing driver

When a large truck was found in a ditch beside the road, the police immediately began searching for the driver in case he had been injured. Eventually the driver was found sleeping at his brother's home after the police had spent several hours searching for him. He might be charged with wasting police time if they decide to prosecute him. Police were to interview the man further before a decision was made. The search was launched about 10 a.m. on Friday as fears grew for the man's safety. In fact, he had abandoned his fully laden truck because it had crashed off the road several hours earlier. Searchers scoured farmland for five hours before someone discovered the man was asleep in a comfortable bed a few kilometres away.

Task 7.16

1 Identify the adverbial clauses in Text 7.9.

2 Put brackets around each subordinating conjunction.

3 In each instance, note what kind of adverbial clause you have underlined (time, conditional, purpose, etc.).

4 Mark whether the adverbial clauses are finite or non-finite.

7.4.2.3.3 Adverbial clauses of time

Not only are adverbial clauses of time very frequent, they also provide problems for learners of English. There are at least three main reasons why they are difficult.

1 Adverbial clauses of time can express different temporal relations, including:

Simultaneity	e.g. *While you were away, the letter came.*
Sequentiality	
priorness	e.g. *I had lunch before John got home.*
subsequence	e.g. *After I'd done the dishes I went to bed.*
Recurrence	e.g. *Whenever it gets cold we get invaded by ants.*
Duration	e.g. *When I was young we lived in Edinburgh.*

2 When the order of mention of two events in a sentence is not the same as their chronological occurrence, time sequences can be confused. This is particularly the case with clauses that are introduced by *after*, *before* or *when*.

Consider these two events:

Event 1	*I had lunch.*
Event 2	*I rang my aunt.*

Using adverbial clauses of time, they can be expressed as follows:

   a *I had lunch before I rang my aunt.*

   b *After I('d) had lunch, I rang my aunt.*

   c *I'd had lunch when I rang my aunt.*

   d *Before I rang my aunt, I('d) had lunch.*

   e *I rang my aunt after I('d) had lunch.*

   f *When I rang my aunt, I'd had lunch.*

The order of difficulty of comprehension goes from (a) (easiest) to (f) (hardest), depending on whether the order of mention of two events is the same as the chronological order.

It is perhaps worth noting that, in the *LOB Corpus of written British English*, adverbial clauses introduced by *after* or *when* reverse the chronological order in about 60 per cent of cases.

3 Some conjunctions have multiple meanings. For example, *when* can mean *before, after, while, whenever, given that, if, although*, etc. This is shown in Table 7.4, which also shows the relative frequency of use of the different uses of the conjunction *when* in the *LOB Corpus*.

7.4.2.3.4 Adverbial clauses of condition

Conditional sentences which contain clauses introduced by *if, unless*, etc. are traditionally considered to be difficult for many learners of English.

1 Sometimes the *if*-clause is ignored by the learner and conditional sentences are interpreted as statements or promises without any condition.

   (If we get this order) *we'll go out and celebrate.*

2 Some learners have difficulty working out the meaning of the condition. Some conditional sentences are **open** or 'possible', e.g.

Factual:	*If you heat air it rises.* (each clause has the simple present tense)
Predictive:	*If it rains, I'll come and get you in the car.* (*if*-clause has present tense, main clause contains *will*)

Other conditional sentences are **hypothetical**. They may express conditions that are counterfactual. That is, they are improbable or impossible to fulfil, e.g.

Improbable:	*If it rained, I would come and get you.* (*if*-clause in simple past tense form, main clause contains *would*)
Impossible:	*If I were you I wouldn't take a holiday in winter.* *If I had known, I would have said something.* (*if*-clause in past perfect, main clause contains *would* (*have* + *-ed* participle))

Table 7.4 Senses of *when* in the *LOB Corpus*

		% of uses of *when*
1	*When* marks the simultaneous occurrence of events or states, e.g. *Mr Douglas was away* **when** *that decision was made.*	27
2	*When* marks the simultaneous duration of two states or processes (synonymous with *while*), e.g. *Rundle learned ice carving* **when** *he worked as a chef in Canada.*	15
3	*When* marks sequence and is synonymous with *after*, e.g. *And* **when** *he finished he went away.*	29
4	*When* marks sequence and is synonymous with *before* or *by the time that*, e.g. *She had only been in her room a few minutes* **when** *there was a knock.*	6
5	*When* marks indefinite or timeless frequency or iteration and is synonymous with *whenever*, e.g. **When** *mildew appears it should be treated.*	8
6	*When* is synonymous with *given that* or *since*, e.g. *Can we trust him* **when** *he is known to be unreliable?*	4
7	*When* marks contingency and is synonymous with *if*, e.g. *It is the most harmless thing you could do to anybody* **when** *you think about it.*	9
8	*When* marks concession and is synonymous with *although*, e.g. *I spent twenty pounds on guidebooks* **when** *I should have spent five.*	2

Note: Senses 1 and 2, which mark simultaneity, together account for 42 per cent of the tokens of *when*. Senses 3 and 4, which mark the very different relationship of sequentiality, account for 35 per cent of the tokens. The more contingent senses, 5–8, account in total for about 23 per cent of the tokens. Further, Senses 3 and 4, while both marking sequentiality, actually mark two contrasting sequential notions, priorness and subsequence, with the meaning of *after* being about five times as frequent as the meaning of *before*.

In a study of conditional sentences in the 1-million-word *Brown* (US) and *LOB* (UK) corpora of written English, Wang Sheng found the distribution shown in Table 7.5.

3 A particular learning problem is knowing which verb form to use in the main clause and *if*-clause. Hill (1960) described 324 potentially acceptable combinations. Wang Sheng (1991) showed that some of these combinations are much more frequent than others and that only 24 of the combinations as shown in Table 7.6 accounted for about 75 per cent of all conditional sentences.

Table 7.5 Semantic categories of conditionals in *Brown* and *LOB* corpora (Wang Sheng, 1991)

	Percentage of *if*-conditional sentences	
	Brown (written US English)	*LOB* (written UK English)
Open conditions Factual Predictive	47.3 28.3	48.3 26.3
Hypothetical conditions Improbable Counterfactual	14.2 10.2	14.3 11.1
	100	100

Table 7.6 Verb form use in conditional sentences in the *Brown* and *LOB* corpora (Wang Sheng, 1991)

Verb form in *if*-clause	Verb form in main clause	Percentage of *if*-tokens	
		US written English (*Brown* Corpus)	UK written English (*LOB* Corpus)
present simple	present simple	22.0	22.0
present simple	*will/shall/be going to* + stem	13.2	12.5
past simple	*would/could/might* + stem	11.3	11.1
past simple	past simple	6.7	6.8
present simple	*should/must/can/may/ought to* + stem	10.0	6.4
past perfect	*would/could/might have* + past participle	3.9	4.1
were/were to	*would/could/might* + stem	4.0	4.0
can + stem	present simple	1.1	3.2
present simple	*would/could/might* + stem	1.9	2.4
present simple	imperative	1.7	2.0
		75.8	74.5

4 With hypothetical conditions, learners sometimes have difficulty interpreting the presence or absence of *not*. In Sentence (a) below, for example, it might be expected that the reader would interpret it as 'the cup did **not** break' and 'I did **not** drop it'. On the other hand in (b), although there is a *not* in each clause we interpret it as 'I **did** drop the cup' and 'the cup **did** break'.

a *The cup might have broken if I'd dropped it.*

b *The cup wouldn't have broken if I hadn't dropped it.*

c *If he wasn't in such a hurry he would do better.*

d *If she'd told me about it earlier I would have tried to help.*

5 Sometimes conditional sentences are expressed with co-ordinated clauses which use *and* or *or*, e.g.

Come late again and I'll have to cut your allowance.

Don't do that or you'll get hurt.

7.4.2.3.5 Adverbial clauses of cause or reason

It is not always easy to decide whether a clause expresses cause, reason, purpose or result. These semantic categories are expressed in many ways (Fang & Kennedy, 1992). About 30 per cent of the time in the *LOB Corpus*, causation is expressed in a subordinate adverbial clause, e.g. *I went home **because I was tired**. Because* is the most frequently used subordinating conjunction for expressing reason or causation. *For* is also frequent, e.g.

Our walk was a tiring one *for the very wet weather had made all the paths muddy.*

Causation can also be expressed by prepositional phrases, e.g.

Because of the rain, I stayed home.

Sometimes causation is marked by a non-finite or elliptical clause, e.g.

Being Christmas, the library was closed.

Correctly anticipating the results, I didn't lose any money.

My purchases having been paid for, I left the shop.

Sometimes causation is not marked at all, and has to be inferred from the juxtaposition of sentences, e.g.

Doubts about whether the President can succeed are expected.

There are divisions in his party as well as in the opposition.

Young learners sometimes have trouble working out which clause is the cause or reason for the other. Compare, for example:

I fell off my bike because I had a sore foot.

I had a sore foot because I fell off my bike.

Task 7.17

Select a conjunction to make the following simple sentences into complex sentences. State what kind of adverbial clause each complex sentence contains (time, place, etc.).

Conjunctions: *although, while, as, since, where, because, if, unless, when*

1 The days went by.
   Fred became more and more miserable.

2 You'll find their farm.
   The road climbs away from the river.

3 Liz was short of money at university.
   Sue spent her time in a series of temporary but well-paid jobs.

4 They ring us before 5 p.m.
   We'll go ahead with our plans.

5 You have a few spare moments.
   Give me a call.

6 I broke my leg.
   I can't go skiing this year.

Task 7.18

Rewrite each set of sentences in the form of a single complex sentence. Use appropriate conjunctions. Try to avoid using *but, and, or, so.*

1 Mary took a pill. She got on the ferry. She wanted to avoid being seasick.

2 The trader had all his goods moved on camels. He had a lot of property. There was no railway in that country.

3 Two senators are elected from each state. Senators are elected for 6-year terms.

4 He did not see the event. He described the event so well in a pamphlet. I was reading the pamphlet yesterday. I will refer to the pamphlet later.

5 Smoke results from burning fuel. There is water vapour in smoke. There is carbon dioxide in smoke.

6 Human beings have the ability to make instruments. Instruments bring stars into view. The light from the stars has taken a thousand years to reach the earth.

7 He has gone away without leaving his address. This fact is a clear proof of his intentions. His intentions are dishonest.

Task 7.19

Underline the conditional clauses in the following sentences and say whether the condition is open (possible) or hypothetical.

1 If they can be persuaded to change the law then a lot of people will be pleased about it.

2 Many members mightn't get to hear about the meeting unless they are sent a personal invitation.

3 If I were in Fred's position I would resign immediately.

4 He couldn't have been there when the crime was committed unless someone at his workplace is not telling the truth.

5 Sue thinks they would be better off if they still lived in Boston.

6 As long as you let us know when you get there we don't mind how long it takes you.

7 If she reduced the second chapter I think the book would be a lot better.

8 If I hadn't seen it with my own eyes I wouldn't have believed it.

7.4.2.3.6 Learning how to use adverbial clauses
Typical errors made by learners:

1 *We should pay attention to the time. So that we get through the work quickly.*

2 *I will consider them as members even they have not paid their fee.*

3 *Even though that I know that one of the best ways is repetition.*

4 *Although he did his best but he failed in the end.*

Discussion topic

What is wrong with the sentences above? What advice would you give learners in order to help them overcome the problems?

Experience with learners' problems such as those above suggests to some teachers that the following points need to be kept in mind.

1 Teach adverbial clauses by focusing on the meaning of the conjunction rather than from the point of view of the 'grammar' of the complex sentence. Remember that most conjunctions have more than one meaning and can be used in different types of adverbial clauses.

2 With adverbial clauses of time, be careful that learners do not confuse the order of mention and the actual order of occurrence.

3 For conditional clauses, in addition to the meaning of the conjunction (*if* or *unless*), the verb forms in the main clause and *if*-clause are also very important for meaning.

4 Although adverbial clauses follow the main clause in about two-thirds of cases, learners may find it easier if they practise using conditional clauses initially with examples which have the *if*-clause before the main clause.

5 With hypothetical conditional sentences, check that the learners understand what the sentence means, e.g.

> If Fred had been careful, the vase wouldn't have broken.
>
> Was Fred careful? Did the vase break? What happened to the vase?

6 For production, learners need to be reminded that each clause needs a verb. It is probably best to insist initially that a finite verb is necessary in each clause. Non-finite and elliptical constructions can come later. Exercise types which can help learners include:

- Making a single complex sentence by linking two or more simple sentences with subordinating conjunctions
- Matching clauses which, when joined by a conjunction, make good sense, e.g.

A	B
I know how to make bread	Mine has been stolen
Can I borrow your bike	She's got arthritis
Our cat spends a lot of time inside	I have a recipe book
The meeting will be cancelled	The airport is closed

- Sentence completion exercises which can help focus on meaning, e.g.

> People would have more confidence in nuclear power stations if. . . .

7.4.2.4 Comparative clauses

In a comparative clause, an aspect of the main clause is compared with an aspect of the subordinate clause, e.g.

> Fred likes skiing   more than he likes studying.
> main clause   comparative clause

Comparisons can be made in terms of:

Non-equivalence

Superiority (more)	e.g.	*Fred is heavier than he used to be.*
		Fred finishes work much later than he used to.
Inferiority (less) or denial of equivalence	e.g.	*Fred is lighter than he used to be.*
		Fred isn't as heavy as he used to be.
		Fred doesn't finish work as early as he used to.

Equivalence   e.g.   *Jane is as fit as the rest of the team.*

Sufficiency   e.g.   *This coat is thick enough to keep me warm.*

Excess   e.g.   *That box is too heavy for you to carry on your own.*

Many comparative clauses contain non-finite verbs or ellipsis, e.g.

1 *The book is easy enough to read in an evening.*
2 *Fred likes chocolate more than Sue likes kiwifruit.*
3 **Fred likes chocolate more than Sue likes chocolate.*
4 *Fred likes chocolate more than Sue does.*
5 *Fred likes chocolate more than Sue.*

Some elliptical comparative constructions, like Example 5, can result in ambiguity.

7.5 Non-finite and verbless clauses

In Section 7.1, we saw that clauses typically have a finite verb. However, many subordinate clauses have no finite verb, e.g. ***To keep out of trouble**, I kept my mouth shut; **Having nothing else to do**, I watched the TV news.* The clauses *to keep out of trouble, having nothing else to do* do not have a finite verb, and are therefore called **non-finite clauses**. In most respects non-finite subordinate clauses are similar in function to finite clauses in that they can stand in place of a noun (nominal clause), adjective (postmodifying relative clause) or adverbial (adverbial clause). Because non-finite clauses have no finite verbs (i.e. no 'tensed verb' or no modal verb) and sometimes do not have a subject, their structure may seem less explicit. Verbless clauses, as the name suggests, have no verb at all. Because non-finite clauses and verbless clauses have 'missing' or ellipted elements, they are often hard for learners of English to understand, and are a major source of error in using English.

7.5.1 Non-finite verb forms

There are four non-finite verb forms used in non-finite clauses.

1 *to* + infinitive   e.g. She wanted *to travel* overseas.

2 bare infinitive   e.g. I saw him *leave*.

3 *-ing* participle   e.g. He finished *reading* the newspaper.

4 *-ed* participle   e.g. I wanted my TV *repaired*.

7.5.2 Verbless clauses

e.g. I'll meet you in town, *if possible*.

With you in mind, I ordered a large pizza.

Most non-finite clauses or verbless clauses can be interpreted as if they are finite. That is, the ellipted part can be 'recovered', e.g.

1 *To paint that building, it will cost you a fortune.*
= If you paint that building, it will cost you a fortune.

2 *When asked, Max agreed to go.*
= When he was asked, Max agreed to go.

3 *Seeing her there, I asked if she needed a ride.*
= When I saw her there, I asked if she needed a ride.

4 *I like to listen to music while reading the paper.*
= I like to listen to music while I am reading the paper.

5 *If possible, call me this evening.*
= If it is possible, call me this evening.

In Section 7.4.2.1.1 we considered finite complement clauses that are introduced by the complementiser *that*, e.g.

That Max smokes in the cafe annoys me.

There are two non-finite constructions which parallel *that*-clauses, but which use different complementisers (*for . . . to* and possessive *-ing*). These complementisers are used with non-finite clauses, e.g.

For Max to smoke in the cafe annoys me.

Max's smoking in the cafe annoys me.

For you to blame other people for your problems isn't fair.

Your blaming other people for your problems isn't fair.

7.5.3 The structure of non-finite clauses

Non-finite constructions are often associated with particular verbs, e.g.

I wanted *to go* to town.

not

*I wanted *go* to town.

*I wanted *going* to town.

*I wanted *gone* to town.

On the other hand, we do not say:

*I can't stand *go* to town.

*I can't stand *gone* to town.

*I can't stand *to go* to town. (Some speakers of English find this
acceptable.)

but we can say

I can't stand *going* to town.

Non-finite clauses can complement a finite verb or an adjective, e.g.

I like to arrive on time. (complement of a verb *like*)

I was happy to see my friends. (complement of an adjective *happy*)

About 65 per cent of non-finite clauses in written texts complement verbs rather than adjectives.

Table 7.7 contains lists of some of the more frequent verbs which go with the various non-finite constructions. Their relative frequency varies from genre to genre, as Biber et al. (1999: 712) have noted. Learners of English usually need to be helped to learn the verbs associated with these non-finite combinations.

A more detailed analysis of possible clause patterns (including subordinate patterns) has been published by Hunston & Francis (1998), who identified 25 main patterns based on the word classes which follow the verbs in the 250-million-word *Bank of English Corpus* (see Table 7.8). They sought to list the patterns that could follow individual verbs. It is argued by Hunston and Francis that the verbs associated with a particular pattern are often semantically related. This kind of detailed analysis was developed initially by H. E. Palmer (1938), one of the great pioneer teachers of EFL, and was developed further by Hornby (1954). The patterns in Table 7.8 which involve non-finite verb forms are 7, 8, 9, 10, 11, 18, 19, 20, 21, 22.

Table 7.7 Common verbs with non-finite clause constructions

1	2	3	4	5	6
Verb + *to* + infinitive, e.g. *I want to go.*	Verb + *-ing* participle, e.g. *He stopped smoking.*	Verb + noun + *to* + infinitive, e.g. *She told me to go.*	Verb + noun + *-ing* participle, e.g. *I heard him leaving.*	Verb + noun + infinitive, e.g. *I saw him go.*	Verb + noun + *-ed* participle, e.g. *I got my car fixed.*
agree	begin	advise	can't stand	feel	find
appear	can't stand	allow	catch	hear	get
ask	continue	ask	dislike	help	have
attempt	deny	cause	feel	let	leave
begin	dislike	expect	hate	make	order
choose	don't mind	force	hear	notice	want
continue	enjoy	get	like	observe	
decide	finish	help	listen to	see	
deserve	hate	leave	look at	watch	
expect	ignore	need	notice		
fail	intend	order	not mind		
forget	keep on	persuade	observe		
grow	like	prefer	prefer		
hate	love	promise	remember		
have	miss	require	resent		
hope	plan	want	see		
intend	put off	would hate	smell		
learn	remember	would like	start		
like	risk	would love	stop		
love	start		watch		
manage	stop				
need	suggest				
offer	try				
plan					
promise					
pretend					
refuse					
remember					
require					
seem					
start					
tend					
try					
want					

Note: The constructions in Columns 1, 2, 3, and 4 are more frequent than those in 5 or 6.

Table 7.8 Patterns that follow verbs

1 Verb on its own	Fred arrived; I sneezed.
2 Verb + noun phrase	I saw her; She is a doctor; Behave yourself.
3 Verb + adjectival phrase	She looks happy; He is young.
4 Verb + adverbial phrase	He walked away.
5 Verb + *that* + clause	I said that I would help.
6 Verb + *wh-* + clause	I explained what I had seen; He outlined what he wanted.
7 Verb + *wh-* + *to* + infinitive	I know what to do.
8 Verb + *to* + infinitive	He began to laugh; I managed to escape; I wanted to have lunch.
9 Verb + verb + *-ing*	She kept running; He stopped smoking; It needs watering.
10 Verb + infinitive	He helped fix it.
11 Verb + verb + *-ed*	I got fired.
12 Verb + preposition phase	He walked across the park; She works as a chef; She shouted at me.
13 Verb + noun phrase + noun phrase	She wrote me a letter; They consider him a threat; It cost him his life.
14 Verb + noun phrase + adj. phrase	They proved me wrong; I want it perfect.
15 Verb + noun phrase + adv. phrase	I put the book down.
16 Verb + noun phrase + *that* + clause	He promised me that he would ring.
17 Verb + noun phrase + *wh-* + clause	He told her what she wanted to know.
18 Verb + noun phrase + *wh-* + *to* + infinitive	I asked her what to do.
19 Verb + noun phrase + *to* + infinitive	They forced us to leave; I advised her to go; I told him to ring me.
20 Verb + noun phrase + verb + *-ing*	I saw a man swimming; He stopped us seeing each other.
21 Verb + noun phrase + infinitive	I heard him leave.
22 Verb + noun phrase + verb + *-ed*	I got my ears pierced.
23 Verb + noun phrase + prep. + noun phrase	They elected him as their representative.
24 *it* + verb + *(that)* + clause	It seems he knew about it; It was decided that I should go.
25 *there* + verb + noun phrase	There was nobody at home; There was a loud noise.

Note: Most of these patterns (especially those involving prepositions) have a number of important sub-patterns. (See Francis, Manning & Hunston, 1996, who identified more than 700 sub-patterns.)

7.5.4 Non-finite clauses without subjects

Each of the four categories of non-finite clauses identified in Section 7.5.1 can be used with or without subjects, with consequent changes in meaning, as follows:

1 *to*-**infinitive**

with subject	*It would be good for you to go there.*
without subject	*It would be good to go there.*

2 **bare infinitive**

with subject	*Rather than you be unhappy, I'll tell you now.*
without subject	*Rather than be unhappy, I'll tell you now.*

3 *-ing* **participle**

with subject	*Our friends having failed to meet us, we took a taxi instead.*
without subject	*Hoping to learn from our mistakes, we tried again.*

4 *-ed* **participle**

with subject	*With the work completed, we took a holiday.*
without subject	*Disappointed by the result, the fans rioted.*

7.5.5 The functions of non-finite clauses

In Section 7.4.2 the use of finite subordinate clauses as nominal, relative and adverbial clauses was described. Non-finite clauses can also function as nominal clauses, relative clauses and adverbial clauses.

7.5.5.1 Nominal clauses

A non-finite clause can function as a

Subject	*To be happy* is his main ambition. *For you to be happy* is his main ambition. *Helping other people* gives her a lot of pleasure. *Your helping other people* gives her a lot of pleasure.
Object	She likes *to sing*. She likes *me to sing*. She likes *singing*. She likes *me singing*.

Subject complement	His main job is *repairing old furniture.*
	Our first priority must be *to tell them immediately.*
	Our first priority must be *for you to tell them immediately.*
Object complement	I know her *to be reliable.*
Apposition	Your desire *to finish the job* is understandable.
	Your desire *for me to finish the job* is understandable.
	His work *counselling students* is full time.
Adjective complement	She is eager *to please the clients.*
	She is eager *for you to please the clients.*
	They were busy *preparing the meal.*

7.5.5.2 Relative clauses

A non-finite clause can function as a relative clause which postmodifies a noun. Where the non-finite clause is a participle, the relative clause may be described as 'reduced' (see Section 7.4.2.2.4), e.g.

The person *sitting in the back row* is my sister.

Anyone *found in the building after 6 p.m.* must have permission.

There was no time *to waste.*

The person *to see* is the office manager.

That's the best way *to do it.*

The next person *to sing* was John.

The next person *to sing* will be John.

Biber et al. (1999: 632) have noted that some nouns are frequently post-modified by non-finite clauses, e.g. *a chance* **to revise your work.** Other nouns besides *chance* include: *opportunity, decision, right, failure, inability, willingness, way.* In some sentences containing a non-finite clause as a postmodifier, the reader or listener has to infer the time reference of the non-finite clause as past or future according to context. This can cause difficulty for learners of English.

When a postmodifying non-finite clause follows a preposition, it is sometimes called a 'prepositional clause', e.g.

There wasn't enough evidence *for finding him guilty.*

There wasn't enough evidence *to find him guilty.*

7.5.5.3 Adverbial clauses

A non-finite clause can function as an adverbial clause of time, condition, cause, reason, concession, etc., even without a subordinating conjunction, e.g.

Walking home, I noticed the leaves were starting to change colour. (time)

The dishes done, we watched TV. (time)

Weather permitting, we'll do some gardening. (condition)

Although freshly painted, our house still doesn't look good. (concession)

Task 7.20

In the following sentences, identify the subordinate clauses. Mark each subordinate clause with F, NF or Vl to show whether they are **finite, non-finite** or **verbless**.

1 When they announced that the environmentalists wanted to set up a peace base at Mururoa, many people said it would be impossible.

2 But after successfully landing a team inside the Arctic Circle in 1990, and placing another in a secure area in the Nevada Desert, they firmly believed it was possible.

3 In fact, the protesters got within a kilometre of the test area before being discovered, arrested and taken off the atoll.

Task 7.21

These sentences contain subordinate nominal clauses, relative clauses and adverbial clauses. Underline each finite subordinate clause and mark what kind of clause it is. If it is a nominal clause state its function in the sentence. If it is a relative clause identify the antecedent. If it is an adverbial clause, identify its function.

1 They say children are afraid of most dogs.

2 Is that what it is?

3 I didn't think I'd enjoy it much.

4 She must have been about sixteen, although her face was older.

5 It doesn't matter what you read.

6 The trouble with you is that you take yourself far too seriously for your age.

7 We live quite close to a building that needs a coat of paint.

8 It was obvious that they all respected her.

9 He was the kind of person whom it was difficult not to believe.

10 I hope to be back before tea because I've got work to do.

Task 7.22

Identify the subordinate clauses in Text 7.10 and mark them with *Nom*, *Rel*, or *Adv* to show whether they function as nominal clauses, relative clauses or adverbial clauses. In each case mark whether the subordinate clause is finite or non-finite. Mark the function (time, condition, etc.) of the adverbial clauses, and show whether the relative clauses are restrictive or non-restrictive.

Text 7.10

Smoking

A fierce debate nearing a conclusion in the courts concerns several leading universities which have conducted research into the effects of tobacco over the last 50 years. Cigarette companies have argued that in the 1950s the state of scientific research meant they could not have been expected to warn of the dangers of smoking. The companies say that they would not have encouraged smoking if they had known of its dangers. The government believes that the companies deliberately conspired to get the young to smoke by associating smoking with glamorous and exciting lifestyles. The university researchers involved in the debate have suggested that a shortage of resources prevented them from making an effective response to the advertising campaigns which the tobacco companies initiated. Meanwhile, scientists have identified a single gene that might protect against cancer. When they experimented with mice, scientists demonstrated that the gene provides a vital defence against the toxic chemicals found in tobacco smoke. The professor leading the team of scientists said the research is encouraging, and he hoped that they could develop a serious programme of cancer prevention, by manipulating these types of genes, if trials are successful.

Discussion topic

1 Devise sentences containing non-finite or verbless clauses of:

time	(begin the clause with *on*)
reason	(begin the clause with *for*)
condition	(begin the clause with *with*)

2 Devise sentences containing non-finite **relative** clauses which begin with *-ing*, *-ed* or *to*-infinitive.

7.5.6 Learning to use non-finite clauses

7.5.6.1 Comprehension

Until learners are quite advanced, teachers should spot-check that comprehension of non-finite clauses is correct. The main difficulties seem to be:

1 Working out who or what is the subject of the non-finite clause, e.g.

    a Sue wanted *to go to Australia.*

    b Sue wanted *me to go to Australia.*

    c Sue promised *me to go to Australia.*

    d Sue asked *me to go to Australia.*

    e Max wanted *the team's coach replaced.*

    f I asked Bill *what to do.*

    g I told Bill *what to do.*

In general (except after the verb *promise* and sometimes after *ask*), the minimum distance principle (MDP) applies. That is, the noun nearest to the non-finite verb is the subject, but this is not always the case as the following examples show.

> *John surprised Fred by passing the exam.* (Who passed?)
>
> *Tina visited Sarah to offer her sympathy.* (Who offered the sympathy?)
>
> *He went around the members to explain the policy.*
> (Who explained the policy?)
>
> *The judges were impressed by Smith's success. By seeming to be aware of Naylor's preferences he had forced Stevens to raise his offer.*

Learners may find it hard to work out which of Smith, Naylor or Stevens is referred to by *he* or *his* and who is the subject of *offer*.

Learners should practise asking 'Who or what does what?' and attempt to recover the ellipted parts of the clause.

2 There is sometimes difficulty working out the time reference of non-finite clauses. The non-finite *-ed* is sometimes interpreted as a past tense, e.g.

> I will get it *fixed.* (interpreted as 'Someone fixed it.')

Discussion topic

Which of the six categories of non-finite constructions after verbs in Table 7.7 might be most easily misinterpreted as to who or what the subject is?

---

3 The construction **verb** + **noun** + **-*ing*** **participle** can lead to ambiguity.

I saw her standing by the door. (Who was standing by the door?)

7.5.6.2 Production

Errors made by learners typically involve the use of an inappropriate non-finite verb form, e.g.

1 **If the teachers ignore to train the learners, then they won't do well.*
2 **Teachers just require students translate the text.*
3 **It will deprive the less able students to share in the discussion.*
4 **Gouin's influential attitude made the reporting committee never mentioned dictation.*
5 **They disliked to do it.*
6 **I missed to catch the train.*

The most common non-finite clause constructions seem to be:

verb + *to* + infinitive	(*I want to go.*)
verb + *-ing* participle	(*I remember leaving.*)
verb + noun + *-ing* participle	(*I heard the rain falling.*)

The construction **verb** + **noun** + ***to*** + **infinitive** can cause difficulty because there is a partial overlap with the verbs which take **verb** + ***to*** + **infinitive**.

Learners find that they can write

I want to do it.

and   *I want her to do it.*

They may therefore assume they can write

I hope to finish it.

*I hope her to finish it.

It may be a good idea to isolate and teach together the following group of verbs which do not occur in the **verb** + ***to*** + **infinitive** construction: *allow, order, persuade, tell*.

Language in use

In the previous chapters we have considered major aspects of phonology, vocabulary and grammar within sentences and how these relate to the teaching and learning of English. In various places throughout the book aspects of language beyond the sentence have been mentioned. These have included categories of meaning and the relation between forms and functions of language. In Chapter 8 we examine aspects of the relation between language and contexts of use in spoken and written texts as they might relate to second language learning. The word **text** is used to refer to units of speech or writing ranging in size from one or more words (e.g. *danger* or *broken glass*) to whole books. The study of how language relates to the contexts in which it is used is called **discourse analysis**.

Linguists know much less about the structure, characteristics and functions of texts and textuality than they know about the grammar of sentences. Traditionally, learners of English have been taught little or nothing about text and its use. In the last two decades, however, attempts have been made to incorporate into language courses a functional dimension to assist learners to perform various speech acts and to produce spoken and written texts which serve different purposes. A great deal of interesting information on language use has been revealed in recent years by scholars working in discourse analysis and pragmatics. However, while not all of this information can be taken account of by language teachers, its value lies particularly in the consciousness-raising of teachers as to how language works.

Objectives

By the end of this chapter you should:

1 Understand how **texts** perform various **functions**.

2 Be able to state a range of important **semantic functions** which are expressed in texts.

3 Know the major categories of **speech acts**.

4 Know the difference between **direct** and **indirect speech acts.**

5 Know the difference between **coherence** and **cohesion** in texts.

6 Be able to identify the main **ways in which cohesion is achieved** in texts.

7 Know about different approaches to the identification of **genres.**

8 Be aware of the main **linguistic characteristics** of major genres.

9 Know the major characteristics of **dialogue.**

8.1 Functions of texts

8.1.1 Macro-functions

A number of linguists, including Jakobson (1960) and Halliday (1973), have described the nature and structure of language use. In any speech event there are a number of factors involved. These include:

1 The sender of the message (speaker or writer)

2 The receiver of the message (addressee)

3 The establishment and maintenance of contact between the sender and receiver

4 The message conveying the speaker or writer's intention

5 The form of the message

6 The code used

7 The situation or setting in which the speech event occurs.

Any spoken or written text can focus primarily on one or more of these factors and in doing so reflect different **functions** of language. Broadly speaking, these functions can be concerned with ideas, interpersonal relationships or aesthetics.

1 If the primary focus is on the sender, the text can reflect the speaker or writer's attitudes and feelings and serve a **personal** or **emotive function**, expressing awareness of what the speaker thinks or feels. This function of language is sometimes called the **expressive** function and typically involves the use of the 'first person' (*I* or *we*). For example, if I say *I can't stand oysters*, the utterance tells the hearer something about 'me'.

2 If the focus of the speech event is on the addressee, then this is typically reflected in use of the 'second person' ('you'), and the utterance has a **directive** (or **regulatory**) **function** in which we may seek to influence the behaviour of others (e.g. *Please pay attention; Why don't you ask your mother?; It's cold in this room*).

3 Focus on the **contact** between sender and receiver of the message is the **phatic** (or **interactional**) **function** in which the participants establish, prolong or discontinue contact in order to keep the channels of communication open, sometimes almost as an end in itself. The phatic function is often expressed in formulaic speech with talk about particular topics (e.g. the weather, families, exams, the state of the world) supported by paralinguistic phenomena (body language), e.g. *Nice to see you*; *How are you?*; *How's your mother enjoying her new flat?*; *Hasn't the weather been awful!*; *Have you finished your exams?*; (On the telephone) *Are you still there?* In this way, social bonding, solidarity and the channel of communication are established and maintained.

4 Focus on the **content** of the message is reflected in the **informative function** (sometimes called the **referential** function). Here there is a focus on denotative (referential) meaning and sometimes a concentration on the third person (*he/she/it*). The informative function of language is often the only one people think of when they reflect on the question 'What does language do?' ('It's for communicating ideas').

5 Focus on the **form** of the message was described by Jakobson as the **poetic** (or aesthetic) **function**. This is focus on language for its own sake, e.g. Why do we say *fish and chips* and not *chips and fish*? The poet Alexander Pope referred to 'What oft was thought but ne'er so well expressed', and language users often have a well developed sense of what seems to be stylistically attractive.

6 We can also focus on language as a code. This is known as the **metalingual function** and covers the use of language to discuss or find out about language itself, e.g. *What does **whanau** mean in Maori?*; *Are we on the same wavelength?*; *What did she mean when she said 'I've had enough'?*; *Hold on a minute, are we talking about the same thing?*

7 The **setting** in which texts are produced or received also influences their function. The same words of a text can serve to describe, predict or warn, etc., depending on where they are produced and by whom. For example, the utterance *John will ring you about this tomorrow* can be a prediction, a promise, a warning, depending on who says it and in what circumstances.

Texts (or parts of texts) typically reflect one or more of these functions, several of which can be further sub-categorised. For example, texts which serve to satisfy our needs or desires (*I'd like . . .*) may be described as having an **instrumental function**. Texts which serve to create an imaginary setting (let's pretend) may be described as having an **imaginative function**. Many literary works of fiction reflect this function. Texts which seek to discover knowledge may be said to have an **heuristic function** – and so on. Language has evolved in response to human needs. We **do** things whenever we speak or write.

Discussion topic

Text 8.1 is a transcript of a few minutes of spoken interaction among a group of six-year-old children playing with dough in a classroom. What speech functions are reflected in the discourse? For example, line 1 may be classified as having an heuristic function, line 3 may be described as having a directive function.

Text 8.1

1	DAVID	Is that Cameron's dough?
	MICHAEL	hahaha
	DAVID	Put it all in the bag.
	MICHAEL	No, it's Cameron's dough.
5	DAVID	He'll eat it.
	MICHAEL	No, make it all softee, make it all softee, soft soft soft *[He puts flour on the dough]*
	DAVID	So it doesn't stick on your hand.
	MICHAEL	Soft soft softee soft. This is gonna be all soft here's all more flour, more flour. This is gonna be all soft, not going to be no more sticky, softee flour.
	CAMERON	Soft means it'll be sticky.
10	MICHAEL	Wow I've got a lot of hundreds of flour.
	DAVID	That would be a one hundred and sixty infinity.
	CAMERON	You can't get infinity in here.
	MICHAEL	Yes you can.
	CAMERON	No you can't, it never ends.
15	MICHAEL	You can. It'll go on the floor eh?
	DAVID	I know hate it all round the world.
	MICHAEL	No it isn't no it isn't.
	CAMERON	Yes, it is.
	MICHAEL	Finity no, it's not even a word.
20	DAVID	It's not a hundred times round the world cause I've got a hundred nails in my um box and it's not all around the world.
	CAMERON	Infinity is.
	MICHAEL	It isn't. Infinity's not a number.
	DAVID	I know it isn't.
	MICHAEL	It's a great thing finity, finity, finity, hasn't finity finity hundred finity.
25	DAVID	Hundred finity, hundred finity, hundred finity, hundred finity.
	CAMERON	Here's some on my little finger. And look . . .
	CHRIS	I've got it all around, I've got it all around.
	MICHAEL	Now it's a rock of moon snow, it's a little bit. All the snow's gone! Oh, put little wee holes in it.

	DAVID	No he's got some eyes.
30	SUSAN	My one's got some eyes.
	CAMERON	Whose is it?
	SUSAN	It's Christine's. Look at that one!
	CHRIS	My name's Christine.
	MICHAEL	I want some flour.
35	CAMERON	Got some.
	DAVID	We've got more than you right. We've got more than you.
	SUSAN	Oh lucky David.
	KATE	I've got some on my clothes. It's mine.
	MICHAEL	Mine's all sticky.
40	CAMERON	It's a mountain.
	MICHAEL	I'll put all snow on the mountains.
	CAMERON	Look at my yellow fingers, yellow fingers.
	KATE	Haha yellow fingers, yellow fingers.
	EDMUND	Chris, look.
45	MICHAEL	I've got a hundred flours.
	CAMERON	I've got two hundred flours.
	MICHAEL	Yea.
	CAMERON	Clean up all the doughs.
49	MICHAEL	What's that smell?

8.1.2 Speech acts

In Section 2.2, the distinction was made between the propositional meaning or **sense** of an utterance and its **illocutionary force**, e.g. *I can't hear you* has the sense of 'not being able to hear'. The force of the utterance may be 'Please speak louder'. In addition to the few broad categories of functions of text discussed in 8.1.1, we can examine or clarify the functions of text at a more specific or fine-grained level of analysis in terms of **speech acts**. A speech act may be brief (*Stop!*) or very long (e.g. a lengthy political speech). Searle (1969) identified five main types.

1 **Informatives** These are speech acts which describe states of events in the world, e.g. asserting, reporting, classifying, generalising, defining, explaining, describing, exemplifying, predicting, advising, warning, comparing.

2 **Directives** These are speech acts which have the function of getting the receiver of the message to do something, e.g. asking, suggesting, inviting, requesting, ordering, commanding.

3 **Expressives** These are speech acts in which the speaker or writer expresses feelings or attitudes, e.g. apologising, agreeing, conceding, denying, welcoming, complaining, thanking, complimenting, congratulating, approving, disapproving, reprimanding, consoling.

4 **Commissives** These are speech acts which commit the speaker or writer to doing something in the future, e.g. promising, threatening, undertaking.

5 Searle also described the highly infrequent **declarative** speech act as one which can (sometimes in legal terms) change the state of affairs in a situation, e.g. *I pronounce you husband and wife; I name this ship 'Titanic'; We are at war; You are under arrest; I now declare the conference officially open.*

Informatives are associated particularly with ideas (cognitive matters), whereas directives, expressives and commissives are more interactional, or deal with feelings (affective matters).

It can be seen that there are many functional sub-categories within the first four of these major categories of speech acts. J. L. Austin (1962) suggested that there are very many possible speech acts – at least as many as there are possible 'verbs of speaking'. By that he meant that many verbs are 'performative' – they name the speech act they perform, e.g.

1 I *predict* that Bob will be home by Friday.

2 I *suggest* we stop for lunch.

3 I *asked* her the time.

4 She *permitted* us to go inside.

5 I *forbid* her to do it again.

6 She *promised* to ring me.

Discussion topic

The following short texts can be classified as **informatives**. What functional sub-categories of informatives would you describe them as belonging to (generalising, classifying, etc.)? Are there any grammatical or other characteristics which appear to be associated with expressing these functions?

1 A camera is a device for taking photographs. Some cameras are small enough to fit into a pocket and can take about 24 still photographs. Others take moving pictures for video recordings. Electronic cameras are becoming increasingly popular but they are still expensive.

2 Fish are cold-blooded animals with gills and fins. All fish live in water. Most fish are a source of food. Some fish are dangerous. Some sharks, for example, will attack people. Victims of shark attacks sometimes die, but such attacks are rare.

3 You will find your life-jacket under your seat and it is to be used in case of an emergency in the aircraft. If required fit the life-jacket as follows:

a Pass the jacket over the head and pull the tapes tightly.

b Tie the tapes near the front and underneath the jacket.

c Half inflate by pulling the cord under the left of the jacket.

d Fully inflate after leaving the aircraft by pulling the second cord on the right of the jacket.

4 Bread consists of four main ingredients: flour, salt, yeast and water. Firstly, these ingredients are measured and mixed together to make dough. The dough is then kneaded and left to rise. It is then kneaded again and placed in a baking tin. Next, it is baked in a hot oven for about 50 minutes and, finally, it is removed from the oven and is ready to be eaten.

5 Means of transport can be classified according to whether they are used on land, at sea or in the air. These three groups can be further divided according to whether they are powered by machine or not. For example, land transport can be divided into manually powered transport such as the bicycle, and machine powered transport such as cars, trucks, buses and trains. Cars, trucks, buses and trains can be further divided into two groups according to whether they are used for private or public transport.

Discussion topic

For learners of English, **expressives** are often hard to use and interpret. The following sentences illustrate this by showing degrees of commitment in issuing and responding to **invitations**. What problems do you think might face learners of English in responding to or issuing invitations? For example, determining when an invitation is not an invitation, but an act of solidarity.

Invitations
Would you be free to come for lunch tomorrow?
Why don't we have lunch tomorrow?
Shall we have lunch some time soon?
We really ought to talk about this over lunch some time.
Let's have lunch together soon.
I'll get in touch to see if we can organise lunch together.
If you're free, come and have lunch tomorrow.

Some possible responses to invitations
I'd really like that.
When does it suit you?
Shall we make a time?
We really must.
What a great idea.
You name the day.
I'll give you a call some time.
Suits me fine.
I'm pretty busy at present.
Why don't we some time?

Discussion topic

Here are some corpus-based examples of the expressive speech act of 'apologising'. Assume these apologies are responses to treading on someone's foot. The appropriateness of the apology depends on the relationship between the persons involved, and the context. If the apology was to a stranger, which responses would be less polite? Are there implications for language teaching?

1 I'm sorry.

2 I apologise.

3 Forgive me.

4 I'm terribly sorry.

5 Oops.

6 I beg your pardon.

7 Sorry.

8 I'm sorry to have done that.

9 Excuse me.

10 I **do** apologise.

11 I **am** sorry.

12 How clumsy of me.

13 I'm sorry. I'm such a clumsy character sometimes.

14 Uh! Uh!

15 Are you OK?

Discussion topic

List some ways in which speakers of English might perform the expressive speech act of **giving** or **responding to compliments**, e.g.

I like your scarf.   – I got it at a sale.

– Do you really?

– I'm not very happy with it.

– It's not quite what I wanted.

– Thanks.

– Here, you have it!

● What kinds of things do speakers of English make compliments about?

● Are there any (unstated) restrictions on what a speaker may make a compliment about?

● Do there seem to be characteristic responses to compliments?

● How is the use of compliments affected by who the participants are?

● What implications are there for English language teaching?

Discussion topic

In a workplace, native and non-native speakers of English express **disagreement** (an expressive speech act) when discussing ways of carrying out tasks. Here are some utterances collected from a number of sources. What differences can be seen in how some users of English express disagreement? Are there different **communication styles**? What implications are there for language teaching?

> Hey, that's not how you do it.
> Last time we did it this way.
> You can't do it that way.
> That's not how you do it.
> What about trying this way?
> That won't work.
> That's wrong.
> It'll take too long if we do it like that.
> It'll cost the earth to use a steel frame.
> Turn it round the other way.
> You'll never get it done that way.
> Just watch what I do and then do the same.
> I agree with you to a certain extent, but I think we ought to try my way.
> We do it this way.
> This is the way.
> Do you think it would be easier this way?
> I don't agree with that.
> Do it this way.
> This is better.
> Sorry, that won't work.
> If we do x first, y won't fit.

From the 1970s, influential language syllabuses were based on the teaching of language functions. The most well known were by Wilkins (1976) and van Ek (1976). By way of illustration, Table 8.1 contains some of the functions which van Ek listed in a language teaching syllabus project for the Council of Europe. It was suggested that learners of any language need to be able to perform speech acts like these if they wish to be fluent in that language.

8.1.3 Form and function

An essential feature of speech act theory is that in English (or any other language) there is no one-to-one relationship between form and function. As we have seen throughout this book, most linguistic forms can have

Table 8.1 Some important language functions (based on van Ek, 1976)

1 *Imparting and seeking factual information*
   identifying; reporting (including describing and narrating); correcting; asking

2 *Expressing and finding out intellectual attitudes*
   expressing or inquiring about agreement and disagreement; denying something;
   accepting or declining an offer or invitation; offering to do something; stating
   whether someone knows or does not know something or someone; stating whether
   someone remembers or has forgotten something or someone; expressing whether
   something is considered possible or impossible; expressing or inquiring about
   capability and incapability; expressing or inquiring whether something is considered
   a logical conclusion (deduction); expressing how certain/uncertain one is of
   something; inquiring how certain/uncertain others are of something; expressing or
   inquiring whether someone is/is not obliged to do something; giving and seeking
   permission to do something; stating that permission is withheld

3 *Expressing and finding out emotional attitudes*
   expressing pleasure or liking; expressing displeasure or dislike; inquiring about
   pleasure, liking, displeasure, dislike; expressing or inquiring about interest or lack
   of interest; expressing surprise, hope, satisfaction, dissatisfaction, disappointment;
   expressing or inquiring about fear or worry; expressing or inquiring about
   preference; expressing gratitude, sympathy; expressing or inquiring about intention;
   expressing or inquiring about wants or desires

4 *Expressing and finding out moral attitudes*
   apologising; granting forgiveness; expressing approval or disapproval; inquiring
   about approval or disapproval; expressing appreciation, regret, indifference

5 *Getting things done (suasion)*
   suggesting a course of action (including the speaker); requesting others to do
   something; inviting or advising something; warning others to take care or to refrain
   from doing something; instructing or directing others to do something; offering or
   requesting assistance

6 *Socialising*
   greeting people; introducing people; taking leave; attracting attention; congratulating

more than one function, and most functions can be expressed by more
than one linguistic form, e.g. *I'll get in touch with you this evening* can be a
promise or a warning. *Are you feeling tired too?* can have the effect of being
a **question** to the listener, or a **statement** that the speaker is tired.

Since one form can have many functions, it is often not possible to say
what function is being performed outside of the **context** of that utterance. For example, learners are often told that imperatives are used for
giving commands or instructions. However, the following sentences show
that imperatives can have several functions.

Don't move.	(command)
Wait for me outside the classroom, please.	(request)
Send me a note if you need help.	(invitation)
Be careful when you cross the road.	(advice)
Look after yourself.	(farewell)

Similarly, **commands** can be expressed in many ways besides by means of imperatives.

Write this again more neatly, please.

You'll have to do this again.

Your writing isn't very good.

You can do better than this.

I'm afraid you'll have to do better.

Don't you know how to write neatly?

My eyes are sore after reading your writing.

Discussion topic

What functions could the following interrogatives have in different contexts?

1 What is your name?

2 Who do you think you are?

3 Do you like Wellington?

4 How many children do you have?

5 What's going on here?

6 Could you do the dishes?

7 How often do you have to be told to wipe your feet? (Could the response be 'Three'?)

8.1.4 Direct and indirect speech functions

Speech act functions in text can be expressed more or less 'directly'. *(Please) open the window* is likely to be considered more direct than *It's a really hot day* or *I think summer has arrived*, but the outcome (opening a window) may be the same. **Indirect speech acts** can 'soften' directives or make them more polite. In the following examples of the speech act of **permission**, the examples range approximately from being more direct to less direct.

I give you permission to cross my farm.

You have permission to cross my farm.

You can go across my farm.

Feel free to go across my farm any time.

Compare the more direct *No smoking* with the less direct *Thank you for not smoking*.

Similarly, there is a very large number of ways in which **requests** can be expressed – more or less directly. For example, a speaker may ask to borrow someone's computer using various degrees of directness, e.g.

1 *I have to get my project finished tonight.*   (hint)

2 *My computer has crashed.*   (stronger hint)

3 *Could you lend me your computer?*   (hearer's ability)

4 *Would you lend me your computer?*   (hearer's willingness)

5 *May I borrow your computer?*   (hearer's permission)

6 *I desperately need to borrow your computer.*   (speaker's need)

7 *You just have to lend me your computer.*   (explicit request)

8 *Lend me your computer please.*   (imperative)

Searle (1969) and others have described how statements of ability, willingness, obligation, desire, need, etc., as well as very oblique hints, can all be more effective in getting people to do things than outright commands expressed through imperatives. Examples include: *Would you mind . . . , How about . . . , Could you . . . , I wonder if . . . , Why don't you. . . .* Some 'hints' can be very effective (e.g. *Were you born in a tent!* as a way of asking someone to shut a door).

Learners of English frequently find it difficult to work out speech act functions in spoken or written texts they encounter. Official documents such as the *Road Code* for motorists can often provide a number of ways of expressing speech acts. Directives, for example, are not always expressed using imperatives or modal verbs of obligation (*must, should,* etc.).

> *Always carry loads as near to the ground as possible.* (direct imperative)
>
> *Remember the effect of tail swing.* (direct imperative but no particular action is required)
>
> *Under no circumstances must additional weights be added to forklifts.*
>
> *It is a good idea to get someone to check the load.*

Speech acts tend to be culturally associated. What is acceptable in one culture may be considered too direct (pushy or aggressive) in another. Whereas an imperative might be acceptable in one culture, e.g. *Clean it first*, an interrogative might be used in another culture, e.g. *Do you think you should clean it first?* Second language learners cannot assume that what is acceptable in their first language will be acceptable in another.

8.1.5 Seeking clarification and making repairs

Language is also used for **seeking clarification** when communication is not clear, and for repairing communication when breakdowns occur.

This can be a considerable learning burden for second language learners. Thompson (1982) classified the clarification requests made by children when speakers were not understood. There were five main types.

1 Requests for specification, e.g. *(Next to it, you have to put another one)* – *Another what?*

2 Requests for confirmation, e.g. *(This one looks like a cow) – A cow?*

3 Requests for elaboration, e.g. *Where should I put it?*

4 Non-specific requests, e.g. *What?, Eh?, Pardon?, What was that? (What* accounted for 35 per cent, *eh* for 32 per cent, *pardon* for 23 per cent.)

5 Requests for repetition of a specific item, e.g. *(Then on the other side draw an A) – Draw a what?*

These occurred with the following distribution:

	%
Request for specification	40
Request for confirmation	33
Request for elaboration	13
Non-specific request	12
Request for repetition of a specific item	2
	100

As the following exchange between children constructing a diagram illustrates, Thompson demonstrated that seeking clarification can be complex and indirect.

ANN   right in the middle of the paper you draw a rectangle

JEN   I've got to think what a rectangle is now mm (. . .) what sort of shape is it you know (. . .) *(Request for elaboration)*

ANN   um a rectangle is like um a squashed square on the top and bottom

JEN   oh is that kind of long *(Request for confirmation)*

ANN   yeah long

ANN   . . . in the middle of the bottom of the rectangle there's this diamond

JEN   This what *(Request for specification)*

JEN   what's the kind of shape like is it square or *(Request for elaboration and confirmation)*

ANN   um it's sort of a squashed square on two sides of the square diagonally on two sides of the square . you squash them in to make them look like a diamond – you know on a playing card . a diamond

JEN   oh now I know

8.2 The internal structure of texts

Just as sentences have grammatical structure, so, also, texts have structure – a web of meaning relationships which relate the sentences to each other, give direction to the text and make it hold together. The study of **coherence** and **cohesion** in texts was greatly advanced by the work of Halliday & Hasan (1976) and much subsequent research has built on their work.

8.2.1 Coherence

At the broadest level, we expect texts to be **coherent**. We expect the sentences or utterances to be connected in meaning so that the text as a whole 'makes sense', is 'meaningful' and 'comprehensible'. Stringing together grammatical sentences does not of itself result in coherent discourse, as the following examples show:

1 *Sione turned abruptly towards her. By late afternoon all the food had been assembled. At first, he went to Apia only once a week. Kandaswami's heart gladdened when he saw Meena. That's how the coconut came to Mailu.*

2 *It's the British election today. From my window I can see it is raining over the harbour. It's my birthday on Sunday. Do you like avocados? Please don't ring me after 11 p.m.*

Even sentences on the same topic do not necessarily form coherent discourse – they have to seem to be 'relevant' and in the 'right' order:

3 *They were of more use to us than a car or truck would have been. All of our wood for the fire was brought down from the hills by the horses too. The horses were very useful to us then. Besides using them for excursions on the beach we used them for everyday work, and when the rain came and flooded the stream our horses were the only means we had of getting to town.*

As a classroom exercise students are sometimes asked to change the order of sentences to improve coherence. Coherent texts often have discernible introductory sections, developmental sections and concluding sections. While it is often easy to recognise lack of coherence in a text, there is a need for much more research on the characteristics of what makes texts coherent.

8.2.2 Cohesion

Texts are said to display **cohesion** when different parts of the text are linked to each other through particular lexical and grammatical features or relationships to give unity to the text. Cohesion can thus contribute

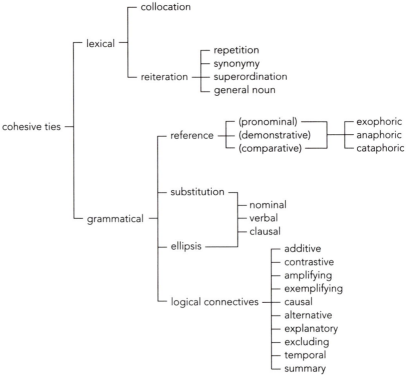

Figure 8.1   Types of cohesion in English

to coherence. Williams (1983) summarised the different kinds of cohesive relations in texts, based on the work of Halliday & Hasan (1976) (see Figure 8.1). Cohesion in texts is achieved mainly through lexical and grammatical means. We will briefly examine these in turn.

8.2.2.1 Lexical cohesion

Lexical cohesion is achieved through the selection of vocabulary.

8.2.2.1.1 Collocation

As we saw in Chapter 2, particular words can become associated with or regularly found in the company of certain other words. Cohesion that is achieved through the association of lexical items regularly occurring together is called collocation. Collocates can be words that belong to the same area of meaning, or words that are frequently used in the same contexts, e.g. *weather forecast, full moon, heavy rain*. In a *trial*, if the *jury* cannot agree on a *verdict* then we say there is a *hung jury* and the *judge* may order a *retrial*. There has been an increasing tendency for such outcomes in *criminal cases*.

8.2.2.1.2 Reiteration

Halliday & Hasan identified four types: repetition, synonymy, superordination, use of general nouns.

1 Repetition, e.g.

> After heavy *rain* the *river* often floods these houses. However,
> last May, in spite of continuous *rain* for 20 hours, the *river* stayed
> within its banks.

2 Synonymy: use of words of a similar meaning, e.g.

> At 6 p.m. I rang a *taxi*, but because of the traffic the *cab* arrived late
> and I missed my flight.

3 Superordination (use of general class words). Hyponymy involves the use of subordinates, e.g.

> This car is the best vehicle for a family of six. (*Vehicle* is a
> superordinate of *car*. *Car* is a hyponym of *vehicle*.)
>
> If I ever buy a dog, it won't be a terrier. (*Terrier* is a hyponym of *dog*.)

4 Use of general nouns – e.g. *person, people, man, woman* for human nouns; *thing, object* for inanimate, concrete countable nouns; *stuff* for inanimate, concrete uncountable nouns; *place* for locations, etc., e.g.

> Can you tell me where to stay in Los Angeles? I've never been to
> *the place*.
>
> What's that *stuff*?
>
> Henry seems convinced there's money in dairy farming. I don't know
> what gave him *that idea*.

8.2.2.2 Grammatical cohesion

Cohesion is also achieved through several kinds of grammatical processes. These include:

1 Reference

There are three main types of reference, involving pronouns, demonstratives and comparatives.

a **Pronouns** such as *it, they, some, many*, e.g.

> When the first simple flower bloomed on some raw upland late in
> the Dinosaur Age, *it* was wind pollinated, just like *its* early pine-cone
> relatives. *It* was a very inconspicuous flower because the use of
> colour or smell to attract birds and insects to achieve the
> transportation of pollen had not yet evolved.

b Demonstratives

Deictic words such as *this, that, those* and other determiners such as *the, each, another*, e.g.

> I saw a man and a child come out of the house. *The* man was carrying *the* child.

> Both kids got sick again. *That* was more than I could cope with.

> You might not believe *this*, but I've never been to London.

c Comparatives, e.g.

> Why don't you use the ladder? You'll find it *easier* to reach the top shelf.

Cohesive reference can point back to previously mentioned items. This is called **anaphora** (e.g. *The man left the house. **He** . . .*). Cohesive reference can also point to forthcoming items. This is called **cataphora** (e.g. *Those of you who have **one**, take out your dictionary*). **Exophoric** reference points outside the text (and may include 'knowledge of the world'), e.g. in ***Our Prime Minister** opened the conference*, the specific referent depends on who says it, and in which country. The use of exophoric reference sometimes includes pointing, e.g. *Why don't you buy that one over there?* In conversation with people in our speech community, we often assume 'knowledge of the world' from outside the text, e.g. *Who do you think will win the World Cup?* assumes that the listener knows which sport is being referred to because there are 'World Cup' events for several sports.

2 Substitution and ellipsis

Related to the grammatical cohesive ties of 'reference' is the phenomenon of **substitution**, where a word or words can substitute for a noun phrase, verb phrase or clause. **Ellipsis**, as we saw in Chapter 7, is the process by which noun phrases, verb phrases or clauses are deleted (or 'understood' when they are absent).

a Nominal substitution replaces a noun or noun phrase, e.g.

> I've ordered a black coffee.   Do you want *the same*?

b Verbal substitution replaces a verb with a 'pro-form', e.g.

> Paul likes muffins.   Sara *does* too.

c Clausal substitution uses a pro-form to replace a clause, e.g.

> I went to the exhibition and *so did* Fred.

> I went to the pictures, and Jane *did too*.

> Has he fixed the window? I (don't) think *so*. If *not*, I'll ring him again.

d Nominal ellipsis omits a noun or noun phrase, e.g.

> They saw three spectators collapse. And then another [ ].

> Which celery did you get? This was the freshest [ ].

e **Verbal ellipsis** omits a verb, e.g.

Is the government going to survive? – It may [ ].

f **Clausal ellipsis** omits a clause, e.g.

Who was on the phone? – Fred [ ].

Apposition is a kind of special case of substitution which can contribute to cohesion and coherence, e.g. *This national park surrounds Menindee and Cawndilla Lakes,* **the saucer-shaped overflow lakes of the park's eastern boundary, the Darling River.** In this example, *the saucer-shaped lakes of the park's eastern boundary* is in apposition to *Menindee and Cawndilla Lakes; the Darling River* is in apposition to *the park's eastern boundary.*

Apposition helps flesh out meaning by repeating a previously stated item in another form.

3 Logical connectives

Grammatical cohesion in texts is also achieved by various **logical connectives** which show the relationship between sentences, help us keep track of time sequences, summarise a series of items, and so on. Table 8.2 shows some of the most common logical connectives. They can be words,

Table 8.2 Basic conjunction relationships

Relationship	Examples of logical connectives
1 Addition/inclusion	*and, furthermore, besides, also, in addition, similarly*
2 Contrast	*but, although, despite, yet, however, still, on the other hand, nevertheless*
3 Amplification	*to be more specific, thus, therefore, consists of, can be divided into*
4 Exemplification	*for example, such as, thus, for instance*
5 Cause–effect	*because, since, thus, as a result, so that, in order to, so, consequently*
6 Alternative	*or, nor, alternatively, on the other hand*
7 Explanation	*in other words, that is to say, I mean, namely*
8 Exclusion	*instead, rather than, on the contrary*
9 Temporal arrangements	*initially, when, before, after, subsequently, while, then, firstly, finally, in the first place, still, followed by, later, continued*
10 Summary/ conclusion	*ultimately, in conclusion, to sum up, in short, in a word, to put it briefly, that is*

phrases or clauses. Many are conjunctions, but some are adverbials. Several of them can indicate more than one relationship, and some of the relationships overlap. Nevertheless, texts are made more cohesive because of them, as Text 8.2 illustrates. The connectives are in bold type.

Text 8.2

Making ships go faster

Just as the railways had to increase the speed of express trains **in order to** compete successfully with the airlines, **so** must ocean liners travel faster if they are to regain the traffic they have lost. In their constant search for higher speeds at sea, marine engineers are designing ever more powerful and efficient engines. **But** the fastest ocean-going liner is still many times slower than the average aircraft. **This** is certainly true of travel between Europe and America. The fastest ships take days to make a journey across the Atlantic which an aircraft can complete in a matter of hours. The friction between a ship's hull and the water through which it is travelling must always act as a brake on the conventional ship's speed. Friction between water and the hull creates what is called drag or resistance. Drag becomes greater the bigger the ship. It can be reduced by careful streamlining of the hull and putting more power into the propellers that drive it. **Nevertheless**, streamlining and greater power do not completely solve the problem. The only solution is to lift as much of the ship as possible out of the water. **One of the earliest** attempts to put that solution into practice was the stepped hull used for high-speed motorboats. The boat **then** travels with only the step below the stern in contact with the water. You can see this in action when a speedboat cuts through the water with its bow high in the air. It achieves high speed **because** only a small part of the boat's hull is in contact with the water to create resistance. The **next** leap forward in the ever-increasing search for high speed on the water was to lift the hull right out of the water supported on skis. With a hydrofoil boat, water resistance is cut to a minimum **and** the chief source of drag or opposition to the movement of the hull comes from the air.

Paragraphing is another way in which written texts are given texture, with 'topic sentences' often heading a paragraph, followed by elaboration within the same paragraph.

Discussion topic

Name the cohesive relationships that are represented by the underlined words in Text 8.3. Locate the other part of the cohesive link. Find one example of ellipsis in the text.

Text 8.3

Lichens

Lichens are not like any other <u>plants</u>. Each <u>one</u> is a partnership between fungus and a green alga. The fungus and alga form a team. The fungus protects the alga so that <u>it</u> can live in <u>more exposed sunny places</u>. And, like all green plants, the algal cells make their own food in sunlight. They share what they make with the fungus. Lichens are very slow growing. <u>Most</u> grow only a few millimetres a year. In fine, sunny weather, they dry out and stop growing altogether. <u>But</u> they are very good at soaking up water. <u>This</u> may come from rain, fog, sea-spray, or even from dew. <u>It</u> allows them to grow in places where other plants could never survive.

Text 8.4

What I have lived for

Three passions, simple but overwhelmingly strong, have governed my life: the longing for love, the search for knowledge, and unbearable pity for the suffering of mankind. These passions, like great winds, have blown me hither and thither, in a wayward course, over a deep ocean of anguish, reaching to the very verge of despair.

I have sought love, first, because it brings ecstasy – ecstasy so great that I would often have sacrificed all the rest of life for a few hours of this joy. I have sought it, next, because it relieves loneliness – that terrible loneliness in which one shivering consciousness looks over the rim of the world into the cold unfathomable lifeless abyss. I have sought it, finally, because in the union of love I have seen, in a mystic miniature, the prefiguring vision of the heaven that saints and poets have imagined. This is what I sought and, though it might seem too good for human life, this is what – at last – I have found.

With equal passion I have sought knowledge. I have wished to understand the hearts of men. I have wished to know why the stars shine. And I have tried to apprehend the Pythagorean power by which number holds sway above the flux. A little of this, but not much, I have achieved.

Love and knowledge, so far as they were possible, led upward towards the heavens. But always pity brought me back to earth. Echoes of cries of pain reverberate in my heart. Children in famine, victims tortured by oppressors, helpless old people a burden to their sons, and the whole world of loneliness, poverty, and pain make a mockery of what human life should be. I long to alleviate this evil, but I cannot, and I too suffer.

This has been my life. I have found it worth living, and would gladly live it again if the chance were offered me.

The Prologue to *Autobiography* by Bertrand Russell, 1872–1970

> **Discussion topic**
>
> Identify examples of cohesion in Text 8.4 and classify them according to the categories of cohesion described in Figure 8.1.

Text 8.5

The monarch butterfly

The life of a monarch butterfly (*Danaus plexippus*) begins on the underside of a milkwood leaf when an adult female deposits a tiny egg. After 3 to 12 days a striped caterpillar emerges and immediately starts feeding on the plant. Within two weeks the larva has increased its original weight by over 2,000 times. The larva sheds its skin five times as it grows. The final shedding occurs when the fully developed caterpillar has stopped eating and found a sheltered place to settle, such as a tree limb or twig. Here, before shedding its final larval skin, the larva produces a fibre to weave into a dense mat of silk to reveal the pupa. This fragile blue-green pouch, studded with gold spots that control colour in the developing wings, turns transparent in about two weeks, exposing the features of a grown butterfly. Cracks then spread across the chrysalis wall and the adult insect appears after pumping body fluid into its limp, fleshy wings. The adult insect on its perch is now ready to fly away to produce a new generation. The metamorphosis from egg to adult has taken about five weeks.

> **Task 8.1**
>
> In Text 8.5 identify possible lexical and grammatical cohesive links. Draw lines between them (e.g. *caterpillar – larva; weaves – silk*).

8.3 Types of texts

Texts differ in their structure and in other characteristics according to the type of activity being engaged in. The relationship between domains of use and the purpose of the text is known as **genre** or **register**. Discussion of genre is not a precise science – but most people can normally tell the difference between reading a novel and an advertising brochure; or between a sports commentary, a weather forecast and a private conversation. We also know when a speaker or writer uses strange or inappropriate language within a particular genre. In the following example, it is not only the spelling and grammar that are not well formed. The writer was a high school student who was a second language learner of English, writing about his first impressions of New Zealand. Clearly, the use of *bloody* in this piece of writing will strike many native speakers of English as 'in-appropriate'. On the other hand, if he had been speaking to a close friend and used the word, it might not have seemed inappropriate.

> Frist of all or the frist time when am arrive in Wellington International Airport I am look so stranger with the bloody wind and cold. In the 7 a.m. my brother pick me up to his house, and early in the morning I wake up after that every-thing so beautiful and I said NZ is lovely country.

There are several ways of approaching genres and understanding how they work. The boundaries for the classifications of different genres are not always tidy and consistent. We will briefly consider three major approaches:

1 Domains of use

2 Co-occurrence of linguistic items

3 Purpose of the text.

8.3.1 Domains of use

Where domains of use are used as the basis for describing genres, it is the place where language is used that is considered to be the most import-ant factor to be taken account of in making the classification. This approach to classifying text types is especially associated with the design of representative corpora of a language. Figure 8.2 shows the categories from which texts were selected for inclusion in the *International Corpus of English* (*ICE*) which, when complete, will include 1-million-word corpora from about 20 regional varieties of English from throughout the world. Each corpus will contain 500 samples, each of 2,000 words, with distribu-tion as shown in Figure 8.2.

It goes without saying that such categorisations can be extremely broad. If we take just one text type category from the *ICE* corpus, **learned** (sometimes called **academic**), it is not hard to see major differences between an academic text in **accountancy** from one in **chemistry** or **history**. Potentially, the number of different possible genres is very large, and broad generalisations tend to be made about the characteristics of texts produced in different mediums (e.g. speech or writing) or in differ-ent domains of use. Nevertheless there have been major differences found between domain-based genres in their use of particular grammatical rules and structures: for example, see Table 5.17 for a description of how the use of passive voice differs in different genres of the *Brown Corpus*.

8.3.2 Co-occurrence of linguistic items

Biber (1988) and his colleagues developed a way of identifying genres by using a statistical basis for showing how particular linguistic items or processes tend to occur together in certain texts. Biber studied how

Spoken genres (300 samples)

DIALOGUE (180)

Private (100)
   direct conversations (90)
   distanced conversations (10)
Public (80)
   class lessons (20)
   broadcast discussions (20)
   broadcast interviews (10)
   parliamentary debates (10)
   legal cross-examination (10)
   business transactions (10)

MONOLOGUE (120)

Unscripted (70)
   spontaneous commentaries (20)
   unscripted speeches (30)
   demonstrations (10)
   legal presentations (10)
Scripted (50)
   broadcast news (20)
   broadcast talks (20)
   speeches (not broadcast) (10)

Written genres (200 samples)

NON-PRINTED (50)

Non-professional writing (20)
   student untimed essays (10)
   student examination essays (10)
Correspondence (30)
   social letters (15)
   business letters (15)

PRINTED (150)

Informational (learned) (40)
   humanities (10)
   social sciences (10)
   natural sciences (10)
   technology (10)
Informational (popular) (40)
   humanities (10)
   social sciences (10)
   natural sciences (10)
   technology (10)
Informational (reportage) (20)
   press news reports (20)
Instructional (20)
   administrative/regulatory (10)
   skills/hobbies (10)
Persuasive (10)
   press editorials (10)
Creative (20)
   novels/stories (20)

Total 500 samples, each of 2,000 words

Figure 8.2 Structure of the *ICE Corpus*

67 linguistic items (e.g. past tense, *wh*-questions, passives, relative clauses, attributive adjectives) tend to occur together in texts, and suggested that texts differ according to the extent to which they have more or fewer of these features. The main dimensions of difference include the extent to which a text is:

1 'involved' or 'informational'

2 'narrative' or 'non-narrative'

3 'situation independent' or 'situation dependent'

4 'abstract' or 'non-abstract'.

More involved
private verbs (e.g. *think, want*)
that-deletion in relative clauses
contractions
present tense verbs
second person pronouns
do as pro-verb (e.g. *I didn't **do** it.*)
negation (with *not*)
demonstrative pronouns
general emphatics
first person pronouns
pronoun *it*
be as main verb
discourse particles
indefinite pronouns
general hedges (e.g. *you know, sort of*)
amplifiers (e.g. *very, terribly*)
wh-questions
possibility modals
non-phrasal co-ordination
wh-clauses
final prepositions
adverbs
conditional subordination
nouns
longer words
prepositions
attributive adjectives
place adverbials
agentless passives
past participial non-finite clauses
present participial non-finite clauses
More informational

Figure 8.3   Dimension 1: involved vs. informational style (based on Biber, 1988)

Abstract
conjuncts
agentless passives
past participial non-finite clauses
by-passives
adverbial subordinate clauses
predicative adjectives
Non-abstract

Figure 8.4   Dimension 4: abstract vs. non-abstract style (based on Biber, 1988)

We can illustrate how this approach works by seeing how texts of different kinds fit. Figures 8.3 and 8.4 show some of the linguistic characteristics of Dimensions 1 and 4.

It can be seen from Figure 8.5 that scientific and medical texts have high scores on the informational and abstract dimensions, while broadcasts

Figure 8.5 Linguistic characterisation of ten spoken and written texts with respect to Dimension 1, *involved or informational*, and Dimension 4, *abstract or non-abstract style* (based on Biber et al., 1994: 182)

tend to have high occurrence of non-abstract features while being relatively neutral on Dimension 1. Figure 8.5 shows how a statistical analysis of the occurrence of these characteristics can reveal how texts from ten spoken and written fields can have strikingly different distributions of linguistic features, with some spoken and written texts having more in common than two written or two spoken texts.

8.3.3 Purpose of the text

A number of researchers have proposed that it is useful to characterise genres in terms of the **purpose** of the texts. From a Hallidayan perspective, Derewianka (1990) has suggested a number of genres which can have major significance in education, e.g.

1 Explanations

2 Narratives

3 Information reports

4 Instructions

5 Arguments

By way of illustration, the following analysis shows Derewianka's characterisation of texts which belong to the 'Explanations' and 'Information reports' genres. The information is presented in a way that can be used to help learners of English to structure their written texts. Success at school can of course depend on the ability to write in different genres.

Explanations

Purpose: To show how something works, or why something occurs.

Types: There are at least two basic types of explanation –

1 explaining **how**, e.g.

> Mechanical explanation (How does a pump work?)
>
> Technological explanation (How does a television work?)
>
> System explanation (How does Parliament function?)
>
> Natural explanation (How are mountains formed?)

2 explaining **why**, e.g.

> Why do some things float and others sink?
>
> Why is the ozone layer thinning?
>
> Why do we have different seasons?
>
> Why does iron go rusty?
>
> Why are plants green?

Text organisation: According to Derewianka, explanations have a 'process' focus rather than a 'thing' focus. They are often concerned with a logical sequence. To position the reader, there is usually some statement about the phenomenon in question (often in the form of a heading or question), followed by a (sequenced) explanation of how or why something occurs.
  Prominent language features:

- Time relationships (e.g. *first, then, following, finally*) (especially in explaining how)
- Cause-and-effect relationships (e.g. *if/then, so, as a consequence, since*) (especially in explaining why)
- Adverbial subordinate clauses (e.g. *because, so that*)
- Action verbs (e.g. *falls, rises, changes*)
- Passive voice
- Simple present tense

Information reports

Purpose: To provide generalised information about a whole class of things.

Text organisation: Information reports are typically structured to move from the general to the specific, with paragraphing to focus on different aspects of the topic.

Prominent language features:

- Simple present tense
- Relationships such as time differences, comparisons with other things
- Generalised participants rather than specific examples
- Technical terms used when appropriate
- Factual and precise descriptions
- Little or no use of subjective opinions
- Formal style

Text 8.6 illustrates some of these characteristics in part of an information report.

Text 8.6

Irises

The *Iridaceae* is a large plant family. In addition to the true irises there are many closely related genera, including most of the more popular South African bulbs such as *Gladiolus*, *Freesia*, *Ixia* and *Watsonia*. These plants nearly all share the strap-like leaves that typify the true irises but cover a wide range of lower types and growing conditions. The true irises range in size from the very small rockery forms like *Iris innominata* and *reticulata* through to the large swamp irises such as the Japanese (*ensata* formerly *kaempferi*) and the flag (*pseudocorus*). In general the smaller forms tend to grow best in normal garden conditions or rockeries, as do many of the intermediate sized forms. Some of the larger species are marginal pond plants and can grow in several inches of water.

Irises are divided into two main groups: bulbs and rhizomes. The common cut flower varieties, the Dutch, English and Spanish, are bulbous, as are many of the smaller species such as *reticulata* and *histrioides*. Many of the rhizomatous irises have quite fibrous roots that are not obviously rhizomes, but most of the larger flowering forms such as the bearded irises are so typical of the rhizomatous group that the term 'bearded iris' is generally used to cover a wide range of species and forms.

Of all the many and varied irises the tall bearded flowers are the most spectacular and therefore the best known. The bearded irises are so called because of the tuft of hairs at the base of each of the flowers. These hairs are part of the plant's pollination strategy. They brush the pollen from any insects that visit the flowers.

Another 'purpose of text' approach to classifying genres particularly relevant for educational contexts was suggested by Johns & Davies (1983). They proposed that there is a limited number of 'topic types' into which texts can fit. They described the characteristics of 12 topic types which can be relevant for second language learners especially at high school level.

	Topic type	Characteristic language features
1	Physical structure	properties, location and function of parts
2	Process	description of form, location, time, properties, instrument of change
3	Characteristics	defining features, measurements, data, examples
4	Mechanism	physical structure, action, material
5	Theory	hypothesis, context, test, results, interpretation
6	Principle	law or principle, conditions, instances, applications
7	Force	source, conditions, examples, effects
8	Instruction	steps or procedures, material, measurement, condition, results, interpretation
9	Social structure	member(s), location, role, assets
10	Situation	participants, conditions, time, place, cause, effects, event
11	Adaptation	example, environmental condition, effects, adaptive feature, function
12	Production	producer, product, location, distribution

The suggested characteristics of text types in this approach by Johns and Davies tend to be vague and non-specific in many cases, and to overlap, but it is possible nevertheless to recognise the occurrence of some of these constituents or a mixture of them in particular texts.

Discussion topic

Analyse the text organisation and language features in Text 8.7 and assign the text to one or more of the genres suggested by Derewianka or Johns and Davies.

Text 8.7

How paper is made

Paper is one of the most important materials we use to communicate with others. All kinds of paper consist basically of fibres of cellulose, the material that forms the hard part of trees and plants. In paper, these fibres crisscross in all directions, forming a closely interwoven mat that holds them together. If you tear a piece of paper, you can see the tiny fibres sticking out from the torn edges. The largest source of cellulose fibres for papermaking is wood. But many other plant materials are also used, including hemp, straw and esparto grass. Some of the best paper is made from cotton rags. Wastepaper can also be reprocessed to make new paper.

There are various processes used for making paper, but they all involve the same basic steps. The first stage breaks up the raw material to release the cellulose fibres. This makes pulp. Both mechanical and chemical methods are used to produce pulp. Mechanical pulp is produced by grinding logs between heavy grindstones. This results in a coarse pulp that is most commonly used in newsprint. Chemical pulp is made by treating wood chips with chemicals at high temperatures in a tank called a digester.

The next stage is to mix the pulp with water and beat it thoroughly. This stage of papermaking breaks up the cellulose fibres even more and cuts them to the correct length. The finer the fibres are, the stronger the paper. Various materials may be added at this stage, including clay, glue, starch or coloured dyes. These all affect the type of paper produced.

The final stage is the drying and rolling. The liquid pulp flows on to a large wire net. There, the water drains from it. After drying, the fibre sheet passes through heavy rollers. This sheet then passes over a number of drying rollers and, in a finishing stage called calendaring, it passes over smooth rollers which give it a smooth surface.

8.3.4 Spoken texts and their characteristics

Linguists have long reminded us that most of our use of language is in spoken genres, and that spoken language evolved before writing, just as it develops first in children. Special characteristics of spoken language have been noted which can make spoken genres different in many ways from written genres, remembering, as noted in Section 8.3.2, that spoken and written texts can have more in common linguistically than two particular spoken or two particular written texts.

One fundamental distinction among spoken texts is the difference between **monologue** and **dialogue**. Whereas monologue, such as a political speech, is usually public, planned and content-focused, conversational genres involving dialogue have some quite distinctive characteristics.

8.3.4.1 Conversation

Conversation is the most well-known type of dialogue and the most widely used of all genres. It is what we do most with language. Conversation can be 'public' (or eavesdropped), but it is most frequently 'private'. It is typically a face-to-face activity, but can also be conducted remotely by means of the telephone, radio, or even email – (a modern genre that falls perhaps somewhere between written and spoken genres). In conversation as in other spoken genres, there is normally repetition, redundancy, incomplete utterances, interruption, hesitation phenomena (e.g. *um*) and fillers (e.g. *and so on, you know*) which give the speaker time to organise what is to follow. There is also self-correction, often in mid-sentence. Conversation tends to make more use of formulaic expressions than written genres (e.g. *How are you?*; *(Have you got) everything under control?*; *I was absolutely shattered to hear about it*).

Successful conversation depends on **co-operation** between participants. Speakers need to observe various principles or 'maxims' such as 'be truthful', 'be brief', 'be relevant', 'be informative and clear' (Grice, 1975). Speakers also need to be acceptably polite and to make the listener feel good (Lakoff, 1973), to be tactful, sympathetic, and to avoid face-threatening acts.

Conversation is typically unplanned and is characterised by spontaneous, often incomplete utterances or sequences of utterances. Facial expression, 'body language' and 'tone of voice' contribute to the messages. Vagueness and generalised statements are given meaning by the context in which they are uttered.

A   *Did you get it?*

B   *They didn't have any left.*

In this exchange, A was referring to an electric foot massager, but contextual knowledge was needed for B to 'know' that and give a sensible response.

C   *I'll bet that tie cost a packet!*

D   *Do you like it? I got it at Kirk's sale.*

In the above exchange, D does not directly answer C's implied question (*How much did it cost?*), but in giving a 'satisfactory' response is co-operating with C. Participants in conversation typically give each other **feedback** to encourage and keep the communication channel open (e.g. *Yeah!*; *Really!*; *You're kidding!*; *mm*; *aha*).

One of the most striking ways in which the principle of co-operation is manifested in conversation is through **turn taking**. Although simultaneous speech (more than one person talking at the same time) does occur, especially when there is overlap at the time a new speaker takes over the conversation from a previous speaker, it is remarkable just how smoothly the transitions from speaker to speaker normally occur among native speakers of a language. Second language learners typically find it difficult to know how and when to bid for a turn and how to take the floor in English. There are important differences associated with status in some cultures, as to how turn taking is achieved. For example, in some cultures it is considered very rude to interrupt a more senior person or be seen to try to take a turn.

Speaker and listener often change roles at the **end** of an utterance; there is minimal silence and the principle of 'one speaker at a time' is generally observed. Some skill is required to bid for a turn, or to stop someone taking over if the previous speaker wishes to continue. 'Turns' can often be classified according to function as a series of 'moves' (initiations, responses, etc.) which can be grouped together to form 'exchanges'.

To bid for a turn we use mainly lexical means, but grammatical and phonological signals can also be used (e.g. raising the pitch or loudness). Lexical means include the following (Sacks et al., 1974; He Anping, 1996):

Address tags	e.g. *John, darling, (have some cherries) . . .*
Hesitation markers	e.g. *Well; sort of . . . ; in, in, in; actually . . .*
Emphasis (the most frequent)	e.g. *Really; Right; Fine*
Connectors	e.g. *And . . . ; Because . . . ; So . . . ;* *Yes but . . . ; I mean . . .*

Sometimes the person bidding for a turn will complete the previous speaker's last sentence. Very often previous speakers give an indication that they are willing to give way to another at what Sacks called a 'transition relevance place' (e.g. by using sequences such as *you know, and so on, you know what I mean, or something*) or by means of body language, lowering the voice, or slowing down.

Some turns typically occur in 'adjacency pairs', e.g.

Question – Answer	e.g. *Where's the coffee? – In the cupboard.*
Blame – Denial	e.g. *Someone left the tap running! –* *It wasn't me!*
Greeting – Greeting	e.g. *Hello. – Hello.*
Invitation – Acceptance	e.g. *Would you like to come for tea? –* *That'd be lovely.*
Congratulations – Denial	e.g. *You did well. – Ah, it was nothing.*
Congratulations – Thanks	e.g. *You did well. – Thanks very much.*
Leave-taking – Leave-taking	e.g. *OK, see you. – So long.*
Summons – Answer	e.g. *John. – OK, I'm coming.*
Complaint – Apology	e.g. *I wish you'd told me. – (I'm) sorry.* *I forgot.*

Richards & Schmidt (1983: 189) give further examples of different possible adjacency pairs arising from the same initial statement.

Compliment	*That's a nice shirt.*
– Acceptance	*Thanks.*
– Agreement	*It is quite nice, isn't it.*
– Rejection	*Well, I think it makes me look old.*
– Shift	*Judy found it for me.*
– Return	*Thanks, I like yours too.*

Complaint	*You ate the cake I left in the fridge!*
– Apology	*Sorry.*
– Denial	*No I didn't, it must have been Susan.*
– Excuse	*You shouldn't have left it there.*
– Justification	*I was hungry. It was just a small piece.*
– Challenge	*So what?*
Offer	*Like a lift?*
– Acceptance	*You saved my life.*
– Rejection	*Thanks, but I'm waiting for my friend.*
Request	*Can you mail these for me please?*
– Grant	*Sure.*
– Delay	*Sure, but I won't have time today.*
– Challenge	*Why do you always ask me?*
– Refusal	*Sorry, but I won't be near the Post Office.*

In conversation, speakers often seem to need to give reasons for what they do or say. For example, in initiating an unplanned visit to a friend, speakers sometimes follow rituals or formulae.

Hello.

I was just passing.

I saw your light on.

When we make an unarranged visit or a phone call, we sometimes seek permission to continue, e.g.

Am I taking you away from your dinner?

Is this a good time?

Have you got a moment? (**not** *Have you got anything else to do!*)

Are you free?

When we want to take leave from a conversation we sometimes need to state a reason to go. That is, we do not just say *Goodbye*, but use routines like the following:

Well, it's getting dark.

I'm going to be late for my class.

I gotta go, to check on the kids.

Well, I'll let you go. I don't want to tie up the phone.

This must be costing you a packet.

Discussion topic

Describe the features that would help you to determine the kind of speech event or context that the following piece of text comes from. Identify the linguistic features that suggest the text is transcribed from a spoken source.

You you personally would like some kind of hou some housing to be put there? Personally, yes, this isn't er a policy view but living in the or living around the area, working in this area, I think the area could be improved, if the flats were replaced by something which looked more attractive. Because they don't look attractive. Mhm. And er they seem to be the cause of all the problems. If they could be improved by er sorry replaced by housing of a higher standard, erm generally made to look more attractive, landscaped and such like, then I think the area as a whole will improve and it'll attract people to the area. Mhm. Which I think should be er an important er an important idea in their minds. In the minds of the people who decide what's going to replace them with. Mhm. What about for local businesses, erm what do you think could be done to actually to attract more businesses to the area? I think the first thing is to improve the appearance, because the area itself appears to me to be to be thriving. There's a lot of larger shops, we've got the chemist's just over the road and er a lot er of good businesses round about. There's one or two empty shops, but they appear to be moving fairly quickly and getting taken over. So the important thing I would say, is just to improve the physical appearance. Because a lot of the shops and house fronts which the the bus routes are on, the main roads are on, do look tatty. And if they could be given a a better appearance, then the the people who see them, the people who drive through on the main road, they could see that the area isn't as run down as often the press makes it out to be. Erm to me it is a thriving and very good community, and all it really needs is to look at it's thriving. Mhm.

Figure 8.6 is an example of a 'service encounter' in a hardware store. It illustrates the formulaic structure or **script** of the conversation during this kind of discourse. Learners of English cannot be assumed to know automatically how to do this even if they have quite proficient grammatical knowledge.

8.3.4.2 Classroom discourse

In a number of ways the spoken language of classrooms typically differs from other spoken and written texts. Outside of classrooms, for example,

(Shop Assistant (X) approaches a potential customer (Y))

Offer of service	X	*Hello, can I help you?* (NOT: *What do you want?*)
Request for service	Y	*I'm looking for a wide paintbrush.*
Clarification request	X	*A white paintbrush?*
Response	Y	*No, a wide one.*
Apology, plus request for information	X	*Sorry, OK. How wide?*
Response	Y	*About this wide.* (Uses both hands to demonstrate the desired width.)
Response plus request for information	X	*That's about a 12 cm one. We've got three or four types. How much do you want to pay?*
Response plus provision of information, request for information	Y	*As little as possible to do the job. I'm going to paint my roof – so I don't need high quality just a brush with um heavy enough bristles. Is there a brush for roof painting?*
Response plus provision of information	X	*Not specifically. But we well . . . , the Apex brand – a lot of painters prefer the Apex for roof painting.*
Request for information	Y	*What are . . . what do they cost?*
Response	X	*$15.95.*
Response	Y	*OK. I'll take it.* (Hands over money.)
Response plus request	X	*OK, is that all?* (After the brush is put in a bag) *Thanks.*
Response	Y	*Yes. That's all for now, thanks.*
Leave-taking	X	*Thanks. I hope it'll do the job you have in mind.*

Figure 8.6 Turn-taking routines in a retail context

it is unusual for speakers to ask questions for which they know the answer, whereas it is acceptable for teachers to do this. For example, *What is the capital of Italy? (Paris.) Do the rest of you agree? Try again.* Classroom discourse is typically characterised by an initiation by the teacher, with a response from students, and a follow-up by the teacher, e.g.

TEACHER : What is the name of our mayor?

STUDENT : Leila Robson.

TEACHER : Good. What does she do?

or No, come on, try again.

etc.

A considerable part of classroom discourse consists of directives which teachers use for imparting information and for maintaining control. Holmes (1983) published data from British and New Zealand classrooms showing a wide variety of imperatives, interrogatives and declaratives being used

1 <u>Imperatives</u> (the most frequent)

   i base form of verb
                          Speak up.
                          Don't shout.
                          Don't draw on the paper.

   ii *you* + imperative
                          You go on with your work.

   iii present participle
                          Sitting up straight please.
                          Looking this way, please.

   iv verb ellipsis
                          Everybody out front.
                          Hands away from your mouth.
                          Jane (= pay attention).

   v imperative + modifier
                          Put your hands on your hips, everyone.

   vi *let* + first person pronoun
                          Let's finish these.
                          Let's see if you can sort this out.

2 <u>Interrogatives</u> (less frequent than imperatives)

   i modals
                          Would you open the window?
                          Can you read what it says for me?

   ii non-modals
                          Have you tried it?
                          What are you meant to be doing?

3 <u>Declaratives</u>

   i embedded agent
                          I want you to draw a picture.
                          I'd like Arnold's group out front.

   ii hints
                          Sally, you're not saying much.
                          I'm not going to do it by myself.

Figure 8.7 Classroom directives

by teachers as directives (Figure 8.7). Holmes found that up to 70 per cent of the spoken language in the classrooms she studied was produced by teachers, and 25 per cent of this was directives. The role of these spoken texts was to maintain order and keep social distance, as well as to inform and instruct.

8.3.4.3 Silence

Finally, silence can be an important part of spoken texts, but how it is used varies greatly cross-culturally.

Sometimes silence is an appropriate response in English:

What a lovely coat.

What a lovely day.

Good morning. (by a teacher to a class)

It has sometimes been suggested that silence in discourse is determined by factors such as:

place: In churches, temples, libraries, Parliament, courts there is not always freedom to speak.

events: During ceremonies or performances such as funerals, operas, concerts or movies there are normally conventions which restrict unlimited speaking.

status: We are not usually expected to initiate speaking to a head of state.

taboo: In some cultures people are not free to initiate speaking with their mother-in-law.

Sorrow, respect, disapproval, dislike, timidity, fear or embarrassment may also inhibit speaking.

In some cultures, audiences typically speak or applaud only at the **end** of a concert or speech. Yet in Parliament interruptions can be appropriate during a speech. Silence can be misinterpreted cross-culturally. In some cultures, silence does not mean agreement or assent, whereas in some other cultures if there is no dissent it is assumed that there is agreement. Learning English thus involves not only learning how to pronounce words and link them together in sentences, but learning when to keep silent, how to bid for a turn in conversation, how to use the language to do certain things – all the while making sense and using language appropriately to achieve communicative goals.

Useful sources of information about English

1 General

Crystal, D. (ed.) (1995) *Cambridge Encyclopedia of the English Language.* Cambridge: Cambridge University Press

McArthur, T. (ed.) (1992) *Oxford Companion to the English Language.* Oxford: Oxford University Press

2 Phonetics and phonology

Brazil, D. (1994) *Pronunciation for Advanced Learners of English.* Cambridge: Cambridge University Press

Brazil, D. (1997) *The Communicative Value of Intonation in English.* Cambridge: Cambridge University Press

Catford, J. (1988) *A Practical Introduction to Phonetics.* Oxford: Oxford University Press

Celce-Murcia, M., Brinton, D. and Goodwin, J. (1996) *Approaches to Pronunciation Teaching.* Cambridge: Cambridge University Press

Dalton, C. and Seidlhofer, B. (1996) *Pronunciation.* Oxford: Oxford University Press

Gimson, A. (1980) *An Introduction to the Pronunciation of English*, 3rd edn. London: Arnold

Kelly, G. (2000) *How to Teach Pronunciation.* London: Longman

Kenworthy, J. (1987) *Teaching English Pronunciation.* London: Longman

McCarthy, M. and Carter, R. (1997) *Exploring Spoken English.* Cambridge: Cambridge University Press

O'Connor, J. (1980) *Better English Pronunciation*, 2nd edn. Cambridge: Cambridge University Press

Roach, P. (1998) *English Phonetics and Phonology: A Practical Course*, 3rd edn. Cambridge: Cambridge University Press

3 Vocabulary

Carter, R. (1998) *Vocabulary*, 2nd edn. New York: Routledge

Corson, D. J. (1997) 'The learning and use of academic English words'. *Language Learning* 47, 4: 671–718

Hatch, E. and Brown, C. (1995) *Vocabulary, Semantics and Language Education*. Cambridge: Cambridge University Press

McKeown, M. G. and Curtis, M. E. (eds.) (1987) *The Nature of Vocabulary Acquisition*. New York: Lawrence Erlbaum

Nation, I. S. P. (1990) *Teaching and Learning Vocabulary*. New York: Heinle & Heinle

Nation, I. S. P. (2001) *Learning Vocabulary in Another Language*. Cambridge: Cambridge University Press

Schmitt, N. (2000) *Vocabulary in Language Teaching*. Cambridge: Cambridge University Press

Schmitt, N. and McCarthy, M. (eds.) (1997) *Vocabulary: Description, Acquisition and Pedagogy*. Cambridge: Cambridge University Press

4 Monolingual learners' dictionaries of English

Cambridge Advanced Learners Dictionary (2003). Cambridge: Cambridge University Press

Collins Cobuild English Dictionary for Advanced Learners (2001). London: Harper Collins

Longman Dictionary of Contemporary English (2001, 3rd edn rev.). London: Longman

Longman Language Activator (1993). London: Longman

Macmillan English Dictionary for Advanced Learners (2002). Oxford: Macmillan

Oxford Advanced Learner's Dictionary (2000, 6th edn). Oxford: Oxford University Press

Oxford Collocations Dictionary for Learners of English (2002). Oxford: Oxford University Press

5 Reference grammars

Biber, D., Johansson, S., Leech, G., Conrad, S. and Finegan, E. (1999) *Longman Grammar of Spoken and Written English*. London: Longman

Chalker, S. (1984) *Current English Grammar*. London: Macmillan

Greenbaum, S. (1996) *Oxford English Grammar*. Oxford: Oxford University Press

Greenbaum, S. and Quirk, R. (1990) *A Students' Grammar of the English Language*. London: Longman

Halliday, M. A. K. (1985) *An Introduction to Functional Grammar*. London: Arnold

Huddleston, R. (1988) *English Grammar: An Outline*. Cambridge: Cambridge University Press

Huddleston, R. and Pullum, G. (eds.) (2002) *The Cambridge Grammar of the English Language*. Cambridge: Cambridge University Press

Jespersen, O. (1954) *A Modern English Grammar*. London: Allen and Unwin

Kruisinga, E. (1931–2) *A Handbook of Present-day English*. Groningen: Noordhoff

Leech, G. (1991) *An A–Z of English Grammar and Usage*. London: Nelson

Leech, G. and Svartvik, J. (1975) *A Communicative Grammar of English*, 2nd edn. London: Longman

Quirk, R., Greenbaum, S., Leech, G. and Svartvik, J. (1985) *A Comprehensive Grammar of the English Language*. London: Longman

Sinclair, J. M. (ed.) (1990) *Collins Cobuild English Grammar*. London: Collins

Zandvoort, R. W. (1972) *A Handbook of English Grammar*. London: Longman

6 Pedagogical grammar

Alexander, L. (1988) *Longman English Grammar*. London: Longman

Celce-Murcia, M. and Larsen-Freeman, D. (1999) *The Grammar Book*, 2nd edn. New York: Heinle & Heinle

Francis, G., Hunston, S. and Manning, E. (1996) *Grammar Patterns. 1: Verbs*. London: Harper Collins

Francis, G., Hunston, S. and Manning, E. (1998) *Grammar Patterns. 2: Nouns and Adjectives*. London: Harper Collins

Hurford, J. (1995) *Grammar: A Student's Guide*. Cambridge: Cambridge University Press

Murphy, R. (1994) *English Grammar in Use*, 2nd edn. Cambridge: Cambridge University Press

Odlin, T. (ed.) (1994) *Perspectives on Pedagogical Grammar*. Cambridge: Cambridge University Press

Parrott, M. (2000) *Grammar for English Language Teachers*. Cambridge: Cambridge University Press

Rinvolucri, M. (1984) *Grammar Games*. Cambridge: Cambridge University Press

Rutherford, W. (1987) *Second Language Grammar: Learning and Reading*. London: Longman

Rutherford, W. and Sharwood Smith, M. (eds.) (1988) *Grammar and Second Language Teaching: A Book of Readings*. Rowley, MA: Newbury House

Swan, M. (1995) *Practical English Usage*. Oxford: Oxford University Press

Swan, M. and Walters, C. (1997) *How English Works*. Cambridge: Cambridge University Press

Thornbury, S. (1997) *About Language*. Cambridge: Cambridge University Press

Thornbury, S. (1999) *How to Teach English Grammar*. London: Longman

Thornbury, S. (2001) *Uncovering Grammar*. Oxford: Macmillan

Yule, G. (1998) *Explaining English Grammar*. Oxford: Oxford University Press

7 English in use

Coulthard, M. (1985) *An Introduction to Discourse Analysis*, 2nd edn. London: Longman

Crystal, D. and Davy, D. (1973) *Investigating English Style*. London: Longman

Halliday, M. A. K. and Hasan, R. (1976) *Cohesion in English*. London: Longman

Halliday, M. A. K. and Hasan, R. (1985) *Language, Context and Text: Aspects of Language in a Social-Semiotic Perspective*. Melbourne: Deakin University Press

Hatch, E. (1992) *Discourse and Language Education*. Cambridge: Cambridge University Press

Kennedy, G. (1998) *An Introduction to Corpus Linguistics*. London: Longman

McCarthy, M. (1991) *Discourse Analysis for Language Teachers*. Cambridge: Cambridge University Press

McCarthy, M. and Carter, R. (1994) *Language as Discourse: Perspectives for Language Teaching*. London: Longman

Nunan, D. (1993) *Introducing Discourse Analysis*. London: Penguin

Schiffrin, D. (1994) *Approaches to Discourse*. Oxford: Blackwell

References

Aitchison, J. (1987) *Words in the Mind*. Oxford: Blackwell

Altenberg, B. (1991) 'Amplifier collocations in spoken English', in S. Johansson and A-B. Stenström (eds.), *English Computer Corpora*. Berlin: Mouton de Gruyter

Altenberg, B. (1993) 'Recurrent verb complement constructions in the *London–Lund Corpus'*, in J. Aarts, P. de Haan and N. Oostdijk (eds.), *English Language Corpora: Design, Analysis and Exploitation*. Amsterdam: Rodopi

Austin, J. L. (1962) *How to Do Things with Words*. Oxford: Clarendon Press

Bauer, L. (1983) *English Word Formation*. Cambridge: Cambridge University Press

Bauer, L. (1993) 'Manual of information to accompany the *Wellington Corpus of Written New Zealand English'*. Wellington: School of Linguistics and Applied Language Studies, Victoria University

Bauer, L. & Nation, I. S. P. (1993) 'Word families'. *International Journal of Lexicography* 6, 4: 253–79

Biber, D. (1988) *Variation Across Speech and Writing*. Cambridge: Cambridge University Press

Biber, D., Conrad, S. & Reppen, R. (1994) 'Corpus-based approaches to issues in applied linguistics'. *Applied Linguistics* 15, 2: 169–89

Biber, D., Johansson, S., Leech, G., Conrad, S. & Finegan, E. (1999) *Longman Grammar of Spoken and Written English*. London: Longman

Brazil, D. (1997) *The Communicative Value of Intonation in English*. Cambridge: Cambridge University Press

Brown, H. D. (1987) *Principles of Language Learning and Teaching*, 2nd edn. Englewood Cliffs, NJ: Prentice Hall

Brown, R. (1973) *A First Language*. Cambridge, MA: Harvard University Press

Celce-Murcia, M., Brinton, D. & Goodwin, J. (1996) *Approaches to Pronunciation Teaching*. Cambridge: Cambridge University Press

Close, R. A. (1962) *English as a Foreign Language*. London: Allen & Unwin

Coates, J. (1983) *The Semantics of the Modal Auxiliaries*. London: Croom Helm

Coxhead, A. (2000) 'A new academic word list'. *TESOL Quarterly* 34, 2: 213–38

Denes, P. (1963) 'On the statistics of spoken English'. *Journal of the Acoustical Society of America* 35: 892–904

Derewianka, B. (1990) *Exploring How Texts Work*. Sydney: Primary English Teaching Association

Elley, W. & Croft, C. (1989) *Assessing the Difficulty of Reading Materials: The Noun Frequency Method*. Wellington: NZCER

Fang, X. & Kennedy, G. (1992) 'Expressing causation in written English'. *RELC Journal* 23, 1: 62–80

Francis, G., Manning, E. & Hunston, S. (eds.) (1996) *Collins Cobuild Grammar Patterns* 1: *Verbs*. London: Harper Collins

Francis, W. N. & Kučera, H. (1979) 'Manual of information to accompany *A Standard Sample of Present-day Edited American English for Use with Digital Computers*'. Providence, RI: Department of Linguistics, Brown University

Francis, W. N. & Kučera, H. (1982) *Frequency Analysis of English Usage*. Boston, MA: Houghton Mifflin

Fries, C. C. (1957) *The Structure of English*. London: Longman

George, H. V. (1963) *Report on a Verb Form Frequency Count*. Hyderabad: Monograph No.1 of the Central Institute of English

George, H. V. (1972) *Common Errors in Language Learning*. Rowley, MA: Newbury House

Gimson, A. (1980) *An Introduction to the Pronunciation of English*, 3rd edn. London: Arnold

Grabowski, E. & Mindt, D. (1995) 'A corpus-based learning list of irregular verbs in English'. *ICAME Journal* 19: 5–22

Greenbaum, S. (1996) *The Oxford English Grammar*. Oxford: Oxford University Press

Greenbaum, S. & Quirk, R. (1990) *A Student's Grammar of the English Language*. London: Longman

Grice, H. P. (1975) 'Logic and conversation' in P. Cole and J. Morgan (eds.), *Speech Acts*. New York: Academic Press, pp. 41–58

Halliday, M. (1973) *Explorations in the Functions of Language*. London: Arnold

Halliday, M. & Hasan, R. (1976) *Cohesion in English*. London: Longman

He Anping (1996) 'A corpus-based analysis of simultaneous speech in English conversation'. Unpublished PhD thesis, Victoria University of Wellington

Hill, L. A. (1959) 'Noun classes and the practical teacher'. *Language Learning* 9: 3–4

Hill, L. A. (1960) 'The sequence of tenses with *if*-clauses'. *Language Learning* 10: 3–4

Holmes, J. (1983) 'The structure of teachers' directives', in J. Richards and R. Schmidt (eds.), *Language and Communication*. London: Longman

Holmes, J. (1988) 'Doubt and certainty in ESL textbooks'. *Applied Linguistics* 9: 21–44

Hornby, A. S. (1954) *A Guide to Patterns and Usage in English*. London: Oxford University Press

Hunston, S. & Francis, G. (1998) 'Verbs observed: a corpus-driven pedagogic grammar'. *Applied Linguistics* 19, 1: 45–72

Jakobson, R. (1960) 'Linguistics and poetics', in T. Sebeok (ed.), *Style and Language*. Cambridge, MA: MIT Press

Jenkins, J. (1970) 'The 1952 Minnesota Word Association norms', in L. Postman and G. Keppel (eds.), *Norms of Word Association*. New York: Academic Press

Johansson, S. (1981) 'Word frequencies in different types of English texts'. *ICAME News* 5: 1–13

Johansson, S. & Hofland, K. (1989) *Frequency Analysis of English Vocabulary and Grammar*. Oxford: Clarendon Press

Johns, T. & Davies, F. (1983) 'Text as a vehicle for information: the classroom use of written texts in teaching reading as a foreign language'. *Reading in a Foreign Language* 1: 1–19

Joos, M. (1964) *The English Verb: Form and Meaning*. Madison: University of Wisconsin Press

Kennedy, G. D. (1987) 'Quantification and the use of English: a case study of one aspect of the learner's task'. *Applied Linguistics* 8, 3: 264–86

Kennedy, G. D. (1991) '*Between* and *Through*: the company they keep and the functions they serve', in K. Aijmer and B. Altenberg (eds.), *English Corpus Linguistics*. London: Longman

Kennedy, G. D. (1992) 'Preferred ways of putting things with implications for language teaching' in J. Svartvik (ed.), *Directions in Corpus Linguistics*. Proceedings of Nobel Symposium 82, Stockholm, August 1991. Berlin: Mouton de Gruyter

Kennedy, G. D. (1998) *An Introduction to Corpus Linguistics*. London: Longman

Kreidler, C. W. (1966) 'English prepositions'. *English Language Teaching* 20, 2: 119–22

Lakoff, R. (1973) 'Language and woman's place'. *Language in Society* 2, 1: 45–79

Leech, G., Rayson, P. & Wilson, A. (2001) *Word Frequencies in Written and Spoken English*. London: Longman

Ljung, M. (1991) 'Swedish TEFL meets reality', in S. Johansson and A-B. Stenström (eds.), *English Computer Corpora*. Berlin: Mouton de Gruyter

Mindt, D. (1995) *An Empirical Grammar of the English Verb: Modal Verbs*. Berlin: Cornelsen

Mitchell, K. (1990) 'On comparisons in a notional grammar'. *Applied Linguistics* 11, 1: 53–72

Nation, I. S. P. (1990) *Teaching and Learning Vocabulary*. New York: Newbury House

Nation, I. S. P. (1991) *Language Teaching Techniques*. Wellington: English Language Institute, Victoria University

Nation, I. S. P. (2001) *Learning Vocabulary in Another Language*. Cambridge: Cambridge University Press

O'Connor, J. (1980) *Better English Pronunciation*, 2nd edn. Cambridge: Cambridge University Press

Ota, A. (1963) *Tense and Aspect of Present Day American English*. Tokyo: Kenkyusha

Palmer, H. E. (1938) *A Grammar of English Words*. London: Longman

Pawley, A. & Syder, F. (1983) 'Two puzzles for linguistic theory: native-like selection and native-like fluency', in J. Richards and R. Schmidt (eds.), *Language and Communication*. London: Longman

Quirk, R., Greenbaum, S., Leech, G. & Svartvik, J. (1985) *A Comprehensive Grammar of the English Language*. London: Longman

Quirk, R. & Svartvik, J. (1966) *Investigating Linguistic Acceptability*. The Hague: Mouton

Richards, J. & Schmidt, R. (1983) 'Conversational analysis', in J. Richards and R. Schmidt (eds.), *Language and Communication*. London: Longman

Rosch, E. (1975) 'Cognitive representations of semantic categories'. *Journal of Experimental Psychology: General* 104: 192–233

Sacks, H., Schegloff, E. & Jefferson, G. (1974) 'A simplest systematics for turn-taking for conversation'. *Language* 50: 696–735

Searle, J. (1969) *Speech Acts*. Cambridge: Cambridge University Press

Stockwell, R., Bowen, J. D. & Martin, J. W. (1965) *The Grammatical Structures of English and Spanish*. Chicago: Chicago University Press

Svartvik, J. (ed.) (1990) *The London–Lund Corpus of Spoken English: Description and Research*. Lund: Lund University Press

Swan, M. & Smith, B. (eds.) (2001) *Learner English*, 2nd edn. Cambridge: Cambridge University Press

Thompson, A. (1982) 'Clarification request sequences and related discourse strategies in information exchange between hearing-impaired and hearing children'. Unpublished PhD thesis, Victoria University of Wellington

Tottie, G. (1991) *Negation in English Speech and Writing: A Study in Variation*. San Diego: Academic Press

van Ek, J. (1976) *The Threshold Level for Modern Language Learning in Schools*. London: Longman

Wang Sheng (1991) 'A corpus study of English conditionals'. Unpublished MA thesis, Victoria University of Wellington

West, M. (1953) *A General Service List of English Words*. London: Longman

Wilkins, D. (1976) *Notional Syllabuses*. Oxford: Oxford University Press

Williams, R. (1983) 'Teaching the recognition of cohesive ties in reading a foreign language'. *Reading in a Foreign Language* 1, 1: 35–52

Key to tasks

Task 1.1

of	2	off	2	government	7 (9)
luck	3	few	3	ship	3
sea	2	write	3	sheep	3
mother	4	thumb	3	arrow	3
boy	2	test	4	yard	3 (4)
answer	4	phone	3	days	3
saw	2	banana	6	rough	3
thought	3	then	3	speed	4
black	4	roll	3	house	3
church	3	light	3	serious	6
be	2	bee	2	some	3
multiplication	12 (13)	magnificently	13	although	4

Task 1.2

pit, led, seek, bet, was, breathe, song, measure, mother, rip, wheat, sheep, beat, lover, learn, need (knead), moth, view, ship, bin, thick, bit, jaw, bigger, yard, chin, arm, visit, fill, thin, been (bean), you, wool, then, sugar, purse, garden, leave, feather, fishing, park, thing, deal, nurse, walked

Task 1.3

1	θ	6	ʃ	11	j	16	ŋ	21	ð	26	ʃ
2	ʃ	7	ð	12	θ	17	ʒ	22	ʃ	27	ð
3	j	8	ʃ	13	θ	18	θ	23	z		
4	dʒ	9	ð	14	ʃ	19	θ	24	θ		
5	tʃ	10	j	15	ð	20	ʃ	25	ŋ		

Task 1.4

/m n/	/f l/	/w θ/ or /w ð/	/s k/
/p n/	/r z/	/s d/	/b θ/
/h t/	/g v/	/b z/	/ʃ m/
/p s/	/θ f/	/l s/	/l z/
/v z/	/ʃ t/	/f v/	/m l/
/k ʃ/	/k tʃ/	/ð z/	/dʒ dʒ/
/b ŋ/	/s t/	/b ŋ/	/ʃ d/
/l z/	/θ k/	/k d/	/r ʒ/
/l ŋ/	/t ŋ/	/s s/	/b t/
/b ð/	/s s/	/l f/	/f z/
/s k/	/s t/	/r f/	/w z/
/j ŋ/	/w d/	/w θ/	/d t/

Task 1.6

The three sounds [kʰ] [k] and [k°] are allophones.
[kʰ] occurs at the beginning of syllables.
[k°] occurs before [kʰ].
[k] occurs in all other positions (ends of words and non-syllable-initial).

Task 1.7

2 j ⇒ dʒ	8 s ⇒ z
4 n ⇒ ŋ	9 sh ⇒ ʃ
5 s ⇒ z	11 delete g
6 f ⇒ fj	

Task 1.8

1 /b/   2 /ʒ/   3 /ŋ/   4 /j/   5 /s/

Task 1.9

/k/ is a voiceless velar stop.
/v/ is a voiced labio-dental fricative.
/j/ is a voiced palatal approximant.
/tʃ/ is a voiceless post-alveolar affricate.
/ð/ is a voiced dental fricative.
/p/ is a voiceless bilabial stop.

/ʒ/ is a voiced post-alveolar fricative.
/ŋ/ is a voiced velar nasal.
/s/ is a voiceless alveolar fricative.
/θ/ is a voiceless dental fricative.
/h/ is a voiceless glottal fricative.
/w/ is a voiced bilabial approximant.
/g/ is a voiced velar stop.

Task 1.10

1 /m/   2 /t/   3 /ʃ and ʒ/   4 /ŋ/   5 /ð/

Task 1.11

1 2, 3	4 1, 3, 4	7 1, 2, 3	10 1, 2, 4	13 3, 4
2 2	5 1, 3, 4	8 1, 2, 3, 4	11 1, 4	14 2, 3, 4
3 1	6 3	9 2, 4	12 2, 3	

Task 1.12

about	finger	custom	dangerous	absent	island
consider	disappear	husband	other	correct	elephant
policeman	worker	neighbour	banana	quarter	yesterday
allowed	forgive	open			

Task 1.13

/əbaʊt/	/maɪself/	/əgəʊ/	/ðəʊ/	/klɪə/	/faɪt/
/feɪl/	/heə/	/haʊ/	/feɪtl/	/meə/	/ndʒɔɪ/
/kraɪd/	/fɪə/	/tʊə/	/graʊl/	/kəʊm/	/eɪk/
/baʊ/	/həʊp/				

Task 1.14

1 development	6 family	11 group
2 duty	7 finished	12 imagine
3 effort	8 flew	13 increase
4 expensive	9 foreign	14 journey
5 fact	10 friend	15 language

Task 1.15

1	a	/uː/
	b	/ʊ/
	c	/ɔː/
	d	/ɜː/
	e	/ɑː/
	f	/æ/
2	a	a long high front vowel
	b	a short mid-to-low back vowel
	c	a short mid-central vowel
	d	a short low front vowel

Task 1.16

/fæmlɪ, hɪstrɪ, prɒplɪ, dəlɪbrət, pəʊsmən, temprɪ, gʌvmənt, pɑːləmənt, sekrətrɪ, kʌmpnɪ, temprəlɪ, dətiːriːeɪtɪŋ, grænmʌðə, ɑːst, seprət, ɪntrɪst/

Task 1.17

1 /wʌmʌnθ/	4 /teŋkʌps/	7 /gɒmbæk/
2 /nekswiːk/	5 /stæmbæk/	8 /naɪʃuːz/
3 /meɪŋɡeɪt/	6 /tempensɪlz/	9 /bægkɒld/

Task 1.18

1 /hɑːbprɒblɪmz/	3 /ɡʊɡkɒnsət/	5 /ɪŋkʌbədz/	7 /naɪʃeɪp/
2 /ɡʊbmiːl/	4 /wempɔːrɪnmɪlk/	6 /ðɪʃjɪə/	8 /hɪʒɒt/

Task 1.19

1	[wɒ tɪ zɪt]
2	[jə rəʊn haʊs]
3	[weə jə ɡəʊ ɪŋ]
4	[ɔː re nɪ je və dəns]
5	[dʒʌs tə mɪ nɪt]
6	[dəʊn tʌ tʃɪt]
7	[ðə fɜːs flɔː]
8	[nɒ tə tɔːl]
9	[ɑːf weɪ ə krɒs]
10	[maɪ mʌ ðə reɪ tɔː ləv ðəm]

Task 1.20

A	1 ac'cept, ac'ceptance	16 a'pply, appli'cation
	2 a'muse, a'musement	17 'atmosphere, atmos'pheric
	3 con'venient, con'veniently	18 'effort, 'effortless
	4 'social, 'socialist	19 enter'tain, enter'taining
	5 'cultivate, culti'vation	20 'ceremony, cere'monial
	6 e'conomy, eco'nomic	21 fa'miliar, famili'arity
	7 mathe'matics, mathema'tician	22 'history, his'torical
	8 'profit, 'profitable	23 'incident, inci'dental
	9 'sympathy, sympa'thetic	24 'character, characte'ristic
	10 'accurate, 'accurately	25 'perfect, per'fection
	11 'active, ac'tivity	26 'continent, conti'nental
	12 'alter, alte'ration	27 'industry, in'dustrial
	13 a'pproximate, a'pproximately	28 'theory, theo'retical
	14 a'ttract, a'ttraction	29 'politics, po'litical
	15 a'ware, a'wareness	30 re'sponsible, responsi'bility
B	Suffixes that alter stress: *-ation, -ic, -ian, -ity, -al, -istic, -ion* Suffixes that do not alter stress: *-ance, -ment, -ly, -ist, -able, -ion, -ness, -less, -ing*	

Task 1.21

1 The ˌweather has been absoˌlutely 'terrible.

2 He was very ˌlucky ˌnot to have been 'hurt.

3 Shall we go to a 'movie after we get ˌhome from 'work?

4 ˌNo-one seemed to ˌknow where we could ˌget 'help.

5 The reˌsult of the eˌlection was quite unex'pected.

Task 1.22

'diːrist 'kriːtʃə ɪn kriː'eɪʃən
'stʌdjɪŋ 'ɪŋglɪʃ prə'nʌnsiː'eɪʃən
aɪ wɪl 'tiːtʃjuː ɪn maɪ'vɜːs
'saʊnz laɪk 'kɔːps 'kɔː 'hɔːs nd 'wɜːs
aɪ wɪl 'kiːp juː 'suːziː 'bɪzɪ
meɪk jɔː 'hed wɪð 'hiːt grəʊ 'dɪzɪ

Task 2.9

In the last 30 year<u>s</u> of the twenti(eth) century there was (un)sustain(able) press(ure) on the natur(al) environment in most part<u>s</u> of the world. A number of environment(al) report<u>s</u> all point<u>ed</u> in the same direct(ion). Carbon (di)oxide emission<u>s</u> doubl<u>ed</u> and great(ly) exceed<u>ed</u> the abil(ity) of the environment to absorb them. Fish consum(ption) also doubl<u>ed</u> and most fish species are now in decline. Freshwater resource<u>s</u> have be<u>en</u> more and more exploit<u>ed</u>, and there is much waste especial(ly) in irrigat(ion) scheme<u>s</u>. The great(er) consum(ption) of wood for paper, packag(ing), fuel and timber has result<u>ed</u> in the destruc(tion) of rainforest<u>s</u> and the life they sustain. Regrett(abl)(y), govern(ment)<u>s</u> and citizen<u>s</u> have not yet do<u>ne</u> enough to reverse this assault on the natur(al) world on which all life depend<u>s</u>.

Task 2.12

About 50 per cent.

Task 3.1

Noun phrases	Prepositional phrases
<u>Water</u>	<u>on</u> Earth
the most important <u>solvent</u> on Earth	<u>of</u> the bodies of all living things
<u>Earth</u>	<u>of</u> all living things
<u>it</u>	<u>without</u> water
a large <u>part</u> of the bodies of all living things	
the <u>bodies</u> of all living things	
all living <u>things</u>	
<u>life</u>	
<u>water</u>	
carbon <u>dioxide and water</u>	
carbon <u>dioxide</u>	
<u>water</u>	
the two starting <u>materials</u>	
green <u>plants</u>	
<u>sugars</u>	

Task 3.2

When <u>I</u> was at school, <u>our class</u> spent an interesting afternoon visiting a sanctuary for birds. <u>We</u> walked for about an hour along a narrow track until <u>we</u> reached a large, flat, stony area at the top of steep cliffs. There <u>we</u> found thousands of gulls and other seabirds on nests or in the air. <u>Some</u> headed out to sea to look for food, and <u>others</u> returned to feed young birds. <u>The noise that the birds made</u> was incredible, especially while <u>we</u> were moving towards the sanctuary and <u>the birds</u> seemed uncertain about our intentions. After <u>we</u> had stopped and sat down to watch, <u>the noise</u> subsided considerably and <u>the birds</u> ignored us. <u>Each bird or pair of birds</u> got upset only if <u>another bird</u> came too close. Otherwise <u>the whole colony</u> seemed to function like a well-ordered community.

Task 3.3

1 I (need a rest).
2 <u>Fred</u> (is asleep).
3 <u>You</u> (didn't recognise me yesterday).
4 <u>The products sold here</u> (are imported from overseas).
5 <u>The new computer</u> (is very fast).
6 <u>It</u> (rarely rains in the Sahara desert).
7 (In my opinion) <u>that</u> (was a waste of time).
8 (Before Christmas) <u>the price</u> (was much lower).

Task 3.6

1 <u>Mary</u> owns (a hotel).
2 <u>They</u> appreciated (your hospitality).
3 <u>The new book</u> contains (a very good index).
4 <u>Some people</u> have (big feet).
5 <u>This bag</u> holds (all my books).
6 <u>That new tie</u> suits (him).
7 For some reason, <u>she</u> wants (a box of matches).
8 <u>I</u> really enjoy (Mozart's piano sonatas).
9 <u>You</u> will like (what I am going to tell you).
10 <u>We</u> need (your help) tomorrow morning.

Task 3.7

1 (t)	2 (i)	3 (t)	4 (i)	5 (i)
6 (t)	7 (t)	8 (i)	9 (t)	10 (t)

Task 3.8

1 <u>I</u> go [there] [at weekends].
2 <u>She</u> told (me) [several times].
3 <u>The day after tomorrow</u> is my birthday.
4 [In the morning] <u>we</u> began (the search).
5 <u>He</u> is retiring [at the end of the year].
6 <u>These things</u> are not suitable.
7 <u>I</u> always watch (TV) [on Sunday nights].
8 [For reasons of safety] <u>you</u> can't enter (that building).
9 <u>They</u> study (how to cure headaches) [in that course].
10 <u>Supplies of food</u> are needed [urgently] [in that region].

Task 3.9

1 SVO	2 SVO	3 not SVO	4 SVO	5 not SVO
6 SVO	7 not SVO	8 not SVO	9 not SVO	

Task 3.10

1 SVC	2 SVO	3 SVO	4 SVC
5 SVO	6 SVC	7 SV	8 SVC

Task 3.11

1 SVC	2 SVA	3 SVA	4 SVC	5 SVA
6 SVC	7 SVC	8 SVC	9 SVC	10 SVA

Task 3.12

1 SVOA	2 SVOA	3 SVOO	4 SVOO	5 SVOO
6 SVOA	7 SVOA	8 SVOO	9 SVOO	10 SVOO

Task 3.13

1 SVOO	2 SVOC	3 SVOA	4 SVOO	5 SVO
6 SVOA	7 SVOO	8 SVOC	9 SVA	10 SVC

Task 3.14

1 (oblig.)	2 (opt.)	3 (oblig.)
4 (oblig.)	5 (oblig.)	6 (oblig.)

Task 3.15

1 Has he often had to go to the doctor about it?
2 Were these shirts cheaper than the ones I got last time?
3 Are they likely to tell me about it?
4 Can she prove that she was there?
5 Did he throw the old pages away?
6 Could you argue that it was his fault?
7 Did your aunt sell the car that she won?
8 Are the polls showing declining support for the government?
9 Did someone (or anyone) speak to her as she walked through the park?

Task 3.16

1 Where is her car?
2 Where does his aunt live?
3 What can I read while I'm waiting?
4 Why did she leave New Zealand?
5 How did he take the news of his defeat?
6 What does their son do?
7 When do they sell most of the strawberries?
8 Which of their daughters is a brain surgeon?
9 (How's his leg) since he hurt it playing football?
  (What happened to his leg?)

Task 3.17

e.g.

1 Who wrote *Pride and Prejudice*?
2 Where did you go?
3 How did they break the window?
4 What do you need?
5 Did you get a good mark?
6 What did he ask her?

Task 3.18

not many people
uncomfortable
don't miss breakfast
not as good
avoid being inactive
do not underestimate
don't just wear one layer
by not leaving doors and windows open

Task 4.1

volcanoes	1 2 3	statement	1 2 3	Asia	2 4 5
world	1 2 4	fact	1 2 3	Australia	4 5
countries	1 3	volcanoes	1 2 3	coast	1 2 4
volcanoes	1 3	world	1 2 4	Antarctica	4 5
places	1 4	couple	2 4	exceptions	1 2 3
Japan	5	kilometres	1 2 4	Africa	4 5
Iceland	5	sea	1 2 4	volcanoes	1 2 3
Hawaii	5	volcanoes	1 2 4	France	4 5
Italy	5	centres	1 2 4	Germany	(4) 5
New Zealand	5	continents	1 4	group	1 2 3
areas	1 2 3	America	1 2 5	volcanoes	1 3
countries	1 2	mountain	1 3	plates	1 2 3
volcanoes	1 2 3	belt	1 2 4	surface	1 2 4
thing	1 2 3	Earth	2 4 5	sea	1 2 4

Task 4.2

In Text 4.1 (approx.) 42 out of 178 words are nouns (24%).
In Text 4.2 (approx.) 43 out of 172 words are nouns (25%).

Task 4.4

start (C)	way (C)	pain (UC)	trousers (C)
item (C)	wedding (C)	ceremony (C)	hospital (C)
newspaper (C)	arm (C)	bridegroom (C)	ceremony (C)
way (C)	leg (C)	registry office (C)	reception (C)
marriage (C)	hospital (C)	wheelchair (C)	anaesthetic (UC)
bridegroom (C)	doctors	blood (UC)	bridegroom (C)
accident (C)	injections (C)	clothes (C)	

Task 4.5

C	UC	C or UC	Collective	Proper
job	music	sugar	crew	Oxford University
airport	scenery	water		Telecom
poet	honesty	truth		
pen	equipment	theatre		
lecture	permission	cake		
road	moonlight	disease		
	happiness	television		
		business		

Task 4.6

Possible answers:

Many medicines contain expensive drugs. (C)
There's no medicine left in the bottle. (UC)

She told me about it three times. (C)
We are short of time. (UC)

In Wellington we went to see all the sights. (C)
They have both lost their sight. (UC)

Sue has an interest in fossils. (C)
I don't get much interest from my bank account. (UC)

I had a glass of beer. (C)
Glass is fragile. (UC)

No-one is interested in the skills I have. (C)
Gymnastics requires a lot of skill. (UC)

I usually work at home in my study. (C)
A lot of study is necessary to pass this course. (UC)

Task 4.9

1 (George's <u>father</u>) gave (<u>him</u>) (some <u>money</u>) to go to (a <u>lecture</u> on electricity).

2 (<u>He</u>) saw (a <u>person</u>) put (<u>something</u>) inside (a <u>coil</u> of wire).

3 (<u>It</u>) was (a <u>piece</u> of iron).

4 (The iron) became (a magnet) when (an electric current) was passed through (the coil).

5 (A simple method of making (electricity)) was demonstrated by moving (a magnet) inside (a coil of wire).

Task 4.10

(An earthquake) destroys (buildings) by shaking (them) to (pieces). (Engineers) are finding ((ways) to keep (them) standing) when (the ground) moves. As ((an engineer) in (California)) observed in ((the aftermath) of (the 1989 quake)): '(Earthquakes) don't kill (people). (Buildings) do.' (Nobody) wants to spend (extra money) to prepare for (something that may never happen), and (earthquake engineering) has long been neglected. (That attitude) is now changing. (Earthquake engineers) may not have needed to be reminded that (building design) can make ((all the difference) between (life and death)) but (recent quakes) have increased ((public interest) in (earthquake-resistant designs)). (These) range from reinforcing (masonry walls) with (steel beams) to strengthen (them), to supporting (an entire building) on (rubber) so that (the structure) can float in (isolation).

Task 4.11

Some people argue that everyone who claims to have seen or to have photographed the Loch Ness monster has been either drunk, deceived by a log or interested in promoting the Scottish tourist industry. On the other hand, many people are quite prepared to concede that some animal or group of animals has been seen in the loch. The issue is whether this animal can be identified as the 'monster'. There is (to date) only one photograph of the creature. It has been studied carefully by experts, and the general consensus is that the picture reveals a row of playful otters. For this reason, arguments for the existence of the monster based on visual evidence have met with a good deal of scepticism. Another approach has been to consider how monsters might be able to survive in a freshwater environment. Could they obtain enough food to sustain themselves? Those that believe that they could, point out that Loch Ness is very deep, and moreover that it may be connected by a series of subterranean passages with the sea, allowing the monster to feed. Some say that the animal could be a whale or a basking shark which has lost its way or even come inland to die, and that this could explain the rare sightings.

Task 4.13

Some people argue that everyone who claims to have seen or to have photographed the Loch Ness monster has been either drunk, deceived by a log or interested in promoting the Scottish tourist industry. On the other hand, many people are quite prepared to concede that some animal or group of animals has been seen in the loch. The issue is whether this animal can be identified as the 'monster'. There is (to date) only one photograph of the creature. It has been studied carefully by experts, and the general consensus is that the picture reveals a row of playful otters. For this reason, arguments for the existence of the monster based on visual evidence have met with a good deal of scepticism. Another approach has been to consider how monsters might be able to survive in a freshwater environment. Could they obtain enough food to sustain themselves? Those that believe that they could, point out that Loch Ness is very deep, and moreover that it may be connected by a series of subterranean passages with the sea, allowing the monster to feed. Some say that the animal could be a whale or a basking shark which has lost its way or even come inland to die, and that this could explain the rare sightings.

1 Preceded by *the*	37%
2 Preceded by *a* or *an*	15%
3 Preceded by Ø	23%
4 Preceded by another determiner	25%

Task 4.14

reports (1), villages (1), attempts (1), houses (1), evidence (2), days (1, 4), friends (1, 4), news (2), kilometers (1, 4), Prayag (3)

Task 4.15

the most magnificent buildings, the walls, the roof, the floor, the pattern, the lights, the wind, the windows, the smell, the flowers, the surrounding garden, the walls, (the rain), the doors

Task 4.16

a dollar (4)	a tailor (3)	a kilo (5)
a third (4)	a franc (4)	a year (4)
a hotel (2)	an item (5)	a half (4)
a man (2)	a hundred francs (4)	a week (5)
a day (5)	a week (5)	a better paying job (1)

Task 4.17

an old story	(individualising *a*)
a man	(individualising *a*)
a crane	(individualising *a*)
the cook	(anaphoric *the*)
a plate	(individualising *a*)
the dinner table	(specifying *the*)
the man	(anaphoric *the*)
the dinner table	(specifying *the*)
the bird	(anaphoric *the*)
the other leg	(specifying *the*)
the cook	(anaphoric *the*)
a (or the) crane	(generic use of *a* or anaphoric use of *the*)
the man	(anaphoric *the*)
the cook	(anaphoric *the*)
the riverbank	(specifying *the*)
a crane	(individualising *a*)
the water	(specifying *the*)
the man	(anaphoric *the*)
the bird	(anaphoric *the*)
the man	(anaphoric *the*)
the cook	(anaphoric *the*)
the cook	(anaphoric *the*)
the crane	(specifying *the*)
the place	(specifying *the*)

Task 4.18

1	he	third person singular, subject
2	them	third person plural, object
3	him	third person singular, possessive
4	her	third person singular, object
5	me	first person singular, object
6	we	first person plural, subject
7	us	first person plural, object
8	she	third person singular, subject
	she	third person singular, subject
	it	third person singular, object
	her	third person singular, possessive

Task 4.19

1 (5) 2 (1) 3 (8), (6) 4 (8) 5 (7) 6 (5) 7 (5)

Task 4.20

1 (1)	2 (3)	3 (11)	4 (9)	5 (6)
6 (12)	7 (9)	8 (13)	9 (5)	10 (12)

Task 4.21

1 some	pronoun (students)
others	pronoun (students)
2 enough	determiner
3 no one	pronoun
anything	pronoun
4 everybody	pronoun
5 some	pronoun (bats)
6 someone	pronoun
any	determiner
nothing	pronoun

Task 4.22

1 her	2 They	3 his	4 They	5 he	6 He
7 his	8 he	9 his	10 his	11 she	12 she
13 He	14 he	15 his	16 him	17 she	18 him
19 she	20 her	21 her	22 her	23 him	24 he
25 her	26 he	27 him	28 she	29 him	

Task 5.1

At a time when scientific advance <u>was</u> <u>seen</u> as universally beneficial, the nuclear industry <u>was judged to be</u> at the cutting edge of technology. It <u>was</u> crucial to a country's status as an advanced nation. But there <u>is</u> a second powerful strategic argument which <u>propelled</u> nuclear power forward in Britain, as in other countries. This <u>is</u> the fact that it <u>is based</u> on what <u>has appeared to be</u> a uniquely simple fuel, and one whose exploitation <u>could avoid</u> dependence on a variety of other uncertain choices. One of the arguments for the development of nuclear energy in the immediate aftermath of the Second World War <u>was</u> a predicted shortage of coal. Coal <u>provided</u> the fuel for much the greater part of the country's electricity. There <u>were</u> power cuts over the winter of 1947 because the industry <u>could</u> not <u>cope</u> with the demand. Worse <u>was expected to come</u> as industrial and domestic consumption of electricity picked up after the attrition of the war years. Now, however, there was an alternative. A single pound of uranium, it was claimed, would produce the same energy as a thousand tons of coal, whilst a hundred tons of uranium could provide all the electricity that the country could possibly need. In fact, apart from industrial disputes, the nuclear industry's pessimistic predictions about supplies of fossil fuels have been proved wrong in practice. Fossil fuels came to be a problem, not because of shortages, but because they cause pollution. Similarly, after the Chernobyl disaster, nuclear energy was seen to bring dangers of a different kind.

i The most frequent form is *to be* (*is, was, were, been*).
ii Verb phrases containing modal verbs make up 17 per cent of the verb phrases.

Task 5.2

1 (c)　　2 (b)　　3 (b)　　4 (b)　　5 (a)　　6 (b)

Task 5.3

1 may not remember	C or E
2 can't control	C
3 will be saved	E
4 may be	C
5 could do	C
6 mustn't let	C
7 'll get away	E
8 must have seen	E

Task 5.4

A collection of 80-million-year-old eggs has shed new light on the parenting style of dinosaurs, suggesting that some of them built nests and cared for their young much as birds do today. The ancient Troodons, whose nearly intact nests were discovered in Montana, were in some ways closer to modern birds than to crocodiles and other reptiles, according to a report in *Nature*. Many scientists believe birds are evolutionary descendants of dinosaurs. Troodons were fast, slender-limbed creatures about the size of adult humans, and may have been among the most intelligent of dinosaurs. Several nests of fossilized Troodon eggs were discovered on Montana's Egg Mountain, in Teton County. Researchers studying the nests concluded, based on their positions, that the eggs were laid two at a time in a bird-like pattern that

<u>suggests</u> parental incubation of the eggs. The eggs also <u>are</u> relatively large with thick, tough shells. By contrast, crocodiles <u>lay</u> a large number of smaller eggs in a single batch. The eggs <u>are</u> buried under sediment and the offspring <u>are</u> left to fend for themselves after hatching.

Task 5.5

1 cost	cost	cost
2 spread	spread	spread
3 feed	fed	fed
4 buy	bought	bought
5 make	made	made
6 get	got	got/gotten
7 draw	drew	drawn
8 give	gave	given
9 swim	swam	swum
10 grow	grew	grown
11 put	put	put
12 sing	sang	sung
13 understand	understood	understood
14 fall	fell	fallen
15 ring	rang	rung
16 steal	stole	stolen

Task 5.6

1 has finished (4–1)
2 was bitten (2–1)
3 will be going (5–3–1)
4 have helped (4–1)
5 are you going (3–1)
6 were you being followed (3–2–1)

Task 5.7

should be	(5–1)
have teamed up	(4–1)
has been set up	(4–2–1)
is recommended	(2–1)
is weakened	(2–1)
can (often) be prevented	(5–2–1)

Task 5.8

1 be shown
2 have lost
3 is driving/was driving
4 had been stung/have been stung
5 (could) be improved/(should) be improved, etc.
6 is being checked/was being checked
7 has been calculated
8 (can)not predict
9 (must) be done

Task 5.9

a Life expectancy in Britain has increased dramatically in the last century. Men and women born between 1910 and 1912 could <u>expect</u> <u>to live</u> an average 53 years. Those born between 1987 and 1988 can <u>expect</u> <u>to live</u> an additional 20 years. Life expectancy at birth is now an average 72 years for males and 78 years for females, but many people can <u>be</u> expected <u>to live</u> much longer. It is anticipated that life expectancy at birth will <u>rise</u> by 2–3 years over the next 40 years and possibly <u>increase</u> further. Increases in the elderly population – in both absolute and proportionate terms – have resulted from long-term downward trends in the birth rate coinciding with decreased mortality at all ages. The elderly population is expected <u>to continue</u> growing, in the foreseeable future, but at a slower rate than in the recent past. However, by 2031 the number of people aged at least 65 will <u>have</u> reached over 12 million, a rise of 38 per cent since 1991. Between 1981 and the turn of the century the portion of the population aged over 65 remained fairly steady at 15–16 per cent. Thereafter, the ageing of the post-war baby boom generation becomes apparent, and by 2031 over one-fifth of the population is expected <u>to be</u> over 65.

b i Non-finite stems are 55 per cent of the infinitives in the text.
   ii *To* + non-finite stems are 45 per cent of the infinitives in the text.

Task 5.13

| 1 (1) | 2 (5) | 3 (2) | 4 (3) | 5 (2) |
| 6 (4) | 7 (4) | 8 (1) | 9 (2) | 10 (3) |

Task 5.14

are riding bicycles	(5)	are campaigning	(5)
than driving cars	(5)	a target of doubling cycle use	(3)
cycling	(3)	for reducing car use	(3)
transport planning	(3)	way of moving people	(3)
the growing demand	(1)	overcrowding on trains	(3)
safe cycling routes	(3)	given to providing a frequent . . .	(7)

Task 5.15

prepared	(1)	improved	(1)
killed	(3)	associated	(1)
reduced	(1)	polluted	(4)
needed	(1)	infested	(2)
overwhelmed	(1)	triggered	(1)
cut	(1)	coupled	(1)

Task 5.16

has undergone   have become   has come   have been   has . . . led

Task 5.17

1 (c) optional   2 (a) optional   3 (b) obligatory
4 (a) optional   5 (c) optional   6 (a) optional
7 (a) optional

Task 5.18

were eaten
were harvested
were put aside
are sold
have been developed (has a *by*-agent)
is used
have been added
may have been shipped

Task 5.19

	Tense	Aspect	Voice	Mood
1	present	non-perfect, non-progressive	active	indicative
2	past	non-perfect, non-progressive	active	indicative
3	present	non-perfect, progressive	active	indicative
4	present	perfect, non-progressive	active	indicative
5	present	perfect, progressive	active	indicative
6	past	perfect, non-progressive	passive	indicative
7	past	perfect, progressive	passive	indicative
8	present	non-perfect, non-progressive	active	subjunctive
9	past	perfect, non-progressive	active	subjunctive
10	present	non-perfect, non-progressive	active	imperative

Task 6.1

Attributive adjectives

compulsory, recent, European, effective, literate, complex, elementary, economic, economic, Victorian, tremendous, economic, social, old, agrarian, new, urban, ruling, squalid, new, illiterate, powerful, educational

Predicative adjectives

essential, essential, necessary

Nouns

state, state, housing, middle

Task 6.2

(i) main, resulting, leading, certain, actual
(ii) afraid, alone, awake, asleep
(iii) sensible, giant, last, annual, scientific, due, unpayable, urgent, overdue

An old friend is ambiguous. If *old* means 'longstanding' then it is used only attributively. If it means 'old in years' then it can be used both attributively and predicatively.

Task 6.3

Text 6.2

modified, accelerated, disrupting, disturbing, existing, unaccustomed, increasing

Text 6.3

menacing, incoming, growing, resulting, affected, increasing, devastating, menacing, known

Task 6.4

Dolphins have <u>always</u> fascinated humans, and the fascination may be mutual. Our cousins who live <u>in the sea</u> seem to have created a society <u>far</u> closer to human ideals of Utopia than anything we have managed to achieve <u>on land</u>, and their social behaviour and lifestyle embody many of the virtues and qualities we humans value. Their movement <u>in the oceans</u> speaks <u>to us</u> of freedom, grace and beauty. Their society is co-operative, with many examples of <u>seemingly</u> altruistic behaviour, and dolphins are <u>usually</u> ready to come to the assistance of those <u>in distress</u>, both their own species and humans. <u>Apart from a few minor displays</u>, they are free of aggression <u>towards their own kind</u>. We see them communicating <u>easily</u> <u>with one another</u>, trying to communicate <u>with us</u> and solving problems. The ancient Mediterranean cultures believed that the dolphin represented the vital power of the sea. The dolphin was a guardian of the sea and a guide <u>to other worlds</u>. <u>In those times</u>, killing a dolphin was tantamount to killing a person, and both crimes were punished <u>with the death penalty</u>.

Task 6.5

She writes legibly; He runs brilliantly; They studied the play carefully; She speaks persuasively; It has rained very heavily; They rang us frequently; It rained quite lightly during the night; She works fast.

Task 6.6

Adjuncts

for at least 2,000 years; as perfect octahedrons with considerable visual appeal; in India; from India; along trade routes through the Middle East; en route; by the time the eastern goods reached the Mediterranean;

in the western world; at first; as objects of beauty; in Roman days; because they were reputed to be indestructible; against a whole range of misfortunes; through the ages; with the rise of scientific investigations; in the sixteenth century; by this time; to western Europe; as jewels; not until 1796; finally; in that year; by burning equal weights of diamond and charcoal; despite an enormous amount of effort; not until the 1950s; successfully

Subjuncts

highly; only; far; only; just

Disjuncts

more importantly; evidently

Conjuncts

consequently; even so; however

Task 6.7

Space

in India; from India; along trade routes through the Middle East; en route; in the western world; against a whole range of misfortunes; in western Europe

Time

for at least 2,000 years; by the time the eastern goods reached the Mediterranean; at first; in Roman days; through the ages; with the rise of scientific investigations; in the sixteenth century; by this time; not until 1796; finally; in that year; not until the 1950s

Manner

as perfect octahedrons with considerable visual appeal; as objects of beauty; as jewels; successfully

Means

by burning equal weights of diamond and charcoal

Contingency

because they were reputed to be indestructible; despite an enormous amount of effort

Task 6.8

Humans have valued diamonds for at least 2,000 years. Some natural diamonds are found as perfect octahedrons with considerable visual appeal. Stones like these began to be highly valued in India, the earliest source of diamonds. Merchants carried diamonds from India along trade routes through the Middle East. They sold the best diamonds en route, so that by the time the eastern goods reached the Mediterranean only the most uninspiring of the diamonds were left. Consequently in the western world diamonds were at first not regarded as objects of beauty – other stones such as emeralds and red garnets were preferred. Even so, in Roman days diamonds had a far greater monetary value than gold, because they were reputed to be indestructible, and, more importantly, it was believed that they would safeguard their wearer against a whole range of misfortunes, from poison to madness. These magical attributes persisted through the ages and died out only with the rise of scientific investigations in the sixteenth century. By this time diamonds were well known in western Europe, and were worn as jewels, but it was not until 1796 that the chemical nature of diamond was finally established. In that year a London chemist, Smithson Tennant, burned diamonds and found that carbon dioxide was the end product; the same amount of carbon dioxide was produced by burning equal weights of diamond and charcoal. Evidently diamond was just another form of carbon. However, despite an enormous amount of effort, it was not until the 1950s that diamonds were successfully synthesised.

Task 6.9

a of electricity; of carbon emissions; of Denmark; in the Horns Rev wind farm; for 150,000 homes; of construction; of the wind offshore; of Europe; of the oil industry; of the world's electricity; of climate change

b in many countries; for the production of electricity; without the disadvantages of carbon emissions; off the coast of Denmark; at sea; in water which is over 30 metres deep; because of the strength and consistency of the wind off-shore; under construction; on land; in several parts of Europe; In Spain; for some time; by means of wind turbines; in many countries; in the United States; in operation; in Texas; to centre stage; by 2020; from wind

Task 7.1

The railway station was one of the hubs of English village life.	(F)
It was a centre of news, gossip and advice and the home of a bookstall and telegraph office.	(F)
Its disappearance has been followed in many cases by that of the village shop, the village post office and the village pub.	(F)
It has been part of the slow, inexorable process of rural decay	(F)
that became inevitable	(F)
when economic viability replaced communal need,	(F)
and left whole areas more isolated	(F)
than they had been at any time since the eighteenth century.	(F)
The country railways, of course, never made a profit.	(F)
But they provided a vital social service	(F)
and their closure marked the end of an era.	(F)
What was it about the station	(F)
that was so fascinating?	(F)
The station was truly a gateway	(F)
which people passed through in endless profusion in a variety of missions.	(F)
It was a place of motion and emotion, arrival and departure, joy and sorrow, parting and reunion.	(F)
Here are some boys and girls	(F)
going away to school,	(NF)
their fathers and mothers filling up the moments of waiting with many last minute instructions,	(NF)
in order to shut out their anxieties	(NF)
which their children must not see.	(F)
At another place a wife is saying good-bye to a husband.	(F)
Elsewhere a son or daughter is setting out into the great world	(F)
to win a name and place.	(NF)
In the corner of a carriage a lonely soul sits,	(F)
his face screened by a magazine,	(NF)
with no one to say goodbye to him at this end of his journey	(NF)
or welcome him at the other.	(NF)

Task 7.2

1. <u>Max</u> (and) <u>Fred</u>   (object noun phrases)
2. <u>Max</u> (and) <u>Fred</u>   (subject noun phrases)
3. <u>long</u> (and) <u>boring</u>   (adjectives)
4. <u>come inside</u> (and) <u>sit beside the fire</u>   (infinitives)
5. <u>very hard</u> (and) <u>late into the night</u>   (adverbials)

6 <u>Empty beer cans</u> (and) <u>heaps of paper</u>   (subject noun phrases)
7 <u>onwards</u> (and) <u>upwards</u>   (adverbials)
8 <u>Apples</u> (and) <u>pears</u>   (subject noun phrases)

Task 7.3

About 200 years ago, the occupants of a rural French village <u>looked up one morning</u> (and) <u>saw an unusual object overhead</u>. It <u>was huge, silent</u> (and) <u>spherical</u> (and) <u>seemed to float out of the sky</u>. After it landed in a field the <u>villagers were afraid</u> (but) <u>they nevertheless attacked the monster with sticks</u> <u>(and) farm implements</u>. Burning fabric added to the confusion. The object was, of course, a hot air balloon. Apparently someone tied it to <u>a horse</u> (or) <u>other farm animal</u>, which <u>ran through the fields</u> (and) <u>caused further damage</u>. Since those early attempts at flying, <u>there have been amazing developments,</u> (and) <u>we now tend to take air travel for granted</u>.

Task 7.4

and	sequence
and	addition
and	addition
but	unexpected contrast
and	addition
or	exclusion
and	result
and	result (or addition)

Task 7.5

(The ellipted parts are underlined.)

1 I'm happy to go if you are <u>happy to go</u>.
2 John went to the movies but Freda didn't want to <u>go to the movies</u>.
3 Has Sue found her keys? She ought to have <u>found her keys</u> by now.
4 <u>Have you</u> got a match?
5 I like Beethoven. Do you <u>like Beethoven</u>?
6 <u>Do you</u> want a drink?
7 <u>It is</u> good to see you.
8 I'll play the piano if you will <u>play the piano</u>.
9 My friends own <u>their beach cottage</u>, <u>my friends</u> pay the expenses on their beach cottage, but <u>my friends</u> don't use their beach cottage.
10 I'll see you tomorrow or <u>I'll see you</u> later in the week.
11 I wanted him to do it today but he can't <u>do it today</u>.

12 The wind dropped and <u>the wind</u> switched to the south.
13 She used to sit after dinner and <u>she used to</u> drop off <u>after dinner</u>.
14 John washed the dishes and Bob <u>washed</u> the clothes.
15 I'm going to the movies tonight and Fred <u>is going to the movies</u> tomorrow.
16 I like avocados but Max doesn't <u>like avocados</u>.
17 <u>It</u> looks like rain.
18 The people <u>who were</u> injured in the crash gradually recovered.

Task 7.6

1 rugby league (second occurrence) ⇒ it too **or** likes rugby league (second occurrence) ⇒ does too.

2 Sarah (second and third occurrence) ⇒ Ø

3 earned (second occurrence) ⇒ Ø

4 storm front passed (second occurrence) ⇒ Ø
through the district (second occurrence ⇒ Ø

5 storm front passed quickly through the district (second occurrence) ⇒ Ø

Task 7.7

(there are) at least one million deaths . . .
(and) many of them (are) children.
(of malaria) are in sub-Saharan Africa
(which are) carrying the disease . . .
(It was) ravaging Roman armies . . .
(it was ravaging) Genghis Khan's soldiers . . .
(that) there were unacceptable ecological consequences . . .
(which were) used to control them.

Task 7.8

(Unless otherwise stated, these clauses are finite.)

1 what he's talking about
2 Although we didn't have any rain this week
  the weather has been fine
3 which he told us about
4 If the phone goes
5 Since we're in agreement
6 who rang me last night
  to sell insurance (non-finite)

    7 if they won't let us
    8 because I didn't find the other one to be relevant
      to be relevant (non-finite)
    9 that you had retired
  10 If possible (a verbless clause)
      to have a few days off (non-finite)
  11 than he did last year

Task 7.9

(Text 7.4)

when they were found near death	(Adv)
after spending four days in shark-prone waters	(Adv)
who rescued them	(Rel)
when he saw a fishing buoy in the water	(Adv)
As he got closer	(Adv)
clinging to it	(Rel)
that five minutes later the young woman asked him to look for her boyfriend	(Nom)
to look for her boyfriend	(Nom)
who had gone missing	(Rel)
that sank four days previously	(Rel)
after it had been hit by a freak wave	(Adv)

(Text 7.5)

who suffered a heart attack on the slopes of Mount Everest	(Rel)
involving his friend's wife in Hong Kong, and a solar-powered mobile phone	(Rel)
as temperatures began falling with only two hours' remaining daylight	(Adv)
after failing to get a land line to nearby Kathmandu	(Adv)
to get a land line to nearby Kathmandu	(Nom)
they needed help urgently	(Nom)
who was a doctor in Hong Kong	(Rel)
whether it could send a helicopter	(Nom)
to rescue the climber	(Adv)
which could hover at high altitude for only 15 minutes with room for a patient and oxygen cylinder	(Rel)
After being treated by two doctors in the climbing party	(Adv)
and surviving temperatures of –15°C	(Adv)
to reach the summit of Everest	(Nom)
before the weather deteriorated	(Adv)

Task 7.10

1 that they are committed to the present policy	complement of an adjective
2 that they wouldn't believe him	complement of an adjective
3 what they like	object
4 What I really wanted to know	subject
'What I really wanted to know was this'	object
5 that your visits were carefully recorded	complement of an adjective
6 that we do not have unlimited funds	complement of an adjective
7 that the joke has to be explained	apposition
8 that some fundamental problems of cognitive psychology can be accounted for in terms of macro-processing	object

Task 7.11

what he was told	object
what he wanted him to do	complement of a preposition
to do	object
'That sack is nearly in the water! Press down hard on it!'	object
that he would do the opposite	object
what his father had told him to do	object
to do	object
why he had pushed down on the sack	object
that he wanted to show his father that he now thought he should obey him	object
to show his father that he now thought he should obey him	object
that he now thought he should obey him	object
he should obey him	object

Task 7.12

1 He showed me (a small room) <u>which I could sleep in if necessary.</u> (NR)
2 Later I spoke to (the people) <u>that owned the house.</u> (R)
3 The proposal would have to be supported by (all the owners), <u>who could not easily be located.</u> (NR)
4 (The yacht) <u>he bought</u> was made of fibreglass. (R)
5 He was past (the age) <u>at which he could easily get these things himself.</u> (R)
6 The earthworm can bend its body in (any direction) <u>it wants.</u> (R)
7 That was (the most famous picture) <u>Rembrandt had painted.</u> (R)
8 His attention was attracted towards (a sound) <u>he couldn't identify.</u> (R)

Task 7.13

(Text 7.7)

According to a news (report) (R) that I saw on TV, a (mouse) (R) which was discovered on an (aircraft) (R) scheduled to leave for London (R) caused panic among (passengers), (NR) who jumped out of their seats and ran to one end of the aircraft to escape. Airport (workers and cleaners) (NR) who were called in unfortunately failed to catch the mouse. Passengers were therefore transferred to another (aircraft), (NR) which took off three hours late. It is hard to believe that adult passengers could be afraid of a (mouse) (NR) which couldn't possibly hurt them.

(Text 7.8)

Influenza remains a serious and debilitating (disease) (R) that is often underrated. Additional (deaths) (NR) which are above the normal winter increase are recorded regularly in association with influenza epidemics. Over the past decade in the US up to 47,000 deaths per influenza season have been observed with 80–90 per cent occurring in (persons) (R) who are 65 years and older. Influenza is caused by a number of different (viruses) (NR) which are classified by structure as Influenza A, B or C. Influenza A causes less extensive epidemics of disease mainly in children and occasionally in adults but is rarely associated with additional deaths. The influenza virus has the ability to undergo major (changes) (NR) called 'shifts'. These usually occur at intervals of ten years or more and result in serious epidemics. Minor (changes), (NR) which are called 'drifts', can also occur each year, (NR) which can result in new strains of the (virus) (R) involved. (Vaccination), (NR) which can offer 60–80 per cent protection in normal healthy adults when the vaccine and epidemic strains are closely related, can reduce the number of (deaths) (R) which are normally caused by influenza.

Task 7.14

(More than one answer may be possible.)

1 I saw a person who was waiting to use a phone.
2 The ferry, which is quite a big ship, crosses the Channel in about two hours.
3 Some people who cross the Channel each year on the ferry get quite sick.
4 I plan to take my holiday, which begins on 3 June, in Italy where I think the weather will be better.
5 Last Friday I finished my assignment which took me several days to complete.

Task 7.16

(Text 7.9)

(When) a large truck was found in a ditch beside the road	(F)	time
(in case) he had been injured	(F)	reason
sleeping at his brother's home	(NF)	place?
(after) the police had spent several hours searching for him	(F)	˙time
searching for him	(NF)	purpose?
(if) they decide to prosecute him	(F)	condition
(before) a decision was made	(F)	time
(as) fears grew for the man's safety	(F)	time
(because) it had crashed off the road several hours earlier	(F)	reason
(before) someone discovered the man was asleep in a comfortable bed a few kilometres away	(F)	time

Task 7.17

(More than one solution may be possible.)

1 As the days went by, Fred became more and more miserable.	time
2 You'll find their farm where the road begins to climb away from the river.	place
3 Liz was short of money at university while Sue spent her time in a series of temporary but well-paid jobs.	contrast
4 Unless they ring us before 5 p.m., we'll go ahead with our plans.	condition
5 If you have a few moments to spare, give me a call.	condition
6 Because I broke my leg, I can't go skiing this year.	cause/reason

Task 7.18

(The answers given here are only suggestions as more than one answer is possible.)

1 Because she wanted to avoid being seasick, Mary took a pill before she got on the ferry.
2 Although he had a lot of property, the trader had all his goods moved on camels as there was no railway in that country.
3 Two senators, who are elected for six-year terms, are elected from each state.
4 Even though he did not see the event, he described it so well in a pamphlet I was reading yesterday that I will refer to the pamphlet later.
5 Smoke, in which there is water vapour and carbon dioxide, results from burning fuel.

6 Human beings have the ability to make instruments which bring into view stars whose light has taken a thousand years to reach the earth.

7 The fact that he has gone away without leaving his address is a clear proof of his dishonest intentions.

Task 7.19

1 If they can be persuaded to change the law	open
2 unless they are sent a personal invitation	open
3 If I were in Fred's position	hypothetical
4 unless someone at his workplace is not telling the truth	open
5 if they still lived in Boston	hypothetical
6 As long as you let us know when you get there	open
7 If she reduced the second chapter	hypothetical
8 If I hadn't seen it with my own eyes	hypothetical

Task 7.20

1 (When they announced (that the environmentalists wanted (to set up a peace base at Mururoa,)NF)F)F many people said (it would be impossible.)F

2 But ((after successfully landing a team inside the Arctic Circle in 1990,)NF and (placing another in a secure area in the Nevada desert,)NF)NF they firmly believed (it was possible.)F

3 In fact, the protesters got within a kilometre of the test area (before being discovered,)NF (arrested)NF and (taken off the atoll.)NF

Task 7.21

1 children are afraid of most dogs
　　　　　　　　　　　　a nominal clause functioning as an object
2 what it is　　　　　a nominal clause functioning as a complement
3 I'd enjoy it much　　　a nominal clause functioning as an object
4 although her face was older　　an adverbial clause of concession
5 what you read　a nominal clause functioning as a postponed subject
6 that you take yourself far too seriously for your age
　　　　　　　　　　　a nominal clause functioning as a complement
7 that needs a coat of paint
　　　　　　　　　　　a relative clause with the antecedent *building*
8 that they all respected her
　　　　a nominal clause functioning as the complement of an adjective
9 whom it was difficult not to believe
　　　　　　　　　　　a relative clause with the antecedent *person*
10 because I've got work to do　　an adverbial clause of cause/reason

Task 7.22

nearing a conclusion in the courts	(NF, Rel, Restrictive)
which have conducted research into the effects of tobacco over the last 50 years	(F, Rel, Restrictive)
that in the 1950s the state of scientific research meant they could not have been expected to warn of the dangers of smoking	(F, Nom)
they could not have been expected to warn of the dangers of smoking	(F, Nom)
to warn of the dangers of smoking	(NF, Nom)
that they would not have encouraged smoking if . . . dangers	(F, Nom)
if they had known of its dangers	(F, Adv, Conditional)
that the companies deliberately conspired to get the young to smoke by . . . lifestyles	(F, Nom)
to get the young to smoke	(NF, Adv, Purpose)
to smoke	(NF, Nom)
by associating smoking with glamorous and exciting lifestyles	(NF, Adv, Manner)
involved in the debate	(NF, Rel, Restrictive)
that a shortage of resources prevented them from making . . . initiated	(F, Nom)
from making an effective response to the advertising campaigns which the tobacco companies initiated	(NF, Nom)
which the tobacco companies initiated	(F, Rel, Restrictive)
that might protect against cancer	(F, Rel, Restrictive)
When they experimented with mice	(F, Adv, Time)
that the gene provides a vital defence against the toxic chemicals found in tobacco smoke	(F, Nom)
found in tobacco smoke	(NF, Rel, Restrictive)
leading the team of scientists	(NF, Rel, Restrictive)
the research is encouraging	(F, Nom)
he hoped that they could develop a serious programme of cancer prevention by manipulating . . . successful	(F, Nom)
that they could develop a serious programme of cancer prevention by manipulating . . . successful	(F, Nom)
by manipulating these types of genes	(NF, Adv, Manner)
if trials are successful	(F, Adv, Conditional)

Task 8.1

(These cohesive links are suggestions only. Other links are possible.)

1 Lexical

    a collocation, e.g. shed–skin; female–egg; wings–fly; weave–silk; monarch–butterfly; weave–fibre

    b repetition, e.g. milkweed–milkweed; larva–larva; skin–skin; wings–wings; times–times; shed–shedding; weeks–weeks

    c synonymy, e.g. monarch butterfly–*Danaus plexippus*; caterpillar–larva; pupa–pouch; pupa–chrysalis; feeding–eating; grown butterfly–adult; increase–grow; milkweed–the plant

    d superordination, e.g. insect–butterfly; colour–gold; fibre–silk

2 Grammatical

    a anaphoric reference, e.g. here–tree limb; its–the larva

    b cataphoric reference, e.g. pupa–this fragile blue-green pouch

    c ellipsis, e.g. the female (butterfly); a new generation (of butterflies)

    d logical connectives, e.g. after, and, as, then

Index